For corrections, additional info
books by Tony Hadland, see
http://www.users.globa
If you do not have Internet acce
addressed A4 envelope (or 3 International Reply Coupons)
to *Rosemary Hadland, 39 Malvern Road, Balsall Common,
Coventry, CV7 7DU, United Kingdom*

*Grand Batch
was Rocned*

THE SPACEFRAME
MOULTONS

Published in 1994
by Tony Hadland

39 Malvern Road
Balsall Common
Coventry
CV7 7DU
United Kingdom

British Library Cataloguing-in-Publication Data

A catalogue record for this book is available from the British Library

ISBN 0 9507431 6 X

Printed by
CP Service Ltd, Birmingham

"Once a person gets hooked on a Moulton, he changes the way he views many things in the world of bicycling.

"The first thing is the absurdity of bicycle design progress for the last hundred years or so (excluding the Moulton of course). We have had a hundred years of people 'fine tuning' a couple of triangular sets of tubes. We have tried all kinds of butting, all kinds of materials. We have fiddled with geometry within two or three degrees for the same 100 years.

"If car design had taken the same route, we would be driving Model A cars with titanium frames and the hand crank would be carbon fiber."

Leigh F. Wade
Paynesville, Minnesota, USA
from a letter in Bike Report magazine, May 1990

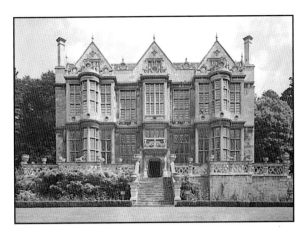

The Hall

Contents

Alex Moulton at The Hall with the stainless steel AM-GT, 1993.
Photo by, and courtesy of, Julian Hartnoll.

FOREWORD

I do admire the pertinacity of Tony Hadland in having researched our archives so rigorously, and to have written this second and yet more comprehensive volume on the history of the Moulton.

For my part as perpetrator of the theme, it is enlightening sometimes to look back and to be reminded of incidents of the past, some of which I must confess I had forgotten. In my unfinished quest to improve on the Starley, or "classic" normal riding position bicycle, as a designed entity manufactured in series and available on the market, one must appreciate that it demands unremitting effort - and I still have ambitions to fulfill in the time left to me. So it is the tasks for the present, and taking steps for the future, which concern me most.

The history of the Moulton does span a significant period in the existence of that most remarkable device which a bicycle continues to represent. In those 40 years we have seen our once great manufacturing industry wither from posturing superiority to one decimated by importers. This decline is not confined to the UK or Europe even, so I find it particularly satisfying that on a tiny scale the current Moulton bicycle is exported to Japan. There are other welcome signs in the UK and in the US of a resurgence of small innovating manufacturers of machines and especially of components.

Of the bicycle itself, we have seen the fashion-directed trade embrace the "mountain bike", which on analysis is (un)remarkably like a low-geared and robust Starley but fitted with modern components from the Orient. The price of the complete bike seems to be determined severalfold by the perceived value of the component group set! Also it is amusing for me to watch the rush to add on "suspensions" of one style or another.

As for materials, we note the appearance on the market of new types, each with its own problems of reliable construction. It is my belief the way ahead for the Moulton remains with the small diameter steel tubes as pioneered by Pedersen, but in the architectural form of the title of this book.

Recently I again studied, with the help of some students of Bath University, the recumbent, which as a type is achieving an increased following. However, I came to the same conclusion as I did back in the '50s when I rejected it as the form for a bicycle to be "more pleasing to have and to ride for universal use".

So in commending this book to those interested in the theme, I would urge them above all to ride and enjoy cycling on whatever type of machine is their preference.

In conclusion, my quest would have realised little without the assistance I have received and continue so to do from my small staff (past and present) and other friends and "Moultoneers". In addition to the author, I would like to express my appreciation of the contributions of them all to my endeavours, including David Duffield, Phil Uncles, John Benjamin, Tim Bigwood, Richard Grigsby, Doug Milliken, Jim Glover, Dave Bogdan and Paulo Kiefe.

Dr Alex Moulton, CBE, RDI, FEng
The Hall
Bradford-on-Avon
31 May 1994

Alex Moulton in Switzerland, 1991.

PREFACE

Tony Hadland, who bought his first Moulton in 1964.
Photo by Roger Charters Photography, Leamington Spa.

My 1981 book The Moulton Bicycle traced the machine's evolution from the late 1950s until Raleigh ceased production in the mid 1970s. The second edition of the book was published in 1982, and the following year Alex Moulton launched the first of his spaceframe bicycles. Almost immediately enthusiasts started suggesting I should write a book about the new bikes.

I resisted. My feeling at the time was that not enough had happened. It would be like writing the biography of a new-born baby. What could I add to the information in the sales brochures?

A decade later I re-examined the situation and, despite two spells as editor of the Moulton Bicycle Club's magazine, was amazed at the rich history of Alex's second generation machines and the achievements of their riders. Therefore, having drawn on many sources, I now present the story of the spaceframe Moultons. I hope you find it interesting and enjoyable.

My thanks go to the many people who helped, by providing information, illustrations, guidance and general support. They include Tim Bigwood, Jack Lauterwasser, Gillian Marsden, Jenny Strawson, Alan Hopewell, Ray Craig, Peter Knottley, Alan Holden, Roger Taylor, Geoff Pratt, Miles Kingsbury, Richard Grigsby, Joe Beer, Elgar Vaivars, Jim Glover, Dave Bogdan, Caba Sajo, Adrian Williams, Keith Findlay, Nigel Sadler, Brian Walker, David Eccles, Mike Lewis, Mike Augspurger, Chris Juden and many others. Doug Milliken deserves a special mention for his assistance with the chapter "Against the Clock". Heartfelt thanks go to my wife Rosemary, who again endured a long spell as a "word processor widow".

Acknowledgement is also made to all authors listed in Appendix C, on whose work I have drawn, and to the owners of copyright in the photographs and other illustrations used in the book. Unless otherwise indicated, these are reproduced courtesy of Alex Moulton Limited.

Last but by no means least, I am greatly indebted to Alex Moulton himself for access to his records, for answering my many questions and for reviewing my draft. I should add that the book is an independent production and was neither sponsored nor commissioned by Alex Moulton Limited.

In writing the book I have tried to cater for all readers but at the same time produce a definitive technical history. Therefore, if gear tables or details of carrier (rack) construction are not your scene, don't get bogged down - simply skip the paragraphs that don't interest you! Sub-headings are provided throughout the text to make browsing easier, and there is a comprehensive alphabetical index at the back of the book.

Naturally enough, being English and writing in England I have used British spelling. However, the US form has been conserved in direct quotations from American texts. Fortunately, apart from minor differences of spelling, most technical terms are common to all English-speaking territories. In the few cases where different terms are used for the same thing (such as "mudguard" in the UK, "fender" in the USA) at its first mention in a passage I give the American equivalent in brackets, but thereafter use just the British term.

Conversions from imperial to metric units (and vice versa) should be regarded as approximate. It is in any case wise to check any measurement quoted before using it for precision engineering purposes. Gears are expressed in inches only, but can be converted to the metric "development" figure by multiplying by 0.08. (For further explanation see Chapter 2.)

Finally, I welcome all feedback on the book, especially corrections and additional information. If you would like a reply, please enclose a self-addressed envelope, either with appropriate UK postage stamps or an International Reply Coupon.

Tony Hadland
Balsall Common, Coventry
Midsummer's Day 1994

Prologue
MOULTON THE MAN

The Hall, Bradford-on-Avon.
Photo by Tony Hadland.

Alex Moulton's great-grandfather, Stephen Moulton, was an enterprising English broker with an interest in engineering. Born in 1794, he travelled frequently to the USA after the Napoleonic wars. About 1835 he went to work in New York, where his acquaintances included Charles Goodyear, inventor of a process for vulcanizing rubber. This converted the natural India rubber gum into a useful elastic material.

At that time the USA, then a nation little more than half a century old, was not industrially developed. Goodyear therefore granted a licence for his process to Stephen Moulton. Armed with the right to exploit the new technology, Stephen returned to England. He sought a suitable seat for his family and, failing to interest the government or anyone else in taking up the Goodyear process, decided to go into rubber manufacture himself.

In 1846 he purchased The Hall, Bradford-on-Avon, Wiltshire; a stately residence built by a wealthy clothier, John Hall, in about 1620. It proved an ideal site. Although the house needed restoration, it came complete with an empty woollen mill on the River Avon, and a workforce in need of employment. Stephen Moulton restored The Hall, planted the trees we see today, and converted the mill into the first English factory for vulcanized rubber.

Early orders included thousands of waterproof capes for the British army's Crimean campaign of 1853-6. Primarily the works produced rubber springs for the burgeoning railways, but other diverse rubber products even included dentures. In the twentieth century pneumatic tyres and tennis balls were added to the product range.

The business pioneered by Stephen Moulton continues in the form of Avon Rubber, the largest employer in Wiltshire. However, it is no longer Moulton-owned, having been sold by the Board, including Stephen's great-grandson Alex, in 1956 – 108 years after it commenced production.

Alexander Eric Moulton was born on 9 April 1920 at Rother Place, Stratford-upon-Avon, Warwickshire; the home of his maternal grandfather, a medical doctor. Alex's scientist father died young, but the boy spent a happy early childhood with his grandparents at The Hall, where the atmosphere was still strongly Victorian.

"Three Moultons and their bicycles. . ."

Alex Moulton's father John (standing) with a Humber Safety Bicycle, c.1896.

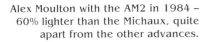

John Moulton, Alex's grandfather and youngest son of Stephen, as a young barrister in 1864 with a Michaux Velocipede.

Alex Moulton with the AM2 in 1984 – 60% lighter than the Michaux, quite apart from the other advances.

His interest in engineering started in childhood, nurtured by the presence (literally at the bottom of the garden) of the family factory and Brunel's Great Western Railway crossing the Wiltshire Avon. He was further influenced by the estate carpenter, who worked in one of the old mill buildings. It was Cooper the carpenter who introduced Alex to the pleasure of making things out of the solid.

While a boarder at Marlborough College, the nearby public school, Alex built himself a steam car chassis. To make the metal parts he set up an old 3 " Drummond lathe in the school's woodworking shop. After Marlborough he was accepted for King's College, Cambridge University via the qualifying examination for the Mechanical Sciences Tripos.

Between school and university, Alex spent some time as a paying pupil apprentice at the Sentinel Waggon Works, Shrewsbury. He applied to Sentinel "to enter the scene of the high pressure steam engine work of Abner Doble", and there learned something of the craft of the practical execution of engineering. This was of enormous value to his subsequent career.

The Second World War broke out in September 1939, after Alex had finished the first year of the Tripos at Cambridge. He immediately applied to join the Royal Air Force. The recruiting board at Cambridge singled him out to be an engineering officer but there was no vacancy until April 1940.

He therefore went to work at the Bristol Aeroplane Company, under the influence of chief engineer Roy Fedden, godfather of a great school friend. This was intended to be a temporary position, pending entry to the RAF, but the Luftwaffe was to ensure that Alex never entered the service. A major daylight raid on the Patchway works caused the death of Adrian Squire, a project engineer. Next day Alex was summoned by Roy Fedden to become his personal assistant, and work on the Centaurus air-cooled radial engine project which Squire had been running.

Alex spent the rest of the war at Bristol Aeroplane. He was sent on many missions to liaise and negotiate with great engineers of the aviation world, in companies such as Vickers and Hawker. Thereby he was exposed to the highest standards of engineering excellence at a very young and impressionable age.

After the war Alex joined the family firm, George Spencer, Moulton & Co. Ltd. He persuaded the board to let him set up a research department to develop rubber suspension and springing. He was particularly interested in bonding rubber to metal, at that time a little-used technique. It allows rubber to be strained in shear as well as in compression, and enabled Alex to develop a family of innovative rubber springs. Perhaps the best known of these early devices was the Flexitor, a rubber torsion spring, widely used in caravan and trailer suspensions.

In his late twenties, Alex went back to Cambridge to finish his degree. He found it particularly useful returning as a mature student, because by then he knew exactly what he wanted to learn, and had the motivation to apply himself vigorously to it. In 1949 he was awarded his Master of Arts degree.

In 1956, the Spencer Moulton company having been sold to Avon, Alex established Moulton Developments Limited in the stables at The Hall. There, sponsored initially by the British Motor Corporation and soon after by Dunlop, he continued research and development work on his inventions in automotive suspension technology. His friendship and collaboration with the famous car designer Sir Alec Issigonis were important influences. Over the years Alex's Diabolo rubber springs, and interconnected Hydrolastic and Hydragas suspensions, were used on millions of cars.

Alex also designed the Moulton coach, a double bogie road vehicle with a geodetic structure of square-section tubes. It gave an unprecedented combination of passenger comfort, safety and road-holding. Although never put into production, its roadholding standards were adopted by the British government for benchmarking military vehicles. The Moulton coach was one of the few prototypes to go straight into the Science Museum without being put into production!

Alex was elected a Royal Designer for Industry in 1968 and was made a Commander of the Order of the British Empire in 1976. He was elected to the Fellowship of Engineering in 1980 and was later elected a Vice President of what is now the prestigious Royal Academy

The Moulton Coach

of Engineers. The winner of numerous awards, he is a Fellow of the Royal Society of Arts, of the Society of Industrial Artists & Designers, and of the Plastics & Rubber Institute. He is also an Honorary Doctor of the Royal College of Arts and an Honorary Doctor of Science of Bath University.

But what of the Moulton bicycle? In July of 1956, the year in which Alex set up Moulton Developments, the Egyptian dictator Colonel Nasser nationalised the Suez Canal Company. Three months later Anglo-French forces took military action against Egypt. This led to emergency petrol rationing in the UK which lasted until mid May 1957.

Fuel rationing forced many Britons back to the bicycle. Alex acquired one from Geoff Warren, a friend and ex-colleague from his days at Bristol Aeroplane. The machine was a beautiful handmade lightweight by Hetchins. Alex was both delighted and surprised by its response. Much of his previous cycling was on old roadsters with no particular merit, which served for touring when he was a boy (starting with a £3 19s 6d Hercules) or as basic undergraduate transport at Cambridge.

Therefore at the age of 35, as a mature engineer, Alex experienced a renaissance of interest in cycling. He decided to apply his creative efforts to making an improvement on what he termed the "classic" – the linear descendant of the late Victorian diamond frame safety bicycle, as first manifested in G. L. Morris's "Referee" and Starley Brothers' "Psycho", and often referred to as the "Starley". As Alex later put it, his aim was "to take the evolution of that most remarkable device beyond its classical form. In other words to produce a bicycle which was more pleasing to have and to use."

In all his innovative engineering work, Alex regards himself as a fundamentalist, first studying deeply the basic theory of the existing before presuming to change for change's sake – the reverse of the superficial fashion-driven designer. In the case of the "classic" bicycle he had no particular quarrel with existing componentry, considering it sensibly developed. (Modern Japanese development of components confirms his original view, although he regrets that European companies lacked the enterprise to make these innovations.) He therefore turned to more fundamental issues.

One of his first acts was to question the riding position – the ergonomic attitude of the rider. He acquired a 1930s F. H. Grubb long wheelbase recumbent and rode it to establish whether or not the alternative position was, in his view, better or worse than the classical conventional position. Obviously it was potentially faster because of the smaller frontal area, but Alex soon concluded that it was inferior for hill climbing – a view particularly reinforced during a hilly ride from

Bradford-on-Avon to Bath. He was also concerned about the recumbent's control response, which he considered inferior to that offered by the classic riding position that "keeps the rider sitting the way God meant him to", as Dutch author and cycle engineer Rob van der Plas puts it.

In the early 1990s Alex reinvestigated the recumbent position with a view to responding to demand for a Moulton recumbent. There had been a number of recumbent conversions of 1960s Moulton bicycles and in 1991 Israel Urieli of Athens, Ohio, devised a bolt-on conversion kit for his AM7 which enabled it to be converted into a recumbent within half an hour. But despite examining some fine modern recumbents, Alex eventually confirmed his original conclusions, and abandoned development work on his own recumbent, after a prototype had been made as a research project with Bath University engineering students.

Back in the 1950s the fundamental flaw Alex perceived in the "classic" bicycle was not in the riding position, but in another aspect of its basic architecture. While the classic configuration patently works very well in many ways, the wheel diameter, typically 27" (700 mm), seemed to him to be arbitrarily large. Early safety bicycles had adopted wheels of about this size as a major reduction from the huge driving wheel of the Ordinary or High Wheeler, typically 52" (1,320 mm) in diameter. But Alex could see no fundamental reason why an even smaller size could not be used. He noted that, with the exception of vehicles for use on soft ground, such as tractors, wheel sizes for virtually all vehicles have decreased as design has evolved – all modern cars, railway locomotives and aircraft are "small-wheeled" compared to their Victorian or Edwardian predecessors. Furthermore, the reduction of the encumbrance of large wheels is always sensible, Alex argued.

So he investigated how much smaller, without detriment, a bicycle wheel could be made. He enjoyed excellent relations with the Dunlop company at Fort Dunlop, Birmingham, through the large amount of business generated for the company by his innovative automotive suspension units. This special relationship enabled Alex, together with Dunlop's very competent technical team led by Tommy French, to carry out a fundamental study of wheel size related to other parameters.

It was no good simply taking an existing juvenile tyre designed for a toy bike: for the experiment to be valid, best quality tyre carcase construction was needed. So special moulds were made to construct 14" and 16" diameter versions of the 26" and 27" Dunlop Sprite, at the time one of the best touring tyres available. Tests were then carried out on rolling resistance, wear and other factors.

Not surprisingly, it soon became apparent that the most significant parameter in rolling resistance was inflation pressure. Given a high inflation pressure and top quality tyre carcase construction, a major reduction in tyre diameter was feasible without a significant increase in rolling resistance. The smaller wheels would liberate space above them for more luggage to be carried safely on the machine.

Hence the significant decision was taken to adopt a wheel with a nominal diameter of 16 x 1$^3/_8$" (406 x 35 mm) using an existing British juvenile rim format known as E3J (Endrick profile, size 3, Juvenile range). Dunlop would make tyres and rims to adult quality, following intensive fatigue testing at Dunlop Rim and Wheel, Coventry, to determine the spoking requirements to give a substantial superiority in strength over the conventional wheel.

But a small wheel with high pressure tyre was no good without the benefit of wheel suspension – the ride was too harsh. Therefore Alex combined the high pressure small diameter tyre with wheel suspension, giving "a total advance over the high pressure unsprung large wheel in road-holding and comfort". Alex describes this as "perhaps the most significant thing the Moulton bicycle has done."

He was also dissatisfied with the conventional diamond frame, which he later dubbed "that quadrilateral bit of piping". He muses that if the "classic" bicycle were launched new on the market today, for consumer safety reasons it probably would not be allowed to incorporate the top tube. (The lengths to which some mountain bike designers have gone to distance the top tube from the rider's groin area are noteworthy in this respect!) Alex therefore concluded that the frame should be open and step-through. It thereby became unisex, enabling production of a single frame size useable by the majority of adults and adolescents.

This then was the thinking that led to the form of the original Moulton bicycle. It carries through to Alex's present range of bicycles, spanning nearly 40 years of what must surely be the most persistent and single-minded effort of development invested in any familiar product. It is a design philosophy which is, as he puts it, "entirely apparent to those that come to study it, and which is totally consistent". He adds:

"All that I've really done, from a design point of view, between that early period and today, is to improve the efficiency in all respects of the manifestation of that idea."

Chapter 1
A CUCKOO IN THE HERON'S NEST
1959-1977

Alex Moulton's involvement with Raleigh and
the design legacy of the Moulton MkIII

Early in 1959 Alex Moulton produced his MkI prototype bicycle. Its sheet duralumin monocoque body was noisy and needed a sub-frame to cope with transmission loads. But already certain key features of the Moulton bicycle were there – a unisex frame, integral carrier and, most importantly, suspension (albeit only for the front wheel) to smooth the harsh ride of the small diameter, high pressure tyre.

On 16 November 1959 the first patent for the Moulton bicycle concept was filed, GB907467. Based on a design drawn up in August 1959, it had a "lazy F" unisex frame with a single tubular main beam linking cantilevered head and seat tubes. The small wheels allowed more luggage space over them than the classic bicycle. Rubber suspension front and rear not only eliminated the harsh ride of the small wheels, but under most conditions provided a smoother ride than the classic big-wheeler.

The first Moulton Bicycle, The Monocoque, 1959.

At Alex's invitation, and a mere three days after the patent was filed, the chairman of Raleigh, George Wilson, visited The Hall to see and test the MkI bicycle. He said it was the most interesting thing he had seen in his professional life, and asked to borrow it for a week to discuss with his co-directors. George revealed that Raleigh themselves were working on a new bicycle but it was entirely different from Alex's. A drawing dated March 1960 showed it to be a U frame bike with 20" wheels.

Taking the prototype and Alex's patent drawings away with him in his big Jaguar car, George requested that Alex keep the design secret, especially from Raleigh's rivals Hercules. Like Raleigh, Hercules was soon to be absorbed into the Tube Investments group.

George's intention was to mass produce the Moulton bicycle. This suited Alex who agreed to collaborate with Raleigh. But from the outset there was friction between the Moulton and Raleigh teams. As Alex later put it, the new bike was "the embodiment of what provokes opposition in the Corporate Man – coming from **outside** – spotted by the **Chairman,** NOT presented to him from below – and NOT even having the respectability of coming from an acknowledged competitor, or **insider**".

Relations were not helped by George's newly recruited heir apparent Leslie Roberts who, throughout his career, opposed Raleigh's involvement with the Moulton bicycle. Leslie's son Sandy, a long-serving Raleigh executive, recalled that his father never had any doubts about the Moulton's novelty or excellence, but was never convinced of its ability to yield a reasonable profit.

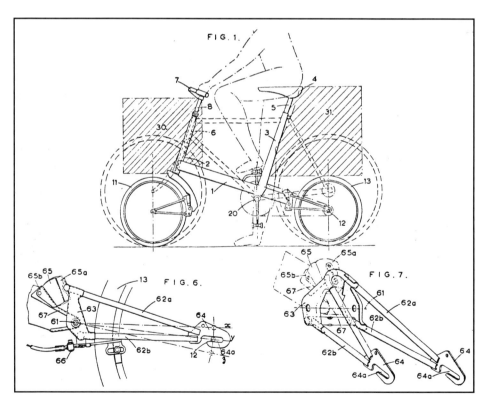

Original 1959 patent drawing for the Moulton Bicycle.

Note the leading link front suspension, triangulated rear suspension and use of small diameter tubes. None of these were used in the 1960s Moulton but all re-emerged in the AM series, albeit in different configurations.

Nonetheless, by August 1960, "practical finality" of the Series 1 Moulton had been reached in all but minor details. In October a licensing agreement was drawn up, allowing Raleigh to manufacture the bike. Because of the hostility of Raleigh staff to the project, Alex offered an initial batch of 10,000 machines royalty free. Production was scheduled to commence in November 1961 at a rate of 200 a week.

At the November 1960 Cycle & Motor Cycle Show, George Wilson continued to show his commitment to the Moulton by having three MkVI prototypes in his private office. However, in September 1961 Raleigh imposed a moratorium on the project, ostensibly because of their development costs. Alex found this difficult to understand, because **he** had paid for most of the work! Raleigh had merely set test standards and prescribed certain specification details relating to standard components.

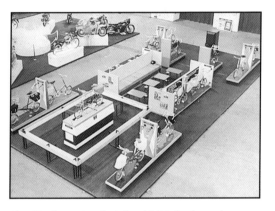

The Moulton stand at the 1962 Cycle and Motorcycle Show, Earls Court.

Two months later, fed up with waiting for Raleigh, Alex commissioned his own pilot market survey. This was carried out by Allied Industrial Consultants at a bicycle shop in Irvine, Scotland. Their report indicated that, even in a relatively conservative area, the new bicycle would find a reasonable market. Raleigh disputed this and in late January

The new factory on The Hall estate, completed in 1963.

1962 abandoned the project. They were, however, prepared to supply components to Alex on favourable terms.

He immediately applied for planning permission to build a bicycle factory on The Hall estate. On 3 February he wrote to George telling him he was going it alone. Moulton Bicycles Limited was formed that April.

The new machine was launched on 12 November 1962 at the Cycle & Motor Cycle Show at Earls Court, London and was an immediate success. It soon became apparent that the new factory at Bradford-on-Avon, still under construction in what would prove to be one of the worst winters on record, would have insufficient capacity. The British Motor Corporation (BMC), with whom Alex had close links, immediately came to the rescue: chairman Sir Leonard Lord (later Lord Lambury) sent a message to Alex telling him not to hesitate to take orders, because BMC would make the bike for him. Alex accepted the offer and in January 1963 BMC's Fisher & Ludlow subsidiary began preparing for manufacture. Deliveries of the new bike began in March, despite suspiciously strange difficulties in obtaining components from Raleigh.

Three months later George Wilson and Leslie Roberts had lunch with Alex at The Hall. To George's surprise Leslie hinted that if Alex's bike sold well, Raleigh would launch a competing machine. Alex countered by threatening action if his patents were infringed. After the meal George offered to let Alex see the prototype of any competing machine developed by Raleigh.

Unfortunately George was killed in a car accident that December but in late March 1964 Alex did indeed visit Raleigh where he was shown the prototype RSW16 (Raleigh Small Wheels 16") – a heavy, balloon-tyred, unsprung machine, at first sight similar in appearance to the Moulton.

It was not immediately clear whether the RSW16 breached Alex's original patent in respect of its frame configuration, and both sides subsequently sought legal opinion. That June the Raleigh directors sought a production licence from Alex. He was prepared to grant one for the production of an **unsprung** F frame small-wheeler, provided the genuine Moulton could be sold through Raleigh-only dealers. In mid August Leslie Roberts met Alex over dinner and hinted that what Raleigh really wanted was a licence for the original Moulton bicycle with suspension.

Negotiations continued into the autumn and included the possibility of Raleigh buying the Moulton bicycle interests outright. In October Alex again met Leslie, who this time expressed an interest in buying badge-engineered Moultons (made by Fisher & Ludlow but with Raleigh nameplates) for sale through Raleigh's exclusive agents. Alternatively, Raleigh would be prepared to handle the entire marketing operation on Alex's behalf. This proposal came to nothing, although in early 1965 a "special relationship" was established between the two companies, allowing Moultons to be sold by Raleigh-only dealers.

This helped Alex more than Raleigh, who were becoming increasingly desperate as their market share was eroded. Alex had become the second largest single-brand bicycle maker in the country. By mid 1965 he was producing more than 1,000 units a week and tens of thousands of Moultons were already on the road. The almost terminal post-war decline in UK bicycle sales had been reversed, but Raleigh was not benefiting.

Alex now began winding up Raleigh by juggling with his serial numbers to suggest even more Moultons were being made. Serial numbers of bikes made in mid June 1965 mischievously suggested a production rate of nearly 10,000 units a week! A month later, reasonably confident that there would be no action over patent infringement, Raleigh finally released the RSW16. The launch on 17 July 1965 was supported by an unprecedented £100,000 of publicity (nearly £1m at 1994 prices).

A trade war between Moulton and Raleigh broke out, resulting in the rationalisation of the Moulton range and the introduction of a cheaper 14" wheel version. This smaller bike was ergonomically optimised for the majority of British women, to compete more directly with the RSW16. The original Moulton was designed to adjust for most British men, but was a bit of a stretch for smaller women. Conversely, the RSW16 was designed for the majority of British women, but was too cramped for taller men.

A Series 1 Moulton Standard with added front carrier and rear holdall, typical of the thousands of machines produced during the mid 1960s. From the 1965 catalogue designed by Colin Banks and John Miles.

In 1966 full control of home and export production of the Moulton passed to BMC who planned to make 100,000 bikes a year. But this was not to be. The heavily marketed RSW16 proved popular, being well made and cheaper than the Moulton. More than 100,000 RSW16s were sold in its nine year production run, the majority in the mid 1960s. Other established bicycle makers entered the market, such as Dawes with their 20" wheel Kingpin, which stayed in continuous production longer than any other British small-wheeled bicycle.

Dealer resistance to the Moulton had meanwhile been nurtured by 11,000 defective front forks made by a sub-contractor and by numerous defective rear forks made by BMC. Meanwhile Raleigh and Moulton accused each other's sales forces of "knocking" the competition.

By summer 1967 weekly sales of the Moulton, though still healthy, were down a quarter to 750 a week. This represented about 6% of the UK cycle market, but another 6-9% had been gained by the Moulton's small-wheeled competitors. Both Raleigh and Moulton were suffering as a result of the cut-throat competition: Raleigh's 1966 profits had dropped 8% and Moulton Bicycles Limited were losing about £1,200 a week (£11,000 at 1994 prices).

Two similar offers were now made for Alex's business, one from the toy makers Lines Brothers of Birmingham (Triang), who produced a child's Moulton under licence, the other from TI-Raleigh Limited of Nottingham. Alex meanwhile was tiring of the struggle and wanted to devote more time to automotive design work, such as his innovative interlinked suspension systems (Hydrolastic and Hydragas) and the Moulton coach, with its geodetic structure and double bogies.

The spirit of the decade was also changing. The swinging sixties, for which the Moulton bicycle had become an icon, were entering a gloomier phase. In Britain the summer of '67 saw the immensely popular pirate radio stations outlawed, bitter controversy over the legalisation of abortion, and the suicide of the Beatles manager, Brian Epstein. Overseas the Vietnam conflict escalated and race riots swept the cities of the USA.

On 23 July Tommy Simpson, a great believer in the speed potential of the Moulton, died competing in the Tour de France. Six days later Moulton Bicycles Limited became part of TI-Raleigh, and Alex became a consultant to his erstwhile rivals.

Leslie Roberts admitted publicly that Raleigh were wrong to reject the Moulton design and blamed faulty market research. "Together we're unbeatable," he told the press, citing Alex's "inventive genius" and Raleigh's "unparalleled resources". An early priority was joint development of motorised bicycles.

At this time Raleigh still made mopeds, true MOtor assisted PEDal cycles. Only two months earlier they had launched the Wisp, essentially an RSW16 with a two-stroke petrol engine slung under the main beam. One of Alex's tasks was to advise on improvements to this machine. Interestingly, less than three weeks before selling Moulton Bicycles Limited to Raleigh, he had been granted British patent 1074431 covering a transmission system for a small-wheeled moped. This involved a hub gear with two freewheels, one driven by a motor, the other by pedals.

However, the most significant product of Alex's second period of collaboration with Raleigh was the Moulton MkIII. The Nottingham firm's contribution to the design was minimal.

The Production MkIII

The production version of the Moulton MkIII was launched by Raleigh in summer 1970, along with the RSW16 MkIII and the hugely successful Raleigh Chopper. The latter, more a toy than a bicycle, completely eclipsed the other two machines, both in terms of publicity gained and sales achieved – six years later it was still selling nearly 100,000 a year. Paradoxically it used a modified RSW16 frame and was therefore, in a bizarre way, a spin-off from the original Moulton.

The Moulton MkIII embodied the essential features of the original Moulton bicycle: small wheels with narrow section high pressure tyres and independent suspension, an open unisex frame adjustable to suit the majority of adults, and extraordinarily good provision for carrying luggage. However, the MkIII differed in several ways from the earlier Moultons, having features that were to be developed further in the later AM series.

Gone was the short cantilevered rear suspension fork. In its place was a long swinging rear triangle, pivoted immediately behind the

bottom bracket, minimising variations in wheelbase and chain tension. The apex of the swinging triangle (the cam) compressed an egg-shaped rubber block with flattened ends, the "squash ball". This was mounted on a short steel channel brazed to the back of the seat tube. To hold the triangle in place when the bike was lifted, a bolt brazed to the channel passed through the squash ball and the cam: the self-locking nut had a rubber washer to absorb rebound shock.

The MkIII was designed to be less of a stretch for smaller riders than previous 16" wheel Moultons. The seat tube was therefore slightly shorter, but more importantly, it was significantly closer to the head tube, shortening the wheelbase from $44^1/_2$" (1,130 mm)

Moulton MkIII production version, from the Raleigh "Happy Families" catalogue c.1970. Reproduced by courtesy of Raleigh.

to 41" (1,041 mm). Because of this, the MkIII's main beam met the seat tube higher up than in the earlier bikes. The bottom bracket was therefore built onto the bottom of the seat tube, rather than the underside of the main beam.

The MkIII's carrier provision was also different. For marketing and cost cutting reasons Raleigh chose not to provide front carrier mountings. More significantly, the rear carrier was of a new design and completely detachable.

Earlier Moultons incorporated a rear carrier which sat on a tail tube formed by extending the frame's low top tube/carrying handle rearwards through the seat tube and beyond. The front of the cantilevered carrier was given additional support by a thin tubular steel tie from the top of the seat tube to the front of the carrier, and by a similar strut from just ahead of the rear suspension spring.

The MkIII's rear carrier had a small diameter steel perimeter tube which, like its predecessors, was bent upwards to form an upstand: at this point a cross tube braced the carrier. But whereas the earlier design had two parallel infill tubes running from the rear of the carrier to the cross tube, the MkIII infill was a pair of wider tubes in V formation. They were furthest apart where they met the perimeter tube at the rear of the carrier, and closest where they were bolted to the squash ball mounting. The extended infill tubes therefore doubled as a substitute for the earlier Moulton's tail tube.

A single strut prevented the carrier pivoting down onto the rear wheel. The strut was bolted to a low fixing on the back of the seat tube, and extended to the middle of the carrier's underside, where it bolted to a cross-piece linking the infill tubes.

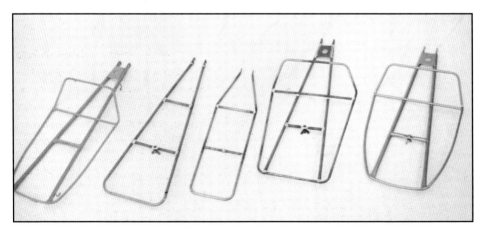

Carrier evolution: Production Mk III far left, V-bar prototype's carrier second from left. The carrier far right closely resembles the AM's.

The production MkIII had a frame constructed from mild steel tubing. Only one model was marketed, equipped with standard roadster components. Variable gearing was provided by the Sturmey-Archer S3B three-speed/small diameter hub brake combination, first fitted to the RSW MkII. It must be said that this was not the most effective hub brake Sturmey-Archer ever produced. (See my book "The Sturmey-Archer Story" for further details.)

The "V-bar" Prototype

Even before Raleigh launched the MkIII, Alex Moulton had produced superior versions in prototype form. He demonstrated one of these in spring 1969, more than a year before the MkIII's launch. Equipped with lightweight components, it had the special Moulton-designed

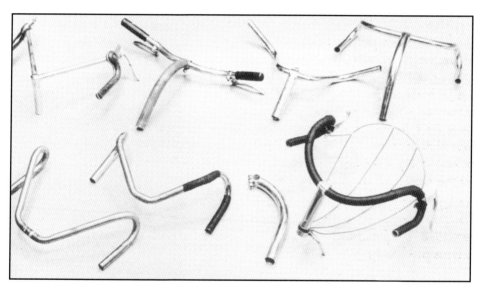

Experimental handlebar and stem configurations. The V-bar is top left.

The "V-bar" prototype MkIII.

1¼" high pressure Dunlop tyre (introduced in 1965 for the Speedsix), and centre-pull brakes. The seat stays and chain stays were half-chromed, and a narrower, simplified version of the MkIII carrier was fitted. This lacked the upstand and V formation infill tubes of the production version.

The bike had a special handlebar configuration with a pair of integral tapered arms branching forwards and upwards in a V formation. The end of each arm had an adjustable laminated "pistol grip", with timber outer sections on an alloy core. Each grip was fitted with an integral drop handlebar brake lever.

The 1969 "531" prototype

Late in 1969 cycle journalist Peter Knottley undertook a 1,000 mile (1,600 km) test of a prototype lightweight MkIII built of Reynolds 531 tubing. Apart from the use of superior lightweight tubing, the frame design was essentially the same as the production MkIII. Differences of detail included bosses for cantilever brakes and a front carrier. At about 28lb (12.7 kg), the machine was some 7lb (3.2 kg) lighter than the production MkIII.

Lightweight equipment comprised a Brooks leather saddle, GB Tourist drop handlebars on a Cinelli stem, Dunlop 1^1/$_4$" tyres on Milremo rims, British Hub quick-release hubs, Bluemels Club Special mudguards, and Lyotard platform pedals. A Williams AB77 cotterless chainset with 52 tooth chainwheel drove a six-speed block, the sprockets having from 25 to 11 teeth and giving gears from 36 to 80": the derailleur was by Huret.

According to Peter it took him about 30 miles (50 km) to get used to the bike. He wrote:

"It seemed to me that this machine ran just a little more freely than my usual mounts, which are 27" machines of the best quality. This, with the advantages of the suspension, made hill-climbing just that bit less energetic and more smooth."

Downhill he "attained some very high speeds" and noted "a complete absence of the jolting to which one gets accustomed on a conventional machine". He was particularly impressed by the wet road-holding and found the steering "not a whit less natural than with a large-wheel cycle".

The Marathon

In 1970, Colin Martin cycled from Wiltshire, England to Kalgoorlie, Western Australia on a Moulton Marathon. This was another prototype MkIII, produced in 1969.

Only four Marathons were made. Colin's was stolen in Australia, terminating what was intended to be a round-the-world tour. A replacement was sent out to him, but instead of completing his

The 1969 Moulton Marathon.

journey, he married and settled in Australia.

The other two Marathons were made for a pair of cyclists planning a major international tour. However, they abandoned their plans and one of the machines ended up being used as a utility bike in London. It came to light a few years ago and is now preserved by a member of the Moulton Bicycle Club.

The Stowaway Joint

An important feature of the Marathon was its dividing main beam, found hitherto only in the Series 1 & 2 Stowaway models. The Stowaway joint enabled the frame to be separated into two parts for easy stowage.

The heart of the Stowaway joint comprised two pieces of pressed steel, forming upper and lower expanding jaws. At one end the jaws were brazed together; at the other they could be forced apart by an Allen bolt acting on a pair of machined steel plates, one clipped into each jaw. The bolt was threaded through one plate, its rounded end acting on a depression in the face of the other.

The Stowaway mechanism was fitted with a small, spring-loaded safety button. In all production Stowaways this was directly below the Allen bolt. However, in some later experimental machines the button was above the bolt, with a hole through the button for the Allen key. In one prototype the safety button protruded from the top of the joint at about 45 degrees to the bolt.

To fit the Stowaway joint it was necessary first to saw right through the main beam of the bicycle. The end of the mechanism where the jaws were brazed together fitted tightly into the rear part of the main beam. It was first pop-riveted into position to locate it accurately, then brazed in.

Separable lightweight MkIII prototype.

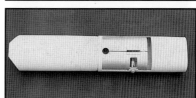

Cutaway Stowaway Joint, shown separated (above), and joined (below).

Next the front part of the main beam was fitted with an internal vertical tie rod. This passed through the top and bottom of the tube and was riveted and brazed into place.

On the top of the main beam, between its cut end and the tie rod, a hole was drilled for Allen key access. In the production version the safety button engaged in another hole, drilled in the underside of the beam.

To reassemble the frame, the jaws protruding from the rearward part of the main beam were inserted into the forward part of the beam. The jaws were slotted so that they passed either side of the tie rod. As the two parts of the frame were pushed together, the safety button clicked into its hole in the forward part of the main beam, thus holding the two parts of the bike loosely together.

The Allen key was then placed in the hole in the top of the beam and rotated clockwise approximately two full turns. This opened the jaws which locked against the inside of the forward main beam. The tie rod, passing through the centre of both jaws, prevented them from appreciably distorting the main beam. Thus the two parts of the frame were held rigidly together.

The Marathon's Equipment

The Marathon used a German Fichtel & Sachs Duomatic 102 two-speed/coaster brake combination. Gear changing and rear wheel braking were both actuated by back-pedalling. There were therefore no cables from the front of the bike to the rear to complicate frame separability.

The front brake was a cantilever, operated from the top of the drop handlebars by a randonneur-style lever. Rarely seen in the UK or USA, these light and powerful levers are particularly suitable for tourists. They clamp to the bars near the stem.

Special carriers were created for the Marathon. For compactness Alex wanted a pair of panniers either side of the head tube. The front carrier therefore projected forward of the head tube only enough to support the forward bottom corners of the panniers and to provide a small platform for items such as a cape. Behind the head tube the carrier incorporated a cage for a Primus stove.

The rear carrier formed a cradle for Colin's rucksack, the perimeter tube being higher than the infill members. To get heel clearance, the carrier was mounted about 30 degrees to the horizontal, its front fixed to the seatpin binder bolt. The underside held an aluminium mess-kit, and several spare tyres could be looped over the rucksack and carrier. Like the production carrier, the Marathon's was supported by a strut. (The Marathon's unusual rear carrier configuration reappeared in modified form with the 1991 AM-GT. And in 1994 a GT front carrier was produced which bore some resemblance to the Marathon's front rack.)

The greatest significance of the Marathon was its combination of a **touring specification with frame separability.** Virtually all Moultons designed thereafter were to incorporate a separable frame. Alex had reached the conclusion that this convenient feature should normally be incorporated into any future design, as an advantage over the traditional diamond frame bicycle.

The Moulton MkIV

The next evolutionary design therefore incorporated the Stowaway joint. Produced in July 1974 and known as the MkIV, it was essentially a MkIII with an exceptionally short head tube and a specially designed long swan-neck handlebar stem, clamped by an external binder bolt rather than an internal expander. Typical main frame weight (excluding rear triangle and front fork) was 5lb 12oz (2.61 kg).

Swan-neck handlebar stems were by no means new. Probably their most recent use had been in the RSW16. But whereas the RSW had a heavy steel swan-neck stem with integral flat handlebars, the Moulton swan-neck was lighter and useable with any commercially available style of bars. However, as it was made of over-sized tubing, it needed a special large diameter headset.

At least two MkIV Moultons were built. They incorporated further detail refinements: the rear suspension's squash ball was encased in a rubber bellows; front carrier fixing bosses were provided; and there was a twelve-speed derailleur system, controlled by shifters on the bar ends.

The derailleur system and use of a conventional cable-operated rear brake necessitated another design development destined to be used in the AM series – separable control cables. Turnbuckle cable joints were positioned below the Stowaway joint, the necessary cable stops being brazed to the underside of the main beam.

One of the MkIVs was fitted with centre-pull brakes, another with cantilevers. The latter was donated to the National Cycle Museum at Lincoln. The swan-neck handlebar stem was eventually abandoned because of its tendency to kink in a head-on impact.

Moulton MkIV, July 1974.

The Y-frame

In late February 1975 the MkIV was succeeded by the Y-frame. The principal innovation concerned the new bike's main beam. Rather than spanning from the head tube to the seat tube, it ran only from the head tube to the top tube. A short down tube, similar in length and cross-section to the top tube, linked the truncated main beam to the bottom bracket. Thus head and seat tubes were linked by a Y configuration of tubing.

First prototype Y-frame Moulton, built 23 February 1975.

The main frame of the February 1975 version was substantially lighter than that of the MkIV, weighing 4lb 10oz (2.10 kg). A slightly revised version was produced in May 1975.

One of the Y-frame machines was fitted with another of Alex's experimental handlebar systems. Its long forward extension could, with the aid of an Allen key, be pivoted in the vertical plane. Hence the handlebars could be very high and close to the rider, very low and far ahead, or anything in between.

Another Y-frame machine was fitted with the swan-neck handlebar configuration. Finished in olive green, it became one of Alex's

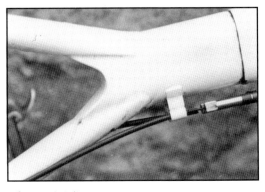

Y-frame details.

particular favourites. He rode it regularly until the launch of the first spaceframe machines, often with just a front carrier for light luggage.

The Parting of the Ways

By June 1974 Raleigh had decided to cease production of Moulton bicycles. Alex's collaboration with the company was formally terminated on 31 January 1975, the optional halfway break point in the 15 year consultancy period.

Raleigh had produced about 55,000 of the 150,000 Moultons

Des Isley working on Alex Moulton's personal Y-frame bike.

manufactured in the UK. (70,000 were made by BMC, 25,000 at Bradford-on-Avon.) But annual sales of the MkIII were disappointing at about 1,300, and total production was only some 5,200. Sales of Raleigh's 14" wheel Moultons, the Mini and Midi, were also poor. And the company's decision (against Alex's advice) to omit front suspension from these smaller bikes had led to frame cracking and recalls.

In contrast, Raleigh's 20" wheel unisex bike, launched about 1969 as the Triumph 20, was the company's biggest seller. For example, in 1975, despite record UK inflation averaging 24.2%, the five versions of the Raleigh 20 had combined sales of 140,000 on the domestic market – almost as many in one year as the total UK Moulton production since 1963. It was still Raleigh's best seller two years later.

By June 1974 Alex had accepted that there was little future for his collaboration with Raleigh. He wanted instead to start small-scale, high quality production of his Y-frame bike at Bradford-on-Avon. Negotiations were already under way with Pirelli and Dunlop for a new supply of his unique 17" tyre, which had never been exploited by Raleigh.

But despite abandoning the Moulton, Raleigh refused to sell Alex's patents and registered designs back to him. However, a condition of the consultancy termination entitled him to licences on reasonable terms. In June 1975 Alex therefore asked Raleigh for a non-exclusive licence to use certain of his suspension patents: GB937117 and GB1047783 relating to the telescopic front suspension, and GB1205286 covering the MkIII's rear suspension. In return Raleigh wanted a royalty, information on any of Alex's design improvements and an undertaking that his bikes would not be marketed as Moultons. This was not entirely acceptable to Alex and by December he was trying to design his way around Raleigh's demands, by using an air suspension system for the front wheel, and a more advanced rubber system for the rear. (The air suspension worked well but needed pumping up every week or so.)

Negotiations continued until the following autumn. On 18 October 1976 Raleigh finally signed an agreement allowing Alex to use the patents, and letting him use the new trade mark "Alex Moulton".

Alex was therefore free, as he put it, "once again to 'go it alone' but this time in a very small way at the top of the market."

A Quadrilateral Interlude

While the divorce from Raleigh proceeded, Alex continued his development work. In 1975 severe torsion trials were carried out on the separable Y-frame. The bike was scientifically subjected to sideways twisting of the head tube relative to the seat tube, a graph being produced relating increasing torsion levels to measured frame deflection. As a result he decided to abandon the original Stowaway joint.

In September 1975 he built a non-separable quadrilateral main frame of round aluminium tube. This weighed just 1lb 13oz (0.82 kg). The following month a separable version was produced, having detachable clamps at each end of the top and down tubes. These solid aluminium clamps were necessarily heavy and pushed the main frame weight up to 4lb (1.81 kg). A non-separable 24 swg steel tubed version, made in March 1976, weighed 3lb 13oz (1.73 kg).

Leading link suspension on the corrugated Y-frame Moulton.

The Corrugated Joint Y-Frame

By this time Alex was working on a more rigid version of the Stowaway joint. In February 1976 a variant of the Y-frame was built using a corrugated (dumb-bell) section main beam and weighing 4lb 11oz (2.13 kg). As before, the two parts of the frame plugged together. But instead of the rear part's spigot jaws being expanded by the jacking action of a vertical bolt, a horizontal bolt tightened a pair of external cam plates against the web of the beam's front part, squeezing it onto the spigot.

Mechanic Des Isley, then a prominent and long-serving member of the Moulton development team, rode this machine 20,000 miles (32,300 km) in 18 months. Equipment included drop handlebars mounted on a swan-neck stem and an American Cool Gear saddle, which was highly rated.

The Monosphere

Part of the test programme involved improved front and rear suspensions. The rubber spring for the rear suspension was no longer the truncated ovoid squash ball of the original MkIII. Instead a more sophisticated hollow rubber cone was used, the Monosphere, similar to the Moulton-designed unit in the Rover Mini.

The new spring had a domed rubber face, against which rested the cam at the apex of the rear triangle. As the cam pressed harder, the surface area of rubber in contact with it increased, thus continuously and automatically uprating the spring.

The MkIII's squash ball provided the same facility in a less refined way. However, the new spring offered a second means of automatic uprating. The hollow rubber cone reacted not only to compression (squashing) forces but also to shear (sliding) forces. This dual automatic spring rate adjustment meant that the rear suspension adjusted unusually well to the weight of rider and luggage, and yet could be very light and substantially maintenance free.

Leading Links

The front suspension was also radically different. Hitherto a single telescopic system had been used. Splines on a guide tube brazed to the fork crown engaged in a serrated nylon bearing at the base of the steerer tube (steering column). This gave steering linkage while allowing the fork to move up and down relative to the steerer tube. A rubber or neoprene bellows between the base of the steerer tube and the crown of the fork prevented grit and dust from clogging the nylon bearing.

The suspension medium was a rubber column inside a long steel coil spring. The rubber took most of the load (typically 80%) and by bulging between the coils of the spring, automatically damped the system. There was a second short coil spring to absorb rebound shock. Although there was no provision for fine tuning the system, those in the know could increase the pre-loading by inserting a spacer to pre-compress the rubber column and coil spring. This could be useful for heavier riders, maximising suspension travel and reducing suspension sag on mounting the bike. The ride could also be made stiffer by shortening the rubber column and coil spring, and making up the length with a spacer.

In the new front suspension the wheel was bolted to a fork stirrup. The top of the stirrup was connected by a hinged link plate to pivots on the back of the fork blades, a little below the fork crown. The bottom of the stirrup was attached to the fork ends by leading (forward facing) links. The arrangement formed a parallelogram and allowed the stirrup (and therefore the wheel) to move up and down relative to the steerer tube, while imparting steering linkage.

The new suspension medium was a simple steel coil spring in the steerer tube. The spring acted on a guide bearing (base plug) connected to the middle of the hinged plate. Damping was by friction discs in the leading link pivots.

Parallel Developments

The corrugated joint Y-frame Moulton was a significant improvement on the MkIII prototype demonstrated eight years earlier. The frame was lighter, stronger and separable; the front and rear suspension more subtle. Yet in parallel with its development and testing, Alex evolved other frame options, all with short head tubes. These variants were routinely tested for torsional strength, just as the earlier Y-frame had been.

In March 1976 a non-separable X-frame was built out of 20 swg steel tube. The 1¹/₂" (38 mm) diameter head and seat tubes were linked by two 1¹/₄" (32 mm) diameter tubes which intersected each other to form an X when viewed from the side. This frame weighed 3lb 3oz (1.45 kg).

The following month, April 1976, saw a new version of the Y-frame. This had a large diameter round-section main beam with a threaded locking ring for the separable joint and weighed 4lb 2oz (1.87 kg). Alex also built a non-separable frame with the head and seat tube linked solely by a very deep section oval tube. This weighed 3lb 14oz (1.76 kg). A slightly later version had a main beam that was wedge-shaped when viewed from the side – reminiscent of the Moulton-inspired Pavemaster Spacemaster small-wheeler of the 1960s. The deeper end of the beam was joined to the seat tube, and the frame weighed 3lb 2oz (1.42 kg).

In May 1976 Alex sketched a frame with a die-cast aluminium Y-shaped centre section, separable from the head and seat tube by means of four U-clamps. But to make the desired weight savings this frame would have needed wall thicknesses of only $^1/_{16}$" (1.6 mm). Such thin-walled construction would have been very difficult to manufacture reliably and consistently.

That month he also built a non-separable frame, somewhat similar to the MkIII's but with a large diameter round main beam and a bracing gusset between the base of the seat tube and the underside of the main beam. This frame, built of Reynolds 531 tubing, weighed 2lb 13oz (1.28 kg).

Frame experiments continued through the remainder of 1976. In June a "torque box" frame was built of 24 swg Reynolds 531, the main beam increasing in depth and width dramatically in the zone of maximum frame torsion near its junction with the seat tube. Other frame variations were tried in July, August and October. Towards the end of the year "arrow" frames were built, in which a large diameter main beam was braced to the seat tube by a pair of very thin tubes or flat strips. One of these frames, built in November 1976, weighed 4lb (1.81 kg).

But Alex was not happy with any of these designs. As he put it:

"Big tubes in aluminium were rejected on the basis of poor fatigue at the welded lugless joints. Big tubes in light gauge steel were rejected because of the ease of denting with the high diameter/thickness ratio."

The Y-frame was still hard to beat. Test riding of the corrugated frame version was going well. In late February 1977 Alex began fine tuning the design.

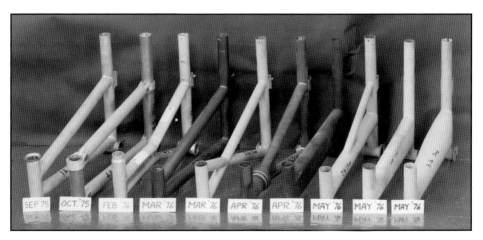

Experimental frames from September 1975 to May 1976. The corrugated Y-frame is third from the left.

Footnote: In case you have been puzzled by the heading of this chapter, the Raleigh trademark incorporates a heron's head!

19

Chapter 2
GOING IT ALONE
1977-1983

Designing the Alex Moulton bicycle

By spring 1977 Alex Moulton was free again to "go it alone". In bullish mood he outlined his proposals to cycle journalist Peter Knottley. Peter's subsequent article in the weekly magazine Cycling revealed Alex's intention to produce two versions of his new bike, a "Super-Tourist" and an upmarket commuter model. Both would use the special 17" Moulton tyre.

The tourer, with 12-speed derailleur gears, would be built of Reynolds 531 tubing and would incorporate a more advanced suspension system. Luggage capacity would be superlative and the pump would be concealed in the oversize seat tube. The bike would be separable, capable of being stowed in a bag.

Alex's intention was to use the separable Y-frame as the basis for the new bikes. But the plan then suffered a setback, and the hitherto linear evolution of the Moulton bicycle swerved sharply sideways.

This was caused by a casual remark. Alex was on holiday in France, riding a Y-frame Moulton. His companion, Philippe Carpentier, commented unfavourably on its weight. Even though the machine was no heavier than a typical conventional tourer built of Reynolds 531 (about 29lb or 13 kg), the Frenchman perceived it to be too heavy.

Alex was haunted by this intuitive response. He therefore turned his creative efforts to designing a bike with a significantly lighter frame. This was not easy, as he wanted it to have all the advantages of the Y-frame – full suspension, separability and superlative luggage carrying capacity.

The Spaceframe

The breakthrough came on 1 June 1977. This was when Alex returned to the X-frame theme of March 1976. However, instead of a simple two-dimensional X formed of round tubing, he sketched a frame that used intersecting trussed beams laid on their sides.

Each beam had outer members (chords) of $^1/_2$" (13 mm) diameter 24 swg Reynolds 531 tubing. These chords were linked by a perforated 22 swg pressed steel infill (web). The web, and therefore the beam itself, was widest in mid span and narrowest at the ends.

One beam spanned from the base of the seat tube to the top of the head tube; the other ran horizontally from the middle of the seat tube to the base of the head tube. Therefore, when the frame was viewed from the side, the two beams formed a cross; and the frame was described in the subsequent patents as "cruciform".

The beams were cut at their intersection, and brazed to a three part horizontal tube. The rearward halves of the beams were brazed to the two outer parts of the tube; the forward halves to the centre part. Through the tube ran a "kingpin", a removable bolt holding the front and back of the frame together.

Because of its width at the mid point, this frame configuration gave tremendous lateral strength. However, it provided no vertical rigidity whatsoever, the kingpin acting as a hinge. Therefore, to triangulate the structure in the vertical plane, a thin tie bar was employed. This

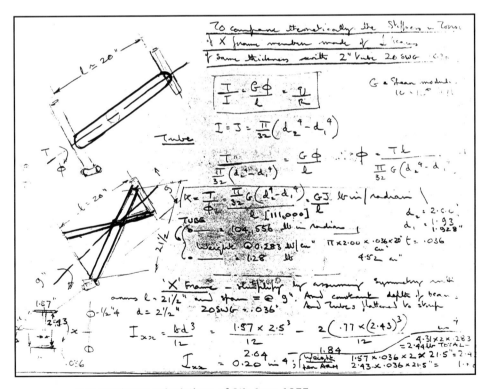

Alex Moulton's calculations of 8th June 1977.
"To compare theoretically the stiffness in torsion of X frame member made of I beams of same thickness with 2" tube 20 swg .036".

tied the base of the seat tube to the base of the head tube. So that the frame could be separated, the tie rod was separable below the kingpin.

As Engineering magazine later put it, Alex had reconciled...

"... the conflicting requirements of stiffness, lightness and separability using laterally stiff beams of 'torsionally feeble elements' in an X-frame. The 'feeble elements' would ensure low weight, their assembly into beams would provide torsional rigidity and crossing the beams in an X-shape would allow separability via a kingpin."

Alex had created a novel spaceframe - a three-dimensional structure, triangulated in more than one plane - in an area dominated by two-dimensional structural design.

Truly three-dimensional cycle frames are relatively rare. The late nineteenth century Pedersen is perhaps the best-known example. It pioneered the use of thin tubing but had a completely different (and much less rigid) structural form than Alex's spaceframe. In the late 1960s Professor D. E. Newland claimed that his lightweight folding bicycle, designed in 1965 and extensively tested by Raleigh's Carlton subsidiary, had a spaceframe. However, it was essentially a two-dimensional folding lattice truss, with a partly bifurcated top chord to permit the seat tube to fold.

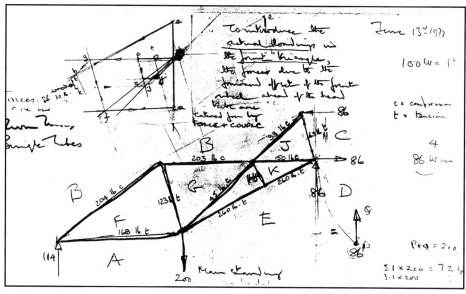

Further calculations, 13th June 1977.

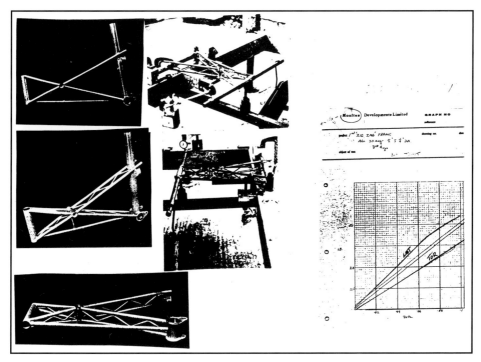

The first Moulton spaceframe with thin tube zig-zag infills, tested for lateral and torsional strength.

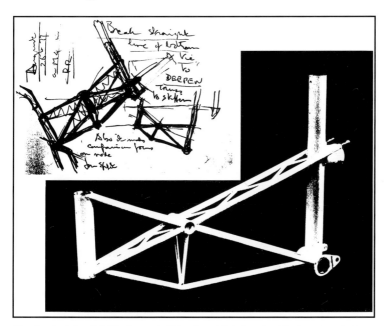

Alex's sketch of 26th August 1977 in which he decided to break the straight line of the bottom tie. This deepened the truss, making it stronger. It also made, as he put it, "comparison focus on mode for split".

The photograph shows a non-separable prototype frame with the "bent" tie.

Lower Weight, Higher Strength

In June 1977 two prototype non-separable frames were built. One had beams with perforated sheet steel webs as in Alex's sketch. However, there was no tie bar, gusset plates being used to reinforce the intersection of the two beams. This frame weighed 3lb 11oz (1.67 kg) - slightly more than the plain tube X-frame of March 1976.

The other June 1977 frame was more promising. It weighed 3lb 4oz (1.48 kg) and had a web formed by a zigzag formation of $^1/_4$" (6 mm) Reynolds 531 tubes, each thinner than a pencil. The frame was tested for torsional and lateral stiffness and was found to be nearly two and a half times better than a typical conventional frame.

Torsional and lateral stiffness (the abilities respectively to resist twisting and sideways bending) are significant and much ignored factors in bicycle frame design. American cycle journalist Doug Roosa says the typical diamond frame is roughly 30 times more rigid vertically than laterally. Its vertical rigidity is therefore considerably greater than is needed. Yet the frame suffers from "a fair amount of side-to-side flex". This absorbs rider energy.

Frame flexing has long been a recognised problem, yet little has been done to overcome it. As Doug Roosa puts it, "it's hard to triangulate a frame horizontally and still fit the thing between the rider's legs". But Alex's spaceframe did exactly that.

In August 1977 a separable version of the thin tube spaceframe was produced. This was 11oz (0.31 kg) heavier than its non-separable predecessor. The original thin tube spaceframe was built up into a complete bike. By 12 August Des Isley was test riding it.

The patents relating to the new Alex Moulton bicycle were not applied for until about five months before its commercial launch. This was to prevent news of the new machine leaking and detracting from its impact. Therefore from 1977 increasing secrecy surrounded the technical innovations at Bradford-on-Avon.

British patent 2130982 for the basic, non-separable cruciform frame concept was applied for on 1 December 1982. This was more than five years after Alex conceived the idea.

The August 1977 non-separable Spaceframe Moulton outside the drawing office, test ridden by Des Isley.

Frame Jointing

Most of the August 1977 prototype's frame joints were lugged in the traditional way. (A lug is a sleeved coupling for two or more tubes, which are brazed into it.) However, these non-standard lugs were expensive to make. Furthermore, a complete set weighed 25.6oz (726 gm). Alex's long-serving chief engineer (and patentee of a number of Moulton bicycle-related innovations) Phil Uncles solved this problem by designing machines to "cod's mouth" the ends of the tubes. The smaller tubes then junctioned perfectly and directly with the larger ones without needing lugs. The frame could then be assembled using SIF bronze welding, commonly referred to as "brazing" but superior to true (brass) brazing for this application. Weight was saved, cost reduced and appearance improved.

Alex later wrote:

"The design of the AM was purposely slanted towards hand crafting to increase the perceived value appropriate to a small-scale operation. Nevertheless every process is jigged to ensure accuracy. All the many mitred joints are milled in fixtures to control the gaps. The bronze welded joints are exposed for visual inspection, and each completed frame is tested for torsional alignment, typically within 4 minutes of a degree ($^1/_{15}$th of a degree). The space-frame, properly jigged and with an organised sequence of welding, is inherently accurate in comparison with a conventional frame."

In contrast, conventional frames are commonly merely twisted into precise vertical alignment after assembly.

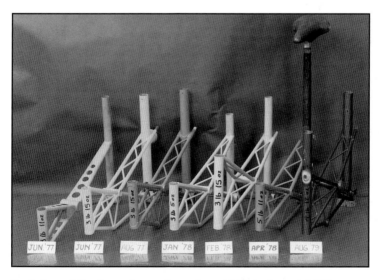

Evolution of the Spaceframe, from June 1977 to August 1979.
The lugged separable frame is third from the left.

The Hook Joint

Another refinement was devised by Alex's nephew, Christopher Hartnoll, whose brother Julian is a director of Alex Moulton Limited. Christopher's suggestion solved the problem of how best to make the frame's tie rod separable.

The solution is a hook joint beneath the kingpin. The rearward part of the tie terminates below the kingpin in a socket. This is braced by a pair of thin tubes to the kingpin housing. Into the socket fits a hook on the end of the forward part of the tie.

When the frame is reassembled, the kingpin is first removed. Next the hook end of the forward tie is inserted into the socket. The two parts of the bike then swing together under their own weight, the hook joint acting as a hinge.

The cuts between the three tubular sections of the kingpin housing are angled, so that the inner section of the housing (on the front part of the frame) automatically aligns itself between the two outer sections (on the rear part of the frame).

The kingpin is then reinserted and tightened up. Finally, a threaded locking ring is screwed down hand-tight onto the knuckle, taking up the slight tolerance in the joint.

Hook joint detail.
Note cutaway knuckle showing hook inside socket.

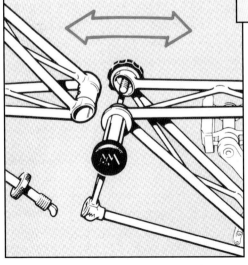

The production hook joint.

The Captive Kingpin

Ultimately a system was evolved that did away with the loose kingpin, making separability more convenient (although the loose kingpin was reintroduced for the 20" wheel versions of the spaceframe Moulton). In the original production version the captive kingpin takes the form of a $^7/_8$" (22 mm) diameter steel tube which does not rotate. Brazed to its left end is a pressed steel flange. To this a black plastic knob is friction-fitted and glued. The knob is pulled to the left to withdraw the kingpin.

Threaded to the flange is a thin guide rod which passes through a hole in the frame immediately below the kingpin. The right-hand end of the guide rod is formed into a stop, thus preventing the kingpin from being completely withdrawn to the left. The flange prevents withdrawal to the right.

But merely making the kingpin captive is not enough. A means of tightening the assembly is also necessary. This is provided as follows.

At the right-hand end of the kingpin housing is another black plastic knob, knurled to aid rotation by hand. The knob is fixed by three small Allen bolts to a steel disc. The disc passes over, and is welded to, a large Allen bolt. The threaded end of the bolt engages in a thread in the right-hand end of the kingpin. The head of the bolt is recessed into the face of the plastic knob.

The knob and the disc are assembled either side of a flange on the end of the kingpin housing. Hence they are captive but free to rotate.

To lock the frame together, the left-hand plastic knob is moved fully to the left, thus pushing the kingpin through both parts of the frame. The right-hand knob is then rotated by hand, screwing its bolt into the end of the kingpin and pulling the whole assembly tightly together. Final tightening of the bolt, about an eighth of a turn, requires insertion of a 6 mm Allen key in the bolt head in the right-hand knob.

British patent 2130981 for the separable version of the cruciform frame was applied for on 1 December 1982. The corresponding US patent was 4540190.

Leading Link Front Suspension

By 1977 the leading link front suspension, piloted on the 1976 corrugated joint Y-frame bike, had been considerably refined. The sprung fork stirrup no longer had a parallelogram action, the link plate connecting the top of the stirrup to the top of the unsprung fork blades having been designed out. This simplified and lightened the system. Incremental development continued, and by 1979, apart from its retention of a curved stirrup, the front suspension closely resembled the version used on production machines.

In the production version the wheel is bolted to the fork stirrup which is connected to the fork solely by a pair of leading links. The links impart steering control to the fork stirrup, while allowing it to move up and down independently of the fork. The crown of the fork stirrup is connected to a graphite-impregnated nylon guide bearing (base plug), which acts on a steel coil spring inside the steerer tube (another idea suggested by Phil Uncles). This ensures that the fork stirrup remains vertically aligned with the steerer tube.

The crown of the stirrup fork is formed by a hollow boss, through which passes the brake calliper bolt. Projecting upwards from this boss is a threaded rod which extends into the base of the steerer tube. Over this rod is threaded the fork stirrup bushing - a steel disc faced with a rubber washer. The bushing is screwed down onto the crown of the fork where it forms a bump stop: this cushions the crown if the suspension "bottoms out" against the base of the steerer tube.

A pre-load adjuster is also threaded onto the rod. This is a steel sleeve, the top of which is formed into a ball. The ball clips into the underside of the fork spring guide bearing. This bearing acts on the base of the steel coil spring inside the steerer tube. The nylon bearing is protected to some extent from the ingress of water and grit by an internal boot, a seal at its base. The steel spring is retained in the steerer tube by a pin riveted across the tube.

Pre-loading the suspension involves turning the steel adjuster sleeve to the right, so that it climbs up the threaded rod on the fork crown. This compresses the spring and lengthens the stroke of the front suspension.

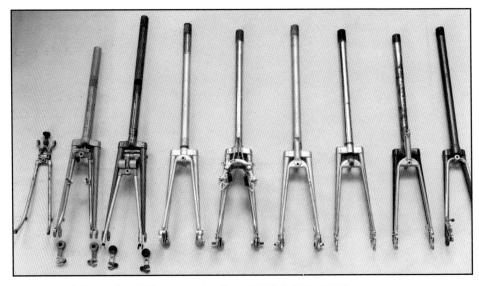

Evolution of the leading link suspension from 1976 (left) to 1979.

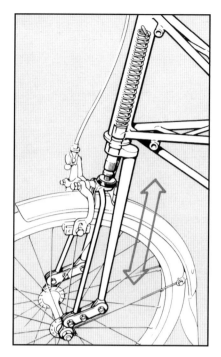

The production front suspension.

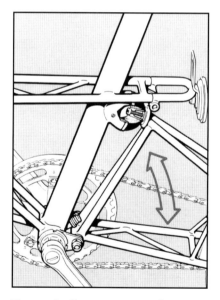

The production rear suspension, showing the rubber Monosphere cutaway.

Thus even reasonably heavy riders can enjoy the full benefit of the suspension without the risk of it frequently bottoming.

Each leading link comprises a pair of stainless steel pressings held together by a stainless steel bolt passing through a polyurethane spacer. The rearward end of the link pivots on a pressed-in Glacier DV shell bearing in the stainless steel fork end. The forward end of the link pivots onto another Glacier DV shell bearing, pressed into the stainless steel end of the stirrup fork blade, just above the wheel dropout. Stainless steel bolts at each end of the links act as pivot journals. There is a polyurethane friction damper washer between each internal face of the link and the fork or stirrup (four per link).

Damping can be varied from minimal to locked solid by equally adjusting the tightness of the four pivot bolts. These have nylon insert self-locking nuts (Nylok) operated by an 8 mm pocket spanner. With practice, adjustment can be done in less than half a minute. This form of friction damping, using multiple discs, is called Coulomb, after the French pioneer of multi-plate electrical capacitors.

British patent 2130983 for the suspension system was applied for on 1 December 1982. The corresponding American patent was 4576393.

Rear Triangle

The principal change in the evolution of the rear triangle during this period was the introduction in January 1978 of thin tube bracing, along the lines of that adopted for the main frame. An X-shaped brace of thin tubes linked the bridges between the chain stays and seat stays; and there was a zigzag infill between the chain stays, their bridge and the suspension pivot housing.

On the first Saturday of the following month, while reading gloomy news in the Financial Times, Alex sketched on the newspaper an

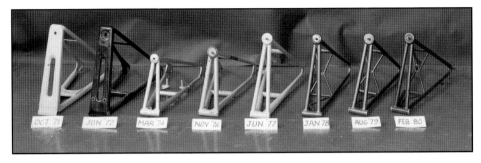

Evolution of the rear triangle, from October 1971 to February 1980.

idea for replacing the top half of the seat tube with a "wigwam" of four thin tubes, meeting at a crown into which the seatpin would fit. A prototype was subsequently constructed but the idea was not pursued further.

The Decision to Proceed

Between the first sketch of the spaceframe concept and the commercial launch of the Alex Moulton bicycle were nearly six years of development and testing.

In summer 1977 Alex set a target weight of 24lb (10.9 kg) for his new bike. This was to be the weight of a UK street-legal machine with wide-ratio gearing, without carriers but with mudguards (fenders), pump and reflector. By November 1979 Alex was well on the way to meeting his weight target. At 17lb 4oz (7.8 kg) a prototype spaceframe, complete with suspension, wheels, tyres, sprocket cluster, mudguards, seat pillar and front carrier precisely matched the weight of a high quality Reynolds 531 lightweight touring frame with all the corresponding components, but no carrier. Alex's sprung, separable prototype was therefore already slightly lighter than the benchmark unsprung, fixed-frame conventional tourer. (The weight of the main frame of this Moulton was 4lb 12oz (2.15 kg).)

On 11 November 1979 Alex rode the first definitive prototype of the new AM bike in the Peak District of Derbyshire, an olive green machine with chromed rear triangle and front suspension stirrup. It was here that he decided to put the spaceframe Moulton into production.

Nonetheless, in parallel with the development of this frame, he continued experimenting with variations on the theme. For example, a version with perforated alloy sheet beam webs, instead of thin tube infill, was produced in January 1980. This main frame weighed 2lb 15oz (1.33 kg). And in July 1981 a variant with steel angle chords, instead of tubular chords, was made. It weighed 3lb 12oz (1.7 kg).

The need for secrecy limited the amount of road testing that could be carried out on the complete machine. However, it was subjected to

6,000 miles (9,600 km) on a rolling bump rig without any failure.

Individual components or sub-assemblies, such as the suspension, tyres and extra-small rear sprockets, could be tested more discreetly on earlier Moultons, such as the Y-frame MkIII derivatives. Some later road testing of the whole bike was done with the spaceframe disguised by a set of frame skins. Held on by Velcro fixings, these enabled small items of luggage to be carried safely within the frame. They were therefore offered as an accessory when the AM bike was launched. The skins evolved from a pair of in-frame bags, sketched by Alex on 29 December 1977, while on the Isle of Wight with his 1975 Y-frame bike.

The procurement and refinement of the tyres, rims and special small sprocket clusters were vital to the success of the new bike. We therefore now turn to these components.

November 1979 – A prototype AM with front carrier matches the weight of a high quality 531 tourer with no carrier.

At this stage the AM's front suspension stirrup was curved and the kingpin had a quick-release lever.

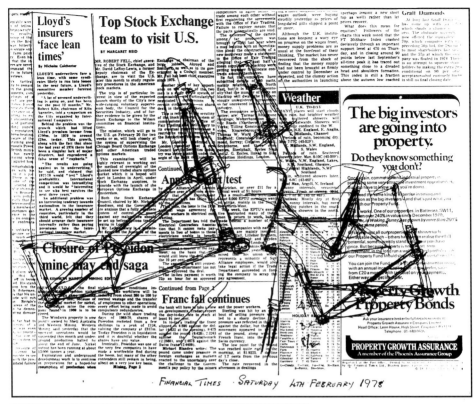

Sketches on the Financial Times for a "wigwam" of thin tubes to replace the top of the seat tube, and allow a lighter seat pin, 4th February 1978.

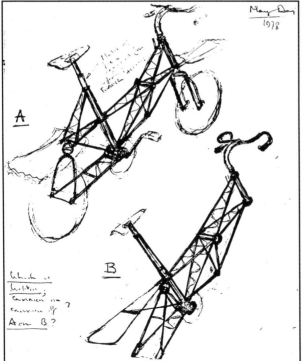

An alternative rear suspension and carrier configuration (A), sketched on May Day 1978.

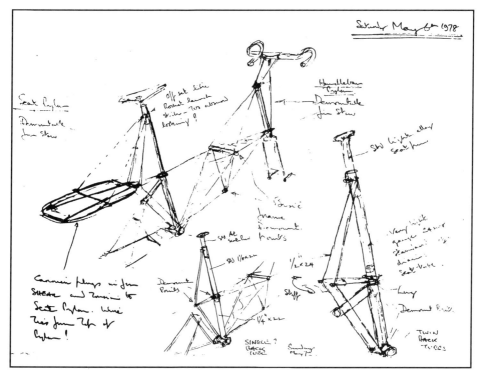

Sketches for a lightweight 'pylon' to support the seat pin. The carrier is partly supported by wire ties from the top of the pylon. 6th May 1978.

The day Alex decided to put the Spaceframe Moulton into production, 11th November 1979. He was at Boswell, Derbyshire with his friend Stuart Smith.

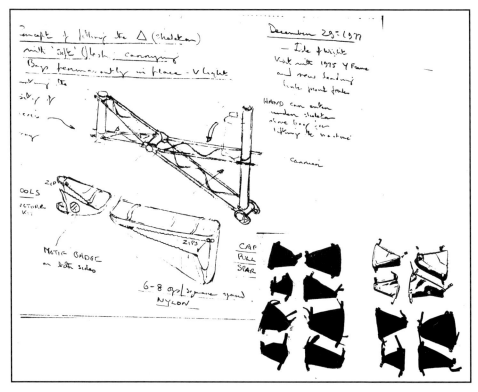

The original sketches for the in-frame bag concept, 29th December 1977 and photos of early prototypes.

The first definitive prototype AM, photographed at The Hall in late March 1980.

The in-frame bags can clearly be seen. These later evolved into frame skins.

Tyres

The special Moulton high pressure tyres were manufactured by Wolber at their factory in Soissons, France. New moulds were made by Alex Moulton Limited in spring 1978. The tyre, with its exceptionally low rolling resistance, was a crucial component in the bicycle system. It was based on the Moulton-designed Dunlop HP tyre introduced for the Moulton Speedsix in 1965.

This format is exclusive to Alex Moulton bicycles, although Alex permits its use in certain Human Powered Vehicles (HPVs) such as the record-breaking Bean faired recumbent bicycle and the Mike Burrows Speedy Windcheetah recumbent tricycle. The reason for the unique format is that early racing Moultons used tubular (sew-up) tyres glued to sprint rims. These tyres were of a little-used English format, originally known as 18", with a bead seat diameter of $14^1/_2$" (369 mm). English tubulars had originally been of nominally $1^3/_4$" (45 mm) section. However, over the years they slimmed down to about 1" (25 mm). Hence, while the rim diameter stayed the same, the tyre diameter had shrunk to nearer $16^1/_2$"(419 mm).

Italian tyre makers, such as Milremo, continued calling the format 18". Dunlop however, in recognition of the shrinkage of the format, renamed the tyres 16".

Because of the very poor durability of tubular tyres, Alex decided to design a high pressure wired-on tyre which could match the racing performance of the tubular, yet be equally suitable for touring. Development was done in conjunction with Dunlop. In those days the idea that a well-designed high pressure tyre could match the performance a tubular was generally regarded as heretical.

To ensure that the new tyre could be retrofitted into Moultons already equipped for tubular tyres, without repositioning the brake blocks or replacing the brakes, the rim was designed so that its braking surfaces aligned with those of the sprint rim. Hence the unique Moulton format with the International Standards Organisation/European Tyre & Rim Technical Organisation code 32-369 - a tyre for a rim with a nominal internal width of 32 mm and a 369 mm bead seat diameter. As the new tyre was a direct replacement for the 16" Dunlop tubular, it was called $16 \times 1^1/_4$".

By the time the spaceframe Moulton was under development, Dunlop had ceased to manufacture bicycle tyres, hence the involvement of Wolber. There was also potential confusion with a Clement wired-on tyre, also designated $16 \times 1^1/_4$", that Falcon imported into the UK from Italy. This $1^1/_4$" tyre fits the standard English E3J $16 \times 1^3/_8$" rim (ISO code 37-349), but not the Moulton $16 \times 1^1/_4$" HP rim.

To clarify the situation Alex renamed his tyre 17 x 1^1/$_4$". The only other 17 x 1^1/$_4$" tyre is a Swedish format for children's bikes, ISO code 32-357, which will not fit the Moulton rim. Although common in Sweden and also used in Germany, it is virtually unknown in the UK.

Considerable development work went into improving the tyre for the new bike. The original Dunlop version, with a nylon reinforced lightweight carcase and thin ribbed natural rubber tread, gave good road-holding and achieved excellent rolling resistance figures. In tests carried out by Alex in 1972 as part of a total re-evaluation of his bicycle concept, the Dunlop tyre inflated to 70 psi (4.8 atm) matched the performance of the corresponding tubular tyre at 100 psi (6.8 atm), and was 3% more efficient than a 27" tubular at that pressure. It was also 50% better than a 16 x 2" tyre at 35 psi (2.4 atm) as used in the Raleigh RSW16.

However, the Dunlop 17" tyre wore fairly rapidly and was prone to carcase damage. Replacement every 700 miles (1,100 km) or so was not uncommon, although Colin Martin averaged about 2,000 miles (3,200 km) per rear tyre on his ride from England to Australia.

The Wolber version for the new bike was subjected to 27,000 miles (43,000 km) of testing on real roads. Much of this was done by Des Isley. At least once he even cycled to and from the Wolber plant in France on 17" sample tyres as part of the evaluation process. Many rubber compounds were tested so that a balance could be struck between durability and wet and dry roadholding.

Rolling resistance was tested using the "coast-down" method pioneered by the American Professor Chester R. Kyle, Ph.D. Chet Kyle was a founder of the Human Powered Vehicle (HPV) movement in the United States. HPVs include all manner of human powered vehicles, aircraft and boats; but most are streamlined cycles of various configurations.

Speaking in November 1981 to the First Human Powered Vehicle Scientific Symposium, Alex described Chet's test method as "a very handy means of sorting out tyres". He added that in his new 17" tyres he was achieving rolling resistance figures about 4.7 times better than those achieved by contemporary automobile tyres.

Two years later (and six months after the launch of the new AM bicycle) Chet sent Alex his own initial test results on the 17" tyre. These confirmed Alex's own findings.

Chet sent further results in July 1984. These showed that the Wolber tyre had a rolling resistance comparable with a 27"/700C cotton road tubular or high quality wired-on high pressure tyre, such as a Specialized 1.125" tourer. The tests also showed that at 120 psi

(8.2 atm) the rolling resistance of the 17" tyre was 17% lower than at 70 psi (4.8 atm).

Chet's tests were carried out in California, using a tricycle and rider with an all-up weight of just over 204lb (92.6 kg). Eight tests were run on a 100 ft (30.5 m) smooth linoleum ramp, using five traps per test, spaced 20 ft (6.1 m) apart. (Alex typically used 10 traps 5ft (1.525 m) apart.)

The ramp sloped uphill and the rider passed through the first trap at approximately 10 mph (16.7 kph). He coasted down to about 3 mph (5 kph) by the time he reached the last trap.

Almost three years later, in April 1987, further tests were carried out on the 17" tyre at General Motors' Milford Proving Ground in Michigan. These were described and commented on by Chet Kyle in the American magazine Bike Tech. They were part of GM's quest to find a suitable tyre for their solar-powered car, Sunraycer. This was designed to enter a race across Australia and subsequently won it by two and a half days. A 20" Avocet tyre was used, not because it rolled better than the 17" tyre, but because it gave better handling characteristics to the Sunraycer car.

The GM tests, conducted on a revolving drum, subjected the Moulton tyre at various pressures to different loads, slip angles, cambers and speeds. The rolling resistance figures obtained were excellent and correlated closely with Chet's earlier tests. GM's tests also showed that fitting wheel discs (aerodynamic covers for the spokes) is beneficial, even when the wheel is shielded from the windstream, as in a faired HPV.

Chet noted that another tester, Paul van Valkenburg, had spun the Moulton tyre at more than 120 mph (194 kph). Under these conditions the diameter increased only a few thousandths of an inch as a result of centrifugal force. This confirms that the high pressures used in bicycle tyres control tyre deformation. Therefore the energy loss from dynamic distortion does not increase significantly with speed.

But back now to the period before the introduction of the AM bicycle. In June 1982, nearly a year before the launch, the Wolber version of the 17" tyre was quietly offered to members of the Moulton Bicycle Club at £6 a cover. Wolber inner tubes were also available, at £2 each. This gave another opportunity for feedback on the tyre prior to marketing the new machine.

Rims

The first rim used with the Moulton 17" tyre (the then 16 x 1¹/₄" Dunlop) was a steel Dunlop Special Lightweight. This had very good chromium plating and dimpled spoke holes. However, it seems that all production Moultons equipped with the $1\,^1/_4$" tyre were fitted with a very light section Milremo rim, the Model M-Club.

Generally this Italian rim performed well. However, it had no reinforcement boxing in the corners of the rim well and was of very thin construction. Under prolonged heavy use, hairline fractures could spread from spoke hole to spoke hole. Also, as the brakes wore away the flanges, they could bell out under pressure from the tyre.

Alex therefore sought a better quality rim for his new bicycle. His natural inclination was to use a British component if possible, and one with guaranteed continuity of supply.

About 1978 TI-Raleigh set up a production facility at Nottingham to make aluminium rims. They did this to create a source of alloy rims at lower price than the imported products hitherto used. Raleigh's development department therefore designed a cost-effective lightweight extrusion in a nominal 17 mm width to suit tyres from 28 mm to 32 mm. Production at Nottingham began about 1978, initially using extrusions supplied by another TI company, BA (British Aluminium). However, quality proved inadequate and SAPA of Tibshelf, Derbyshire became the supplier.

The alloy used was HE9 containing silicon and magnesium, fully hardened and now known as 6063 T6. The extrusion had a corner-boxed section similar to the classic Wolber Super Champion Model 58, with an internal width of 17.5 mm (0.69"), external width of 22.5 mm (0.89") and total depth of 14 mm (0.55"). The extrusion was rolled into a circle, the ends being joined with friction pins in the hollows in the box sections. As American cycle technology writer Frank Berto points out: "There's no problem with the joint separating because the compressive force of the spokes pulls the joint together." The valve hole was placed opposite the rim joint, so that the extra weight of the joint was more or less counterbalanced by the valve.

In 1981 Raleigh transferred rim production to Sturmey-Archer, at which point Chris Juden, later technical officer of the Cyclists' Touring Club and an independent cycle design consultant, became closely involved with the project. The alloy rim was given the name Mistral.

Shortly after Raleigh went into rim production Alex Moulton reached an amicable arrangement with technical director Keith Hutcheon for production of a 17" version of the type M17, version 117 Mistral rim. This was the only way Alex could obtain a British-made alloy rim of suitable quality. As Raleigh's machinery could only make 622 and 630 mm diameter rims, Alex had to install his own equipment for circling, pinning and polishing.

In August 1982 Raleigh decided to abandon manufacture of Mistral rims. As far as the company was concerned the exercise had served its purpose in bringing down the price of imported rims. Sturmey-Archer therefore closed the rim making department. Keith Hutcheon used his redundancy money to buy the rim-making equipment and stock, and set up an independent company in Nottingham called Mistral Rims Limited, where Chris Juden and others continued to work. It operated for a further year but paid no wages and was largely ignored by the British cycle trade and industry.

However, Alex continued to produce the original Mistral M17 pattern rim in his 17" format and does so to this day. In 1983 Keith Hutcheon sold the rights in the Mistral system to Sun Metal Products Inc. of Warsaw, Indiana, with whom he now works. The company still makes Mistral M17 rims but in the improved 217 version designed in 1981 by Chris Juden. This is slightly stiffer with a more rounded profile and is joined by larger pins. Sun Metal M17 rims have spoke hole eyelets (as did later type 117s made by Sturmey-Archer) and are hard anodised. A 17" version for the Moulton tyre format is available in the USA. It is a nice rim but is not recommended by Alex Moulton, who cannot guarantee compatibility with his tyres.

Sprocket Cluster

Before entering the world of gearing in detail, a few paragraphs for those not familiar with basic terminology.

In English-speaking countries, since Victorian times, bicycle gearing has been expressed in inches as the equivalent front wheel diameter of a direct drive bicycle - one with the cranks fixed directly to the wheel. With a chain-drive bicycle this figure is obtained by dividing the number of teeth on the chainwheel by the number on the cog and multiplying the product by the wheel diameter. If a hub gear is used, the figure will be correct only for direct drive: adjustment must be made for the percentage shift up or down offered by the other gears.

In some European countries gearing is expressed in terms of the development - the distance in metres travelled for each turn of the pedals. This can be obtained from the English gearing figure by multiplying it by pi and converting the result from inches to metres. A sufficiently accurate conversion results from simply multiplying the English gear in inches by 0.08. Hence a 60" gear has a development of 4.8 m.

As a basic reference, a single speed bicycle typically has a gear of about 64". Low gear on a bike with a three-speed hub is usually about 48", high gear about 85".

Now, back to the development of the AM. A problem when designing around a wheel substantially smaller than the commonly used formats is how to achieve sufficiently high gearing. With a wide-ratio five-speed hub gear in a 17" wheel this is not too difficult. A standard 52 tooth chainwheel driving a readily obtainable 14 tooth sprocket will give a top gear of just over 94". This is because in top gear the hub increases the 63" direct drive by 50%.

However, with a derailleur gear the same 52 tooth chainwheel driving the smallest sprocket of most freewheels commonly available in the 1970s (13 tooth) gave a high gear of only 68" - a typical mid range gear.

Although freewheels with smaller cogs were sometimes available, supply tended to be erratic. Nothing smaller than an 11 tooth sprocket was produced, which in any case gave a gear of only 80". This is high enough for some tourists and utility readers, but inadequate for racing or to do justice to the speed potential of a lightweight Moulton.

With a 17" wheel to achieve a top gear of about 94" requires:

- an 11 tooth sprocket with a 61 tooth chainwheel,
- a 12 tooth sprocket with a 66 tooth chainwheel, or
- a 13 tooth sprocket with a 72 tooth chainwheel.

These "dinner plate" chainwheels are relatively heavy and difficult to obtain. The only supplier in the 1970s to offer standard rings with up to 68 teeth was TA of France. Bigger rings were to special irrevocable order – up to 140 teeth, but understandably at a high price. You paid by the tooth and through the teeth.

Long before he conceived the spaceframe concept, Alex Moulton considered the alternative and lighter way to achieve high gearing - use of smaller sprockets. In 1967 he filed British patent 1202886 for a freewheel with very small cogs. The tiniest had just 9 teeth, which with a standard 52 tooth chainwheel gave a 17" wheeled bike a 98" top gear. A 9 tooth sprocket was fitted to the modified MkIII used for the 1972 re-evaluation of the Moulton bicycle concept, and which was the subject of Alex Moulton's 1973 Royal Institution discourse. The tiny cog was also used on some of the MkIII derivatives described in the previous chapter. Not until 1993 did another manufacturer, Goldtec Cycle Components, announce a 9 tooth sprocket.

American cycle technologist Frank Berto points out:

"The main problem with very small sprockets is 'chordal action'. The sprocket isn't completely round so the chain moves with a jerky action. The uneven movement amounts to 2 percent for a 16-tooth sprocket, 3 percent for a 13 tooth and 4 percent for an 11 tooth sprocket."

However, he notes that he cannot detect the chordal action in 11 tooth gear trains. I can detect it in a 9 tooth train when turning the crank by hand with the bike hanging up and no load on the transmission.

However, it feels smooth when I ride it, and when riding a 17" wheel Alex Moulton bicycle I use the 9 tooth cog probably more than any other.

The 9 tooth sprocket was further developed for the spaceframe Moulton as part of a screw-on cluster, consisting of three small sprockets brazed together on a threaded carrier. The other two sprockets were typically 11 and 13 tooth. The version fitted to early AMs was chrome-plated and used in conjunction with a standard Regina CX six-speed threaded-on freewheel to make an ultra-wide ratio seven-speed block. The four largest sprockets were standard splined or threaded Regina cogs, locked in place by the Moulton cluster.

This arrangement, used in conjunction with a carefully designed extra deep derailleur hanger integral with the rear wheel drop-out, enabled a compact slant parallelogram derailleur mechanism (then exclusive to SunTour) to give an extraordinarily wide gearing range of 3.12:1 without the need for a double chainwheel, front derailleur and associated cable and lever. (2.62:1 was the widest range offered by any Shimano seven-speed block in 1993.) Thus Alex's special small sprocket cluster contributed to significant further weight savings.

Producing and perfecting the world's first 9 tooth sprocket for modern $1/2$"pitch chains was by no means easy. Some 45,000 miles (72,000 km) of development testing were involved. Achieving adequate chain wrap-round was vital and ultimately it proved possible to arrange the derailleur mechanism so that the chain engaged with 6 of the 9 teeth at any one time.

Rumours

By the late 1970s rumours of the new AM bike were beginning to spread. Michael Strutt, who later designed the Worksong folding lightweight bicycle, was then a journalist for the Financial Times and a Moulton rider. In January 1979 he published an article in the FT entitled "Some new angles on the bicycle". In it he noted that small-wheeled bicycles then accounted for 20% of bicycle sales in Britain, while drop-handlebar "sports" machines comprised 40% of the market.

Michael interviewed Alex for the article, describing him as "the man who made the most startling impact on the shape of the bicycle this century". Alex revealed:

"I am designing a much-improved Moulton for the upper end of the market which is now in prototype form. It will have the classical riding position because I am quite sure from my research among doctors that this is the correct one.

"The new machine will be very light and have all the Moulton features but we don't know yet when it will be ready."

Fourteen months later, in March 1980, The Sunday Times carried an article by another Moulton-riding journalist, Mark Ottaway. Writing under the headline "Yesterday's bike of the future", he disclosed: "The brightest hope for a long time has been the rumour that The Master is designing another bike. When I visited him in Bradford he could not deny it - nor promise anything either."

Mark pointed out that Alex was "much pre-occupied with car suspension systems" and added: "If there is another Moulton bicycle it will have to be an 'Alex Moulton' (for trademark reasons) and will be produced on a relatively small and upmarket scale."

He formed the opinion that any new machine would be a direct descendant of the original but with steeper head and seat tube angles.

Mark's article helped renew my interest in Moultons by alerting me to the existence of the two user groups, Moulton Preservation and the Moulton Bicycle Club. This led me to write the book "The Moulton Bicycle". The first edition went on sale early in 1981, and in it I referred to Mark's comments on the proposed new machine. I added that the new bike was shrouded in secrecy but that apparently it would be an ultra lightweight version with a rumoured price of around £400.

In 1980, while writing the book, I joined the Moulton Bicycle Club and for the first time attended its annual meet at Alex's home, The Hall, Bradford-on-Avon. The club had been founded in 1975 by Daved Sanders as a successor to the touring-oriented Moulton Safari Club. Membership was so small that, until January 1982, no subscription was charged: the modest expenses involved were covered by Alex as recognition of the interest expressed in his concept.

At the 1980 annual meet the new machine was not on show. However, the design studio and workshops were accessible to the 30 or so enthusiasts who attended - about a third of the total membership in those days. The quest for lightness of componentry could clearly be seen in comparative figures and calculations chalked on a blackboard, now preserved in the Moulton Museum at Bradford-on-Avon.

At the annual meets in the two subsequent years, as the launch came nearer and the club doubled in size, security became tighter. The windows of the workshop were obscured with sheets to maintain secrecy.

From January 1981 regular weekly secret meetings were held within Alex Moulton Limited on the progress of the new bike. In his 1981 address to the club, Alex warned the nearly four dozen members present that there was no guarantee he would launch the new bike. The machine had to be financially viable and much would depend on the state of the economy. With unemployment heading towards three million this was not good. However, the following year Alex hinted that the AM would be launched in 1983, possibly at a Moulton Bicycle Club meet in the spring or summer.

The second edition of my book "The Moulton Bicycle" was reviewed in Cycling in December 1982. The same issue contained a small news feature stating that Alex was to launch a new bike. The article was almost certainly based on comments in my book. It caused a certain amount of panic at The Hall, where it was feared that someone had leaked information to the press.

As 1983 arrived rumours continued to spread. Yet the new machine's frame was such a closely guarded secret that some Moulton devotees thought it might be built of carbon fibre. The secret had been well kept!

Prototype AM undergoing bump rig testing.

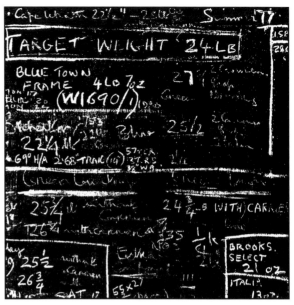

Above: Blackboard with target weight for the first production AMs.

Left: Production AM on bump test rig, 1983.
An electric motor drives the bottom bracket axle via a flexible rubber coupling. Photo by Tony Hadland.

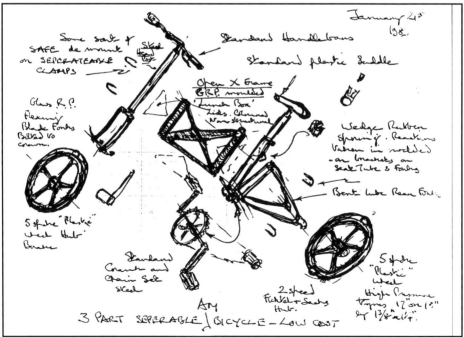

Just four months before the launch of the AMs, Alex produced this provocative design for a low cost separable Spaceframe Moulton, 21st January 1983.

Chapter 3
THE AM REVEALED
1983

Launch of the AM2 & AM7 – Specifications – Improvements
Accessories – Marketing

As preparations proceeded for the launch of the new Alex Moulton bicycle, the British cycle market was in a state of flux. The bad news was that exports had dropped by three-quarters in three years. The good news was that imports were down slightly, and overall sales had risen by 15% in a year.

Raleigh, boosted by the BMX craze, had half of all UK sales. The rest of the British cycle industry had just 15%.

Within this small segment Alex Moulton hoped to carve a tiny niche accounting for no more than 0.3% of annual UK sales – perhaps 5,000 units at most.

A Glimpse Under the Sheet

A few weeks before Christmas 1982 I received a telephone call from John Benjamin, company secretary of Alex Moulton Limited. Bristol-based BBC West was sending a television film crew to the Moulton works at Bradford-on-Avon. I was invited to be on hand to demonstrate a 1960s Moulton.

When Alex Moulton was interviewed, the yet to be launched AM bicycle "appeared" with him, concealed by a sheet! After the filming the two-man film crew remained chatting to Alex. As motor cycle enthusiasts, they were interested in the Moulton bicycle and its suspension system.

Alex showed them his green Y-frame machine. Then, having bound them to secrecy, he removed the sheet from the new AM bicycle. His best-kept secret was revealed.

The machine was an AM2 and, after the film crew left, I was invited to have a brief test ride. The immediate impression was of a very light yet outstandingly rigid bike, with an exceptionally silky ride. The longer travel front suspension was much more effective than the original Moulton's at eliminating high frequency vibration, as caused by the coarse granite chippings used to surface many rural English roads.

Warming Up the Press

Meanwhile the rumours and speculation about the new bike continued. Early in January 1983 Alex briefed the press from his office in The Hall. On 7 January the Wiltshire Times & News announced that a new Moulton was on the way. The following day The Daily Telegraph added that Alex was "keeping prototypes secret because of intense trade competition."

Similar stories were carried by a number of provincial newspapers. A fortnight later Cycling devoted half a page to the story. The magazine asked Alex why he was launching an expensive bicycle during a severe economic recession. He replied that "the financial pressures today have made the public very aware of travel economics and helped me bring forward my plans a little". Cycling ventured the opinion that "the only sure thing about the new machine is that it will not differ much in looks" from the Moultons of the 1960s and 70s.

Last Minute Problems

In March I wrote to John Benjamin, company secretary of Alex Moulton Limited, with some observations about the pre-production 17" tyres released to members of the Moulton Bicycle Club. I had noticed cracking of the rubber on the sidewalls.

On 21 March John replied that the tyres were from a small batch of 300 which Wolber had made. He continued:

"We had observed some cracking of the rubber on the walls and immediately drew this to the attention of Wolber who have overcome the problem in the production run of the tyres. Meanwhile tyres from the 300 batch have been used on our prototypes and have been extensively tested by a number of riders in this area. The appearance of the wall of the tyre has had no ill effect on the performance of the tyre from a wet grip and rolling resistance point of view."

Production in full swing –
AM frames in 1983.
Photo by Tony Hadland.

In the same letter John referred to the launch of the AM bicycle range:

"The initial bicycle production is now getting under way despite many problems such as ten days ago the company that was going to paint the frame went into liquidation and we have had to spend ten days getting another suitable painter and organising a supply of paint. Nevertheless, we are determined to succeed and at this point in time envisage the launch will be somewhere towards the end of May."

A Media Opportunity

The opportunity arose to feature the AM in the inaugural edition of a Channel 4 television series about cycling. The TV slot was 4.35 p.m. on Saturday 21 May in the first of an eight-part series called "On Your Bikes". This series, by John Gau Productions, dealt primarily with non-competitive cycling and was unprecedented on UK network television.

The unique nationwide promotional opportunity became the determining factor for the timing of the formal launch. It was therefore agreed that the AM would make its first public appearance at a reception and press conference in London two days before the broadcast. This would ensure press coverage for both the bike and the TV programme on the day before transmission.

Eight days before the launch John Benjamin wrote:

"Everyone here is working all hours in order to try and get at least a few machines into the shops as well as having enough available at the preview."

The Launch

The launch duly took place on Thursday 19 May 1983 at the Kensington Palace Hotel, London. Those present were allowed to ride the bikes along the relatively quiet De Vere Gardens and adjoining roads. Alex addressed the assembled press and his words were reported in the July issue of Cyclist Monthly:

"My intention was to make a better bicycle for a wider range of usage. ... Design is a continuing challenge in my life. ... Two years ago we decided to go ahead, although it is a hassle to go into production. Very different from the period 20 years ago when we brought out the original Moulton bicycle.

"This time, it is being done on a more modest scale to start with. We are not entering the volume market, but concentrating on producing the highest quality machine for those who want the best available."

The following day the AM was revealed to the world via two of the London quality broadsheets. The coverage given by The Times consisted of two photographs and a caption. The pictures showed Sarah Lam, former star of the hospital soap opera "Angels", with the AM2. Ms Lam was one of the presenters of "On Your Bikes" and was shown carrying a separated AM2 and riding the assembled machine. The caption was headed "Folding bicycle", despite the fact that the photograph clearly showed the bike separated, rather than folded! A much more informative piece, written by Michael Strutt, appeared in the Financial Times. This showed Jim Poslett, then chairman of the Moulton Bicycle Club, riding an AM7. Michael described the AM bicycle in outline and stated:

"Production next year will be in the low thousands ... It will provide work for 20 [15 were directly involved in production] and the machine will be sold through a network of 20 or 30 dealers.

"There are plans for export to the US. The machine's construction makes it air freightable."

He went on to reveal that there were two models, a two-speed town model at £399 and a seven-speed tourer at £489.

The first edition of "On Your Bikes" was transmitted the following afternoon. It showed the launch and included footage shot at The Hall. The main presenter was Phil Liggett, well-known for his television commentaries on major cycle races, such as the Tour de France. Phil interviewed Alex and road-tested the AM7.

To illustrate how compactly the machine could be stowed, it was shown being lifted from the tiny boot of Jack Lauterwasser's Renault 5 hatchback.

Jack, a Londoner of Anglo-German descent, joined Alex from Raleigh in 1965. He was in charge of wheel building for the AM series bicycles. A pioneer of the diamond frame lightweight, in 1928 he broke the British 50 and 100 mile (81 and 162 km) Road Records Association bicycle records and rode with the British team in the Amsterdam Olympics. He also gave his name to a style of handlebars, and in 1930 launched a $17^1/_2$"lb (7.9 kg) track racing bike.

In the weeks following the launch of the AMs they were mentioned a number of times in the quality press. On 14 June publicity was boosted by Alex making a public appearance at the London Bicycle Company in Covent Garden. A fortnight later New Scientist devoted an illustrated feature to the new bike and The Guardian stressed its portability.

Not surprisingly, the AMs received numerous mentions in the cycling press. Many were straightforward reports of the launch and outline descriptions of the product. The more detailed reviews are discussed in the next chapter.

There was another photo opportunity when the Wiltshire Cycleway was formally opened in mid July. This took place at Longleat, the stately home of the Marquess of Bath. The 78 year old Marquess (who in the 1930s cycled to Austria and Sweden), his son Lord Christopher Thynne, Alex and cycle journalist Peter Knottley all rode AMs in what was described as "the best turn-out of them to be seen so far".

Left: Jack Lauterwasser with Rosemary Hadland, 1993. Cycling does keep you fit!
Photo by Tony Hadland.

Above: A cartoon of Jack in the 1920s

The Production Frame

The initial range of AMs comprised two models: the AM2 for town use, and the AM7, a tourer for the countryside. The difference in nomenclature reflected the number of gears provided.

Both bikes had identical frames, apart from detail differences indicated below. The spaceframes were as described in the previous chapter, built of Reynolds 531 tubing. Presswork, such as the stainless steel fork ends (dropouts) and the stainless steel seat pillar, was by Haden Brothers. Most bolts were supplied by Webbs Fastenings of Calne. Thumb nuts were by Tayroh, the coil spring came from Flexo, and Chippenham Precision Plastics supplied the kingpin knobs.

Wheelbase was $41^1/2$" (1,051 mm), $^1/2$" (13 mm) longer than the MkIII but 3" (76 mm) shorter than the Series 1 and 2 Moultons of the 1960s. The head and seat tubes were parallel, the angles being $72^1/2$" degrees. This was approximately $2^1/2$" degrees steeper than the MkIII and a full $3^1/2$" degrees steeper than the Series 1 machines.

Bottom bracket height of the unladen bike was $11^1/2$" (292 mm).

Weight of the bare AM frame without front fork or rear triangle was 3lb 15oz (1.8 kg).

In the best tradition of Henry Ford there was no colour choice: the frame was finished only in "steely grey". The paint was a smooth, tough, oven-baked polyester powder coating. This was highly resistant to scratching and chipping; particularly important for when the bike was transported in separated mode. In October 1983 it was announced that the frame painting contract had been awarded to Gloucester Finishing of Colegrave, Gloucester.

SIF bronze welding an AM frame.

Cable casing sheaths were translucent. The optional carriers (racks) and the Bluemels Club ribbed plastic mudguards were finished in black. For aesthetic and weight-saving reasons, only one pair of rear mudguard stays was fitted to the early machines. Mudguard clearance was $3/8$" (10 mm). The front mudguard had a black plastic mudflap.

A new, riveted head badge was introduced for the AM range. Finished in black on silver, it featured the south front of Alex's Jacobean home The Hall, Bradford-on-Avon. Above the house, echoing the form of its gables, were the initials AM, picked out in red. A German cycling magazine described the badge as "a wonderful British understatement".

The new AM logo echoing the gables of The Hall's south facade.

The AM monogram was cast into the front of the fork crown, and onto each side of the frame tie knuckle. In each case it was picked out in red. The monogram was also moulded into the left-hand plastic knob of the kingpin. A Reynolds 531 decal was applied to the rear of the seat tube, just above the rubber spring of the rear suspension.

An option offered on both models was a longer steering column. This was achieved without the need for a frame variation. Instead the fixed fork had a longer steerer tube and a 2" (52 mm) alloy sleeve was fitted between the lock nut and the threaded cup of the upper steering bearing. The long steerer had enough length of thread to be sawn down and converted to the standard, shorter version, if necessary.

Wheels

The rims were Moulton-fabricated as described in the previous chapter. They were fitted with the Moulton-Wolber 17 x 1$^1/_4$" special high pressure tyres and inner tubes, with a recommended pressure of 70 psi or 4.6 atm marked on the walls. However, the instructions that came with the bike recommended 70 psi (actually nearer 4.8 atm) for the front wheel and 90 psi (6.1 atm) for the rear.

Spokes were 14 gauge stainless steel, there being 28 per wheel. The front wheel was radially spoked, thus making a slight weight saving over the usual tangential pattern. There was no problem in adopting the weaker radial pattern, as the 17" wheel was inherently much stronger than a 27" or 700C.

Rear wheels were built with spokes laced two cross (each spoke crossed over two other spokes attached to the same flange of the hub).

Components Common to the AM2 & AM7

The alloy handlebar stem used was a British-made GB (Gerry Burgess) Stelvio RTE. It was offered with either an 80 mm (3$^1/_4$") or 100 mm (4") forward extension.

RTE stands for Reverse Thrust Expander. In the then usual way, the stem was held in the steerer tube by a threaded cone pulled into the split tubular end of the stem. The ingenious and novel aspect of the RTE stem was that there was no need to use a mallet to knock the unscrewed expander bolt down to release the cone.

Above the recessed head of the expander bolt was a circlip in an annular groove. As the expander bolt was loosened with a 6 mm Allen key, the circlip prevented the bolt head rising up, and instead forced the conical wedge out of the bottom of the stem, releasing the stem from the steerer tube. To tidy up the appearance, a removable (and easily lost) black plastic cap was fitted to the bolt hole in the top of the stem. (Today most stems use wedge nuts rather than cones, and generally release easily without the need for RTE or mallet!).

Early AMs were fitted with Campagnolo Record track headsets with loose ball-bearings. From about 1984 the specification was changed to Stronglight Spidel with captive roller bearings, much easier to service. The seat pillar comprised a standard Sakae Ringyo (SR) Laprade alloy micro-adjust post riveted and glued into the necked-down top end of a $13^1/_2$" (343 mm) long, $1^3/_8$" (35 mm) external diameter thin-walled stainless steel tube. The top few inches of the seat tube were almost imperceptibly swaged down to accommodate the seat pillar. This configuration offered 8" (203 mm) of saddle height adjustment, covering a nominal conventional frame range of $18^1/_2$" to $26^1/_2$".

A "get you home" lightweight 15" (380 mm) Bluemels alloy pump was concealed within the seat pillar. The pump was held in place by a neoprene collar in the base of the seat pillar. This incorporated an internal groove in which the flange of the pump handle engaged. A foam rubber insert within the top of the seat pillar helped prevent rattles.

Bolted to the micro-adjust saddle cradle was a pressed and drilled alloy strip into which a neoprene grommet was push-fitted. This grommet held the 6 mm Allen key for adjusting the saddle and handlebar heights, separating the frame and removing the AM7's pedals.

The leather-covered saddle was a Selle Italia Anatomic. It had a nylon foundation shell supported on steel rails, and incorporated dense foam padding. Saddlebag loops were provided. Because of its more upright riding position, the AM2 was fitted with the wider (female) version of the saddle. This had a shorter nose and wider base than the narrower (male) version, standard on the AM7.

The AM2 Specification

The AM2 "town" bike was designed for easy stowage, whether in the home, car boot or on public transport. It was exceptionally light, weighing about 23lb (10.4 kg). Initial recommended retail price was £399.

The frame differed from that of the AM7 in several ways. The rear triangle had slotted, forward-facing dropouts for the wheel axle, so that chain slack could be taken up without the need for a sprung arm chain tensioner. Also, the width between the dropouts, at 120 mm (4.72") was narrower to accommodate a hub gear.

Certain brazed-on fittings necessary on the AM7 were omitted. Hence there were no mounting and parking points for the gear lever assembly, and no cable stops and guides. Also, the rear triangle's mudguard bridge was not reinforced to take a calliper brake.

The British-made GB alloy handlebars were "flat" and extra narrow in the Moulton Stowaway tradition. The shaped black grips were of

The 1983 AM2.

high-density foam. The alloy front brake and lever were by Weinmann of Switzerland: the 605 side-pull calliper incorporated a cable adjuster and quick release, and could easily be centred with a Weinmann 687 4 mm alignment adjusting key.

The front hub was by Milremo of Italy (although it seems a few machines had French Maillard hubs) and was a diablo-shaped alloy type with track nuts.

The rear hub was a German Fichtel & Sachs Torpedo Duomatic R2110 two-speed coaster brake. This was a development of the Duomatic 102 hub specified by Alex Moulton in the 1960s for his Automatics, Mini Automatics and later Stowaways. The 102 was also selected by Colin Martin for his ride from England to Australia on the Moulton Marathon in 1970.

The Duomatic R2110 was operationally similar and visually almost identical to the 102, apart from the lack of an oiler point, the newer hub being "lubricated for life".

The Duomatic offered direct drive or a 36% increase. To change gear required slight back-pedalling, but not enough to apply the brake. Therefore, if the rider had to use the back-pedal brake to halt while cruising in high gear (for example at a road junction) low gear was automatically engaged ready to restart. Unfortunately the converse was also true: if the rider braked while climbing a hill in low gear, high gear was automatically engaged. This necessitated a quick backward flick of the pedals to re-engage low gear before restarting.

With the Duomatic there was no need for a rear brake calliper, nor for a rear brake lever, gear lever and associated cables. The hub offered reliable wet weather braking and provided a very efficient transmission system for hill climbing, its low gear being direct drive with an in-line chain.

The AM2 had a $^3/_{32}$" (2.38 mm) Sedisport chain and a Nervar alloy cotterless chainset with detachable 46 tooth chainring. The chainwheel was a five-arm type with a bolt circle diameter of 122 mm (4.8"), a comparatively rare dimension used only for certain chainsets by Nervar and Stronglight. Bolted to the chainring was a black plastic protector ring. The cranks were 170 mm (6.69").

The standard rear sprocket had 14 teeth, which gave gears of 56 and 76". Lower gears could be achieved by fitting larger rear sprockets. For example, a 15 tooth cog gave 52 and 71"; a 16 tooth, 49 and 66"; and a 17 tooth, 46 and 63". The sprockets had the standard three-lug fitting adopted for hub gears by Fichtel & Sachs, Sturmey-Archer and Shimano, and were retained by a circlip. However, they were specially modified by Alex Moulton Limited for use with the $^3/_{32}$" chain, traditionally used only with derailleur gears.

The Sakae Ringyo (SR) pedals fitted to early AM2s were alloy-shelled, lightweight, utility-type with black rubbers and integral reflectors. A spanner was provided for removal.

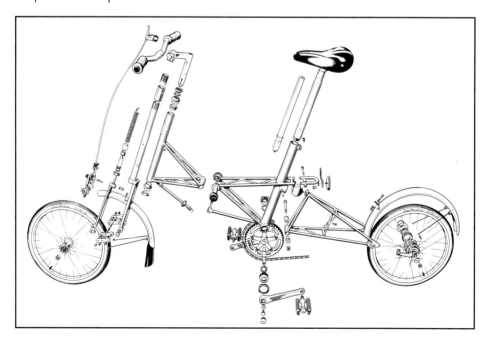

Exploded drawing of the 1983 AM2.

The pedals and the SR saddle clamp were the only non-European components used on the bike in its original form. The AM2 was discontinued in early 1992, after Fichtel & Sachs ceased production of the Duomatic hub.

The AM7 Specification

The AM7 was the "country" or touring version of the Alex Moulton bicycle. It weighed about 24^1/$_2$"lb (11.1 kg) – not far off Alex's 1977 target – and the initial recommended retail price was £489.

The rear triangle differed slightly from the AM2's, being designed for use with derailleur gears. There was an integral hanger for the rear mechanism and stops were brazed on for the control cable. The width between the dropouts was 130 mm (5.12"), to cater for a seven-speed freewheel without resorting to narrow sprocket spacing. Although now commonplace on mountain bikes, at the time a 130 mm wide-spaced seven-speed block was comparatively unusual. (Most seven-speed blocks then were 126 mm (4.96") wide with narrow sprocket spacing.) The AM7's dropouts were the vertical (touring) type, thus obviating any risk of installing the wheel out of line.

The bike's main frame had extra brazed-on stops and guides for the rear brake cable and derailleur cable, and brazed-on threaded bosses on which to anchor and park the gear lever demount plate.

The demount plate was a stainless steel device, complete with an AM motif decal, fixed by an Allen bolt to an anchor boss on the highest part of the upper lattice beam behind the head tube. The gear lever was mounted on the plate and was therefore located in a position similar to the down tube mounting on a conventional diamond frame bike.

Pivoting from the centre of the demount plate was a short crank, connected by a cable to the rear brake calliper. A similar crank, connected by a cable to the rear brake lever, pivoted from the underside of the anchor boss. The two short cranks socketed together, one on top of the other, giving cable linkage from the brake lever to the calliper.

When the demount plate was unbolted (using the 6 mm Allen key normally hidden under the saddle), the brake cable system was automatically separated. Tension was maintained in the front cable by a coil spring between the cable stop and the lower cable crank. Once unbolted the demount plate was turned through 180 degrees on plan and screwed onto a parking boss brazed onto the horizontal section of lattice beam between the kingpin and the seat tube. The two parts of the frame could then be separated.

GB alloy drop handlebars were fitted, these being fairly narrow (380 mm or 15") and shallow. They were clad in a black, dense cellular foam similar to, but not quite as good as, Grab-On. The alloy brakes and levers were by CLB of France. The levers had black rubber hoods and cable adjusters. The callipers were long-reach and were fitted with cable adjusters and quick-releases.

The alloy small-flange hubs used on the AM7 were by Zeus of Spain. They were diablo-shaped and, being derived from a Campagnolo design, used $7/_{32}$" (5.6 mm) ball bearings in the front hub, rather than the standard $3/_{16}$" (4.8 mm).

The freewheel was an Italian screw-on Regina CX, which in standard form carried six sprockets, the smallest option having 12 teeth. In the original AM7 the CX freewheel body was used in conjunction with four standard Regina sprockets and the special Moulton "silver" triple sprocket cluster. The Regina sprockets used were typically 28 and 23 tooth large diameter splined, 19 tooth large diameter threaded, and 16 tooth small diameter splined. All were alloy with symmetrical teeth. The Moulton cluster was offered with 13, 11 and either 9 or 10 teeth, the sprockets being of heavily chromed steel. A Regina-style symmetrical tooth profile was used for the 13 tooth sprocket, while the two smaller cogs were asymmetrically chamfered. The special Moulton clusters were made in Wales by Roger Maughfling Engineering Limited of Knucklas, Powys.

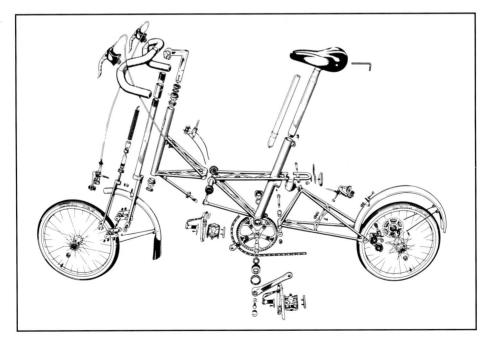

Exploded drawing of the 1983 AM7.

The chainset was a French five-arm Stronglight 103, with the same comparatively rare 122 mm (4.8") bolt ring diameter as the Nervar used on the AM2. (The 1994 AM7 uses a Stronglight 190 chainset with the same bolt ring diameter, but with a Shimano UN51 bottom bracket set, rather than the Stronglight originally fitted.) The chainring had 52 teeth and was fitted with a clip-on black plastic protector ring. The chain was a standard Sedisport. Gears offered by this configuration were 32, 38 (an increase of 21%), 47 (+21%), 55 (+19%), 68 (+23%), 80 (+18%) and 88" (+10% with 10 tooth) or 98" (+22% with 9 tooth), a range of up to 3.1:1 controlled by a single lever.

The cranks were 170 mm (6.69") long, fitted with Lyotard 82 alloy quill pedals, complete with bolted-on reflectors, leather toe straps and Christophe toe-clips. The pedals and toe-clips were French.

Apart from the SR saddle clamp, the only items of Japanese equipment on the original AM7 were the SunTour short arm rear derailleur mechanism and its gear lever.

The earliest AM7s were fitted with a SunTour Superbe rear mechanism. In 1984 this was superseded by the more aerodynamically-styled SunTour Cyclone MkII. Both were compact, short-arm mechanisms, but could handle the ultra-wide-ratio freewheel when used in conjunction with the AM7's carefully designed, extra-long integral gear hanger. This was approximately ¹/₄" (6 mm) longer than a typical touring

The 1983 AM7.

hanger and $1/2$" (13 mm) longer than a typical racing hanger.

SunTour rear mechanisms had the great advantage of the slant parallelogram shifter cage, which keeps the jockey pulley closer to the sprockets giving smoother gear changing. This feature was unique to SunTour, having been patented by the company in the 1950s. The patent expired in the mid 1980s and slant parallelograms are now commonly used by other manufacturers, such as Shimano.

Reliable modern indexed derailleur shifting systems were not available when the AM7 was launched. The first, Shimano's SIS, did not appear until 1985 and did not become well-established in the market place until 1987.

Certificate of Ownership/Guarantee

Purchasers of an early AM received two pieces of literature: Assembly Instructions and a Certificate of Ownership/Guarantee. The latter had the frame number of the machine written in by hand. From this could be deduced the year and week of manufacture: eg. my AM7, number 424005, was the fifth machine made in the twenty-fourth week of 1984.

The guarantee was in addition to the consumer's statutory rights. It offered the first retail buyer of an Alex Moulton Bicycle free replacement or repair of any defective part made by Alex Moulton Limited during the first year of ownership. Business use, hiring, racing, misuse, accident, neglect and improper operation were all excluded from this cover. Altering the original specification without the company's written consent voided the guarantee, as did altering or removing the AM trade marks. To register the guarantee a registration slip had to be cut from the side of the Certificate of Ownership, completed and returned to Bradford-on-Avon.

Assembly Instructions

The Assembly Instructions took the form of a four-sided document $8^1/2$" high by $11^3/4$" wide (210 x 298 mm). This was the same face size as the Certificate of Ownership before removal of the guarantee registration slip. The instructions were printed in black and red on stiff white glossy paper.

The front cover featured an exploded drawing of an AM2. On the back cover were the maintenance and riding instructions. The latter were almost identical to those issued with the Moultons of the 1960s.

The instructions opened out to give a double-page spread of 20 monochrome photographs with accompanying text showing how to assemble the bicycle and how to adjust the front suspension. Advice on the latter point included the following:

"With rider in position, the leading links should be adjusted to be approximately horizontal. The knurled ring should be turned clockwise to lower forks, anticlockwise to lift forks."

"Alter damping by tightening or loosening the friction pads. The front and rear friction pads on both sides of the wheel should be altered by the same amount."

Improvements and Minor Changes

A number of improvements were made to the AMs in the first few years of production. One of the earliest was the introduction of a second pair of stays for the rear mudguard, a single pair having proved inadequate. Another early change, made within five months of the launch, was the introduction of a pair of bottle cage bosses on the forward face of the AM7's seat tube.

Some tall, heavy riders of early AMs found that the lightweight stainless steel seat pillar bent slightly (particularly if the binder bolt was overtightened) preventing it from being lowered into the seat tube. A slightly heavier gauge of stainless steel was therefore adopted, the stronger seat pin being indicated by four rivets holding the alloy saddle cradle, rather than two. Shortly afterwards the necked section at the top of the stainless steel tube was increased in length from 1" (25 mm) to 2" (51 mm). This reduced the risk of the SR micro-adjust pillar working loose in the stainless steel tube.

After I reported that my AM7's seat binder bolt had snapped (a loud crack followed by a sinking feeling!) the bolt specification was changed to a higher tensile steel.

The Spanish-made Zeus hubs used on the AM7 sometimes failed to meet expectations, despite Alex setting up his own quality control procedure for these components. Bearing cones and, more terminally, cups tended to pit after as little as 1,000 miles (1,600 km). Also the spoke holes sometimes elongated slightly, reducing spoke tension. Eventually the Zeus hubs were superseded by similar looking but superior products by Sansin. (The 1994 AM7 has Mavic hubs.)

Following requests, particularly from the German market, a brazed-on dynamo bracket was provided between the chainstays to facilitate mounting of a tyre tread driven dynamo, such as the then popular Sanyo Dynapower.

The original spade-type alloy rear lamp bracket tended to fatigue when used with the large battery-operated lamps then in common use. A stronger bracket was introduced, formed out of a rectangular loop of thin stainless steel rod.

New UK regulations concerning bicycle reflectors became effective in October 1985. Bikes made or first used thereafter had to be sold with front, rear, pedal and wheel reflectors that complied with British Standard 6102/2. It was still not mandatory to have any reflectors for daytime cycling: for night-time use, only the rear and pedal reflectors were required. (AMs produced before October 1985 only needed a red rear reflector marked BSAU40LI or LIA: a circular one was fitted.)

The new rear reflector required a slightly larger mounting hole than its predecessor. Early AM front and rear reflectors to the new standard were hexagonal, later ones trapezoid and supplied by Adie-Nephew.

A special lightweight mounting was devised for the AM's front reflector: a fixing strip brazed to an internally threaded sleeve which replaced the nut of the handlebar stem clamp bolt. A similar method was used to fix a specially designed lightweight front lamp bracket. This was Allen key adjustable for angle and, like the redesigned rear lamp bracket, was formed of folded thin stainless steel rod. The front lamp bracket was marketed as an optional extra from 1985, and cost £4.95.

Initially Alex Moulton Limited merely supplied the wheel reflectors with AMs for owners to dispose of or fit, as they wished. However, the enforcement authorities insisted that the devices be factory-fitted to the wheels.

The AM2's original SR double-sided pedals were later superseded by single-sided counterbalanced Shimano utility pedals. At first the black plastic PD-100 was fitted. Later the alloy Adamas AX or similar Fulfit PD-A-100 was used.

Pre 1984 Moulton-Wolber tyres could be distinguished by their black rather than amber interiors.

After Bluemels ceased trading in 1986, mudguards were sourced from Spencer, a subsidiary of W. R. Pashley Limited. The latter company's product lacked the central ridge found on the Bluemels Club mudguard.

Early GB Stelvio RTE stems tended to expel their circlips. This was because the groove in which the circlip sat was sometimes not deep enough. Free issue replacements were supplied.

Very early AMs had a shallower rim to the circular alloy cam at the apex of the rear triangle.

ACCESSORIES

A comprehensive range of optional accessories was available for the AMs. The alloy prop-stand was a standard commercially available component but most other accessories were specially designed.

Carriers

The front and rear carriers were finished in black and were low, wide and frame-mounted in the Moulton tradition. They were much lighter than earlier Moulton carriers, being built from Reynolds 531 tubing, principally of $^{11}/_{32}$" (8.5 mm) and $^{1}/_{2}$" (12.7 mm) diameter. All joints were brazed.

Front Carrier

Two fixing points were provided on the AM frame for the front carrier. Both were brazed-on horizontal tubes: one between the head tube and upper frame lattice beam; the other between the lower frame lattice beam and frame tie.

The front carrier had a flat platform formed by a perimeter tube and two longitudinal infill tubes. The latter extended rearwards and were bolted to the lower fixing point. The perimeter tube extended upwards to form an upstand against the head tube. A pair of tie tubes connected the infill tubes to the upstand and bolted to the upper fixing point.

The front carrier was designed to carry 15lb (6.8 kg) of luggage, 5lb (2.3 kg) less than the Moulton front carriers of the 1960s. Initial recommended retail price was £16.95.

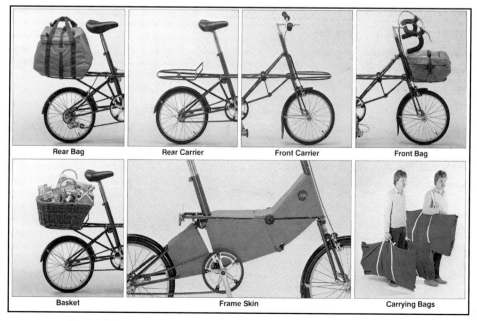

| Rear Bag | Rear Carrier | Front Carrier | Front Bag |
| Basket | Frame Skin | | Carrying Bags |

Accessories.

Tailpiece

In the AM frame, the chords or outer tubes of the horizontal lattice beam passed either side of the seat tube. When no rear carrier was in use, a tailpiece was fitted to the ends of the chords. This had four functions: it stopped rain and debris getting in the tubes, provided a mounting point for a rear light and reflector, formed a platform more than 4" (100 mm) long on which a rolled-up cape or other small piece of luggage could be strapped, and improved the appearance of the bike, giving it a finished look. The weight penalty was about $3^1/_2$oz (90 g).

The tailpiece, complete with rear reflector and alloy spade-type lamp bracket, was supplied as standard with all AMs. It consisted of a $2^1/_2$" (64 mm) long horseshoe-shaped length of the same Reynolds 531 tubing as the chords of the lattice beam. Brazed to the curved back of the horseshoe was a tab, drilled to accept the reflector's integral bolt, which also held the lamp bracket in place. An alloy thumb-nut threaded onto the bolt. This allowed the reflector and lamp bracket to be released from the tailpiece and repositioned on the rear carrier without using a spanner.

Brazed to the underside of the tailpiece was a tube with a slot cut completely through it. As the tailpiece was pushed onto spigots in the ends of the lattice beam chords, a tab brazed to the frame fitted into the slot. A 6 mm Allen bolt was then passed through the right-hand half of the tube, through a hole in the tab, and into the threaded left-hand half of the tube. Tightening the bolt ensured that the tailpiece was held positively in place.

Rear Carrier

The AM rear carrier was a refined lightweight version of that use on the Moulton MkIII (see Chapter 1). The main differences concerned the fixings to the bicycle frame.

The carrier fitted to the frame in exactly the same way as the tailpiece. However, because of its much greater size, like the MkIII's carrier it required a support strut. This had to be fitted to the frame before the carrier could be bolted on. A large diameter coarse-threaded stud was brazed to the base of the seat tube and the strut was threaded onto this by hand.

The top end of the strut was slotted. In the middle of the underside of the carrier was an alloy thumb-nut, which ran on a threaded stud fixed to the carrier. This stud had to fit into the slot in the strut as the carrier was pushed onto the spigots. Once the Allen bolt was securely in place, the thumb-nut was firmly tightened by hand, thus completing installation of the carrier. (The strut end was later modified – see Chapter 5.)

Two other features of the AM rear carrier were new. Firstly, short bracing wires were fitted in the corners of the carrier; two in the rear corners of the platform and two in the lower corners of the upstand. These provided a little added rigidity but more importantly, formed useful anchorage points for the hooked ends of elasticated straps. In later carriers longer wires were fitted.

Secondly, there was a zigzag infill of small diameter tubing linking the two main carrier tubes between the carrier upstand and the mounting point. Apart from giving added rigidity, this visually emphasized the continuity of the carrier with the horizontal lattice beam of the bicycle frame.

The rear carrier was designed to carry 30lb (13.6 kg) compared with 50lb (22.7 kg) for earlier Moultons. Its initial price was £19.95.

Rear Bag

Specially designed bags were available for fitting to the front and rear carriers. Made by Karrimor, they had a combined capacity of 36 litres (approximately 1) cubic feet). They were constructed of Silvaguard, an easily cleaned, superior quality, "waterproof" nylon fabric. However, the manufacturer did not claim that the bags were 100% waterproof. Regular treatment of the seams with Karrimor seam sealant was recommended, and it was suggested that clothing and sleeping bags

CAD drawing of the 1994 AM7 by Nigel Sadler.
Apart from componentry changes the only significant difference from the 1983 model is the parallel sided fork blades.

be packed "in sac liners for extra protection".

The rear bag folded flat for storage or for carrying empty on the rear carrier. The bag was kept flat by a flap on its lower left side, which fastened onto the upper right side by means of Velcro.

The wide webbing reinforcement which passed down both sides of the bag and across the underside of its base was extended to form a pair of loops. These could be clipped together by a suede leather strip, sewn to the right-hand loop and fitted with a pair of press-studs. Thus a comfortable handgrip was formed for carrying the bag when used off the bike.

A strap was stitched centrally to the base and sides of the bag. This had adjustable plastic couplings on either side of the bag. One enabled the strap to be separated so that the bag could be strapped to the carrier; the other passed over the top of the bag and enabled the height of the bag to be reduced if it was only partly full.

To hold it rigidly in place on the carrier, the bag incorporated a pocket in its front which slipped over the carrier upstand. Two plastic footpieces were stitched to the base of the bag, to protect it from abrasion when used off the bike.

The bag's top flap had four rings fixed to it so that an object such as a tent could be strapped or tied to it. Two zip toggles running on a single track, along both sides and the rear of the bag, held the top flap shut. The zip toggles could be parked anywhere on the track, for side or rear access as required, and were large enough to be padlocked together.

Original production of the Karrimor bag was mid grey, later production being darker. The webbing was dark blue, and in early bags had white stitching. The plastic quick-release couplings were black, and the Karrimor and AM logos were embroidered on the flap in white. Later production incorporated a hidden document pocket in the underside of the top flap, a detachable shoulder strap, and Velcro loops for carrying a spare tyre horizontally around the bag.

A criticism of the rear bag was its floppy condition when less than full. Despite the adjustable strap, carrying small, lumpy items such as cans, bottles, or egg boxes could be problematic. The bag's sides and base were foam-filled to give some rigidity but it was not enough for this type of utility use.

However, the bag was good when loaded for touring. It was also excellent for use off the bike. It could be stored in the back pocket of a briefcase and yet carry a heap of box files or enough personal effects for a long weekend away. Bicycle Action described it as "smart enough to use for hand luggage on Concorde". The bag originally cost £21.95.

Front Bag

The front bag was considerably smaller. However, in most respects it was similar in concept, folding flat for storage. The fixing to the carrier upstand was by a webbing strap passing round the carrier upstand, another under the carrier platform halfway along its length, and a Velcro strap holding the front of the bag to the carrier perimeter tube.

The front bag lacked the rear bag's webbing reinforcement and loop handles, but had a detachable shoulder strap. The top of the bag incorporated a transparent pocket for a map. Later production incorporated a hidden pocket for documents in the underside of the top flap. The colour varied during production, as for the rear bag. The initial price was £18.95.

(From about 1993 Karrimor were unable to supply bags in a shade acceptable to Alex. This probably explains why very light coloured Karrimor-AM front bags were being sold at bargain prices at the 1993 CTC York Rally. The 1994 AM bags are produced by an ex-Karrimor employee in black with red piping.)

Basket

To solve the grocery carrying problem, the AM accessories included an open-topped shopping basket for the rear carrier. This was specially made on Sedgemoor, an area of Somerset noted for traditional basketwork. The basket was detachable and incorporated a pair of carrying handles. At launch it cost £16.95.

Frame Skins

Another load carrying option for small items was the use of frame skins. Made of a sailcloth material, they enclosed the spaceframe between the head and seat tubes, and also the part of the rear triangle ahead of the rear wheel. Journalist Graham Vickers described them as "evoking those tailored coats that women of a certain age put on their poodles".

The skins were held in place by Velcro fixings and were available in red or yellow with black piping, or black or blue with red piping. Black with red piping seems to have been the most popular choice. The AM logo appeared on the sides of the skins just behind the head tube, in red on a black circular background.

The price was not available when the AM range was launched, but in June 1984 a set of frame skins cost £24.95.

Carrying Bags

For transporting the separated AM, a pair of identical carrying bags were available. Made of sailcloth, they measured approximately 48 x 24" (1,219 x 610 mm) when laid flat.

Each bag had a flap at one end, along the short dimension of the bag, which was held in place by Velcro. The front part of the bike went into one bag, along with the seat pillar. The rear part went into the other bag. There was sufficient space in the bags for carriers, if first unbolted from the frame.

Each bag was reinforced by webbing which was stitched to it and passed right around it. The webbing was extended to form a pair of carrying handles at the middle of the long side.

The pair of bags could be carried separately, or fixed together by means of integral straps and Velcro fasteners. Loops were fitted so that a single shoulder strap could be fixed to both bags.

It was quite difficult to fit the rear part of an AM7 into the early carrying bags. The height of the bag was only just enough to accommodate the dimension from the top of the seat tube to the bottom of the 52 tooth chainwheel. Later bags incorporated a substantial gusset which eliminated this problem and enabled AMs with much bigger chainwheels to be bagged with ease.

Using two bags to carry the AM had three advantages:

- the parts would not scrape each other in transit,
- they could be stowed separately,
- as neither bag contained a bicycle (merely parts of a bicycle) the AM could in some cases legally be carried on public transport which prohibited bikes on board.

The carrying bags were offered in navy blue with cardinal red webbing, or blue with white webbing. Both bore the AM logo. They were made by Sherborne Designs Limited of Westbury, Wiltshire. The price was not available at the time of the bike's launch, but a year later was £43.95.

Tool Bag

A tool bag was introduced in 1984. Initial production was in black sailcloth with a red embroidered AM motif. Velcro fixings on flaps were used both to close the bag and fix it to the frame.

The tool bag was designed to fit between the chainstays of the rear triangle, and was tapered accordingly. However, it could get quite muddy there and would not be noticed if it fell off. (Early examples had rather short flaps which tended not to engage too well.) Therefore some users preferred to fix the tool bag on the flat section of spaceframe immediately behind the head tube.

The tool bag was big enough to carry a spare inner tube, basic puncture repair kit and a small spanner or two. In June 1984 it cost £4.95. Later production varied slightly in proportions and colour.

MARKETING

Brochures

The AM2 and AM7 were initially marketed via two brochures, each approximately 8" high x 9" wide (203 x 229 mm) when folded. Both were printed on stiff, glossy paper.

A four-sided brochure printed in black and red on white, described the merits of Alex Moulton's "Advanced Engineering Bicycle" concept. With the aid of silhouetted drawings it pointed out that the AM has a similar riding position, wheelbase, frame angles, tubing, gearing and componentry to a high class lightweight, but with "unique bonus features".

Chief among these were:

- strong small wheels with the special 17" tyre for quick acceleration, and low rolling and air resistance,
- suspension giving shock isolation, a "silky" ride and improved road-holding,
- the unisex, universal size, rigid and lightweight step-through spaceframe,
- front and rear carrying capability on the centre-line and low down for safety, with a wide range of luggage options,
- separability, into two parts for easy lifting and stowage.

A second brochure, printed in colour, provided further details of the machines and optional accessories. It had six sides, folding out into a three panel strip.

The front cover featured a colour photograph of the central part of the spaceframe, emphasising the kingpin mechanism. The back cover was headed "The Moulton Story". Monochrome photographs showed The Hall, and Alex at his desk, with a model Series 1 Moulton under a glass dome in the foreground. (This exquisite $1/5$ scale model was built in 1965 by his friend Henry Trevaskis.) The accompanying text, written by Alex, set out his objectives in creating the AMs.

Opening the front cover revealed, on the right, a partial perspective of the AM bicycle, divided into three panels to feature the front suspension, the frame separability and the rear suspension. Each panel was accompanied by descriptive text.

When the brochure was opened out fully, the left page revealed a photograph of the AM2 complete with rear carrier, the right page a photo of the AM7, while the centre page featured seven photographs of the accessories. This brochure was also produced in German.

Price lists and dealer lists for the AMs were merely typed at the factory and photocopied as necessary.

Display Advertising

Display advertising for a limited production, relatively expensive product such as the Alex Moulton bicycle has to be sparingly used to be worthwhile – sales are unlikely to increase in proportion to advertising expenditure. Over the years Alex therefore made relatively little use of press advertising.

However, from summer 1984 until spring 1985 he ran an advertisement, typically 8$\frac{1}{4}$" wide by 6" high (210 x 150 mm), in certain cycling magazines and some upmarket non-specialist publications, such as the Observer colour supplement.

The advertisement incorporated a monochrome photograph of the lower half of a track-suited rider astride an AM7. This was set against a graph paper background to emphasise the "designer" aspect of the product. Handwritten notes around the photograph highlighted the design features. The heading was an attributed quote from Peter Knottley of Cycling magazine: "A new and improved cycling experience".

The accompanying text pointed out the benefits of the Advanced Engineering Bicycle:

"Light and quick like a racing bike.

Small and compact like a folding bike.

Strong and durable like a touring bike.

Front and rear suspension like a motor bike."

The 1984-85 advertisment.

The text also mentioned that Tom Race (a CTC tour leader) had chosen the AM7 for a 3,000 mile (5,000 km) trip around the Himalayas. He was quoted as saying the AM was the most versatile bicycle he had ever owned, and that all other cycles seemed, by comparison, to be obsolete.

Early UK Dealers

The initial UK dealer list was deliberately restricted to just five carefully selected firms, three in London and two local to the factory. Serving the capital were the London Bicycle Company, Condor Cycles and Swift Cycles Limited; the latter two firms having been staunch Moulton supporters in the 1960s. The county of Avon and surrounding areas were served by John's Bikes of Bath and by Les Wilkins Cycles Limited of Weston-super-Mare, who also had a shop at Bridgwater in Somerset.

Air Freighting

For overseas sales the separability of the AM bicycle came into its own. The AM7 when separated could be packed into a carton measuring 39 x 22 x 12" (990 x 559 x 305 mm). This enabled Alex to despatch machines direct to dealers by air freight in cartons approved by UPS (United Parcel Service), the major US parcel delivery company.

Shows

The AMs were displayed at the International Festival of Cycling, Harrogate in July 1983. Alex spent several days there and said he was confident of selling a few thousand bikes a year to those who sought the ultimate in design and craftsmanship. At the show he received "a fistful of orders". Peter Knottley, reporting on the show in Cycling, wrote: "Although these bicycles are not cheap, they cost no more than many keen riders already pay for conventional machines and no one was heard to say that they were too expensive ..."

The Australian magazine Freewheeling reported that Alex's stand was one of the best attended exhibits. The British trade magazine Cycletrader printed a photograph of the stand.

The following year saw Alex Moulton Limited again at the Harrogate show. According to the company, there was a four-deep file across the hall to see the bikes. Cycling magazine's report on the show included a picture of the stand.

AMs were first displayed in the United States in Las Vegas at Inter-Bike '83, the largest US cycle show.

Manufacture

By August 1983 demand for the new bikes was ahead of production. 40% of the 4,000 sq ft (377 sq m) 1960s factory was devoted to cycle production, the rest being devoted to automotive and aircraft work. In charge of production was 60 year old Phil Uncles, a long-time Moulton employee, who also designed much of the machinery used in manufacture. The offices remained in The Hall.

The 1960s factory on The Hall estate, building AMs.

Majority Achieved

Every year Alex commissions a Christmas card design from cycling illustrator Brian Walker. The 1983 card, featuring a street scene in Bradford-on-Avon, was the first to show the new bike. The legend declared: "The Twenty-first Anniversary of the Moulton Bicycle 1962-1983".

But what did the critics think of its latest manifestation?

Chapter 4
REACTION
1983-1986

Reviews of the AM2 & AM7

Many early reviews of the "Advanced Engineering Bicycle" were effusive, but none more so than Cycle Trader's of June 1983. It concluded:

"The Moulton of today is a big improvement on its august predecessor: we are dealing here with an aristocrat of bicycles, produced by the prince of designers: the cycling movement and the cycle trade should judge themselves fortunate to attract still, after 21 years, the inventiveness and initiative of Alex Moulton."

Three months later Cycle Trader devoted a photo spread to the manufacture of the AMs, showing key personnel John Benjamin, Jack Lauterwasser, Phil Uncles and accountant Andrew Hemmings.

"The Only Bicycle You Will Ever Need"

The front cover of Bicycle, July 1983, featured an AM front wheel under the heading "Alex Moulton's Latest Invention". Inside was a major report on the bike by Stuart Morris, illustrated with superb photographs by Jon Stewart.

Stuart Morris appreciated the "high quality, lightweight and durable materials and cleverness ... subsumed into function". The AMs were not, he observed, ostentatious: "the concept, colour and the ride are subtle". He felt that the new bikes combined quality, function and dedication in the same way as Leica, Rolex, Hewlett-Packard and Mercedes.

Having tested the AMs, Stuart concluded:

"Physically the AM7 felt as comfortable, taut and precise as my favourite bike back in the Paddington Left Luggage. The AM, though, is lighter and smoother with higher and lower gears. I could have carried it on the HS 125 [High Speed Train], I could have carried a crate of wine back from France without the frame shimmying like a jelly. With the range of accessories and its inherent versatility, the Alex Moulton is the only bicycle you will ever need."

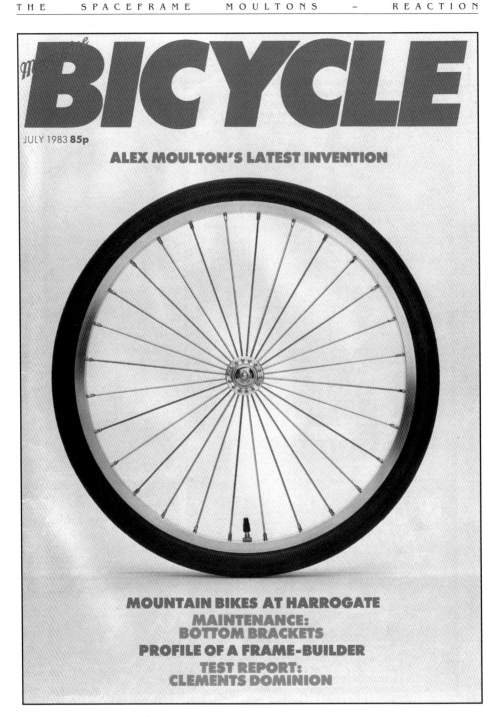

Bicycle Magazine's classic cover, July 1983.

"A Superb Touring Machine"

The July 1983 Bicycle Times printed what was claimed to be the first thorough testing of the AM7 by any journalist or magazine. The tester was editor Peter Lumley, who put the bike through its paces over "a fair expanse of County Durham".

Peter praised the frame separability, noting that almost every designer of folding bicycles had "made a hash of the hinge". To test the AM's frame joint, he had "leapt up and down on the machine to see if there was any give, any flexing", but he had found none.

The AM's braking received some criticism: Peter felt that the problem lay with the brake blocks. However, the gearing was satisfactory, even for the long hill climbs of County Durham. This was "a bicycle to cruise on, selecting the right ratio so that you don't need to throw it around". That way the rider would not have to fight the suspension.

The road-holding and ride comfort were praised: "If you hit bumps when cornering there is no tendency to go off line … The Moulton suspension gobbles up quite wide differences of road condition, although the rear wheel acts a little more like a conventional machine, kicking if the road is bad."

Just over a year later Peter reported that the first year's manufacturing target of 1,000 machines had been met, and that half had been exported to America, Australia, Canada and elsewhere.

"Even Better!"

Cycling's detailed review of the AMs was headed "Even Better!" and appeared in August 1983. Peter Knottley praised the new bike's separability, luggage carrying capacity and its "steady, smooth and satisfying ride". He felt that the "return for effort on the new Moulton is just a bit up on the conventional bicycle".

In the same issue Harold Briercliffe reported on the organisation of Alex Moulton Limited, with special reference to the factory. A fortnight later Cycling printed a letter from Graham McDermott of Epsom, praising the design and finish of the AMs.

An Engineering Debate

August 1983's Engineering included an article headed "Moulton Makes a Better Bicycle … Again". This recounted the evolution of the AM and described its claimed advantages. The following month the magazine printed a letter from Michael French, Professor of Engineering Design at the University of Lancaster and author of "Conceptual Design for Engineers". Michael, an AM2 owner, praised the new machine, calling it "a pegasus to the palominos of common bicycles, worthy as they are".

This was too much for Tony Pennell, a lecturer in the Department of Mechanical Engineering at the University of Newcastle upon Tyne. He wrote to Engineering putting forward what he called "an alternative 'non-establishment' view". It must have come as quite a shock to Alex to be accused of propounding establishment views on bicycle engineering!

Tony, a non-cyclist, viewed the AM as "yet another over-complicated, over-glamourised, enthusiasts' machine doomed eventually to commercial failure". November's Engineering printed Tony's letter, complete with replies from Alex and Michael.

Tony stated that the use of diagonals for torsional stiffness was so well known that it could not be considered innovative. Presumably as a non-cyclist he did not realise that such use was most unusual in bicycle design. He went on to question why the seat and head tubes were not linked by "one or two straight thin-walled tubes of circular, oval or rectangular cross-section", which he suggested would probably be lighter and certainly cheaper than "Moulton's lattice nightmare". Tony, not mincing words, was inclined to define a good engineer as "one who can do for £49 what Dr Moulton can do for £490".

Alex replied that "the original Moulton theme ... has diverged so that it is now eponymous as the simplest and lowest cost form of bicycle, outstripping the diamond-frame 'classic' in these respects". However, what he had set out to do with his Advanced Engineering Bicycle concept was "to make an altogether superior version of the original ... for the enthusiast at a price (maybe not ten times the minimum!) amongst those of the highest class of similar weight classic, in comparison with which it has unique bonus features".

As for thin-walled single tube, Alex suggested that Tony had "overlooked the vital factor of the limiting diameter/thickness ratio in regard to manufacture and above all 'oil-canning'", the flexing of the tube walls which militates against the maximum stiffness/weight ratio.

Tony went on to criticise the frame separation mechanism. Why, he asked, was the kingpin "just where the effects of lateral bending and torsional loads are greatest, and its weakening effect most serious"? He attacked as "crazy" the splitting of the "simple tension link underneath at mid span", because it necessitated reinforcing four ends instead of two.

Alex replied that the kingpin and hook below were "positioned to optimise ergonomically and spatially the separation function". He pointed out that the proportions of the kingpin were "more than sufficient to satisfy the lateral and torsional stiffness requirements".

Finally the engineering lecturer asked, "What is the structural and

economic justification of the **twin** vertical struts between the two rear suspension pivots; the **multiple** diagonal bracing in the lower trailing arm; the crossed vertical bracing in front of the rear mudguard?"

Alex replied, "Twin vertical struts are primarily to allow passage between them of the single strut which supports the carrier. The bracings in the trailing arm are to secure the tested values of torsional and lateral stiffnesses, required by the high values of the offset chain load."

Engineering's original review included some of Alex's design sketches. Tony Pennell attacked them for being too like Leonardo's drawings and not conveying enough engineering information. (It must **really** hurt to be compared to Leonardo!)

Michael French agreed that pictorial sketches "are not able to store and convey as much useful information as engineering drawings", but this was not their function. "The pictorial sketch is an aid to thinking during the design process itself ... the exercise of eye, brain and hand in the delineation of form and the appreciation of the potentials of solid bodies are closely linked."

One of Alex's sketches was subsequently shown in Designing's April 1984 issue, as an example of the usefulness of visualisation in the design process.

"Not for the Common Man"

In September 1983 Michael Strutt, writing in the Financial Times, praised the AM's comfort, manoeuvrability, lightness, handling, luggage carrying capacity, gearing, componentry and finish. However, he had a few criticisms. The gear lever would, he said, be better if mounted on the handlebars, "especially since with small-wheel bikes both hands should be kept on the bars". He would also have welcomed "more bite from the brakes" but, like Peter Lumley, felt that changing the brake blocks should help. And the mudguards were, he thought, comparatively frail.

A fortnight later the FT again featured the AMs, this time in an article by Lynton McLain examining the market for the new bike in the UK. He quoted Andrew Ritchie, designer of the Brompton folding bicycle, who described the AM as "a very nice piece of engineering" but a "personal indulgence" on Alex's part. Jim Ryan, director of the Bicycle Association of Great Britain, told Lynton, "This cycle is not for the common man."

The September edition of Technology described the AM as "a classic example of design by and for engineers, but not for any significant market". Yet in the same month Cycle & Motorcycle Trade Monthly reported that sales were so buoyant that deliveries to the trade were falling behind demand.

"A Damned Good Touring Bicycle"

Alan Gayfer of Cycling World reviewed the AM7 in the magazine's November 1983 issue. Describing the AM7 as "a damned good touring bicycle", he warned, "if you are prejudiced, or stuck in your ways, you will find it strange and therefore unsatisfactory. If you give yourself time, however, the results are really very good indeed."

The AMs were, he thought, like Citroen cars: "you need a little time to get used to their steering, brakes, ride and so forth".

Alan, a former editor of Cycling, noted the effectiveness of the AM7's suspension:

"I learned this in striking fashion. In fact, while I was riding the AM7, I was struck from the side by a learner driver who just carried on and did not even slow down. I lay on the deck with broken ribs, but I was a good eight miles from home. It wasn't funny, but I was nevertheless able to ride home, thanks to the rubber suspension. I would never have been able to do that on an orthodox bike, so the system undoubtedly works well."

In Alan's opinion, the AM7 was "properly" geared, although he suggested a SunTour PSL M ratcheted gear lever would be worth fitting. He reckoned that an acceptable cadence was about 70 revolutions per minute or less. Faster pedalling could induce bouncing, but, "If you pedal at the touring gait ... it just rolls along." With the AM, as with earlier lightweight Moultons, you might end up using slightly higher gears than on a conventional bike. Alan ascribed this to the AM's small wheels, which complete with tyres, were about 30% lighter than conventional lightweight wheels.

(From figures he gave, the Moulton wheel and tyre was 27% lighter than a conventional lightweight wheel with small flange hub, Mavic E rim and Michelin Bib TS 280 g tyre. It was 34% lighter than a wheel with large flange hub, "normal" Weinmann rim and Michelin Sports tyre.)

Alan noted the reduced gyroscopic effect of the 17" wheels but thought that riders would soon get used to this. Lighter wheels might, he thought, make cycling downhill slower than with a bigger wheel but this did not worry him. (In practice, AMs, like the 1960s Moultons, are noted for being fast descenders, but a little "dead" at the bottom of the descent.)

The advantage of the lighter wheel was its lack of inertia: "If you are strapped in you can drag your foot round through bottom dead centre with greater ease, since there is less wheel to accelerate, and that can't be bad, especially if you are loaded, and do not want to get out of the saddle."

He suggested that, when first riding the AM, owners should tighten up the front suspension dampers: "After a few hours, loosen them again gently bit by bit until the desired softness is found ... it takes a few miles to get used to the rolling gait of the Moulton".

Alan praised the load carrying system and noted that the carrier could be removed much faster than any other he knew of. He also thought that separating the bike was quite easy.

However, the rear brake was less than stunning. This puzzled him. The CLB brakes were neither cheap nor nasty, he mused, and the front brake worked very well. But even with the rear brake adjusted quite tightly, he could not lock up the rear wheel when descending a hill. He suggested using long, bonded, Mathauser brake blocks and added, "Bikes are odd things, and whether it is the spring, the pivots, the length of the cable or a combination of all three, I cannot tell, but the rear brake is both heavier and less precise than I would wish."

(This prompted Isaac Fairclough to write to Cycling World. He reported that he had noticed that Weinmann brake cables were braided differently from those factory-fitted to the AM. Fitting the Weinmann cable had, he said, greatly improved his AM's braking.)

The saddle, however, was so good that Alan considered buying one for his regular machine. Rider comfort on the AM was, he said, outstanding: surfaces unridable on an ordinary bike felt merely rough, whereas normal surfaces seemed board smooth. Road-holding was no problem, "for the flexibility of the suspension ensures that there is less bounce at the wheel-surface contact point".

He concluded that, "for the cyclist who wants something different which is still a practical machine and not just a toy, this must be high on the list for lightness, fun and practicality."

This article produced a critical response from Birmingham cyclist and science teacher Stan Bray: Alan described it as "vaguely vituperative, generally vague". Stan accused Alan of whitewashing the AM7's faults. One of these perceived shortcomings was that the bike could not safely be ridden hands off. According to Stan, riding hands off saved energy – to which I replied that perhaps we should all be riding unicycles.

Stan's overall conclusion was that "small wheelers need a lot more development before they are ready for cycle touring, as opposed to car touring with a cycle". Alan, writing both under his own name and as Hugh Blackeby, replied at length to Stan's arguments, accusing him of being an unscientific publicity seeker.

Whether he was or not, Stan wrote a number of letters to the cycling press (Cycling, Cyclist Monthly, Cycling World) at this time attacking the Moulton bicycle concept.

Irish Agency

In November 1983 Cycling World reported that Wallacesport of Ballymoney, County Antrim, Northern Ireland, had been given the sole agency for Alex Moulton bicycles in the whole of Ireland. The dealership's owner, Wallace McNaul, had raced on Moultons in the 1960s.

"The Great Event"

For Peter Knottley, the advent of the AM was "the great event" of 1983. In Cycling's last issue of the year he wrote:

"It is not just another cycle or another Moulton, still less another small-wheeler. It is the first integrated approach to the best design of machine for its purpose in the history of cycling ... the new Moulton is a summation of ideas transformed into an efficient and skilfully made machine. It is not a question 'why did he choose 17 inch wheels?' or 'why is the front wheel radially spoked?' or 'why is the frame designed as it is?' Each feature depends upon and descends from the others."

Noting the conservative nature of most cyclists he observed nonetheless that "those who have tried the new Moulton agree that it offers a new and improved cycling experience."

Such comments might have been regarded as somewhat sycophantic, were it not for the fact that Peter was one of the UK's most experienced and highest mileage cycle tourists.

"A Reason for Everything"

In the January 1984 issue of Cycling World, Alan Gayfer presented "The Alex Moulton Story". This was largely based on an interview with Alex and a visit to the factory at Bradford-on-Avon.

Alan stressed the amount of background work and hard testing that went into the AM bicycles. He ventured that Alex cycled "more than any other major name in the cycle industry, excepting the few specialist makers". Consequently there was "a reason for everything that is on the new AM7".

Tim Bigwood, later in charge of the plant, had worked for Alex since 1962. He told Alan how one customer sent his frame for metallurgical X-ray analysis – the brazing (strictly speaking, bronze welding) was flawless, which was no more than the customer or Alex expected. At the time the plant was producing about 25 bikes a week. Tim and his colleagues were each responsible for one stage in the frame building process.

Alan watched the rolling road test rig on which the AM's suspension had been subjected to about a thousand bumps a mile (600 per km) for several hundred thousand miles without failure. He reported that company secretary John Benjamin habitually ran his tyres at 110 psi (7.5 atm) with no detrimental effects.

At this time a sixteen-speed automatic expanding chainwheel gear, the Deal Drive, was due to come onto the market. Alex told Alan that the AM was unlikely to be offered with this transmission because "it should be up to the rider, not up to the bike to decide". In the event, the Deal Drive was never mass-produced, although a number of leading British cycle manufacturers announced that they would fit it.

EUROPEAN VIEWS

West Germany

In November 1983 the prestigious West German newspaper Frankfurter Allgemeine Zeitung printed a major article on the AMs. It stated, "The history of the bicycle is rich in innovations which have failed to find a market. That a bicycle which had disappeared now reappears is one of the sensations of bicycle technology. A British grand seigneur has just delivered the impossible."

The article noted that in the Germany of the 1960s only connoisseurs, such as Daimler-Benz designer Nallinger, rode Moultons. The Zeitung's reporter wrote enthusiastically about the new bike, noting that the spaceframe was "somewhat reminiscent of the Eiffel Tour". His only criticism was that the AM lacked a chaincase – an indication of the German view of bicycles as a means of day-to-day transport, rather than fashion accessories or sports equipment.

The German cycle trade magazine Radmarkt (Cycle Market) described the new bikes in late January 1984. In the same month they were advertised in Radfahren (Cycling), the importer being named as Jonasch & Meyer. Prices were quoted as DM 1,755 for the AM2 and DM 2,117 for the AM7. There was further reporting of the AMs in Radfahren's March issue and in Tour Rund ums Rad (Cycle Touring) the same month.

That summer Bild Post (Picture Post) featured the new bike, and Radfahren focussed on the AM2. This was shown slightly modified for the German market with swept-back flat handlebars and a Sanyo Dynapower lighting set, complete with tail light on the rear mudguard.

The September 1984 Wirtschafts Woche (Economy Week) contained an advertisement offering by mail order **three** versions of the AM. The AM2 cost DM 1,957, the AM7 Country DM 2,360 and the AM7 Tour DM 2,456. The Tour differed from the regular AM7 in that it had swept-back flat bars and the Dynapower lighting set.

In August the following year Fahrad Sport & Reisen (Cycle Sport & Touring) featured the AM, describing it as a "Rolls Royce on two wheels".

France

The French magazine Cyclotourisme made a passing reference to the AM and printed a photograph of it in January 1984. Reporting an Audax event (see page 226), it noted the presence of three Moultons "of a new model showing as always the combination of small wheels and effective suspension".

Le Cycle, April 1984, showed the AM2 and AM7, with drawings of the suspension and kingpin mechanism. Prices were quoted as from F 5,200 to F 6,900. The following month Velo (Bicycle) reported on "La moulton", citing the "talent of an inventor of great reputation across the Channel". The magazine named Pierre Maisonneuve of Paris as a contact for further details.

Almost a year later Velo described Alex as the "enfant terrible of the industry across the Channel". Noting "some success in amateur racing events in Britain", the magazine added, "We the people of the Continent are perhaps a little more old-fashioned and wait to see, for example, in the Tour de France." In the meantime they were happy to designate the AM "classe touriste" to begin with.

The next issue of Velo contained an advertisement for the AM7, which was available from Paris dealer "La Grande Roue" – paradoxically the **big** wheel!

The Netherlands

Dutch magazine Fiets (Bike) first reported on the AMs in its coverage of the 1983 Harrogate show. Early in 1985, Fiets ran a thorough review of the bikes. In an article headed "Expensively Different", Guus van de Beek concluded, "You can race with a bike costing 500 or 5,000 guilders, tour with a single-speed or 18-speed bike, and ride round the world on an ATB, folding or touring bike. With a Moulton you can do all these things and more."

Prices quoted were Fl 2,495 for the AM2 and Fl 2,995 for the AM7.

Scandinavia

In spring 1985 reviews appeared in the Swedish press. Cykling, magazine of the cycling organisation Cykelframjandet, gave a favourable view. The weekend supplement of national newspaper Svenska Dagbladet described the AM as the Mercedes of bicycles. And Dina Pengar, a magazine issued by a Swedish bank, gave a brief technical analysis and a very positive report.

The Finnish magazine Tekniikan Maailma also reviewed the bikes.

REPORTS FROM AUSTRALIA

It was winter 1983/4 in the northern hemisphere when Pedal Power's report on the AM7 hit the streets of Australia. Describing the bike's "feel", its reviewer wrote, "My test riders were all wildly enthusiastic, using words like 'smooth', 'floaty', 'busy', 'responsive', 'unreal', or just 'How do I get one?' Dr Moulton himself describes the feel as 'dynamically synergistic'."

The reviewer added that the AM7 was "as comfortable as a fat-tyred bike on your average road, but noticeably faster". It was also "an excellent hill-climber, if you get the gear shifts right". However, he found the gear lever a "bit awkward to reach" and shifting was "twitchy and uncertain". Moreover, he thought many Australian tourists would prefer a gear range of up to 5:1, which would necessitate a front derailleur – difficult to fit to the oversize seat tube.

The detachable rear carrier was, he thought, "a sop to the sporting types", and should have been an integral part of the frame.

But the conclusion was fundamentally favourable. The AM was "enormous fun to ride", the only serious drawback being cost.

Another Australian cycling magazine, Freewheeling, reported on the AM7 in its November/December 1983 issue. Nigel Jenkins described the AM as the Rolls Royce of bicycles, but had a few reservations: "Detailing is well thought out, the finish of the lugless frame superb, however a number of items fail to meet general standard."

He was particularly concerned about the use of pop rivets on the seat pillar and for fixing the mudflap to the "comparatively ordinary" mudguards. He also disliked the Stronglight snap-on plastic chainguard, and criticised the design of the demount bracket.

On the whole though, Nigel was impressed. He had road-tested the AM7 in England on the London-Brighton Ride, where the first reaction of many riders was "what a peculiar machine". After 10 km (6 miles) he was "convinced of its excellence": "The ride is silky smooth, the gearing wide enough for the steep descents and rises on the route. It is quick and very responsive."

He pointed out that the AM7 did not handle potholes or narrow transverse trenches very well, but added that neither does the conventional lightweight bicycle.

Shortly after the Freewheeling report, the Adelaide newspaper The Advertiser carried a report on the AM7 by Bill Hickling. Noting Freewheeling's description of the AM as the Rolls Royce of bicycles, he wrote: "I'm sure they weren't thinking of its looks when they described it thus because its appearance won't win it many converts. However, the rigidity of the frame and the ability to absorb the shocks of surface irregularities is certainly Rolls Royce-like."

Five months later Freewheeling carried an advertisement for Calypso Cycles of Newtown, New South Wales, stating that they were exclusive agents for the AM range. Prices quoted were Aus $ 965 for the AM2 and Aus $ 1165 for the AM7.

FURTHER UK REVIEWS

A Bike of the Century?

The 1984 edition of the International Cycling Guide featured three "bikes of the year", one of which was the AM7.

Hol Crane reviewed it enthusiastically:

"The brilliance of the detailed engineering design, the rigidity of the main structure, the impeccable craftsmanship, the manoeuvrability, the ease of mounting and the superb handling at all speeds make you want to leap aboard, to feel at one with its excellence."

He had ridden the bike on a two-day tour of 120 miles (200 km) with a load of 28lb (12.7 kg) on the rear carrier. The bike handled well on rough urban roads and at speed on downhill runs. In contrast to many reviewers, he found the CLB brakes "powerful". He also liked the carrier, which had "no discernible sideways sway". However, he found that it twisted easily, "allowing the top of a high load to swing from side to side unless it is firmly attached to the saddle". As to the separability, Hol likened its significance for bicycle design to the adoption of the 35 mm film format for the Leica camera.

His overall conclusion was that the AM was not only a comfortable, practical touring machine: it was "so far ahead of its competition" that it would be "treasured by future generations as one of the great bikes of the century".

Hol's review contained the results of his own (non-laboratory) rolling resistance tests. From these he concluded that the AM 17" tyre at 78 psi (5.3 atm) had a rolling resistance on tarmac roads about the same as a 26 x $1^3/8$" tyre running at about 45 psi (3.1 atm). However, he claimed no great accuracy for his tests the results of which are quite at variance with those obtained by more scientific test methods by Chet Kyle, General Motors and Alex Moulton himself.

Putting on the Style

In London on 26 January 1984 at Stationers' Hall, Alex presented a paper to the Wynkyn de Worde Society. (Wynkyn de Worde was one of the first English printers.) The theme was "Putting on the Style". The paper, which was later published, dealt with the development and evolution of the Moulton bicycle, and the extent to which styling came into the exercise. Alex concluded:

"Styling in the design sense is actually about evolving an image of **something else** in the mind of the observer. In the case of my bicycle, a pure engineering object, I am not wishing to evoke an **image** of anything; only to reveal its hopefully harmonious form of fitness for its purpose. Hence even its colour is limited to steely grey. I do admit that the mudguards (black) can cause controversy; perhaps they are the only parts for which I have consciously **put on the style!**

Menage a Trois

David Foster took up cycling in middle age. He bought an AM7 **and** an AM2, and wrote about his "Love of Two Moultons" in the February 1984 edition of Bicycle.

David noted the reactions of non-cyclists to the prices of the AMs: "'Is it made of gold?' asked a bus conductor. 'Does it fly?' asked a London cabbie. But to me it fulfilled both these criteria as we glided through the glorious summer of '83".

However, he was less poetic about the AM's pump:

"In my opinion a pump should be more readily available – and a better pump should be supplied. I christened mine the Vampire because, far from putting air into the tyre, it seemed to suck out the air which was already there."

He also advised forethought in locking the machine, to ensure that both halves were firmly anchored to an immovable object.

David's AMs were not immune from teething troubles, but most of the problems involved components made by companies other than Alex Moulton Limited. He was pleased with the service he received, both from the London Bicycle Company (where he was served by the well-known cycle tourist Tim Gartside) and from Alex Moulton Limited.

As for the ride quality:

"I felt as if I was on the conventional touring bike which had given me so much pleasure over the last four years. ... There was a little instability when I changed from the 'drops' to the 'tops' and vice versa. But it was just a matter of getting used to it."

The High Mileage Tourist and Big-Wheel Snobbery

By 1984 cycle journalist Peter Knottley had ridden 300,000 miles (480,000 km) by bicycle, mostly on traditional lightweight touring bikes. In June his views on the AM7 were published in a letter to Cycling World.

He reported that he now ran two AM7s and did virtually all his touring and utility riding on them. He found them "at least as easy riding and certainly more comfortable as using a diamond-frame cycle". Although he still kept "a very nice 'conventional' bike", he found it "rather ungainly and awkward" compared with the Moulton.

Peter praised the bike's "imaginative and effective load-carrying system and its compact portability". He bemoaned the lack of objectivity of many fellow cyclists, "some of whom are strangely reluctant to give serious consideration to innovation".

Indeed, in the January 1984 journal of the Cleveland Wheelers, he pointed out that, when riding his AM7 he was "virtually never greeted". Neither was a greeting returned, "even by those who are obviously 'real' cyclists".

Strong Attachment

An article about Alex in Bicycle's July 1984 issue revealed his strong attachment to his new creations:

"I feel tremendously identified with them. They are **my** solution. I am deeply sensitive to reacting criticism of the bicycle. It is a highly idiosyncratic solution and one which has been deeply studied, and it is **my** solution.

"The thing which gets up my snout – if that's the right expression – is the lack of curiosity of the expert and of the man in the street. It absolutely amazes me that they are not rushing to try it out. I rode one on the Centenary Club [the cycle trade's club] autumn run and they scarcely took any interest. I have never met anyone who hasn't come back smiling after a test ride or taken it for a longer ride than intended. I feel that everyone has got to try the blasted thing."

A Satisfied Customer

Strangely enough, it was not until summer 1984 that the views of Moulton Bicycle Club members started to appear in the club magazine, Moulton Cyclist. Phil Boot, a member from Nottingham, wrote that he had ordered an AM7 which arrived at his home with the frame damaged by the road carrier's rough handling. This was just three days before Phil intended to take the bike on holiday.

He managed to contact John Benjamin, Alex's company secretary, at the Harrogate International Festival of Cycling. A solution was swiftly evolved.

Phil sent the damaged bike back to Bradford-on-Avon by Datapost. Meanwhile John sent colleague Andrew Hemmings from the cycle show to the factory, some 200 miles (320 km) away, specially to rebuild the components into a replacement frame-set. During the operation Phil was given three progress reports by telephone. The rebuilt bicycle finally arrived back at Nottingham just in time for the holiday to proceed as planned.

Phil was extremely pleased with the "wonderful Rolls Royce service" and said that he considered the AM7 "absolutely superb".

6,000 miles on the AM7

The same edition of Moulton Cyclist included an in-depth report on the AM7 by its new editor, Nick Peregrine. Nick described himself as "a 10,000 mile a year cyclist ... and a Moulton fanatic". By the time he wrote his review, Nick had ridden some 6,000 miles (10,000 km) on his AM7:

"The terrain covered has varied enormously from stripped down dual carriageway to rough mountain tracks in the Pyrenees with full camping gear on board. Thus the following observations have been made in the light of these experiences plus of course the 69 hours spent in the saddle on the Paris-Brest-Paris 1,200 km (750 mile) marathon."

Nick praised the lightness and portability of the AM7. But he suspected that the dual cable system for the rear brake was "partly responsible for inefficiency of the rear brake". He also had doubts about the practicality of the foam handlebar grips.

He saw the special small sprockets as "a neat idea", avoiding the need for "giant 68 TA rings" and saving on overall weight. "However, the gaps between the gears are very large, a change from 7th to 6th results in a drop of 18" which is somewhat disastrous for one's cadence, even on a touring bike never mind a racing machine."

Nick considered the new suspension system "a vast improvement", the rider almost enjoying "a floating sensation". Hill climbing ability was good, "something until now we never associated Moultons with". As to luggage carrying: "The bike feels virtually the same (until you try and lift it!) laden or unladen and of course a vast amount of luggage can be safely and easily carried."

On a major tour of the Pyrenees, Nick had been able to take all his camping gear and other equipment in the two AM holdalls, "without the need to tie bits and pieces elsewhere". The bags had stood up well to wear and tear, and looked good on or off the bike. The fixings were easy to use. The only quibble he had was that the front bag leaked, which precluded keeping cameras, passport and suchlike in it. He suggested that it be redesigned, "perhaps with a longer flap over the front zip or alternatively to open back to front".

The carrying bags had proved their effectiveness on trains where "it is undesirable to let officialdom know you have a bike". Nick had found it "just possible to carry the bike in its two bags, rear holdall and front holdall" all together. However, as he pointed out, the whole lot could be loaded onto a luggage trolley.

Whilst he appreciated the anti-theft benefit of the AM's concealed pump, he was less enthusiastic about it at night or in the rain. He thought it a nuisance "having to remove seat pillar and pump, replace seat pillar, invert bike, mend puncture, invert bike, remove seat pillar, insert pump and carefully adjust seat pillar to exactly the right height". He also found it embarrassing when a cycling companion on a conventional machine could offer a pump "in a split second" before he had even removed his seat pillar.

Nonetheless Nick was pleased with his AM7: "The suspension is very smooth, it carries vast amounts of luggage, is easy to take on trains, buses etc, handles as well as my diamond frame machines when light and better when heavily laden."

Up Ditchling Beacon at Last!

Cyclist Monthly's August 1984 edition included a report by Eric Simpson on the annual London to Brighton Bike Ride. 15,000 cyclists took part, raising funds for a heart charity.

The ride includes the feared Ditchling Beacon, where the road rises some 700 feet (200 m) above sea level, climbing relentlessly for about a mile (1.6 km) at a gradient of up to 1 in 8 (13%). Eric was riding an AM and proudly reported, "I got up this time for the first time thanks to the Moulton AM7 and its extremely low gear."

A "Biblical" View

1984 saw the publication by the Bicycle Cooperative of The Bicycle Buyer's Bible. It relegated the AMs to a chapter on portable bicycles.

The reviewer stated that "the new Alex Moulton bicycles were certainly worth waiting for." They compared very well with a good quality lightweight cycle and delivered "quality performance". However, the AM's drop handlebars and derailleur were "pandering to the high speed whims of the racing element".

Factory Visits

The September 1984 edition of Bicycle Action reported that Alex was "obviously enjoying himself more than ever since his new small-wheeled designs came out". The magazine continued:

"By common consent they represent an even greater advance than his original Sixties contribution. ... The new Moultons are absolutely amazing, as more and more people who've tried them have found out."

Bicycle Action added that Alex would "now accept visits by groups of cyclists, by arrangement, during which you get a chance to ride the machines as well as look over a museum which illustrates the story of the Moulton bikes." Visitors could even camp in the grounds of The Hall, if they wished.

One cyclist who visited the factory was Martin Brain of Bristol. He went with the Bristol District Association of the Cyclists' Touring Club and revealed his impressions in a letter to Cycling World magazine.

Martin was impressed by Alex's "mechanical genius and genuine love of cycling", and test rode an AM7. To his surprise he immediately felt at home on it. It was the first time he had tried a different cycle and "not felt a little ill at ease".

He described the stability at low speed as "uncanny" and added, "no need to take foot out of toe-clip at traffic lights; just dribble along at 1 or 2 mph". Martin found the bike equally stable under acceleration and was greatly impressed by the "superb" suspension. However, he conceded that "If you like 'honking' up hills or riding through bogs, then maybe this is not your bike".

"A Self-Imposed Problem"

The AM2 was the subject of a test report in the August 1984 issue of Bicycle by Graham Vickers. He noted that for the price of an AM2 you could buy "a very good conventional bike indeed". He concluded that the AM's appeal was "to those who are put off by the seeming complexity of ten-speed derailleur bikes for pottering around town". It was, he felt, somewhat condescending to produce a bike like the AM2 because it was "better to educate people to understand superior solutions than to supply them with soft options".

Graham saw the AM as tending to "make a virtue out of a very necessary solution to a self-imposed problem", particularly in respect of the suspension. This was "clever and effective" but only needed "on this sort of small wheel bike". Despite the adjustability of the front suspension, he preferred conventional 531 forks.

Nonetheless, Graham admitted that the AM2 "immediately commands respect". Everything tangible was of "top quality" and the bike was "a lovely piece of engineering".

His first test ride consisted of about 13 miles (22 km) non-stop in town. "Unexpectedly the first response was to want to cycle fast," he reported. "This is surely a unique quality among small wheel bikes."

He soon got used to the Duomatic hub, and evolved a technique to get the pedals in the best position for starting off. (With any coaster hub it is impossible simply to flick the pedals backwards to get them to the best position.) The suspension was found to be very good, easily handling all the bumps he rode over at speed.

The test bike was not fitted with carriers but the reviewer was convinced that the AM carriers could not be "as rigid as a Blackburn carrier fitted to a standard geometry frame". He praised the easy rolling tyres and rightly drew attention to the need to maintain the pressure accurately, a factor that cannot be over-emphasized. He also noted that the AM2 was "genuinely unisex, not some half-hearted compromise".

Apart from expressing a preference for slightly lower gearing, Graham was well-pleased with the bike, which he felt should be "judged by the highest standards". It "immediately exceeds expectations" and the "road-holding and general handling capabilities are excellent".

(Graham's "self-imposed problem" comment about the AM was repeated two and a half years later in the Architect's Journal. This produced a robust reply from Alex, who said that, had TI not acquired Raleigh in 1960, the history of the bicycle itself might well have been very different. George Wilson of Raleigh was "utterly convinced of the advance represented by the Moulton bicycle and would have made and marketed it on a considerable scale".)

Graham's wife, not usually interested in bicycles, "succumbed to the accessibility" of the AM2 and later passed it on to their daughter. In Bicycle, January 1986, Graham wrote about bicycles for youngsters: "Maybe Moulton's one-size frame is best for children, it grows as they do and though it is not cheap it is probably no more expensive than a series of fashion-bikes."

In the same issue David Gibbon wrote, "The amazing thing about the Moulton, in this age of adman's hype, is that it is exactly what it claims to be, a small-wheeler that goes like a touring bike, and more importantly, makes the rider feel at home right from the start."

This comment was prompted by a ride on a borrowed AM2. Eight months later the AM2 was featured in Design magazine, having been selected for inclusion in the Design Centre, London.

Time Out

In late September 1984 Matthew Hoffman wrote in Time Out of his year-long quest for the perfect commuting bike. He concluded that it was "a machine with the strength and positive feel of a mountain bike, the lightness of a racer, the portability of a fold-up and the price of a second-hand three speed".

Acknowledging that this machine did not exist, he reported that he had settled for an AM7. It gave him manoeuvrability and fast acceleration, and combined separability with a rigid frame.

"Of course there is no sane reason to spend this much money on a bicycle – even one as superbly designed and built as the Moulton – but once you have done it anyway, you'll manage to persuade yourself that it was worth it. I have."

FIRST REPORTS FROM NORTH AMERICA

The AM was featured in Popular Science, March 1984. Datelined London, the report by David Scott merely described the machine.

About the same time J. Baldwin, wrote in Co-Evolution "first reports are that it is quite exceptional in every way, especially as a load carrier". He added, "Now if one could only adapt the suspension to a Mountain Bike ..."

"A Delight To Ride"

An advertisement for the AM appeared in Bicycling, March 1984, under the banner of Two-Wheel Transit Authority, the major cycle dealer in Huntingdon Beach, California. Two months later Bicycling printed a road test by Sheldon Brown and John S. Allen entitled "Five New Folding Bicycles". The machines tested were the Montague, Bridgestone Picnica, Hon, Brompton and AM7. The AM's "quality and care of constructing, and attention to cosmetic detail were very high indeed". The report added that the frame-mounted luggage racks vastly increased the bike's stability under load-carrying conditions.

The testers noted the ingenuity of the AM7's gearing system and praised the "surprisingly smooth " running of the nine tooth sprocket and "spectacular 185 degrees wrapround" the chain gave it. However, they thought they might prefer a conventional double chainwheel, and felt the chain angles were excessive when using the low gears.

As to performance, "The Moulton is a delight to ride. It is essentially as fast as any other bike with clincher [wired-on] tyres, but the suspension makes it almost as smooth and comfortable as an all-terrain bike."

The testers quoted the "startling test result" that the AM's tyre had less rolling resistance than most bikes with "full-size" wheels. "In repeated rolling resistance tests conducted by bicycle engineer Chester Kyle on a smooth linoleum surface, the Moulton's rolling drag coefficient was 0.0034 with 90 psi (6.1 atm) in the tires, and 0.0028 with 120 psi (8.2 atm) in the tyres".

They pointed out that, to obtain the total rolling drag, you must multiply the combined weight of the rider, load and bike by the drag coefficient. Bicycling's testers quoted the drag coefficient for 27" cotton tubular tyres (sew-ups) as 0.0032 and for Specialized 1.125" touring clinchers as 0.0031. Tyre pressure was not quoted, but was presumably that recommended for those tyres.

The testers' conclusions on the AM's ride qualities were that it "fosters a riding style with more seated spinning, more care for big bumps, less care for small bumps, and faster cornering and descending". They recommended it to any cyclist who could afford it, even if frame separability was **not** required.

"As Big As They Come"

The AMs received another American review in September 1984. Peter Tonge wrote in The Christian Science Monitor about how Christopher Igleheart of the Portland Bicycle Exchange, Portland, Maine travelled virtually everywhere either on or with his AM7. "The combination of public transportation and what he sees as 'this remarkable little machine' gets him wherever he wants to go." Chris even praised the AM's performance in the snow: "If a car can handle it, the bike will too."

Peter had tested the bike himself and praised its "silky smooth" ride. He quoted a frame-builder friend as saying that, despite the AM's small appearance, in performance terms it was "as big as they come".

A Canadian Convert

The Vancouver-based magazine Bicycling News Canada featured the AM7 in its summer 1984 issue. John Monroe headed his article "Birdcage Moulton – the Well-Mannered Folder". He felt that the AM "may be one of the most interesting bikes to hit the market in the last decade." It was, he said, "literally hip-deep in interesting technical innovations and automotive technology that will have experts and bike freaks in general arguing for years to come."

John praised the "very high" overall quality of the wheels, which needed no truing "even after some very vigorous rides". The rear suspension was acclaimed for its simplicity and for the fact that Alex had "correctly judged power transmission to be more important than the last ounce of shock absorption". The feel of the front suspension when riding out of the saddle concerned some of the magazine's test riders, but most agreed that adjusting the suspension would probably overcome any problems. John found that tuning the dampers did the trick for him.

As to ride quality, apart from the need to adapt riding style when honking, he felt that "on level ground it feels and rides like almost any quality bicycle". Small bumps were absorbed with ease by the suspension. However, "bottoming the suspension on big holes can bring you back to reality with a jolt".

Like many other reviewers, he was impressed and surprised by the bike's "terrifying cornering ability". "I literally could not get this bike to break loose on dry pavement [road surface]. Even leaning over and pushing the bike farther over didn't help, to my gratitude."

John had three complaints about the AM7. Firstly, the brakes were "far too mushy to be considered adequate". Secondly, the gaps between the high gears were "far too large, leaving the bike without a reasonable array of cruising gears". Finally, the carriers, good though they were, would not accept standard panniers, which he felt limited the touring possibilities of the machine. (He made no mention of the Karrimor holdalls, so may not have been aware of their existence.)

He concluded that, despite its fairly high price, the AM7 was ideal for those who want to "get about town with class and comfort".

Louis Bernhardt, editor of Bicycling News Canada, was so impressed with the bike that he bought one for himself. He wrote to tell me that, despite "very minor bugs", he thought it was the most significant achievement in bicycle technology since the introduction of the first Moulton. "I guess I have become a Moulton enthusiast," he added.

US Dealers

In October 1984 a full page advertisement for the AM appeared in Bicycle Sport. It likened the bike to the Volkswagen Beetle: "It looks small, but its Big on design. It's not a folding bicycle. It's an Alex Moulton."

The exclusive stockists for the USA were listed as:

- The Bicycle Center, Santa Cruz, California
- Two-Wheel Transit Authority, Huntingdon Beach (near Los Angeles), California
- Criterium Bike Shop, Colorado Springs, Colorado
- Velo Sport Moscow Bicycles, Moscow, Idaho
- Portland Bicycle Exchange, Portland, Maine
- Collins Cycle Shop, Eugene, Oregon
- Angle Lake Cyclery, Seattle, Washington.

JAPAN

In September 1984 Dr N. Tominari, President of the Japanese company Dynavector Systems Limited, visited The Hall to assess the AM range. He liked it. Exports to Dynavector commenced in November and by the end of 1984 a second order had been placed. Bicycle Times reported, "They expect to build up a sizeable market in Japan where the quality, performance and advanced engineering of the new bicycles is very much understood and appreciated."

A double page advertisement for the bikes appeared in the Japanese magazine Cycle Sport in January 1985. It included a small inset photograph of the BMC Mini, which had Moulton suspension and was much admired by the Japanese.

Japan was destined gradually to become the biggest export market for Alex's bicycles. In 1994 Alex Moulton visited the country to celebrate a decade of satisfying the Japanese demand for AMs.

BACK IN THE UK ...

Bicycle magazine's Claire Gilman gave the AM7 star rating in her round-up of "perfect presents" for Christmas 1984. She showed a fully laden AM7, complete with front and rear bags, tent, stove and spare tyre. The bike was described as a "marvellous example of precision engineering" which could be used either "for serious touring or city cycling with the added feature of being separable".

"A Quite Remarkable Achievement"

Chris Juden, Technical Officer of the Cyclists' Touring Club, summed up reaction to the AMs among CTC members – on the one hand "enthusiastic acclaim", on the other "profound scepticism". He decided to find out for himself by carrying out a comprehensive test of the AM7, complete with carriers and bags. It was published in the CTC magazine Cycletouring (December 1984/January 1985).

He found that the suspension "seemed to give the Moulton the edge" over conventional tourers on rougher minor roads, and added:

"While whizzing along over cobbles and potholes, or down tracks that should loosen your fillings, you are insulated from the frantically oscillating wheels which (at lower speeds) hop in and miraculously out of ankle-high ruts. Deeper holes, soft sand or mud stop it dead (and twigs get caught in the ground-hugging mudguard), but the AM7 is surprisingly at home on roughstuff."

None of the energy that should go into propulsion appeared to be absorbed by the suspension. However, he hoped that the fork spring base plug was easy to replace, "as wear causes brake judder."

He praised the frame for its "uncompromising stiffness". The value of its separability was proved during the test by stowing the bike on the luggage rack of a British Rail High Speed Train.

Chris soon adjusted to the "bouncing front suspension" when riding out of the saddle but conceded that some riders might not like it. He was more concerned, however, about the "disconcertingly light steering" and suggested reducing the fork rake by $1/4$" (6 mm). As he put it: "I reckoned fork rake to be around $1^5/_8$" (41 mm), equivalent to $2^1/_2$" (64 mm) with a 27" wheel, rather long for $72^1/_2$ degrees ..."

(Stan Eagle of Culcheth subsequently demonstrated an AM7 with shorter links to Chris. The octogenarian H. H. "Chater" Willis, concerned that "the slowed reactions of old age" coupled with his "quivering nerves" could bring on an attack of the "Willis Wobbles", followed Stan's example. In The Moultoneer, Spring 1987, Chater wrote:

"I have now done the same [as Stan] since it is an easy experiment to get the necessary holes drilled in the links, without pulling the forks back as is strictly desirable. That means that the short stem within the main fork column is slightly out of line, but if that has ill effects in wear, it can be rectified.")

Turning to the transmission, Chris found the tiny special Moulton sprockets ran "remarkably well" but criticised the chainline for making the two largest sprockets grate "horribly". He concluded that the 120 mm (4.72") crank axle was too long and overcame the problem by moving the chainring to the inside of the crank spider.

Although he was used to a fifteen-speed transmission (five-speed freewheel and triple chainwheel) Chris found that the seven gears gave "even, 21% intervals" and "optimum coverage". The gears changed "quite well", although the chain occasionally skated on the grooved tips of the Regina sprockets.

Braking was found to be "tolerably good". However, the brake levers were criticised for rubber hoods that perished and flimsy cable adjusters that snapped "like a carrot" when knocked.

The carriers were praised for their capacity and rigidity. Chris was less enthusiastic about the "not very waterproof" bags. He found the front one floppy and ended up putting a board stiffener in its base. He also suggested that the rear bag "could do with an internal divider near its zippered opening, to avoid losing small things in its cavernous interior."

Chris concluded that, despite his criticisms, the AM7 was a "quite remarkable achievement" and "probably the lightest, stiffest, most comfortable touring cycle" he had ridden. If he had to restrict himself to ownership of only one bike, it would probably be an AM7.

Subsequent issues of Cycletouring contained a number of letters stimulated by Chris's article. In the June/July 1985 issue, Philip R. Stanesby of North Cheam wrote expressing concern about future availability of "specially produced parts" for the AMs. He had owned a Moulton in the 1960s and was tempted to buy an AM7. However, he understood that certain parts for 1960s Moultons were almost unobtainable. As he put it, "Most people spending £500 on a bicycle would, I suspect, want to ride it for the rest of their active lives. What hope is there of obtaining spare parts in the future?"

The reply came in the following issue in a letter from Nick Peregrine, then honorary secretary of the Moulton Bicycle Club:

"Many of the spares needed for the 1960s bicycles are in fact available at only the cost of reproduction plus postage. If the AM7 range were to be discontinued it would be Moulton Bicycle Club policy to scour the country's bike shops and the factory, in addition to channelling our small resources into reproduction suspension parts, etc."

During his test of the AM7 Chris had broken three spokes in the rear wheel, which had nonetheless remained "just ridable". In a letter in the April/May 1985 issue of Cycletouring, P. Rawlins of Bath expressed surprise that this had happened. He was perturbed that Chris had "accepted" the breakages. Chris replied that he **never** accepted spoke breakages, but as he could not vouch for the treatment previously received by the well-used test model, he had not felt inclined to labour the point.

The following issue of Cycletouring contained another letter on AM spokes, this time from N. S. "Miff" Mowle, an Isle of Wight cyclist. He had just returned from three months working in the South Pacific area, where he had covered over 1,000 miles (1,670 km) on his AM7. Much of this was on very rough roads, without a single spoke breakage and with only one puncture.

Miff was interested in Chris's remarks about fork rake, and would have welcomed some extra stability, "especially on a long tour with loaded carriers". The AM7 was, he said, "a great bike all the same".

An Ex-Cycle Tester's View

A writer for Car magazine might seem a strange person to listen to for comments on the AMs. However, Roger Bell used to road-test bikes for Cycling. In a major article in January 1985 on Alex Moulton, he wrote: "...the Moulton's spirited feel, its secure roadholding – the low centre of gravity really does help on the corners – its precision and solidity mark it out as something extra special."

The Boilerhouse Project

The March 1985 issue of Bicycle Action reported on three bicycles selected for Terence Conran's Boilerhouse Project at London's Victoria & Albert Museum. This was established to celebrate "designs from the real world", and early in 1985 mounted an exhibition of the "100 Best Ever Products", nominated by leading British designers and design experts.

Among the products displayed were the Swatch watch, the Mini car, the Macintosh computer and the Michelin guides. The three cycles selected were all British – a Condor racing bike, a Muddy Fox Monarch mountain bike and an Alex Moulton AM2. The exhibition catalogue described the AM as "the ultimate expression of cycling technology" and added, "Both the original Moulton and its successor provided the rider with outstanding comfort and control, together with compactness and portability."

More Views from the USA

Jim Langley reviewed the "Remarkable Moulton Bike" in the February issue of California Bicyclist:

"The bike is a marvel to ride! ... The bike is also an amazing handler because the suspension forces the wheels to contact the road at all times. In rough, fast turns a road bike will sometimes bounce sideways because the wheels lose contact. The Moulton's wheels refuse to stop gripping the pavement."

Doug Roosa of Bicycle Guide gave a more detailed view of the AM7 in a 1985 article subtitled "Not a quadrilateral bit of piping" (Alex Moulton's pejorative term for the diamond frame). He wrote:

"You never quite forget about the Moulton's suspension. Its assertive personality both woos and bugs you. It handles railroad tracks and broken pavement with ease. But it also responds to propulsive thrusts on the pedals with a mild bobbing. A certain rhythm develops. Silky smooth pedallers – those who can ride no-hands on rollers – can probably minimize this suspension quirk, but mashers are bound to discover all its excitation frequencies."

Doug noted that adjusting the suspension could reduce the bobbing, but at the expense of making the ride harsher. He added: "Fortunately, the bobbing largely disappears when the Moulton is laden with baggage ..." and concluded that this was "what Alex Moulton had in mind since, foremost, the AM7 is a touring/commuting bike and not a racer." While not a supporter of suspension on racing bikes, Doug considered there was a good case for springing a loaded tourer.

He found the 17" wheels initially felt "very skittish during slow speed manoeuvres and when you stand out of the saddle". When cornering tightly, the AM needed "more lean and less steer into the turn" than a conventional bike. There was little difference on smooth corners but cornering on rough surfaces could lead to oversteer because of the light steering. However, the suspension made "the wheels track better, so you're less likely to need to adjust your line."

The AM's frame was praised for its "great strength and rigidity". The carrier fixings and the precision of the separable frame mechanism were also applauded.

The component mix was described as "generally good", although the performance of the brakes was criticised. Doug said that the rear brake did nothing but "polish the rim" and that the front brake was only "marginally adequate". The transmission was also criticised somewhat, especially as the chain occasionally unshipped itself, and the spacing between some of the gears was considered "awkward". A minor frustration stemmed from the difficulty in getting fingers round the gear lever when shifting down from top gear.

Doug found that riding the AM7 he consistently took a minute or so longer than on a conventional machine to complete his normal 9 mile (14.5 km) journey to work. He felt that perhaps he had not fully adapted to the Moulton and that maybe "tighter gearing" might have helped, had it been available.

The views of AM dealer Paul Moore of Two-Wheel Transit, Huntingdon Beach, California were quoted by Doug. Paul felt that the right psychological attitude was needed to get the best out of an AM. At first he had been reluctant to take the bike on training rides. However, when he finally plucked up courage, he found he could "sit in the saddle and climb with most anybody." Paul also appreciated the acceleration and found that "if some rider jumps, I can get on his wheel really fast."

Doug stated that "anybody with an ounce of appreciation for industrial design will go back and marvel at the Moulton again and again". He concluded that:

"The Moulton's best quality may be that it keeps you on a good set of wheels no matter where you go. Most everyone I talked with praised the portability of the Moulton without having to put up with the ride compromises of even more portable folding bikes like the Bickerton or the Hon."

An accompanying article by John Derven contrasted Alex's use of small diameter tubing with that of Mikael Pedersen at the turn of the century. It quoted Alex as saying in 1978, "it is not impossible that some features of the construction of the Pedersen will be revived in a modern machine". John suggested that "Moulton may have had the nascent design of the AM7 in his head as he wrote that."

He was right. As we saw in Chapter 2, by 1978 the AM design was well-advanced. Alex wrote the introduction to a 1979 book, "The Ingenious Mr Pedersen", by David Evans of Dursley, Gloucestershire and by the early 1980s had a Dursley-Pedersen at The Hall. In 1991 he told Larry Taylor of Bicycle, "I was especially interested in their small tube construction and the durability question. Yes, I was interested by it and respected it but my solutions or structures are quite different."

Top Ten

The December 1985 issue of Bicycle listed the magazine's Top Ten machines of 1985. The AM7 was one. Interestingly it was 4lb (1.8 kg) lighter, and less than £80 dearer, than another listed machine, the conventional diamond-frame Mercian "King of Mercia" – unsprung and non-separable!

Consensus

A high level of consensus emerges from the many reviews quoted above. It was generally agreed that staying in the saddle and cruising was what the bike responded to best. It was not a bike for "mashers".

Some reviewers thought the high gears of the AM7 too widely spaced. Many criticised the performance of the rear brake. There were also a few quibbles about the light steering and the concealed pump.

But despite these criticisms, the construction, performance, road-holding, comfort, luggage carrying capacity and portability of the Alex Moulton bicycle were almost universally praised.

Chapter 5
THE RANGE EXPANDS
1985-1987

AM-Zzipper - AM14 - Reorganisation - AM5 - Frame Kits

The performance qualities of the Alex Moulton bicycle were soon almost universally acknowledged by the British cycling press. In August 1984 Cycling stated that the AM was "the only 'stowaway' cycle ... for long-distance riding". In 1987 a similar comment appeared in Bicycle Action, which advised that for touring, "The only folding [sic] bikes suitable ... are made by Alex Moulton."

This chapter examines the progress of the "Advanced Engineering Bicycle" in the period between these two comments, as the AM product range expanded.

AM-Zzipper Fairing

Since quite early in the history of the bicycle it has been realised that streamlining can give a bicycle significant speed advantage. As Frank Whitt & David Wilson pointed out in their 1974 book Bicycling Science, "At racing speeds the power to propel rider and machine is almost all spent in overcoming air resistance, and this power is proportional to the speed cubed."

Twelve years before that was written, Alex Moulton conducted experiments with streamlined fairings on prototype Series 1 Moulton bicycles. John Woodburn, who soon afterwards broke the Cardiff-London record on a Moulton, was the rider for the test programme. He commented on the strangeness of riding in "still air", hearing all the transmission noise that is normally drowned out by the wind.

However, such fairings were not permitted under Road Records Association rules. Rider safety in cross-winds was also a problem, and Alex therefore suspended development work. But over the following two decades materials technology progressed considerably, particularly in the field of plastics. This induced Alex to look again at the possibility of creating a practical fairing for everyday use.

Bicycle Magazine, July 1984, mentioned a prototype fairing for the AMs. It was described in more detail by Doug Roosa in the September

1985 edition of Bicycle Guide. The fairing was developed in conjunction with Glen Brown of Zzip Designs in California. Doug reported:

"It's a large Lexan fairing that attaches to a modified front carrier (made from Reynolds 531, of course) and to the handlebars. Brown was careful to warn us that the prototype we had was not rubber mounted and was therefore both noisier and shakier than he liked. Ignoring that, I still found that the fairing tended to amplify road and gear noise. On the positive side, the fairing really helped when riding into headwinds, and it caught enough tailwind to actually sail the bike."

The AM-Zzipper fairing was launched in March 1985. Its design drew on aerodynamic research by Doug Milliken (see Chapter 9). Its weight, including the special Reynolds 531 front support carrier, was about 3lb (1.4 kg). But to compensate for this, the fairing offered a measured drag reduction of very nearly 20%.

A remarkable feature of the design was that, although the Lexan fairing curved both vertically and horizontally, it could be rolled up compactly for storage.

The literature claimed that the AM-Zzipper improved cold weather comfort and made the AM "virtually impossible to catch with a standard bicycle, particularly into a headwind". The price at launch was £174.95.

One of the first purchasers of the fairing was Douglas Cooke of Sunningdale, Berkshire. He evolved an inexpensive but effective way

AM-Zzipper fairing.

of soundproofing the AM-Zzipper fairing, using self-adhesive 9 x 2 mm ($^3/_8$ x $^1/_{12}$") foam strip supplied by Sound Services (Oxford) Limited of Witney. With the fairing removed, the foam strip was stuck to the aluminium support rails, above and below the fairing fixing press-studs and to the carrier where it abutted the fairing. The modification was claimed to make the fairing virtually silent. Douglas's idea was subsequently incorporated into AM-Zzipper production.

In November 1986 AM News, the dealer newsletter, warned that the fairing carrier was "not intended to carry heavy loads" and recommended that "no weight is carried on the fairing support carrier".

Evaluating the AM-Zzipper

Bicycle reviewed the AM-Zzipper early in 1986. The tester found it disconcerting, because it did not turn with the bike's handlebars. He also found the cold air stream tended to get him in the eye, and was concerned about catching his chin on the top of the fairing when riding out of the saddle.

On the whole he felt that the fairing was a hindrance which could "probably only provide assistance when ploughing along against the watch in a big gear".

Nigel Sadler used an AM-Zzipper for much longer before giving his opinion: "After three year's use, and much consideration, I have concluded that it really does help. It is attached to my AM14-S for about half my journeys – either fast ten mile (16 km) sprints across London, or UK touring."

The fairing came into its own on hard and fast long distance rides, Nigel reported: "Travelling at speed, low on the drops, looking through the screen, in the comfortable still air behind the fairing is a very pleasing experience."

He found the drumming and road noise acceptable. Head winds were easier to ride against than side winds; and as Doug Roosa had noted, tail winds enabled the fairing to be used as a sail. However, Nigel cautioned against using the AM-Zzipper in wind speeds higher than 30 mph (50 kph), as sudden gusts or passing traffic could blow the rider over.

Like any cycle accessory, the fairing could be a nuisance when not used to full advantage. Parking in anything more than a light breeze could result in the AM being blown over. In some conditions the rider could overheat. And the AM-Zzipper was definitely not for the shy.

From windswept Midwest America, Leigh Wade of Paynesville, Minnesota wrote:

"Yes, the fairing does work. It even works better than I had expected it to. For the same amount of effort I exert on other bikes, the Zzipper-faired AM14 gives me 3-5 mph (5-8 kph) more. While riding on the brake hoods, just the top of my shoulders and head are above the fairing; by ducking down completely behind the fairing, I immediately go 2 mph (3 kph) faster. This is a really neat sensation – sort of like kicking in a turbo or something."

The AM14

In March 1985 Alex launched a third interpretation of his spaceframe bicycle, the AM14. It was displayed at the London Cycle Trader Show where, in three days, a dozen orders were taken. This was a specially good week for Alex – the Austin Metro, with its Moulton-designed suspension, being declared best-selling car of the month.

The AM14 was available in two versions, the S (Sports) and the T (Town or Touring). Both versions had much in common with the AM7, the obvious difference being their 14 speed transmissions.

The AM14s were also distinguished by their frame finish. Although the basic colour was still steely grey, there was a red coach line along the outer edges of the horizontal frame girder. This was continued along the outer edges of the optional steely grey rear carrier's main horizontal members. The head badge also had a red line.

The frame incorporated polished, stainless steel, investment cast fittings by Yeovil Precision Castings for the fork crown, hook joint socket and front derailleur bracket. The demount bracket anchor and parking bosses, and the rear carrier stay stud were also stainless steel.

AM14S

The AM14 rider's points of contact with the bike differed from those of the AM7 as follows. The AM14S had a Cinelli alloy-railed saddle and Shimano 600 EX pedals with toe-clips and straps. The AM14T had a Madison G11 saddle, GB Loveday alloy handlebars and Shimano Fulfit PD-A100 counterbalanced alloy pedals, which could be adapted to take toe-clips and straps.

The AM14T's Loveday handlebars were an interesting innovation. They looked like drop handlebars turned upside down, but with the straight ends elongated by about 3" (75 mm) and fitted with moulded foam grips. They therefore offered a very upright riding position. However, the foam padded lower part of the handlebar, either side of the stem, gave a position similar to the tops of conventional drop handlebars. It was also possible to ride with hands on the padded, forward upsweeps. These gave a handhold similar to a time trialist's bull-horn handlebars.

The bars were named after Loveday Llewellyn, wife of George Llewellyn, one of Alex Moulton Limited's directors. He suggested them in February 1984.

Both versions of the AM14 used the GB RTE handlebar stem, with a wider choice of forward extension lengths than hitherto – from 50 to 120 mm (approximately 2 to $4^3/_4$").

The brakes were Shimano New 600 sidepull callipers. The AM14S had Shimano AX hooded levers with concealed cables, whereas the

AM14T

AM14T used a Shimano lever more suited to the "sit-up-and-beg" handlebar style.

The crankset was a Stronglight 106 which, unlike those fitted to the AM2 and AM7, used the racing standard 144 mm (5.67") bolt circle introduced by Campagnolo in 1968. The AM14S had 62 and 52 tooth chainwheels, the AM14T 52 and 42.

The freewheel used on both versions was a Shimano Dura-Ace EX. Its four largest sprockets were Shimano 30, 21, 16 and 13 tooth. They were complemented by a new close-ratio "gold" AM cluster with 9, 10 and 11 tooth sprockets.

The AM14S therefore offered the following gears:

52T: 29, 42, 55, 68, 80, 88, (98)"

62T: (35), 50, 66, 81, 96, 105, 117"

The lower geared AM14T offered:

42T: 24, 34, 45, 55, 65, 71, (79)"

52T: (29), 42, 55, 68, 80, 88, 98"

(The gears shown in brackets are not recommended because of the inefficiency caused by the "crossed chain" – inner chainring driving outermost cog, or outer chainring driving innermost cog.)

Both AM14s had what was basically "crossover" gearing, i.e. most changes are made simply by using the rear derailleur: the front changer is used only when the rider runs out of gears.

A typical sequence from the lowest to highest gear offered by the AM14S was: 29, 42 (45% increase), 55 (+31%), (shift to larger chainwheel) 66 (+20%), 81 (+23%), 96 (+19%), 105 (+9%), 117" (+11%).

A typical upward sequence offered by the AM14T was: 24, 34 (42% increase), 45 (+32%), (shift to larger chainwheel) 55 (+22%), 68 (+24%), 80 (+18%), 88 (+10%), 98" (+11%).

Both bikes therefore offered very widely spaced "granny gears" at the low end of the range, and closer gearing towards the top.

The chain was a Sedisport Silver. The SunTour Cyclone MkII front and rear derailleur mechanisms were operated by a pair of SunTour ratchet levers. The rear changer lever was on the brake demount plate (as with the AM7), the front changer lever on the right-hand handlebar end.

For frame separability the front changer cable was split via a Fichtel & Sachs hub gear cable coupling, adjacent to the demount bracket. There was a cable stop on the right side of the head tube for the front changer cable.

A special brazed-on bracket for the front derailleur mechanism was necessary for two reasons: firstly, because no standard banded-on front changer would fit the oversize seat tube, and secondly, because of the downward angle of the chain from the top of the chainwheel to the freewheel caused by the small rear wheel. This meant that the changer had to be further back than on a conventional machine.

The AM14S and T each weighed 25$\frac{1}{2}$lb (11.6 kg). At launch they cost £997.

New Leaflets

The AM14S and T versions shared a single-sheet, glossy, colour-printed leaflet in the same style and page size as the fold-out brochure for the AM2 and AM7. Another single-sheet leaflet promoted the AM-Zzipper fairing, showing it fixed to an AM14S.

The original brochure was now updated. A revised back page referred to the new AM14S and to some of the long distance and speed achievements of AM riders. There was also an invitation to visit the Moulton estate, see the museum and factory, and test ride the bikes.

"The Ultra Moulton"

The June 1985 edition of Bicycle Action featured the AM14S on its front cover. The staged photograph showed an impeccably attired young City gent astride the machine, nonchalantly reading The Times. A valet waited alongside with the other broadsheets, while an overalled serf polished the bike's AM-Zzipper fairing. The headline read: "The Ultra Moulton: Is this the perfect bicycle?"

Inside Nigel Thomas and Brian Montague reviewed the machine, which in this case was equipped with fairing, rear carrier, holdall and tool bag. The total price, nearly £1,400, produced some misty eyed comment: "For this you get a beautifully made, beautifully designed machine that proclaims its class to everyone, whether they can tell a spoke from a sprocket or not."

Among the magazine's staff "there was plenty of forlorn coveting going on". And there was no doubting that the Bicycle Action reviewers appreciated the bike's appearance: "Simply as an object, the AM14 has the same sort of appeal as the very best Italian furniture."

But what of its performance? Here there was less consensus. One reviewer "fell in love and lost all objective judgement". The other was "intrigued but sceptical", and felt that the front suspension was "absorbing power from every pedal stroke". It seems that neither reviewer was aware that the damping could be adjusted.

The handling was said to be faultless. But, the Shimano rear brake received much the same criticism as the AM7's CLBs, being described as "fairly ineffective".

Bicycle Action's June 1985 cover, featuring the AM14S with Zzipper fairing.

The ride was described as comfortable and fast. But the bike was deemed "totally unsuited to honking" – riding out of the saddle. It was necessary to develop a "smooth supple style revolving the pedals as if your feet were churning butter". However, if you did, the bike would respond "by going much faster than you think."

The Bicycle Action staff who rode the AM14S found themselves using a higher gear than normal. The gearing was described as unusual, because (as pointed out above) it gave close ratios in the high gears "with sudden great jumps to get up the hills". The reviewers would have liked the ultra-low 24" gear of the AM14T on the S model they tested.

They pointed out that to use the full range of gears properly "requires a lot of double shifting ... and also much use of the chainwheels to provide neighbouring gears". But, they said, this was easy to get used to and worked well. (In fact, if the suggested shift pattern I gave above is followed, there are only two intermediate gears worth chasing with double shifting – a 50" and an 88".) The "superb quality" of the derailleurs was praised. So too was the unusual positioning of the gear levers, both being on the right of the machine.

In general the details of the AM14S were "quite amazing". Bicycle Action's reviewers felt that "every feature ... had been thought about". They concluded that anyone interested in bikes should try to test ride the machine – and that at least half who did would be convinced that Alex had indeed produced a better bicycle.

Bicycle reported on the AM14S in January 1986. Although the suspension made the reviewer modify his riding style, he reported that after a day's testing "it was as if we had been as one since birth".

The reviewer praised the comfortable ride, fast acceleration, responsiveness and cornering. To his surprise, he **was** able to ride out of the saddle satisfactorily. He concluded that the AM14S was "not only unique but also a piece of high quality engineering without a technical flaw in sight".

A 1,000 Mile Road Test

The October 1987 issue of Cycling World carried a 1,000 mile (1,600 km) test report on the AM14S by Dennis Romer. He described himself as hitherto "very anti Moulton, believing them to be toy bicycles, or for shoppers".

At the time Dennis was 55 years old, 5'10" (178 cm) high and weighed 168lb (76 kg). In a typical year he cycled about 5,000 miles (8,000 km), almost always in mountainous terrain, such as the Alps, Dolomites, Pyrenees or Himalayas. What he looked for in a bike was "complete confidence in its reliability and comfort". He normally used a high quality conventional tourer, such as a Hetchins or Jack Taylor.

A thousand miles on the AM14S convinced him that it was "the finest touring bicycle" he had ever had the pleasure to ride. He appreciated the rigidity of the frame and the ease of mounting the loaded machine. The smaller wheel took some getting used to, but seemed "to have many advantages". Road-holding was excellent and he had experienced "no problems whatsoever" with the tyres.

Dennis praised the brakes, stating that "when applied at speed the front seems to dig in, bringing the rider to a more rapid halt than on other machines". This he attributed partly to the suspension which "has to be tried to be believed". However, he warned that anyone riding an AM14 for any distance would rapidly sell their existing bikes.

Nonetheless, he was not uncritical. Like many AM owners, he found the black plastic cap of the handlebar stem bolt hole easily lost and therefore frustrating. The "cheap" rear reflector was prone to damage. And he thought the mudguards lacked clearance and were unworthy of the AM14's price.

The carrying bags for the separated bike were, he said, "very poor". He found that they tore easily, came undone "under the rigours of aircraft loading and unloading" and were not large enough. Furthermore, the Fichtel & Sachs coupling for the front derailleur cable persistently broke.

He would have liked the holdalls to have included an outside pocket so that small items could be readily to hand. Echoing the thoughts of many AM purchasers he wrote:

"Dr Moulton also assumes we all have some mechanical ability. Although even I can, from scratch in a busy airport, assemble an AM14 together with luggage and be on my way in 25 minutes, I would like to see more instruction leaflets on the cycle and carrying bag luggage which this excellent company provide."

Mistaken Identity

In June 1985 the US magazine Bicycling featured Dave Moulton, an expatriate British frame builder living in San Marcos, California. Although a builder of classic diamond frames and not related to Alex, he routinely received orders for AM bicycles, which he passed on to The Hall.

Personal Insights

At the beginning of June 1985 the Daily Mail reported that Alex had absolutely no intention of getting a stock market quote. "No, I'd quarrel with my partners", he said. Further insights were given in Bicycle Action, where Alex told Byron Rogers:

"I believe in total ownership and total risk. Share options and bonuses are the lot of corporation managers, but if you own the whole damn thing it is just you who are the loser.

"It gives one an entirely different perception of things. It is quite strange, being in control of one's destiny. I have learnt a great deal over the past two years."

He disliked being called a businessman, because that suggested being purely profit motivated: his preoccupation was design. But having designed, he wanted to market his creation. The operation had to be profitable or the enterprise would fail.

Reorganisation at Bradford-on-Avon

About the end of 1985 considerable organisational changes took place at Alex Moulton Limited. During the two years following the launch of the AMs, some 2,000 machines were produced. Demand had been bolstered by four factors: the unavailability of Moultons from 1974 to 1983, excellent reviews of the AMs by the cycling press, interest in the new bikes generated by my book on the earlier machines, and the burgeoning Moulton Bicycle Club. However, once the initial surge of demand had been satisfied, sales declined quite sharply.

It then became apparent that the purpose-built 1960s factory, which even in 1983 had never been fully utilised for bicycle manufacture, was much bigger than necessary. Production was therefore transferred to the old stable block where, after 23 years with Alex and following the departure of Des Isley, Tim Bigwood became production manager.

The stable block, to which AM production was transferred in 1985.

Teddy Holbrook, another veteran from the early days, became works manager.

The factory was leased to Anthony Best, a former Moulton employee involved in automotive suspension design and manufacture. The bas-relief wall plaque of Tom Simpson testing the Moulton Speed was moved from the factory facade and built into the stable block wall.

The offices were transferred to the former drawing office (see photo on page 1), built during the 1960s opposite the stable block. Alex had his private office there, from where he could oversee the operation.

John Benjamin retired from day-to-day administration. This became the responsibility of accounts manager Ron Miles, a new recruit recently retired from the Westinghouse company. Record-breaking tricyclist David Duffield, marketing manager for the 1962 launch of the Moulton bicycle, became part-time sales consultant.

Alex was concerned that good back-up service be provided to his customers. Certain dealers had apparently been telling customers that Alex was not supplying parts or accessories when, in reality, the orders had never been sent to the factory. Therefore in spring 1986, through the first edition of the new Moulton Bicycle Club magazine The Moultoneer, Alex invited customers to ring the factory direct if their dealer failed to deliver.

One long wall of the new main office was lined with boards displaying the various components of the AM range. This, together with the office's close proximity to the stable block factory, enabled the company to provide a full and fast spares service most of the time.

Left: The Simpson wall plaque, transfered to the stable block wall.

Above: Production facilities in the stable block.

In April 1986 Alex gave a talk on the history of his bicycle to the Pedal Club. He shed more light than ever before on his dealings with Raleigh. He also said he had recently watched Jack Lauterwasser riding an AM up the test hill at The Hall. To see the veteran ride so perfectly convinced him that all the worry and expense of nearly a quarter of a century had been worthwhile.

The following month the dealer newsletter AM News stated:

"We have survived a very bad period for the Cycle Industry and retail trade, and are now rehoused and reorganised in a compact group of buildings in the Hall grounds. ... Incidentally, we manufacture probably more of our bike than other makers do of theirs, and we have now our own high-quality paint shop on site."

The Club Reformed

The reorganisation of the company was accompanied by a parallel reformation of the Moulton Bicycle Club. Hitherto it had been largely the responsibility of its honorary secretary. This had worked well enough when the club had about 100 members. Now that it was much larger and growing steadily, it was no longer reasonable for one volunteer to carry the bulk of the organisational burden.

Alex therefore invited a management committee to run the club. Founder David Sanders, became chairman. Paul Cooper, hitherto responsible for club sales, became membership secretary and treasurer. Michael Woolf, co-founder of the Moulton Preservation user group, became correspondence secretary, and Ian Hodgson was co-opted to deal with publicity. I was appointed magazine editor.

The subscription was raised to £5 per year plus £1 for each additional household or family member sharing the magazine. A major mailshot was launched to boost membership, and the magazine became a quarterly publication, rather than annual or twice yearly. The last issue of the much-improved Moulton Cyclist had been in the A5 format and this was adopted for The Moultoneer, which first appeared in spring 1986.

By autumn the club had some 400 members worldwide, including the USA, Canada, Eire, West Germany, France, Australia, South Africa, the Middle East and Japan.

A Hint of the Five ... and a Favour for a Veteran

On the first Saturday of July 1985, Stephen Stuart staged the second Oxford Moulton Rally. My family and I missed the start in Oxford's Radcliffe Square and were cycling across Ot Moor to catch up when the latest Bentley Turbo overtook us and pulled in. Out stepped Alex. He and a friend had driven over from the Henley Regatta and, in the process, were putting the borrowed Bentley through its paces.

Knowing that I was writing the technical history of Sturmey-Archer, Alex asked me what I thought of their latest five-speed hub gear. He was particularly interested in the single-lever control, launched that February as an alternative to the twin-lever systems used hitherto.

I replied that I thought that the hub was a reasonable product and that the single-lever system was more user-friendly than the old twin-lever system, which many cyclists found baffling. Alex then revealed that he was seriously considering launching a version of the AM equipped with the new Sturmey-Archer system.

That afternoon at the Nut Tree pub in Murcot, where the Moulton riders had stopped for lunch, veteran cycle tourist H. H. "Chater" Willis expressed a wish for a softer rear spring for his AM7. Alex noted this and subsequently produced a "one-off" softer Monosphere. Chater enjoyed many miles on his customised AM, and died five years later, aged 86.

The AM5 Launched

The AM5 was launched in spring 1986. It was described in The Moultoneer as "more than a worthy successor to the original Moulton Deluxe as the definitive city cycle".

The rear triangle was similar to that of the AM2 but with a proper brake bridge and brazed-on cable stops for the twin gear cables. The rest of the frame was virtually identical to the AM7's, except for brazed-on fittings for the hub gear cables and a gold coachline along each side of the frame's horizontal girder.

Components were generally as fitted to the AM7, except for the pedals and handlebars. The Shimano pedals were counterbalanced alloy Adamas AX or the near identical Fulfit PD-A100, both of which could be adapted to take toe-clips and straps. The alloy handlebars were typical British flat "all-rounders" by GB, with foam grips. Straight alloy CLB brake levers were fitted, which had small black plastic hoods. AM7 drop handlebars, pedals, toe-clips and straps were optional.

From 1987 the AM5 was available with swept-back German-style flat handlebars, for a more upright riding position. These were SR Road Champion, marked Sakae Custom England.

A demount bracket, as fitted to the AM7 but without the gear lever, was used to split the rear brake cable. Fichtel & Sachs hub gear cable connectors were used to split the gear cables. The connectors were arranged one behind the other along the right chord of the upper frame girder near the head tube. The two gear cables were held loosely together by a thin steel loop fixed to the rearward connector.

When split, the forward connector was parked on a prong brazed to the rear section of the horizontal frame girder, near the parking position for the demount bracket. As both gear cables were looped together, this prevented either from dangling loosely.

In addition to direct drive, the AM5's Sturmey-Archer S5/2 hub gave decreases of 33.33%, and 21.1%, and increases of 26.6% and 50%. Therefore the standard 15 tooth sprocket and 52 tooth chainwheel, offered gears of 39, 46 (an increase of 18%), 59 (+28%), 75 (+27%) and 88" (+17%).

There was a choice of 14, 15 or 16 tooth sprockets, all specially modified for $^3/_{32}$" derailleur chain by grinding down from the standard $^1/_8$". ($^3/_{32}$" sprockets by Fichtel & Sachs were later used for the AM5 and AM2.) With the 14 tooth sprocket a range of gears 7% higher was provided: 42, 50, 63, 80 and 95". The 16 tooth gave a range 6% lower than the 15 tooth: 37, 44, 55, 70 and 83".

The redesigned rear lamp bracket, and the special AM lightweight adjustable front lamp bracket were fitted as standard to the AM5. The rear bracket, formed from thin stainless steel rod, overcame the metal fatigue problems encountered with the original alloy spade bracket. The front bracket fitted the handlebar clamp bolt of the GB RTE stem and incorporated angle adjustment by means of an Allen key.

Alex received the first batch of fifteen S5/2 hubs for production AM5s in May 1986. At its launch the AM5 cost £644, £95 dearer than the AM2 and just £5 cheaper than the AM7.

AM5

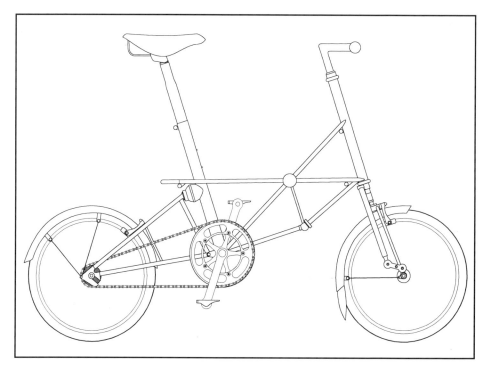

The 1994 AM5.

CAD drawing by Nigel Sadler.
Apart from minor componentry changes the only significant difference is the
parallel sided front fork blades.

The original AM5 weighed about $25\frac{1}{2}$"lb (11.6 kg), some 1lb
(0.45 kg) more than the original AM7. After a few years Alex
therefore began exploring the possibility of lightening the Sturmey-
Archer S5/2 gear. However, in spring 1991 it was superseded by
the 5-Star, itself replaced by the single-cable Sprinter in 1993.

Some early production of the 5-Star, made about April 1991, suffered
from poor tooth formation of the sun pinions. This caused noisy and
rough running, especially in fourth and fifth gears. It was virtually
impossible to detect the fault by visual inspection. Sturmey-Archer
therefore invested £12,000 in a German shadow-graphing machine
which helped overcome the problem. About a dozen AM5s were
inadvertently fitted with defective hubs. Sturmey-Archer therefore provided
replacement gear internals to Alex for free issue to the affected customers.

Although the 5-Star subsequently suffered a poor reputation for reliability
in big-wheeled machines, few major problems were encountered in
the AM5. This was because of the lower torque level in the smaller
wheel.

The 1994 AM5 is substantially the same as the original, but like the
1994 AM7, has a Stronglight 190 chainset, Shimano UN51 bottom

bracket and Mavic front hub. Whereas the AM7 now has a Mavic rear hub and SunTour Radius indexed derailleur, the AM5 has the single-cable Sturmey-Archer Sprinter five-speed hub. Quoted weight of the AM5 is now about 26lb (11.8 kg), 1lb or so (0.45 kg) heavier than 1994 AM7 – both bikes having increased in weight a little over the years.

Reviews of the AM5

When launched in 1986, the AM5 received relatively little press coverage. Cycling Weekly (formerly Cycling) did not report its introduction until early September 1986, some four months after the launch.

The Winter 1989/90 issue of The Moultoneer contained a review by the then editor, Mike Hessey. He had recently bought one second-hand and was already an AM7 owner. He concluded that the AM5 had "all the established virtues of an AM – light, comfortable, easily transported, good luggage carrying capacity and a fast mover".

"The ease of gear changing is a joy, and makes life easier under all conditions. The gear ratios are quite reasonable, although personally I would prefer them to be slightly different, and with an SA hub the only thing you can do is lower or raise all of them by changing the chainwheel or sprocket."

Mike found noise from the hub gear somewhat disturbing. In all but the lowest two gears the pawls in the hub ticked, and on rough roads the hub rattled annoyingly. This rattling is a characteristic of hub gears in small wheels with high pressure tyres. With the S5/2 hub, the problem was worst when freewheeling in third gear, ie. direct drive. But despite this, Mike concluded that anyone contemplating an AM should give the AM5 serious attention.

In the following edition of The Moultoneer, Ian Hodgson, then the MBC's Midlands co-ordinator, heaped further praise on the AM5. Whilst acknowledging that it was a little heavier than the AM7, he felt that the positive action of the hub gear more than outweighed the weight penalty. However, this comment was conditional on discarding the single-lever control with its "slow, rather woolly feel" in favour of either the Sturmey-Archer stem-mounted twin levers or a pair of three-speed triggers.

Ian reported that, using a 48 tooth chainwheel and a 16 tooth sprocket (giving gears from 34" to 77") he could still "keep up with the lads on a club run, do the [CTC] reliability rides, go touring or whatever". He appreciated that the hub gear was slightly less efficient than a well-maintained derailleur but had an "unshakeable faith" in its dependability, provided that it was properly adjusted and lubricated.

The K Carrier

For use with the AM5 a special Reynolds 531 rear carrier was introduced. This differed from the earlier rear carriers in two ways.

Firstly, instead of the supporting strut having a forked end where it bolted to the underside of the carrier, it had a drilled bolt hole. This necessitated the complete unthreading of the knurled nut, which was therefore attached to the carrier by a cord to prevent it being lost.

The revised strut fixing method was more rigid, both laterally and vertically. It reduced the risk of metal fatigue to the bolt and the crosspiece to which it was brazed. It also overcame the problem of the carrier bolt jumping out of the strut fork when the bike hit a large

The K carrier with Kryptonite 4 lock, and below how to lock <u>both</u> halves of an AM to a street sign.

bump at speed. This could sometimes happen even with the knurled nut tightly engaged. The modification was applied to subsequent production of the standard rear carrier.

The second difference was more apparent. MBC member Clive Fletcher had devised a simple, inconspicuous method for fixing a Kryptonite 4 or similar shackle lock horizontally under the carrier. The AM5's carrier incorporated a similar facility. This was achieved by means of two loops of thin tubing, brazed to the underside of the the main horizontal members of the carrier (the "extensions" of the AM's horizontal girder). Both loops were about 45 degrees to the horizontal, the front one sloping forwards, the rear one backwards. The shackle lock was simply locked around them.

Because the carrier was designed to carry a Kryptonite lock, it was known as the K carrier. To match the AM5, it was finished in steely grey and had a gold coachline down each side of the main horizontal members. It nonetheless fitted all 531-framed 17" wheel AMs and for three years was offered as an alternative to the standard rear carrier. In May 1989 the original standard carrier was deleted and the K type became the new standard. When launched it cost £56.75, £5 more than the standard item.

Child Carrier

Since the launch of the AM a child carrier had been promised. The prototype was demonstrated at the 1985 annual MBC meet at Bradford-on-Avon and the production version was launched in spring 1986, alongside the AM5.

The rearward facing seat shell was a proprietary one-piece polypropylene moulding, with child harness. As the promotional leaflet put it:

"With its 17" wheels and low centre of gravity, the AM is the most suitable bicycle for a child carrier. The rearward facing seat is an excellent vantage point for the child and the easy-clean plastic seat shell keeps the child's feet away from the wheel."

Certainly, the child had a better view than in the conventional arrangement!

The seat was supported by an extra-strong, narrow rear carrier, built of Reynolds 531. The support strut was similar to that of the K carrier. The platform consisted of a single tube formed into a lozenge shape on plan. This plugged into the ends of the horizontal girder of the AM's frame, and was narrow enough to permit the foot guards of the plastic seat to hang down either side.

For additional strength, the carrier platform was braced to the top of the seat tube by a "hairpin" tie. This was formed from a single piece of tube, its lower ends being brazed to the inner rails of the carrier platform either side of the strut fixing. The tie's looped upper end had two fixing plates brazed to it, through which fitted an extra-long seat pillar binder bolt.

When launched the child carrier cost £85 complete, or £59 without the plastic seat shell. The latter option allowed the owner to fit his or her own seat shell of the same type, bought for use on a conventional bicycle.

In the Autumn 1989 issue of The Moultoneer, K. J. Flint, a Briton living in Switzerland, wrote of his experience with the child carrier. He had bought one in England three years earlier and the dealer had "screwed it down a little too tightly, resulting in some cracking around the screws". This had not produced any adverse effects and Mr Flint was "very happy" with the child seat, heartily recommending it.

The AM child carrier on an AM5.

Leaflets and Lamps

The K carrier and child carrier were advertised on the reverse of the AM5 promotional leaflet. This matched the page size and style of the original AM2/AM7 brochure.

The AM5 was shown equipped with Marvi battery lamps, which Alex had recently selected as approved accessories. These were Danish and similar in concept to the original French Wonderlights, but used cheaper, more readily available batteries.

Chain Peg

Another accessory launched in spring 1986 was a chain-catcher peg. It had been discovered that if an AM7's chain fell off the chainwheel, the chain could drag along the road and get trapped under the rear wheel, causing a loss of control.

The peg was a simple, lightweight device that bolted onto the right-hand chord of the lower frame girder alongside the chainwheel. Once correctly fitted, the chain could not slip between the chainwheel and the bottom bracket.

H. H. "Chater" Willis pointed out in The Moultoneer that the "chain under the wheel" problem was not unique to AM7s: he had heard of it occurring on a 27" wheel machine with single chainwheel. That it does not happen more often is due largely to the prevalence of front derailleur mechanisms, which prevent the chain falling far enough to be troublesome.

Milliken Wheel Discs

In autumn 1985, and again in summer 1986, a fully-faired AM ridden by Jim Glover broke the 200 metres flying start speed record for the conventional riding position (see Chapter 9). The fairing was designed by Doug Milliken of Williamsville, New York.

Doug also designed the aerodynamic wheel discs used on the record-breaking machine. These discs were made from high impact polystyrene and weighed approximately 2 oz (70 g) each, ie. 5oz (140 g) per wheel. They were attached to the wheel by being taped to each other, the disc rims abutting the spoke nipples.

The discs were designed for AM wheels built on Zeus hubs, but seem to fit all subsequent AM wheels. They were normally supplied in white but other colours could be ordered, as could a flocked finish, intended for display purposes only. (At the time of writing the standard colours are black and white.) In 1990 the high impact polystyrene from which the discs were made was changed to "100% regrind", made from recycled factory scrap blended with extra plasticiser.

Doug first marketed his wheel discs in 1986 via the International Human Powered Vehicle Association newsletter. In the first year he sold 50, about half to AM owners, the rest to owners of recumbents using AM wheels. Via The Moultoneer's Spring 1987 issue, the discs were publicised to a wider audience. By December 1993 600 discs had been sold. As Doug put it, while the discs "won't do much good at touring speeds, they do look nice and can be painted etc." And if the rider was serious about high speed riding, the reduced spoke turbulence could prove worthwhile.

Trouble-shooting The Suspension

The Spring 1987 edition of The Moultoneer revealed a potential problem with the front suspension of early AMs: the fork spring base plug (guide bearing) tended to swell through absorption of lubricant. The problem was exacerbated by high ambient temperatures: leaving the bike in the sun during a lunch break could result in the front suspension being jammed solid for the rest of the day, only to free itself when the temperature dropped overnight.

The solution involved a free-of-charge replacement bearing. This was a slightly looser fit and could be installed either by the factory or in the field.

Alex issued a free Service Sheet (No.1) giving instructions for repairing the suspension. These described a rather laborious way of knocking out a firmly stuck bearing. The front fork assembly was first removed from the bike, and the spring retaining pin drilled out, with the handlebar stem in place to contain the pin safely. The spring was then removed which enabled use of a large diameter rod to knock out the bearing. Easier techniques were soon evolved (see Appendix A).

Service Sheet No.3, released in August, dealt with how to overcome the problem of a loose rear triangle pivot bearing (see Appendix A). From that time a longer Nylok nut was fitted as standard giving an increased recommended torque setting of 20lb ft (27.12 Nm or 2.76 kgf/m).

Better Pumps

The limitations of the Bluemels lightweight pump supplied with the AMs were noted by many riders. Fortunately it is easy to fit a frame-fit pump within the spaceframe between the seat tube and head tube. I use an 18" (460 mm) SKS Airpower, which can be used with both Presta and Schraeder valves.

Doug Milliken tried three samples of the Bluemels pump and the best he could get out of any of them was 30 psi (2 atm). Angle Lake Cyclery of Seattle then supplied him with a better alternative, known as a No.1 Pump. In the Autumn 1987 issue of The Moultoneer he explained how he fitted it:

"To hold it up inside the post (it being a different diameter than the Bluemels) I have removed the rubber cuff (hard work, easy to slip and poke a hole in yourself). The replacement is a cut down piece of plastic foam water pipe insulation, cut to about 4" (100 mm) long. Pushed in (no glue) it holds the pump up in the seat post with no rattles."

Two issues later Australian Stephen Parry offered another option. He found an Italian Silca Impero pump which had a slim, oval-section head that would fit in the seat tube. Out of closed-cell foam, as used in sleeping mats, he cut a circular piece which he put at the base of the seat tube. The valve end of the pump rested on it without rattling.

Having discarded the rubber seal that held the handle of the original pump, he cut a couple of pieces of inner tube and put them over the handle of the pump to stop it making a ringing noise in the seat pillar. Near the head of the pump he fitted a pair of O rings. This helped guide the pump down the tube, the neoprene dragging less on the sides than would rubber from an inner tube.

For those who abandoned the seat tube as home for the pump, the space could be put to other uses. Back in 1984 Clive Tully pointed out that he could stow all the poles of his Robert Saunders tent in the AM's seat tube!

Developments In Marketing

Through its winter 1986 catalogue, the upmarket British leisure garment retailer Rohan announced it was supplying the Alex Moulton bicycle by mail order. This was an unprecedented marketing alliance for both companies. Hitherto Rohan had not ventured into bicycle sales, and Alex's products had not been available through any UK mail order catalogue.

Rohan's catalogue devoted nearly two and a half pages to the AM range and its inventor. The AM14S was featured on the back cover. The catalogue stated:

"We believe that not only is the Moulton bicycle a significant advance in cycle design but that in time it will be considered a design classic like a Le Corbusier chaise, an Eames chair or even the Anglepoise lamp. Its appearance is so technically 'right', so functionally attractive, it is sure to be an investment for any customer."

By September 1986 the AM dealer network had expanded considerably. There were now 72 dealers in the UK. In North America there were a dozen, strategically placed from Toronto, Ontario to Orange County, California, and from New Westminster, British Columbia to Fort Worth, Texas.

From autumn 1986 to summer 1987 the factory reported an order backlog of eight to ten weeks.

Frame Kits

In May 1986 AM News announced the introduction of AM7 frame and wheel kits:

"A number of customers have particular preferences for certain components. In some export markets, the carriage and tariff costs are considerable. We have therefore evolved two types of frame wheel kits supplied in two standard cardboard cartons within the 15 kilo (33lb) limit each."

Kit 62 contained four sets of AM7 frame and wheel kits. Retail cost of a single frame and pair of unbuilt wheels from Kit 62 was £475 and included tyres, seatpin, mudguards and the special triple sprocket assembly. A photograph was shown in Bicycle, September 1986.

Kit 63 contained three sets of AM7 frame and ready-built wheels.

November 1986 saw two issues of AM News, both promoting the frame kits. One suggested colour co-ordinating components and offering a choice of, say, all-European or all-Japanese componentry. A pricing sheet was supplied so that dealers could prepare sample costings. The other newsletter followed Alex's visit to North America for the International Human Powered Speed Championships in Vancouver. He reported:

"I also took the opportunity of calling upon a number of our Canadian and American dealers and was particularly impressed by the way especially that Dale and Kelvin Clark of Angle Lake, Seattle have built up a sizeable AM business with AM7 frame kits. I think you will find the enclosed information interesting."

The enclosures included a specification order form from Angle Lake Cyclery. This listed a comprehensive range of accessories, including high specification American-made Bel Ami front and rear bags by Sandy Bellamy, and Quick Disc wheel and chainring discs.

A special Angle Lake version of the AM, the CX Group, was illustrated in silhouette. It was equipped with the AM-Zzipper fairing, wheel and chainring discs, frame skins, Cobra Aero water bottle, Aero Pro AM saddle and other aerodynamic components.

In January 1987 Bicycle's Max Glaskin described a "stunner" built for him from an AM frame kit by Swift Cycles. The bike was used for a tour of Ireland and the original aim was to use as many Italian components as possible. However, this proved difficult and Max's AM special ended up with Mavic cranks, chainring, stem and handlebars, Maillard 600 hubs and Red S brakes with Modolo blocks. The Mavic equipment "looked stunning", while the Red S brakes "certainly seemed better than the standard CLBs".

Max warned potential frame kit users to check carefully that their "dream components" were compatible with the AM frame.

A Special Award

The February 1987 issue of the American magazine Bicycle Guide gave a special award to the Alex Moulton bicycle for "Most Elegant Bicycle Engineering".

The magazine highlighted Alex's claims that his bike was more useful for carrying luggage, more portable, offered better handling, quicker acceleration and greater ride comfort. It concluded: "And you know, in most of these claims he is absolutely right."

Chapter 6
FROM JUBILEE TO KM150
1987–1990

AM-Jubilee – AM14 Blue – AM-Moulton Marathon – User Feedback

12 November 1987 was the 25th anniversary of the launch of the Moulton bicycle, but celebrations started several months earlier. Moulton Bicycle Club member Robert McCann produced a limited edition cast aluminium plaque depicting a Series 1 Moulton. Another MBC member, Fiona Hedges, organised an edition of 500 commemorative envelopes which were passed through Alex Moulton's franking machine.

On the front of the envelope was a drawing of a girl on a 1960s Moulton and a boy on an AM7, and inside was a brief history of the marque. The envelope was featured in the Rohan magazine's reportage of the jubilee.

In its issue for 11 September 1987, The Bath & West Evening Chronicle devoted a centrefold spread to the event. The following day the Moulton Bicycle Club commenced its annual meet at Bradford-on-Avon. A wet Saturday afternoon found Alex in the factory with members of the club, discussing a new version of the AM, aptly named the Jubilee.

The commemorative envelope, designed by Terry Wilkins.

That evening, the machine was formally unveiled at the club dinner at St Margaret's Hall in the town. Among the 100 or so people present were two racing cyclists who broke records on Moultons in the 1960s, John Woodburn and Vic Nicholson.

The AM-Jubilee

The AM-Jubilee was the most sophisticated interpretation of the "Advanced Engineering Bicycle" to date. Alex called it his flagship, celebrating 25 years of endeavour to make a "bicycle more pleasing to have and to use."

It was based on the special machine on which Dave Bogdan successfully completed the single-stage Race Across America in 1987 (see Chapter 9). The promotional leaflet, produced in the standard format, proclaimed: "The AM series has now accumulated some millions of rider miles since its introduction in 1983. The policy of incorporating improvements and additions to the range continues, in our aspiration to offer 'The Improved Bicycle System'."

AM Jubilee with day bag.

The Wishbone Stem

The most significant development was the Jubilee's lowered head tube and indexed adjustable handlebar stem, trade marked "Wishbone". The race-proved Wishbone was adjustable with the standard 6 mm Allen key, and could be used with any conventional handlebars.

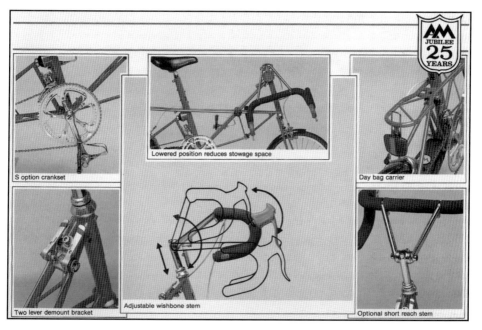

AM Jubilee

It was built of chromium plated Reynolds 531 tubing and there was a choice of two versions, one offering 2" (51 mm) longer reach than the other.

The Wishbone offered two advantages. Firstly, it readily allowed the riding position to be altered from upright (with the Wishbone about 18 degrees out of vertical) to low profile (with the Wishbone horizontal). Secondly, when swung to its lowest position and turned in line with the front wheel, it considerably reduced the stowage space necessary for the front section of the bike. The leaflet claimed, "These features give a feeling of more openness and safety to the rider and are ergonomically superior."

The Wishbone was protected by British patent 2182895 and US patent 4729255. The first filing was on 14 November 1985 and the claimed advantage was compactness when stowed. Harold Briercliffe, writing in Cycle Trader, said, "When the advantages of such a design are fully appreciated by the road and track cycling fraternity I have no doubt that there will be a general demand for Dr Moulton's patented stem." However, it was not for sale except as part of the AM-Jubilee.

The stem shaft fitted into the steerer tube in the usual way and incorporated an RTE-type expander bolt, concealed by a plastic cap. The arms of the wishbone were secured to the stem shaft by serrated clamps.

In early 1986 I showed Alex photographs of the folding handlebars of the 1930s French small-wheeled bicycle, Le Petit Bi (British patent

526773). These handlebars were of the "high-riser" configuration, non-adjustable and folded in a different way to the Jubilee's. Two serrated clamps were incorporated, one for each handlebar.

When he saw the photographs of the mechanism Alex commented on the amount of machining it required. At the time I had no idea he was already patenting the Wishbone stem which also used serrated clamps, but in a different and more versatile configuration.

The AM-Jubilee Frame

The Wishbone stem necessitated the lower steering head, the top of the headset being just above the head tube's junction with the upper frame girder. Otherwise the Jubilee's frame was similar to that of the AM14S or T, complete with stainless steel fork crown, frame tie knuckle, carrier stud, demount bracket anchor boss and front derailleur bracket. However, for the first time steely grey was abandoned in favour of another frame colour – Ferrari Red. As with the AM14s and the AM5, the Jubilee had a coachline, in this case silver.

Day Bag and Carrier

A pair of complementary new accessories were supplied with the Jubilee – a day bag supported by a small cantilevered rear carrier. The day bag attached to the carrier, seat tube and seat pillar by Velcro straps.

The bag was finished in grey and bore the red AM logo on its side on a grey circular background. The carrier was finished in Ferrari Red with a silver coach line to match the main frame. The standard AM front and rear carriers were also available in Ferrari Red to match the Jubilee.

The weight of the complete AM Jubilee, including day bag and carrier, was 26lb 12oz (12.13 kg).

Transmission – Jubilee S

As with the AM14, two versions of the Jubilee were produced, the S (speed) and T (touring).

The S's transmission had a Stronglight 700A sealed bottom bracket assembly on which was mounted a Stronglight 106 chainset. This had 62 and 52 tooth chainrings, as fitted to the AM14S. The Sedisport Silver chain drove a six-speed Shimano cassette with 13, 15, 19, 23 and 28 tooth sprockets. To this was added a new special screw-on cluster with 10 and 11 tooth sprockets, giving a total of seven cogs. This configuration gave the following gears:

52 T: 32, 38, 47, 59, 68, 80, (88)"
62 T: (38), 46, 55, 70, 81, 96, 105"

As with the AM14, this was essentially a "crossover" gearing configuration. A typical sequence from lowest to highest gear offered by the original AM-Jubilee S was: 32, 38 (19% increase), 47 (+24%), 59 (+26%), (shift to larger chainwheel) 70 (+19%), 81 (+16%), 96 (+20%), 105" (+9%).

This range of 3.3:1 was slightly wider than the AM7's but narrower than the AM14s'. In particular, the Jubilee S's lower gears were more closely spaced than either of the AM14s, but with more duplication or near duplication. Top gear was lower than the AM14S but higher than the AM14T.

[An AM7 fitted with the 9 tooth smallest sprocket and a 31 tooth largest cog (in place of the standard 28 tooth) gives a slightly **wider** range (3.4:1) than the AM-Jubilee S, from a low of 29" to a high of 98", with merely a single 52 tooth chainwheel. This arrangement offers a top gear 7" lower than the Jubilee S and a lowest gear 3" lower. Such a configuration pushes a short cage derailleur mechanism to its operational limits, (and will usually necessitate removing the anti wind-up stop) but is feasible using the AM's special integral gear hanger. The biggest disadvantage is the wide steps between the gears.]

The Jubilee S's front derailleur was a SunTour Sprint, the rear a SunTour Cyclone 7000 Accushift. Unlike the AM14S and T, both derailleur levers were on the demount bracket. The levers used were SunTour Superbe Pro Accushift with indexed shifting, the first time that this feature had been offered on an AM. A brazed-on cable stop was provided on the head tube to facilitate installation of optional handlebar-end gear changers.

Simon Edwardes and Ian Booth of Swift Cycles, the premier AM dealers in the UK, were largely responsible for customising the indexed gearing to suit the Jubilee. The Shimano sprockets used were of the twist-tooth type, designed for use with indexed changers. Special AM sprocket clusters with this tooth formation were introduced in 1993.

Transmission – Jubilee T

The Jubilee T's transmission was the same as the Jubilee S's except for the chainset. This was a Shimano 600 EX Biopace with 52 and 42 tooth asymmetrical chainwheels. (See Chapter 7 for comments on the Biopace system.) It offered the following gears:

42 T: 26, 31, 38, 48, 55, 65, (71)"

52 T: (32), 38, 47, 59, 68, 80, 88"

This was a slightly wider range than the Jubilee S (3.4:1 v. 3.3:1). Top gear was 17" lower, bottom 6" lower.

As with the S, there was a good progression of eight useful gears in sequence, involving only one shift of the front changer and no double changes: 26, 31 (19% increase), 38 (+22%), (shift to larger chainwheel) 47 (+24%), 59 (+26%), 68 (+15%), 80 (+18%), 88" (+10%).

Other Components

The AM-Jubilee S's points of rider contact were similar to those of the AM14S: Shimano 600EX pedals, a Cinelli Volare saddle and alloy GB Maes drop handlebars, clad in genuine Grab-On high density foam. The T version had Shimano Sport & Triathlon pedals, a Madison G11 saddle and a choice of GB Maes or special Jubilee flat handlebars. If the latter option was ordered, thumb shifters could be factory-fitted in lieu of the twin levers on the demount bracket.

The brakes were Shimano 600 EX, with matching Aero levers, the concealed cables running under the handlebar foam. The special AM front and rear lamp brackets and reflectors were provided.

At its launch the AM Jubilee cost £1,325. Comparative prices for the rest of the range at that time were:

AM2 – £570

AM5 – £670

AM7 – £720

AM14 S & T – £1,071.

Alex's Christmas card for 1987 bore the legend "Celebrating Twenty-five Years of the Alex Moulton Bicycle". Designed and drawn as ever by Brian Walker, it featured the AM-Jubilee with The Hall, Bradford-on-Avon as the background.

The 1994 Jubilee

The 1994 version of the Jubilee has Shimano Dura-Ace hubs, Shimano 105 brakes and chainset, and a Shimano UN71 bottom bracket set. No distinction is made between S and T versions, but there is nonetheless a choice of gearing ranges – from 29 to 117" or 24 to 98". Both ranges are wider than in the original versions, being in the order of 4:1.

The Jubilee Christmas card, designed for Alex by illustrator Brian Walker. Brian did a lot of testing of the 1960's prototypes, culminating in a Trans-Icelandic camping tour with the first Moulton Safari.

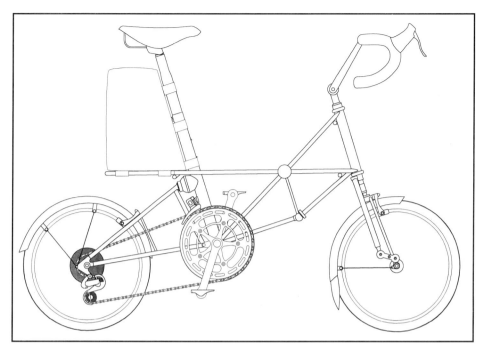

The 1994 AM-Jubilee. CAD drawing by Nigel Sadler.

Early Press Comment

In April 1988 Harold Briercliffe reviewed the AM-Jubilee in Cycling Weekly. He described it as "responsive to the nth degree, smooth throughout the drive and delicate but obedient in steering, a superb all-purpose touring mount." In November The Times Saturday supplement carried a half page colour feature on innovative bicycles. This showed a professor of the Royal College of Arts, Floris van den Broecke, expressing his admiration for the Jubilee. A month later the Japanese "goods & life" magazine Begin featured the bike, complete with AM-Zzipper fairing, on its front cover and in a two-page colour feature.

A Test Ride

The summer 1989 issue of The Moultoneer contained a test report on the AM-Jubilee by Daved Sanders, then MBC chairman. It was the handlebar configuration that most impressed him:

"The most radical feature of the Jubilee is the 'Wishbone' stem, and it requires a little time to become accustomed to the extra space in front of the rider; AM7s now feel claustrophobic in comparison! The adjusting range is excellent, and must make this the ultimate in versatility – ride to the race in the normal position, and then sweep the stem down, adjust the bars and you are in the perfect position for a super fast performance. The very act of adjusting is unnerving for competitors – like a secret weapon."

Although Daved had some initial doubts about the Biopace chainwheels, he reported that "pedalling did feel a little smoother". However, he would have preferred a larger chainring. He liked the quick and positive indexed gear change.

The Jubilee that Daved tested was loaned to the MBC for its stand at the 1989 National Cycling Festival at Himley Hall, West Midlands. He reported that at the show the bike "caused crowds to gather whenever it was displayed or ridden". He added, "I understand that there is a six month waiting period for the Jubilee, and it would certainly be worth considering trading-up if you have an AM at present; the AMs hold their value extremely well on the pre-owned cycle market."

CTC Appraisal

Chris Juden, Technical Officer of the Cyclists' Touring Club, compiled a survey of portable bicycles which was published in the April/May 1990 issue of Cycle Touring & Campaigning (formerly Cycletouring). In it he described the AM-Jubilee as "the machine of choice for the enthusiastic cyclist on the move, who must have the best and can afford it".

Of ten portable bicycles appraised in the survey, only two were rated "excellent" for ride quality and durability – the Jubilee and the Strutt Worksong.

Jubilee SE

In 1990 a Jubilee SE was announced. This was a special version, customised by Angle Lake Cyclery in Seattle. SE presumably stood for Shimano Eight, the bike's special feature being an eight-speed Shimano Dura-Ace freewheel. Angle Lake also catalogued SE versions of the AM7 and AM14.

AM14 Blue

In January 1988 an additional lower-cost version of the AM14 was introduced. Finished in Royal Blue, it was designated the AM14 Blue to differentiate it from the S and T versions. Essentially a 14-speed version of the AM7, it had a lower component specification than the original AM14s. It also lacked their non-functional aesthetic enhancements, such as the stainless steel fittings.

The AM14 Blue had a Stronglight 190 chainset, with 52 and 42 tooth rings and a black plastic protector ring. The chain was a Sedisport Silver. There was a choice of Regina CX or SunTour Winner Pro freewheels, and the sprocket range was 9, 11, 13, 16, 19, 23 and 28 tooth. As with the AM7, the bike could be ordered with a 10 tooth smallest cog rather than the 9. (The SunTour Winner Pro freewheel later became standard on the AM7 and AM14 Blue. The special AM small sprocket cluster for this freewheel was originally finished in gold. From 1993, when Shimano-style twisted tooth form was adopted, the finish was silver.)

Indexed gear shifting was provided by the same derailleur equipment as used on the AM-Jubilee. The gears offered were:

42T: 26, 31, 38, 45, 55, 65, (79" with 9 tooth or 71" with 10)
52T: (32), 38, 47, 55, 68, 80, 98" with 9 tooth or 88" with 10.

This provided a range of 3.8:1 with the 9 tooth sprocket or 3.4:1 with the 10. Like the Jubilee's transmission, it was essentially a crossover system. A typical upward progression, starting on the smaller chainwheel, would be:

26, 31 (+19%), 38 (+23%), 45 (+18%), 55 (+22%), (change to larger chainwheel) 68 (+24%), 80 (+18%), 98" (+23%) or 88" (+10%) with 10 tooth sprocket.

The new machine was £221 cheaper than the earlier AM14s, costing £850 when introduced. It weighed about 26lb (11.8 kg). The 1989 version, which cost £980, had an improved specification, including Shimano 105 brakes with aero levers. From 1989 the Jubilee-style day bag carrier was available for the AM14 Blue.

The Blue, like the AM7, was also supplied to dealers in "frame and wheel kit" form. This enabled customised versions to be produced to meet purchasers' particular requirements. A leaflet in the usual AM house style was produced for the AM14 Blue, including the frame kit.

AM14 Blue.

AM14 frame and wheel kit.

Evaluation of the AM14 Blue

The January/February 1989 edition of the American magazine Bicycle Guide published a list of seven "Bikes We Couldn't Live Without". One of these was the AM14 Blue which was summarised thus: "Full suspension, fascinating construction, clever details, endless fun."

But the most thorough evaluation of the AM14 Blue was published much later, in the October 1992 issue of Cycling Plus, as part of a major feature entitled "Is Moulton Still Magic?" By this time the original AM14S and T models had been deleted from the range, and the Blue was merely referred to as the AM14.

There had been some specification changes. The pedals were now MKS platform type, the brakes were Shimano 105 and the SunTour derailleur system was different: the front changer was now a Cyclone II, the rear a Radius, both operated via Accushift Plus levers.

The machine tested weighed 27lb 9oz (12.49 kg), the extra weight apparently being accounted for by a full-size rear carrier.

Cycling Plus's evaluation was carried out by cycle journalist Ben Searle, a far from uncritical veteran Moulton owner. He considered the bike's performance under six headings, in each case awarding points out of seven.

Handling was the first aspect considered. The bike was found to be light but stable and "came into its own on fast, twisty descents".

When loaded it had "exceptional stability" and bumps were "sweetly outsmarted by the suspension". Ben's only concern was tyre grip in wet or very slippery conditions. He felt that rear wheel breakaway was more likely to induce a sideways skid than with most conventional bikes. The overall rating for handling was, nonetheless, a creditable six out of seven.

The same score was awarded for speed. Ben described the acceleration as "electric", although a smooth pedalling style was desirable. He confessed, "Whenever I'm on my own AM and spot an unsuspecting roadie or mountain biker up ahead I like to swoop on them, leaving them astonished as I speed by on those small wheels!"

Gear performance did less well, just four out of seven. The wide gap between the two top gears (the test bike had a 9 tooth smallest sprocket) was considered fine for tourists but irritating for performance riding. It was also noted that customising the gears was "much more difficult" because of the specialised componentry.

Ben criticised duplication among the gears, an inherent feature of crossover systems. He was also unimpressed by the indexing. It worked well in the higher gears (on the special AM sprockets), but was "hit-or-miss" on the SunTour cogs. Because of the light steering, he would have preferred bar-end changers. However, he praised the suitability of the low gears for touring.

Frame design quality scored highly – six out of seven. Head and seat tube alignment were very good and fork alignment was excellent. Rear triangle alignment was merely adequate, being 5 mm (nearly $1/4$" to one side. Ben reported that: "The 70-odd brazed joints were all very neat and tidy with tubes properly mitred." On the down side, and surprisingly in view of general experience, he said the paintwork was easy to chip.

The separation mechanism was described as "lovely to use" and the rear carrier was easy to fit. There was a minor quibble that the support strut could not be tightened on its stud, thus causing an annoying rattle (see Appendix A).

Ben, like many before him, criticised the concealed pump. Surprisingly he added that "there's no provision anywhere else on the frame". While it is true that, like most modern cycles AMs have no pump pegs, an 18" (460 mm) frame-fit pump will fit cosily within the spaceframe, between the head and seat tubes.

Frame weight (including rear triangle) was quoted as 6lb 10 oz (3 kg) and the front fork assembly as 2lb 12oz (2.25 kg). Ben made the point that the frameset was heavy by conventional standards but that this was more or less offset by the lighter wheels. These he said weighed 2lb 3oz (0.99 kg) for the front and 2lb 5 oz (1.07 kg) for the rear.

As might be expected, the AM14's comfort and ergonomics rated highly, scoring six out of seven. The reason why it did not score seven was that Ben found the saddle merely adequate and the handlebars too narrow. He also disliked the foam handlebar covering. Build and component quality also scored six out of seven. The only significant criticism was of the Sansin hubs, which, according to Ben, wore out quickly and for which he said spares were unavailable. (The 1994 AM14 uses Mavic hubs.)

The Cycling Plus appraisal included second opinions from two other riders. Phil Marshall, a regular tester of racing bikes for the magazine, wrote "I really enjoyed riding the AM14. It combines fun and extremely comfortable ride with excellent handling and stability, making it an ideal touring bike." However, he did not consider it suitable for his style of racing and found the braking barely adequate. Like Ben, he felt that the handlebars were too narrow, as did Cycling Plus's technical editor, Hilary Stone.

Hilary particularly liked the "exceptional armchair comfort combined with a big chunk of liveliness". He thought the AM14 "unique in combining these qualities so well". The machine's stability also impressed him, despite the very light steering giving an unstable feeling at first. His major criticism was of the componentry, and he rated the gear changing very poor by contemporary standards.

The 1994 AM14, descendant of the AM14 Blue. CAD drawing by Nigel Sadler.

Cycling Plus's final verdict was that the AM14 deserved five out of seven, both for value for money and for overall performance. On the debit side it was expensive to run – Ben Searle estimated 3p per mile for freewheels and tyres alone. (By this time the complete freewheel assembly cost £147.95 and tyres were £13.95.) But on the credit side, Ben found the machine so versatile that "it saves me from owning and insuring several other machines". He pointed out that, through the Cyclists' Touring Club, an AM was 10% cheaper to insure than a conventional machine.

Ben concluded that the AM14 was "a superb tourer, which is perhaps its greatest forte". It came close to perfection "but could certainly benefit from more attention to detail". One of the review's picture captions stated that the AM14 gives the rider "a grin-factor so high you could eat a banana sideways"!

Marketing Advice

In January 1988, via the dealership newsletter AM News, Alex Moulton offered this advice on marketing "The Improved Bicycle System":

"I am convinced that the key to sales is in overcoming the understandable barrier to perception as to what the AM bicycle really is. We know from experience that simply to expose AM bikes in the largest store with the biggest floor traffic with unknowing and uncommitted sales people will produce zero results. On the contrary, when preferably the proprietor himself, as is certainly the case of one of our dealers, says, "over there and quite separate is the alternative bicycle, the Moulton range, which does everything better than the conventional and is the only bicycle I use …", then the continuing sales which result are remarkable. This is the ideal to which we are looking from our few selected and committed dealers."

Capacity Increased

The same edition of AM News announced that manufacturing capacity was being "somewhat increased" for 1988. It also revealed some further product refinements.

Frame painting had been brought in-house during 1986, rather than continuing to rely on outside contractors. AM News announced that "our in-house paint shop now exclusively uses Deltron two-part paint finish for high gloss and chip resistance".

Tyre Improvements

There was also news about the tyres:

"The key feature of the AM bicycle is the special Moulton tyre made exclusively from our moulds by Wolber. We have committed further investment to introduce a moulded-in valve in the tubes which will work through as standard supply later in the year."

Moulton-Wolber inner tubes hitherto had replaceable valve bodies, retained by a nut. About 1985 it was discovered that this perfectly standard nut prevented the inner tube bedding down correctly. The inner tube was forced into a tightly radiused blister either side of the valve, as the tube bulged into the rim well, between the high points formed by the spoke nipple and valve nut. This "blebbing" could lead eventually to spontaneous punctures, often while the bike was not in use.

When this came to light, Alex had the size of the valve nut reduced. However, this did not completely eliminate the problem. In the Summer 1986 edition of The Moultoneer I suggested that the rim well between the valve hole and the nipple heads either side be infilled with a double thickness of self-adhesive foam pads (eg. Sticky Fixers). Other Moultoneers improvised their own remedies. The moulded-in valve was the ultimate solution, although it necessitated a slight enlargement of the valve hole in earlier 17" rims (see Appendix A).

Perceived problems with puncture resistance led to another development announced in the January 1988 AM News:

"A useful Wolber development for puncture reducing is a liner strip, Protec (not to be confused with Mr Tuffy) and it will be available shortly to suit our tyre size. Statistically it gives at least a 2:1 benefit; and was used successfully on their tyres in the Tour de France. We will use it in RAAM '88"

(RAAM being the **R**ace **A**cross **AM**erica.)

This announcement followed 18 months of correspondence in The Moultoneer on the merits and demerits of Mr Tuffy and similar puncture-resistant tyre liner tapes. The conclusion was that these products were a Godsend to low mileage riders but could be a curse to those covering high mileages. This was because, although the tape was extremely puncture resistant, its ends chafed the inner tube. After a few hundred miles this would **cause** a puncture, even if the ends of the tape had been feathered by thermal or abrasive means.

Experience with the Moulton-Wolber tyre's resistance to punctures varied considerably. In the Summer 1987 issue of The Moultoneer, Linda Bailey complained she had suffered eight punctures in about ten outings involving no more than 500 miles (800 km). This tallied with my own experience riding without an anti-puncture liner in the damp, flinty, lanes that run through the southern Chiltern beech woods.

On the other hand Peter Knottley, who by this time had "enjoyed some 30,000 Moulton miles (48,000 km) in all", had no complaints at all. In the same issue of The Moultoneer he wrote:

"Not for the first time I am at a loss to understand the troubles which Moulton riders seem to encounter. The troubles with tyres ... leave me wondering just how people ride their machines to meet these failures. ... I get tyre use certainly as good as I ever got with 27" ones; they just wear bald and I fit a new one! ... Punctures as ever, two in a week and then none for some months."

(By the end of 1990 Peter Knottley had almost doubled his AM mileage to approximately 56,000 miles (90,500 km) and by May 1994 he was up to 75,000 miles (120,000 km).)

A most pertinent point was made by Neil "Miff" Mowle, also in the Summer 1987 issue of The Moultoneer: "I have found that if just one of the casing threads is severed, a swelling soon appears and the tyre is rendered unserviceable. If this mishap can be avoided the tyre tread has a long life."

A year later an anonymous member of the MBC reported that in ten months he had covered 6,635 miles (10,675 km). In doing so he had completely worn out two tyres. He wrote, "I have had my share of punctures – these seem to be caused mainly by flints in wet weather." He added that the tyres "afford little or no grip off road in the wet. If this could be cured, I would have the perfect bike."

In January 1989 Alex reported on the successful use of Wolber Protec in his 17" tyres. He stated in AM News, "In a controlled test of two riders in Devonshire lanes with plenty of thorns about, the relative score has been six to zero." Not long after this Peter Knottley reported that Protec was very effective: "One puncture in the rear after 800 miles (1,300 km) was due to a thorn on a forest track, and nothing would have stopped that. ... The front tyre has now done 3,200 (5,200 km) without a puncture, and is still in use." Peter had been in contact with Hampshire AM rider Reg George who mentioned that he had got 5,000 miles (8,100 km) out of a set of Moulton-Wolber tyres.

Keith Giles of Sunnyvale, California, was also impressed by Protec. In the first 500 miles (800 km) on his new AM7 he had suffered three punctures, all caused by thorns. He fitted Protec and nearly 1,500 miles (2,400 km) later had not had another puncture. "I rotated the tyres, front to back/back to front, after 1,000 miles (1,600 km), and now have almost 2,000 miles (3,200 km) and I can see no tyre wear."

Sprocket Clusters

In spring 1988 Swift Cycles Limited were reported in The Moultoneer as having encountered several defective silver AM sprocket clusters which caused chain slippage on the smallest sprocket. The problem had always been easily overcome by exchanging the component.

This report followed a query from a German member of the MBC, and specialist dealer in small-wheeled bicycles, Hans-Heinrich Voss of Itzehoe. He had experienced difficulties with a silver cluster, the chain occasionally "overjumping" a tooth. A similar problem was experienced by C. S. Johnson, who reported: "Closer inspection of the silver cluster showed tiny indentations on the shoulder between 5th and 6th (cogs). Each was opposite a trough between teeth. I suspected that the shoulder was fouling the chainlinks."

Mr Johnson had been using Shimano VG chains. He then tried a Sedis Black chain and found that it performed perfectly. Alex Moulton confirmed that the Sedis was the most suitable chain.

Bel Ami Bags

The AM February 1988 price list included the special American bags produced for the AM road bikes. This Bel Ami luggage was made by Sandy Bellamy (Bel Ami, get it?). The front bag cost £113.21, the rear £170.69. (In 1994 Alex Moulton Limited lists a Bellamy bag at £140.64.)

There was also a Bel Ami Marathon set, consisting of a rear bag with two detachable pouches. These fitted **under** the rear carrier and when removed could be worn round the waist. The Marathon set cost £219.94.

Peter Reyner Banham

On 18 March 1988 the great English architectural historian Peter Reyner Banham died. Author of such classics as "Theory and Design in the First Machine Age", he trained as an apprentice at the Bristol Aeroplane Company where Alex Moulton was personal assistant to the Chief Engineer, Sir Roy Fedden.

Only a few months before his death Peter had written to The Moultoneer. He was coming to the end of a tour of duty lecturing at the University of California's Santa Cruz campus.

Peter owned an AM7 with flat handlebars, his fifth Moulton since 1963. He regularly rode it to the campus, which involved a climb of some 800 feet (246 m). The AM was, he said, five minutes (about 14%) quicker up the hill than "its immediate (non-Moulton) predecessor".

He wrote, "My present mount will go with me to New York City when I transfer there in the New Year, but it will be strictly recreational – not even the AM7's sophisticated suspension can cope with the appalling road surfaces of New York."

Sadly Peter died a month before he was due to give his inaugural lecture at New York University.

The AM-ATB

In spring 1988 the AM-ATB was launched. This was a 20" wheel mountain bike and is dealt with separately in Chapter 7.

Portables Compared

In June 1988 The Observer, Britain's oldest Sunday newspaper, published an article comparing four portable bicycles – the Bickerton, Strida, Dawes Kingpin and AM2.

The verdict on the AM2 from motoring journalist Sue Baker was that "it feels eminently stable and is pleasing to look at". It was more comfortable than the others and "arguably the best bike to ride". It felt like a "normal bike" but was not the most convenient for stowage. "It is quickly dismantled, but does not reduce to as compact a size as the Bickerton or Strida."

Turnbuckles

At the MBC's annual meet in September 1988, Alex rode an AM which dispensed with the demount plate as a means of splitting the rear brake cable. Instead a neat stainless steel turnbuckle was used, smaller than those on the experimental MkIVs and Y-frames of the 1970s.

The cut end of the cable from the brake lever passed through the front part of the turnbuckle, and a nipple was formed on it by slipping a small brass ferrule over the cable and silver soldering it in place. The cable from the turnbuckle to the brake calliper, was actually a strong derailleur wire, the nipple of which was small enough to fit into the rear part of the turnbuckle.

Each of the two parts of the turnbuckle was fitted with a rubber O ring to prevent it rattling against, or scratching, the frame. Plumbers' O rings can be used as a cheap and easily obtainable replacement (see Appendix A).

Turnbuckles eventually became standard for the rear brake and gear cables on all AMs. From 1992 a slightly larger diameter version was produced which incorporated a grub screw, operated by miniature Allen key. This obviated the need for soldering and allowed use of a standard pear nipple brake cable from the turnbuckle to the rear brake.

Vibrational Stress Examined

The Fall/Winter issue of Human Power, the technical journal of the US-based International Human Powered Vehicle Association, contained a paper by Rainer Pivit of the University of Oldenburg in West Germany. Entitled "Vibrational Stress on Cyclists", it noted that "rough surfaces of typical West German city cycle tracks nearly always impair performance and even sometimes the health of the rider." The paper recorded the vibrational stress on cyclists with various cycles on different road surfaces.

One of the machines tested was an AM7. The tyres were inflated to 100 psi (6.8 atm). The machine's weight was quoted as 14 kg (30lb 14oz), some 2.9 kg (6lb 6oz) heavier than the weight as manufactured. No explanation was given for the increased weight, although it might be accounted for by carriers and other accessories.

Rainer reported that the intensity of vibration on the AM7 "is similar to the roadster bicycle" and that the "highly damped rear suspension is especially troublesome". He added that "the only slightly dampened front suspension is unsatisfactory in driving behaviour", whereas "on smooth surfaces swinging of the rear suspension in reaction to pedal forces is noticeable". (Rainer did not seem to realise that the front suspension damping could be adjusted.)

These comments induced AM7 rider Derek Roberts, then Honorary Editor of The Fellowship of Cycling Old-Timers, to write to Human Power. He explained that he had shown Rainer's paper to Alex who had found it puzzling. Derek himself found it hard to take: "What Pivit means by 'the highly damped rear suspension is especially troublesome' I cannot make out – what trouble is there? 'Swinging of the rear suspension in reaction to pedal forces' ... bunkum!"

Nonetheless, Rainer's paper showed that the AM was significantly healthier to ride over rough surfaces than conventional tourers with high pressure tyres – 1.125" (28 mm) running at 85 psi (5.78 atm) front and 100 psi (6.8 atm) rear. For example, one of the road surfaces used for the tests consisted of old, irregular field stones. According to Rainer's findings, riding a touring bike of this type on such a surface for less than **one minute** was health impairing because of vibration at both saddle and handlebars. You could safely ride the AM7 on the same surface for **20 minutes**.

Another of Rainer's tests, on small cobblestones, showed a conventional touring bike producing health-impairing vibrational stress in less than 25 minutes. The AM7 took more than an hour to produce the same stress level.

AM7 Stamps

At Christmas 1988 Clacton County High School in Essex operated a local cycle mail delivery service. The school had been doing this annually since the waiving of the Post Office monopoly on mail delivery for charities in 1982.

The Christmas 1988 delivery carried nearly 3,500 items of mail and used three stamps. The green 20p stamp featured an AM7.

Changes for 1989

The January 1989 edition of AM News advised that the AM7 was available with a choice of SunTour Winner Pro or Regina CX freewheels. It could also be supplied with the Jubilee-style day bag carrier.

The AM5 now had an easier gear change following a revision by Sturmey-Archer to their S5/2 hub gear design. This involved simplifying the sun pinion clutch mechanism by eliminating a spring hold-off device designed to make the gear more tolerant of crash changes.

AM News pointed out that the Duchess of Westminster, who had recently joined the board of Alex Moulton Limited, had progressed from an AM2 to an AM5. Since 1985 Alex had helped the Duchess in a Cheshire-based scheme to encourage young British industrial designers.

Increased Costs

The newsletter revealed that the future of the AM range had been seriously imperilled during 1988 when Reynolds had threatened to withdraw supply of the special sizes of 531 tubing used in the bikes. Alex wrote: "It was only by my intervention in high places that future supplies are assured, but at a cost!"

Consequently for 1989 prices of the AM2, AM-Jubilee and AM14S & T increased by 4 or 5%. Other models increased by much larger margins, 15 to 19%. Alex pointed out to his dealers, "On price, please remember that it is a fact that in the Moulton range alone of all bicycles, the most expensive model substantially outsells the lowest priced!"

Thereafter the 17" wheel Moultons continued to increase in price substantially faster than inflation. For example, by spring 1994 the AM7 was, in real terms, 80% dearer than at its launch 11 years earlier. But it has to be realised that in the early years Alex was producing about 1,000 bikes a year in just two variants, whereas by 1994 he was producing a few hundred machines annually, yet offering a choice of eight models.

Exports

In January 1989 CBI News, a publication of the Confederation of British Industry, included an article entitled "Small is Beautiful". It described the downscaled operation at Bradford-on-Avon and highlighted the fact that 60% of output was exported. This was facilitated by the low weight, small size and high value of the product, enabling all exports to be air-freighted.

A year later Bicycle Trade and Industry magazine published a photograph of eight AM-Jubilees lined up ready for air-freighting. The accompanying text again stressed the high proportion of output exported by Dr Moulton, which by then had risen to about 70%. The heading read "£12,000 the batch" and the magazine stated, "Britain's best export record bike-for-bike must be from the Bradford-on-Avon works of Alex Moulton Ltd ..."

University Challenge

In March 1989 Mike Hessey, then editor of The Moultoneer, visited Alex at The Hall. During their discussions Alex commented that even engineers still seem to have difficulty understanding that the AM bicycle is no harder to propel than a conventional machine. He had recently given a lecture to Cambridge University Engineering Society about cycles, and found less understanding than when he lectured there in the mid 1960s.

Mike, a lecturer in engineering at Warwick University, commented that this confirmed his own experience.

Luggage Options

In the Spring 1989 issue of The Moultoneer I reviewed two additional pieces of luggage for the AM range. Neither was an official Alex Moulton accessory, but both reflected the interest in the bikes and their luggage-carrying capacity.

The Curlew rear bag was a prototype produced by Curlew Camping of Yeadon, West Yorkshire. In common with the Moulton bags of the 1960s, it retained its shape well, even when empty. However, like the official AM bags, it could be folded flat for storage. Externally it was finished in a tough black material, similar to Carradice canvass. The sides were stiffened by interior foam padding.

The production model was intended to incorporate a detachable carrying handle, and possibly an inside lid pocket. I suggested that external side pockets, like those on the old Moulton Safari bag, and tyre holding loops would also be worth considering. However, it seems that the bag did not go into production.

A useful little bag that **did** become available was designed and manufactured by MBC member John Long. About 10" (250 mm) long, its cylindrical base sits on the tailpiece behind the seat tube. Fixing is by three elasticated straps with Velcro ends, which pass around the seat tube and seat pillar.

Made of expanded vinyl in AM Royal Blue or grey, it is suitable for holding small objects such as a lightweight cape or Camping Gaz Bleuet stove. At the time of writing it costs just £7 including postage. Specials in different lengths or colours can be made to order. (See Appendix B for address.)

Another luggage option, highlighted by MBC member John Burnett, was to use a Karrimor Rac Pac: " ... it fits very well, has seven compartments, including one for a U lock (if you don't have the special rack to carry one), and it costs around £45."

Some years later, in 1993, MBC member Andrew Beckman produced bags in the style of the 1960s Moulton holdalls, but to fit AMs and APBs. (The APB is described in Chapter 8 and Andrew Beckman's 1994 address is in Appendix B.)

All At Sea

May 1989's issue of the US magazine Practical Sailor featured a detailed survey of five portable bikes in respect of their suitability for use on small boats.

The conclusion was that the AM was a "connoisseur's bicycle, a machine with a pedigree ... at a pedigree price". As such it deserved better than a corrosive environment. "If you love wonderful bicycles and have deep pockets, buy a Moulton for land use; get a cheaper bike for the boat."

AM-Moulton Marathon

Timothy Walker was Chairman of the World Wide Fund for Nature (WWF) and a long-term friend of Alex. When Timothy died, Alex decided to produce a special bicycle that could be auctioned in memory of his friend. The proceeds, after deduction of tax, were to go to the WWF.

The machine was called the AM-Moulton Marathon and was built "in the spirit of Colin Martin's Moulton Marathon, used in his epic 'Half Way Round' journey in 1970 from England to Australia". (See the book "Half Way Round" by Peter Knottley.)

As noted in Chapter 1, the original Marathon was based on a Moulton MkIII and incorporated a Stowaway frame joint. It had lightweight components and a simple, efficient transmission based on the Fichtel & Sachs Duomatic two-speed coaster hub. Double chainring and twin rear sprockets meant that there were two two-speed gear ranges: the chain was manually moved from one chainline to the other, depending on how arduous the terrain was. There was no need to shorten the chain or use a tensioning device, because the total number of teeth in each drive train (chainwheel plus sprocket) was the same.

The AM-Moulton Marathon followed the same equipment philosophy as the original Marathon, but was based on the AM2. It was finished in standard AM steely grey and equipped with drop handlebars, a single randonneur-style brake lever, rear carrier, rear bag, tool kit and spare tyre.

On Alex's behalf the bike was built from a frame kit by Swift Cycles of Forest Hill, London. Sealed bids were requested by the end of October 1989 and originally there was a reserve price of £1,100. However, the reserve price was not met and the machine was subsequently sold to long-distance cyclist Ian Wright, a member of the MBC. He cycled 135 miles (216 km) from his home near Cambridge to Swifts and back to inspect the bike and make his offer.

Front Derailleur Conversion Kits

It was against Alex's policy to braze fittings for a front derailleur onto an AM7 or AM2. Consequently at least two conversion kits were produced by others for fitting a front derailleur without recourse to brazing.

Stephen Parry of Perth, Western Australia announced one of the kits via the Summer 1989 issue of The Moultoneer. It was marketed by A/M Bicycles WA of Kallaroo, Western Australia. It consisted of a stainless steel adaptor which enabled a front derailleur designed for a brazed-on frame fitting to be fixed to the bike. Also included, along with miscellaneous parts, was an adaptor to allow twin shift levers to be fitted to the demount bracket. The price was Aus $100.

An alternative conversion kit was produced by Angle Lake Cyclery of Seattle. It consisted of a Shimano Deore ATB front derailleur with continuous band fixing, an aluminium adaptor to mount the mechanism, shifters which fixed to the demount bracket and various other accessories. It cost US $165.

In The Moultoneer for September/October 1990 Jacques Bilinski of Vancouver told how he had used the Australian converter to adapt the gears of his AM7. He used the bike for a combination of sport and fitness riding, commuting and loaded touring. Although he appreciated the simplicity of the AM7's single lever gear system, he found the 20% steps between gears too wide when cycling hard. He also wanted a lower gear for use when touring in hilly terrain with a loaded bike.

Jacques decided to adopt the "half-step plus granny" pattern of gearing. In this configuration the two larger chainwheels are sized so that changing from one to the other gives half the difference in gearing of a single shift of the rear derailleur. Hence, as the AM7 gave approximately 20% shifts at the rear, the two larger chainwheels were sized to give a 10% difference – the "half-step". The third chainwheel is essentially the smallest that can be accommodated, and gives a range of closely spaced low "granny" gears.

Jacques pointed out that obtaining chainrings for his AM7's original Stronglight crankset (with the rare 122 mm diameter chainring bolt circle) was difficult. Most triple chainwheels for tourers and mountain bikes used a 110 mm circle for the two larger chainrings and 74 mm for the inner ring. However, his AM7 had the original high-headed rear suspension pivot bolt which would have fouled a 74 mm ring and at the time he was unaware that a low-head pivot bolt had become the norm.

He therefore evolved a suitable triple chainwheel configuration based on a Campagnolo Euclid crankset with three 110 mm Sugino chainrings. These consisted of the largest (54 tooth) and smallest (34 tooth) he could find, plus a 49 tooth ring, 10% smaller than the largest. The original AM7 freewheel was retained but the 23 and 28 tooth sprockets were replaced with 25 and 31 tooth cogs. The gearing range thus obtained spanned 18 to 102".

Jacques rejected the Angle Lake front derailleur conversion kit because the Shimano Deore front derailleur supplied with it was designed for very wide range gearing, and was not in his opinion well suited to the five tooth difference between his "half-step" chainrings. The Australian conversion kit enabled him to fit a Shimano Dura-Ace braze-on racing derailleur. This was used to the limits of its capacity to accommodate the "granny" ring, with the mechanism shimmed out from its mounting slightly for best alignment on the smallest ring.

The original rear derailleur, in this case a SunTour Cyclone 7000, was retained. It worked well, despite being used beyond the manufacturer's stated tooth capacity. Changing was via SunTour ratcheted (non-indexed) bar-end shift levers. Various brazed-on cable fittings were used.

In practice the largest chainring was not used with the biggest sprocket, and the smallest chainring was used only with the three largest sprockets. The principal disadvantages of the converted transmission were the number of double gear changes needed, and the relatively rough shifting resulting from using sprockets and a derailleur mechanism designed for close-ratio racing use, in a wide-ratio touring mode. Weight was increased by 1lb 1 oz (550 gm), of which 11oz (310 gm) was due to the crankset and chainrings.

Some riders succesfully fitted a standard front derailleur mechanism to the rear triangle, without recourse to brazing or a converter kit. The small diameter frame tube was simply packed out as necessary.

The SPEED Launched

The annual meet of the Moulton Bicycle Club in September 1989 saw the launch of the AM-SPEED, a new, non-separable racing version of the Alex Moulton bicycle. This is covered in detail in Chapter 9.

The same September an AM was featured in the Harvest Festival at Bradford-on-Avon parish church. The vicar cited changes over the years in the local economy – wool, rubber, Moulton suspensions and the Moulton bicycle. "At which point **the** bicycle was smoothly and gracefully ridden up the aisle and parked before the altar rail", reported the church magazine.

Shimmy

The subject of front wheel shimmy was raised in The Moultoneer by Keith Giles of Sunnyvale, California in Autumn 1989. He had loaded up his AM7 with the official front and rear bags and, because there was not enough space in either for his tent and sleeping pad, had tried mounting them in a variety of positions – "on top

Alex unveils the AM-SPEED, September 1989. Photo by Tony Hadland.

of the rear rack (under the large rear bag), on top of the rear bag, on top of the front rack (under the front bag) and on top of the front bag." In each case the tent and pad were tried both transversely and longitudinally.

In every case an occasional shimmy would develop in the handlebars. Keith suspected that "if you can't get something into one of the designed touring bags you shouldn't take it". He asked if anyone else had experienced similar problems and whether they had overcome them.

I replied via the next issue that in 1986 I had experienced shimmy when hand-signalling in traffic in France. My bike was an AM7 with the standard AM rear bag full of camping gear and a 12lb (5.4 kg) tent and sleeping mat fixed transversely on the front carrier. The following year I repeated the journey, taking the same equipment but not fitting the front carrier. Instead I put all the luggage in a very large soft case approximately 30" (760 mm) wide, 15" (380 mm) deep and 18" (450 mm) high, firmly lashed to the rear carrier and saddle. No shimmy was experienced.

The Moultoneer for March/April 1990 printed a letter from Niall Mackey in Dublin. He too had experienced front wheel shimmy, overcome by moving some of the weight from the front of the bike to the back. He asked: "Is it simply a result of weight on the front, or of the front/ rear weight distribution?"

In the same issue Nigel Sadler, writing of his experiences with the AM-Zzipper fairing, commented that too much weight on the fairing's carrier would result in "serious front wheel shimmy". (AM dealers had been advised in November 1986 through the AM News newsletter that **no** weight should be carried on the fairing's carrier.)

Alex replied to these points in the May/June 1990 issue of The Moultoneer:

"… our recommendation is to put as much weight as you want on the rear carrier, for which it was designed. On the front you should put as little as possible, since loose loads on the front can excite wobble.

"If the fairing, with its high inertia, is fitted, I recommend only the addition of a light well-damped load, such as an item of clothing or a sleeping bag.

"As on any vehicle, it is a good idea to keep wheels and tyres well balanced, and to keep backlash in the steering and linkage to a minimum."

In respect of this last point, there were few complaints of shimmy in the first two or three years of the AM's manufacture. It seems likely that problems began to arise as the steering and front suspension wore.

About 1989 laterally stiffer stainless steel leading links for the front suspension were introduced with a view to reducing shimmy and preventing overtightening and consequent cracking of the polyurethane spacers midway along the links. The new links had wider flanges top and bottom that met, thus forming a box section. (For trouble-shooting shimmying see Appendix A.)

Folding Tyres

Michael Doube, an experienced Australian long-distance cycle tourist, wrote to The Moultoneer (July/August 1990) about the advisability of carrying a spare 17" tyre if touring outside England. He imagined that economics would rule out the possibility of a Kevlar-beaded folding tyre for the AM series.

However, he had discovered that he could fold a 17" tyre in the same way that a conventional 27" or 700C tyre is folded, that is, by grasping opposite sides of the tyre and twisting to produce three equal-sized loops. As he pointed out, "A little more twisting and the two end loops will tuck into the middle one, producing a compact circle of only $6^{1}/_{2}$" (165 mm) diameter and $2^{1}/_{4}$" (57mm) high."

(If you want to try this, practise with an old tyre first, lest you kink the bead and render a serviceable tyre useless.)

Michael bound the folded tyre with duct tape to protect it and found that it fitted neatly into the frame triangle above the bottom bracket.

Writing in the January/February 1991 issue of The Moultoneer, Mr A. Bullock proffered a neat way of carrying 17" tyres without folding them for those AM riders who had the earlier version of the AM rear bag without the tyre loops:

"Place the tyres horizontally on top of the bag. Pull one of the carrying handles over the tyre towards the middle of the bag. Bring the cross-over strap up through the gap between the carrying handles and the tyres. Take the cross-over strap to the other side of the bag where you will find the other carrying handle drawn over the tyre and coming towards the middle of the bag. Pass the cross-over strap down through the gap between the second carrying handle and the tyre and into its strap fastener."

It may sound like a Paul Daniels magic trick, but it works! In effect the two carrying handles cradle the tyre(s) giving four points of contact and preventing significant horizontal movement in any direction. The carrying handles are tensioned by the cross-over strap. Mr Bullock pointed out that in over 3,000 miles (4,800 km) of touring this method had served him well.

The Californian Market

In March 1990, while staying with my AM-riding brother-in-law Roger Jeffree and his wife near San Francisco, I visited a number of northern Californian bicycle shops. The premier Alex Moulton dealership in the area was the Bicycle Center in Santa Cruz. Its two main shop windows were devoted exclusively to AMs and displayed an AM14, a Jubilee and an AM-ATB. Manager Roger Sands was an enthusiastic advocate of the Moulton bicycle concept and even had an old Moulton MkIII in the shop – a great rarity in North America.

From my visits to about a dozen Californian cycle shops I gained the impression that although the more informed dealers appreciated the merits of the AM, relatively few seemed capable of selling them. More surprising was the fact that the Bicycle Center's AMs were the **only British bicycles of any kind** that I found on sale in California.

AMs at KM150

KM150 was a major cycling festival to celebrate the invention about 1840 of a treadle-driven bicycle by the Scotsman Kirkpatrick Macmillan. The event took place at Drumlanrig Castle near Dumfries from 26 May to 3 June 1990.

For the final weekend the MBC had a stand on which were displayed most of the AM range and about half-a-dozen earlier Moultons. A display of machines illustrating the evolution of the bicycle was staged in front of the castle, Mike Hessey providing an AM7 and a Moulton Stowaway.

The presence of the "Advanced Engineering Bicycle" demonstrated how far the bicycle had evolved in 150 years. Kirkpatrick Macmillan would have been fascinated!

AM5 and the replica Macmillan bicycle. Photo by John Pinkerton.

Chapter 7
AM-ATB

1988-1992

Development – Specifications – Reviews – Customisations

"Rumours had been flying around for some time. Silhouettes had been spotted in American cycling magazines. When were we going to see it?" Thus wrote Hilary Stone in Bicycle magazine, August 1988, describing the feelings of Moulton devotees and cycle journalists during the spring and summer of that year.

As early as March, Eric Duncan had written from Washington DC to Moulton Preservation's Michael Woolf that he had heard of the new machine. The following month Cycle Trader and Bicycle Action both confirmed the rumour.

The subject of all this interest and anticipation? The AM-ATB, the Alex Moulton All Terrain Bicycle.

The silhouette "spotted in American Cycling magazines".
From Angle Lake Cyclery's ATB leaflet.

Origins Of The Mountain Bike

Although the term "all terrain bicycle" is now rather out of fashion, in the mid 1980s it was widely used as a synonym for "mountain bike". Mountain biking evolved out of downhill off-road races that started in the mid 1970s in mountainous Marin County, to the north of San Francisco. Initially the bikes used were only slightly modified American clunkers – heavy roadsters or beach cruisers. Their wide tyres and strong frames made them the most suitable mounts available.

Clunkers were usually factory-fitted with single-speed coasters – rear hub brakes operated by back-pedalling. However, these overheated on the long fast descents, giving off clouds of smoke as the grease inside vaporised. Subsequently cable-operated brakes were used, typically tandem callipers operated by motor cycle levers and cables. Wide-ratio derailleur gears were also adopted, enabling riders to go up the mountains, as well as down! The ability to ride uphill stimulated a move towards lighter frames. Gary Fisher's 1978 Schwinn derivative is said to have been the first with derailleur gears: it weighed a very hefty 60lb (27 kg)!

Probably the first specially designed mountain bike frame to be marketed was made by Joe Breeze. In 1977, at the suggestion of Charlie Kelly, Joe produced a batch of 10 chrome-moly Breezer frames. By the standards of the time the 1977 Breezer was a lightweight, the complete bike tipping the scales at about 38lb (17 kg).

The term "mountain bike" was allegedly coined by Charlie Kelly and Gary Fisher. Their own limited production machines were unveiled to a wider audience at the New York cycle show in 1981. From then on commercial exploitation of the mountain bike began in earnest. By the mid 1980s, spurred on by the eager participation of the Japanese and Taiwanese cycle industries, the mountain bike had gained a major share of bicycle sales in many western markets.

Only a minority of purchasers used the bikes as off-road machines. Most bought them as fashion accessories that were also fun to ride. As far as poseurs were concerned, the cafe racer was a thing of the past – the ATB was now de rigeur. British comedians Baddiel and Newman, Punt and Dennis homed in on the mountain bike in 1991: "Originally designed to cope with the mountainous, rugged and rocky terrain of the Appalachians, it is now very popular in the towns and cities of south-east England as it is by far the most expensive and posey bike you can buy."

But whatever the motives of the purchasers, the advent of the mountain bike certainly led to improvements in the design, construction and availability of bicycle components. This benefited not only ATB riders but also cycle-tourists, utility riders and to a lesser extent racing cyclists. Improvements were particularly noticeable in respect of two very old ideas – wide-ratio derailleur gearing and cantilever brakes. As a result there is now an excellent choice of such products across a wide price spectrum.

Technical improvements and high sales volumes allowed the benefits to percolate right down to the bottom of the market. So much so that by 1993 it was possible to buy a complete new bicycle with cantilever brakes and 18-speed indexed derailleur gears for under £100.

Alex Moulton and Mountain Bikes

Initially Alex was quite uninterested in mountain bikes. He found it difficult to understand why people would want to ride bicycles in rough terrain when it was easier and quicker to use metalled roads. He also felt that much wild country was best enjoyed on foot.

Alex commented more than once on the similarity between the typical ATB and the 1890s Humber in a photograph of his father and uncle – the same old diamond frame and big wheels with fat tyres. Despite the attempts of journalists and marketing men to hype up the mountain bike ("90 years of bicycle technology turned on its head", etc.) in all essential respects the 1980s mountain bike was merely the latest manifestation of the good old diamond frame safety bicycle. This was not lost on the British comedians cited above, who defined the mountain bike as "Basically a 16-geared, wide wheeled Raleigh Wayfarer without the saddlebag, mudguards and bell."

Since the 1950s Alex's aim has been to create a better bicycle system that goes beyond the necessary compromises of the diamond frame. This was another reason why his interest was not initially aroused by the mountain bike boom.

However, he was interested in rationalising the AM design to make the Moulton bicycle concept available to more users at lower cost. In the 1960s he had simplified his F frame to produce the cheaper 14" wheel range: now he designed a new version of the AM that was cheaper to assemble and which used stock 20" wheels and tyres and standard sprockets. Wishing as ever for his products to have maximum British input, he first offered a manufacturing licence to Raleigh. You can guess their response.

Alex then approached Kuwahara, a medium volume Japanese bicycle manufacturer. Initially they expressed considerable interest, but eventually negotiations broke down. Angle Lake Cyclery of Seattle, knowing of the new design, then suggested that it be taken upmarket and developed into a mountain bike. Hence the AM-ATB.

Suspension And Off-Road Bikes

Bicycle magazine made Alex's mountain bike its machine of the month for August 1988, giving it a colour centrefold. One of the picture captions read "Suspension front and rear – is this the way forward for ATBs?"

In fact, suspension for off-road bicycles was not new. Something remarkably similar to mountain biking had been going on in north-east England in the early 1960s, and at least two of the bikes had front suspension.

The Darlington Motor Club organised the annual Scott Motorcycle Trial, said to be the toughest one-day motorcycle event in the world. Impressed by this, local teenagers formed the Darlington Bogwheelers, an off-road club for cyclists. They used ultra-low gearing, for example, by fitting a special 28 tooth sprocket (made by local cycle shop owner and rider Joe Cleminson) to a Sturmey-Archer four-speed hub driven by a small chainwheel from an old-fashioned moped. The toggle chain was protected from mud by a "toggle floggle", a gaiter made from a section of old inner tube. Knobbly cycle speedway tyres called Skidway Gripsters were obtained from Avon, the tyre company who bought the Moulton rubber manufacturing business in the 1950s.

Bogwheeler Peter Young's engineer father devised a front suspension system for Peter's off-road cycle. Colin Davison, a colleague of mine, was another front-sprung Bogwheeler. Bogwheeling received national exposure on BBC television when three of the riders were interviewed by Brian Johnston on Huw Wheldon's "All Your Own". Cycle journalist Geoff Apps recalls similar home-brewed machines in his part of southern England during the early 1960s.

A decade or so later Yamaha marketed a "Moto-Bike" with dual suspension. However, when the AM-ATB was launched in April 1988, suspension for off-road bikes was a rarity: indeed, Alex's bike has a good claim to being the world's first fully suspended production mountain bike.

There had been some experiments by USA designers and by August 1988 Kestrel and Roger Piper (who used to customise Moultons) had both evolved fully suspended machines, the Nitro and Bushido respectively. Both were exhibited at bike shows but neither was marketed.

On the whole there had been little progress with front suspension. Dan Hanebrink's 1987 SE Shocker ATB had a 24" rear wheel with about 4" (100 mm) of suspension travel but an unsprung front fork. Brian Skinner's MCR Descender of the same year was also rear-sprung only. According to Mountain Bike Action, "At that time no one had even begun thinking about front suspension" – a slight exaggeration but not far out.

Indeed, two of the few who had thought about front suspension were now abandoning it on grounds of weight and complexity. Bob Girvin and Dan Hanebrink turned to shock absorbing handlebar stems, which could be fitted relatively cheaply and easily. Girvin's Flexstem subsequently became a well-known mountain bike component, particularly for retro-fitting.

Assuming that the suspension is properly damped and tuned, if a bicycle is to have only one sprung wheel, it is generally better on the front – something the British Bogwheelers got right. This is principally because the front wheel has the full impetus of machine and rider behind it. Therefore, although the front wheel is more lightly loaded under constant speed conditions on a smooth road surface, it takes more shock than the rear wheel when it encounters a bump. Furthermore, as Hilary Stone put it in Bicycle, August 1988, the front wheel "is the one mostly responsible for control" and suspension helps keep the wheel in contact with the road.

Since 1988 the situation has changed considerably. By March 1993 30% of mountain bike models on sale in the United States had front suspension of some sort and 8% were fully suspended. (These figures include those with shock absorbing handlebar stems.) Some of the systems were good, some bizarre, some horrendously expensive, and some nastily cheap. Many required a phenomenal amount of maintenance.

By early 1993 front suspension (of a sort) had percolated down almost to the bottom of the market. In the UK Raleigh and Peugeot were selling front-sprung mountain bikes for about £200. In the USA you could buy a Ross Mt. Pocono with front suspension for a mere $209. And in August 1993 Raleigh launched the Activator II on the UK market, an ATB with suspension on both wheels for just £260. By May 1994 it could be bought for under £200.

Bestselling author of cycling books Richard Ballantine was moved to warn readers of New Cyclist (December 1992) against the "pseudo suspension mountain bike". He stated that "imitation mountain bikes ride like lead, weigh well over 35lb" (16 kg) and "have suspension systems that cosmetically suggest the real thing while concealing a set of rudimentary springs".

Yet back in the late 1980s very few mountain bike manufacturers even at the top end of the market were enthusiastic about suspension. As Mountain Bike Action pointed out "No manufacturer embraced it. Most fought it. They all feared it."

The AM-ATB and Angle Lake Cyclery

Journalist Caris Davis described Seattle as a small city where "a quarter of the population are university graduates, mostly well-mannered

Alex Moulton testing the AM-ATB in Washington state. Photo by Dale Clark, Angle Lake Cyclery.

bicycle users". Therefore it is not too surprising that Seattle was home to the most successful AM dealership in North America, Angle Lake Cyclery.

The transformation of Alex's rationalised spaceframe bicycle into the AM-ATB involved considerable input from Angle Lake. During the summer of 1987 the prototype AM-ATB was extensively tested in the mountains of the west coast of the USA.

The design incorporated the characteristic features of the AM road bikes: smaller than conventional wheels, front and rear suspension, and a separable spaceframe made from small-diameter Reynolds 531 steel tubing. However, it was not merely a carry-over from the earlier machines: there were a number of significant differences. The most obvious was the use of 20" wheels with wide tyres.

20" Wheels

This wheel and tyre format was necessary to achieve a larger tyre-to-ground contact patch and hence better flotation on soft or loose ground. The narrow 17" wheels of the AM road bikes sink deeply into soft ground, making the going very tough; and the Moulton-Wolber tyres would have proved far too fragile for off-road riding. Hence 20 x 2.125" BMX tyres and rims (ISO code 36-406) were selected. This format gave the option of using narrower 1.75" tyres.

The only precedent for Alex using 20" wheels was on the prototype Moulton Twenty. This was produced during his 1967-1974 period as a consultant for Raleigh, and at the Nottingham company's instigation. It resembled a cross between the Moulton MkIII and the Raleigh 20. The frame and rear suspension were based on the MkIII, but the rest owed more to the Raleigh 20. The front fork was unsprung, as was the rear carrier which was fixed directly to the rear triangle. The wheels were 20 x 1^3/$_8$" (E5J rim format, ISO code 35-451).

Whereas Alex had not experimented with 20" wheels since then, at least one Moultoneer had. Eric Duncan of Washington DC bought an

AM7 in 1984. He took it to the Italian Alps and reported that "it performed wonderfully. It climbed well, descended well, and of course carried weight beautifully. Plus the ride ... was one of unparalleled comfort."

However, the 17" rims "heated too fast while braking on long descents". In particular, Eric wanted tyres that were more durable and easily obtainable when touring remote areas. He observed that 20" BMX format tyres are "available all over the world, including the Third World." So he converted his AM7 to run on 20" wheels.

At first he found no great problem in accommodating the larger wheel in the rear triangle: he merely repositioned the small X-brace that links the seat and chain stays. Adapting the front suspension fork posed far greater problems. As he was "never a super fan of the AM7's front suspension" Eric decided to abandon it. Instead he fitted a regular lightweight 20" fork brazed onto a specially made extra long steerer tube.

Unfortunately, after a year the rear triangle cracked near where he had rebrazed the X-brace. (See caution in Appendix A.)

The Hairpin Frame

Another major difference between the AM-ATB and its road bike predecessors was in the frame construction. As with the AM road bikes, the frame incorporated two lattice beams linking the seat tube to the head tube; the two beams intersecting each other to form an X-configuration when viewed from the side. To accommodate the larger wheels, the frame geometry had to be altered slightly. Both lattice beams therefore junctioned with the seat tube at slightly higher points than on the 17" wheel AMs.

A most significant difference was that the $3/8$" (9.5 mm) tubes forming the outer members of the lattice beams wrapped around the head and seat tubes, thus giving the appearance of four hairpins. (The AM road bikes use thicker $1/2$" (13 mm) tubing which would be more difficult to form into a suitably radiused hairpin.) Each of the lattice beams was formed by two of these hairpins, the open ends meeting at the kingpin where any dimensional tolerance could be taken up. The benefits of the hairpin

The Hairpin Frame.
Photo by David Eccles.

construction were a) fewer but longer brazed joints, giving added strength and simplifying construction, and b) fewer tubes to cut to length and cod's mouth for lugless brazing.

The hairpin frame configuration was the subject of British patent 2204004, filed in April 1987: the corresponding US patent was 4813696. The patents allowed for the use of either thin tubing or round rod.

Hitherto the AM road bikes had all incorporated a large diameter captive kingpin, with a plastic knob at either end, as described in Chapter 2. The AM-ATB merely had a loose bolt, released by an Allen key, as in some AM prototypes.

A simplified lower frame tie was also adopted. A single tie rod linked the base of the head tube to the bottom bracket. The upper fixing was a captive bolt, the lower a quick-threaded stud on the bottom bracket which engaged with an internal thread in the end of the tie. Assembly involved first spinning the lower end of the tie onto the stud, then fixing the captive bolt through a hole in the flattened top end of the tie.

Front Suspension

The front suspension was broadly similar to that of the AM road bikes but of heavy duty construction. A particularly noticeable difference was the crown of the unsprung fork. The 17" wheel AMs had each fork blade separately housed in a crown in the traditional way. The AM-ATB followed common mountain bike practice by omitting the crown and adopting the so-called unicrown detail; the two fork blades curving in over the top of the wheel to junction directly with the steerer tube, thus producing a stronger fork.

There were two other ways in which the front suspension differed from that of the AM road bikes: it had a heavier duty steel coil spring, and the ride height/suspension stroke adjuster was shrouded in a rubber gaiter to keep mud and grit out of the steerer tube.

Weight of the complete front fork assembly was 3lb 7oz (1.56 kg). From 1990 the steerer tube wall thickness was increased to make it stronger. This necessitated a reduction in the diameter of the nylon guide bearing for the fork spring – a point to note when ordering spares.

Rear Suspension

The rear suspension consisted of a rubber-sprung, pivoting rear triangle, similar in principle to that used on the AM road bikes. However, for each side of the rear triangle, the chain stay, seat stay and the third member were all made from a single looped $1/2$" (13 mm) diameter tube for added strength. The drop-outs were of heavy duty stainless steel, brazed onto the rearward facing curve of the rear triangle tubing.

Suspension details. Photos by David Eccles.

The self-damping spring unit was an uprated version of the Monosphere rubber cone used on the AM road bikes. In response to suggestions from Angle Lake, the cam was fixed to the rear triangle by an adjustable Allen bolt, thus allowing the frame angles to be steepened by about 1 degrees.

The rubber cone assembly was enclosed by a rubber gaiter to protect it from degradation by ultraviolet rays.

Vital Statistics

The basic head and seat angles were 70 degrees, $2\frac{1}{2}$ degrees shallower than on the AM road bikes.

The distance between the head tube and seat tube (the so-called effective top tube length) was $21\frac{5}{8}$" (549 mm). Absence of a traditional top tube ("crossbar") was claimed as a safety advantage for off-road riders, but the stepover height, at $24\frac{1}{4}$" (616 mm), was significantly higher than on the AM road bikes.

The frame size (based on seat tube length) was nominally 19" (483 mm). In the Moulton tradition, it could cater for the majority of adult riders, typically from about 5' 3" tall to 6' 4", and covered the range of traditional frame sizes up to $26\frac{1}{2}$" (673 mm). Bottom bracket height, with the frame angles at 70 degrees and the machine unloaded, was about $12\frac{7}{8}$" (327 mm), depending on front and rear suspension adjustment, and tyre profile. This, as befits an off-road machine, was about $1\frac{3}{8}$" (35 mm) higher than on the 17" wheel AMs.

The wheelbase was 42.4" (1,077 mm), nearly an inch longer than the 17" wheel AM's, but the AM-ATB was still several inches shorter than a conventional mountain bike. Fork offset was 1.75" (44 mm) and the steering trail (castor) was 1.6" (41 mm).

Total weight of the frame, including front fork, was 11lb 5oz (5.13 kg). Without the fork, the weight was 7lb 14oz (3.57 kg). The bike was offered in chrome yellow or the standard steely grey.

Frame Fittings

The usual cable guides and stops were provided. Cable splitting for frame separation was by turnbuckles.

A brazed-on fitting was provided for the front derailleur mechanism. The right-hand stainless steel drop-out incorporated a hanger for the rear derailleur mechanism.

Mounting points were provided for specially designed, frame-fixed, front and rear carriers, broadly similar to those made for the road bikes. There were threaded bosses for no less than four bottle cages – one either side of the head tube, and two on the seat tube, one on the front, the other on the back. Tapped mudguard fixing eyes were also provided.

Distribution

At first Alex Moulton Limited did not sell the AM-ATB as a complete bicycle. Instead they supplied framesets to a handful of specially selected cycle dealers. In the UK there were initially only two such firms, both in London: Bike UK, which operated a flourishing chain of shops in the capital, and long-time Moulton specialists Swift Cycles of Forest Hill in south London. In 1988 the AM-ATB and the Jubilee were Swift's best-selling Moultons.

The major US distributor was, naturally enough, Angle Lake Cyclery. For a short time, during April and May 1988, this firm had exclusive distribution rights. Sales of the AM-ATB made Angle Lake for a while the biggest Moulton retailer in the world, a position otherwise held by Swift Cycles.

Componentry

Although the customer could specify whatever compatible components he or she liked, a typical AM-ATB specification included the Shimano Deore group set and 20 x 2.125" BMX tyres.

An AM-ATB built by Angle Lake and tested by Bicycle Guide used Mitsuboshi Competition IV Kevlar-beaded tyres running at 35-40 psi (2.35-2.72 atm) on Sun Metal M20 Mistral hard anodised and eyeletted alloy rims. These were laced to Shimano Deore XT quick release hubs via 36 stainless steel 14 gauge spokes. Radial spoking was used on the front wheel and three-cross spoking for the rear (each spoke crossed over three others). The front wheel weighed 3lb 5oz (1.52 kg), the rear 4lb 3oz (1.92 kg).

AM-ATB

The pedals were Deore XT with Deore XT cranks, on a Deore XT sealed cup and cone bottom bracket assembly. Triple Biopace chainrings, with 28, 38 and 48 teeth, were selected via a Deore XT front derailleur. The rear derailleur mechanism was a Shimano 600 EX SIS, used with a Deore XT Freehub having 12, 13, 15, 18, 20 and 22 teeth. This configuration gave the following gears:

28T: 25, 28, 31, 37, 43, (47)"

38T: 35, 38, 42, 51, 58, 63"

48T: (44), 48, 53, 64, 74, 80"

To get the closest changing sequence across the whole range of gears necessitated two consecutive double shifts. Starting on the smallest chainwheel:

25, 28 (increase of 10%), 31 (+11%), 37 (+20%), (shift to middle chainwheel and back one cog) 42 (+14%), (shift to largest chainwheel and back one cog) 48 (+26%), 53 (+11%), 64 (+20%), 74 (+15%), 80 (+8%).

The test bike's specification was complemented by an Avocet Racing saddle on a 17" (432 mm) seat pillar. This consisted of the AM 35 mm diameter over-sized stainless steel post with an SR Laprade micro-adjust pillar bonded and riveted into it in the same way as for the road bikes. However, greater overall length was achieved by having approximately 2" (50 mm) more of the SR post protruding from the stainless steel tube. The handlebars were Salsa Moto Bar, 24" (610 mm) wide with rubber grips, on an SR MTS300 stem.

Many equipment variants were possible for purchasers of the AM-ATB. For example, Angle Lake sometimes used 32 hole Sun Metal Chinook rims with SunTour XC9000 hubs and a seven-speed Freehub. XC9000 derailleurs were also used. The tyres might be Continental Professional and the chain a Sedisport or DID Lanner, rather than the Shimano Uniglide used on the test bike.

The typical specification quoted in Alex Moulton Limited's colour leaflet for the AM-ATB differed in several ways from the Angle Lake specification quoted above. Rims were Araya Aero rather than Sun Metal (although Sun Metal were offered later). The Shimano crankset was fitted with bigger rings by Stronglight of France for higher gearing, thus offering a typical range of 26 to 90". A Madison saddle was fitted, and slightly narrower 580 mm (22.8") alloy handlebars were suggested. The seat pillar was the same as for the AM road bikes, rather than an extra-long version. And plastic mudguards (fenders) by Spencer were an optional extra.

A later specification, issued with AM News in spring 1989, recommended a similar transmission to that used on the tested Angle Lake bike. For those concerned about the derailleur fouling rocks and vegetation off-road, the specification pointed out that with the Shimano 600 rear mechanism engaging the 12 tooth sprocket, the chain was 190 mm (7$^{1}/_{2}$") clear of the ground.

The same AM News recommended a 1.5 mm (0.06") stainless steel

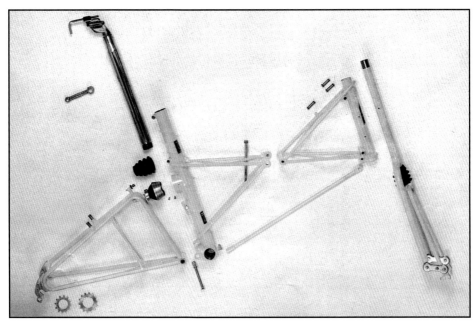

AM-ATB frame kit.

spacer to stop the cam-action quick-release binder bolt distorting the seat pillar. It also advised that rubber knee guards were available as an optional extra to fit over the ends of the kingpin.

The brakes used on all versions of the AM-ATB were a mixture. At the rear was a U-brake, typically the Deore XT; at the front a side-pull calliper, such as the Dia-Compe MX.

The U-brake was a popular, heavy-duty, centre-pull brake, now out of fashion. It fixed to a pair of brazed-on bosses, typically (in the case of a rear brake) on the underside of the chain stays. As Mountain Bike Action put it, they were "wedged into a space that acts like a magnet for mud". But in 1988 U-brakes were fitted to virtually all production mountain bikes. In this respect the AM-ATB was merely following convention – and at least its U-brake was sensibly positioned **above** the seat stays.

However, the front BMX-style calliper was a less conventional choice. Hilary Stone, writing in Bicycle, August 1988, realised that "fitting a brazed-on cantilever, U-brake or Roller Cam brake to the unsprung part of the fork [the stirrup] would be impossible given its present design". But he argued that "surely it would have been desirable to have increased the diameter of the unsprung blades even at the cost of increased unsprung weight" so that "a decent brake could then be provided".

The Launch

The AM-ATB was announced in the March 1988 issue of AM News and made its debut in Seattle the following month. The European launch took place in London at 6.00 p.m. on Monday 20 June 1988 at 40-42 Clapham High Street, the headquarters of the then flourishing chain of cycle shops, Bike UK.

The press release discussed the philosophy of bicycle suspension:

"Whereas the benefits sought by the use of suspension in reducing the shocks transmitted, and improving the dynamic behaviour of the vehicle over the ground, are common objectives, the solutions will be different for each type of vehicle. This is particularly the case of the bicycle in which the live load (rider) may weigh as much as ten times that of the complete vehicle, plus the fact that the propulsive torque fluctuations are great; and at a frequency right in the range of resonance typically used in other types of vehicle.

"Therefore the unique solution used on the AM bicycles is to provide front and rear wheel suspension tuned in response to isolate the frequencies to which the human body is most sensitive, so that the benefits can be enjoyed under all conditions of riding, even including standing on the pedals. The damping at the front, of the coulomb type, is adjustable; and it is mechanically capable of being locked up. We have never heard of any user having once tried this continuing so to do!

"... The most significant part perhaps of the Moulton concept of bicycle suspension is the essential use of a frame construction and wheel size which are inherently much stiffer than the conventional. Thus the eternal compromise between shock transmitted and lack of rigidity of the conventional bicycle is not required on the AM, which gives a feeling of being solid ('like riding on an I-beam') yet insulated, even though the tyres may be inflated for low rolling resistance."

Reports And Reviews

One of the first reports of the AM-ATB outside the trade press appeared in the equipment news section of Cycling Weekly, a month after the UK launch. However, it added nothing to the information in Alex's brochure.

Of more interest was an illustrated review in the August/September edition of Making Tracks, a pioneering UK magazine for off-road riders. Editor Geoff Apps wrote: "Suspension has to be the way forward for off-road bicycles". Geoff tested the Swift Cycles version of the AM-ATB on an off-road jaunt of about 5 miles (8 km). He commented that "performance is excellent in these conditions. The Moulton comes into its own on those dried-out bumpy bridleways – it smoothes out the ride – and is very forgiving if you overcook on cornering."

Hilton Holloway echoed Geoff's conclusions in the September 1988 edition of Bicycle. He was not convinced of its advantages in extreme conditions of competition, but found it a capable off-road machine and a good road bike. He recommended it to riders who enjoy firm tracks, bridleways and need the touring and commuting potential.

By this time a comprehensive review by Doug Roosa had appeared in Bicycle Guide. Alex and three of the Angle Lake team had met Doug and a colleague to test the AM-ATB on a single-track forest trail deep in Mount Rainier National Park, south of Seattle. Alex outlined his approach to creating a machine with improved ride quality:

"I simply make an ever-so-stiff structure and the unsprung parts that hold the wheels are ever so stiff. Then I allow the bloody thing to articulate by a known significant amount. That eliminates all the guesswork on my part, and it becomes an engineering problem rather than artistic. The only artistic decision I make is what colour to paint it."

Doug noted, "The bike floats serenely over washboard trails that excite an unsuspended bike into an arm-numbing frenzy." He added that "the suspension's most endearing feature may be its ability to let the wheels follow every undulation of the trail, keeping the rear wheel biting for traction and the front one in line."

The rider needed to learn to work with the suspension. Compared with a standard mountain bike, the Moulton took "more lean and less steer to navigate." The smaller wheels fell deeper into ruts but since they were lighter and had lower inertia, they could be accelerated and steered more quickly around obstacles that larger wheels might be unable to avoid.

The demonstration bike weighed 30lb 15oz (14 kg) but rode "lighter than it measures because of the suspension and small wheels". While unsure how well the small wheels would cope with really fast rough riding, Doug declared that the AM-ATB was "a joy to ride".

In Bicycle Guide's review of the new bikes of 1988, the AM-ATB was given an honourable mention. "A mountain bike with suspension? You bet, and it works ... Expensive and hard to find, a Moulton nevertheless stretches our imagination of what a bike can be."

The October 1988 edition of Blueprint, the British architectural design magazine, carried a feature by Sebastian Conran describing Alex as "the cycling world's answer to Enzo Ferrari". Of the AM-ATB it said, "the almost pedantically well-detailed machine offers the off-the-beaten-track cyclist the same comfort and stability enjoyed by a motocross motorcyclist."

Another reviewer that autumn was Mike Burrows, who tested the AM-ATB for New Cyclist. He noted that "the idea of an ATB with suspension is a logical one and there have been one or two not especially successful ones before. The use of small wheels 'off road' is less logical but does have its advantages as well as some definite disadvantages."

He found the suspension "quite excellent on hard surfaces, allowing you to maintain control and pedal smoothly on anything from cobbles to short turf and hard-baked mud." However, he found the AM less good on soft ground. Mike was particularly concerned about the fact that the smaller wheel could drop "into a smaller home" than a conventional wheel. Paradoxically, while he was riding his conventional mountain bike in pursuit of Andy Pegg on the AM-ATB, he trapped his **26"** front wheel in a hole, suffering broken bones and a bent bike. Alex, in a lighthearted response published alongside the Burrows critique, asked whether Andy avoided this fate by using the AM-ATB's "designed nimbleness".

Nonetheless, the combination of smaller wheels and lower mounted rear derailleur mechanism led Mike Burrows to conclude that the AM-ATB was "clearly not a candidate for off-road racing", although it was still "very enjoyable and competent on most terrain". It performed best on the streets. "Powering through potholes, cobbles and over the odd kerb with ease, its fat tyres keeping you clear of most of the broken glass. Definitely a child of the city."

Alex responded that he did not know whether the AM-ATB was suitable for off-road racing, but that no doubt some owner would try. He had designed the bike "to be exactly analogous to the Range Rover, which in the words of my American auto friends is 'the top of the heap'."

Biopace

Mike disliked the test bike's Shimano Biopace eccentric chainwheels, designed to vary the effective gearing through each rotation of the cranks. He felt that this did not encourage "the smooth pedalling necessary for a bike with suspension".

Biopace was intended to smooth out the problems of converting the up and down movement of the legs into rotation of the chainwheel. This was done by varying the diameter of the chainwheel to slow down leg speed at the top and bottom of the pedal stroke, and accelerate it through the power stroke. It was a refinement of the old idea of elliptical chainwheels.

Some very knowledgeable commentators stated that Biopace gave a slight improvement, and Shimano themselves stated that "computer calculations disclose that Biopace actually reduces energy demands up to 3% for a given distance". However, the orientation of Biopace rings relative to the cranks was seriously out of phase with the generally accepted optimum for asymmetric chainwheels. Refixing Biopace chainrings one bolt hole anti-clockwise from the factory-fitted position (72 degrees retarded) works much better for many people. (If you do this, it is wise carefully to remove the chain-catcher peg from the outer ring, lest it catches in a shoe lace or trouser leg!) This reorientation has the advantage that it gives maximum effective chainwheel diameter during the power stroke, and minimum effective diameter during the dead-spots, when the cranks are roughly vertical.

As the idea went out of style the eccentricity of the Biopace rings was first reduced, then abandoned. Indeed, "Biopacing" entered the cycling vocabulary as a term describing the undesirable bouncing of a rear suspension system induced by hard pedalling.

Braking

Mike also complained about the performance of the AM-ATB's front brake. The test bike, a Bike UK version, was fitted with a Weinmann 890 deep-reach sidepull calliper which "was very good for cleaning the rim, but had little effect on velocity". He wanted to try a Sturmey-Archer Elite hub brake instead.

A hub brake has a torque reaction arm which has to be bolted to the chainstay or fork blade. Alex pointed out that the brake's torque reaction would have to be taken out symmetrically to the calliper brake anchorage point, a cumbersome thing to do, because it necessitated a very long, specially-made torque arm. Otherwise there would be a tendency for the wheel to be pulled to one side, affecting handling and possibly eventually bending or fracturing the stirrup.

But why was there a problem with the calliper brake? A rim brake's performance is virtually independent of wheel size. Indeed, if no other factors were involved and if such brakes acted on the running surface of the tyre (as plunger or spoon brakes used to) wheel diameter should make no difference at all. This is because there would be no effective leverage between the tyre's point of contact with the road, and its point of contact with the brake. In reality though, the rim brake's braking surface is set in **slightly** from the outer diameter of the tyre. Therefore, for a given tyre cross-section, a change in wheel diameter will slightly affect the effectiveness of the brake.

This is indicated by the lever ratio, also known as the velocity ratio. Lever ratio is defined as d/D, where d is the braking surface diameter, and D is the outer diameter of the tyre. The lever ratio for a 26 x 2.125" tyre would typically be 559 mm/667 mm = 0.84, whereas for a 20 x 2.125" tyre it would be about 406 mm/514 mm = 0.79. The ratio of these two ratios is 1.06:1. Therefore the bigger wheel has a slight braking leverage advantage of about 6%. However, a difference of 6% would be barely discernible and some other factor must explain the disappointment with front wheel braking expressed by Mike Burrows, Hilary Stone and others.

Assuming that the brake blocks were of good quality, the problem may be ascribable to flexing of the brake calliper. Another possibility is cable sheath compression and stretch in the rather long brake cables.

Mike mentioned in his review that he was experimenting with "a one-piece rear brake cable which gives a smoother action". But there is no obvious logical reason why a one-piece cable of a given construction should be superior to a two-piece cable of the same type, as there can be no loss via the turnbuckle unless it rubs against the frame.

As for Mike's suggestion that a hub brake be used, this has much to commend it. As Alex pointed out in his reply, "a given size of hub brake ... will give better braking when fitted to a smaller rather than a larger wheel". This is because the lever ratio increases as the ratio of brake drum diameter to wheel diameter increases. Hence whereas a 90 mm drum brake in a 26" wheel would typically give a lever ratio of 90/667 = 0.13, the 20" wheel would give 90/514 = 0.18. The ratio of these two ratios is 1:1.38. Therefore the 20" wheel would have a massive braking advantage of 38%.

Broadsheet Coverage

Both The Independent and The Times featured the AM-ATB in articles comparing various portable bicycles. The Times's piece appeared in November 1988 and was written by Deyan Sudjic. He quoted fashion and bicycle designer Tom Gilbey on the AM-ATB: "It feels very sturdy, but it's amazingly light, and it has perfect balance. I sat on it and felt completely at home right away. It's very comfortable, has definite gears and the suspension is unbelievable."

The Independent's article by Peter Greene was published the following April. He queried the price and was told by Alex: "I'm making Ferraris ... There is always a market for a manifestly excellent thing executed in an excellent way."

A Long-Term Review

The Summer 1989 issue of The Moultoneer carried a letter from 19 year old George French, an avid mountain biker. By that time he had ridden 1,500 miles (2,400 km) on his AM-ATB.

He admitted to initial doubts about small wheels. However, at the UK national championships his doubts were dispelled by the contrast between his experience and that of a rider of a 26" wheel machine. Both were thrown from their bikes by "an unobtrusive little hollow". However, George was able to jump clear and was uninjured; the other rider came down heavily and broke two ribs.

George concluded that the suspension and the lack of a conventional top tube were both helpful in this situation. He felt that the suspension "probably helps ... by delaying the inevitable dive over the handlebars and giving the rider time to plan his landing". He added that he had now been over the handlebars at least a dozen times without even bruising himself. Most times he had been able to land on his feet.

The "vastly superior" 20" wheels were praised by George for their greater strength. He had damaged only one rim, an extra light one subjected to a head-on impact at more than 20 mph (33 kph). He said that the smaller rim handled far better than the 20" with no trade-off in performance. In comparison "riding with 26 inch seems like riding with your front wheel stuck in some tramlines."

The suspension came in for special praise. George noted that, in an advertising stunt, a Ridgeback ATB had been ridden off the roof of a Volvo estate car. "When the bike landed the frame snapped and the wheels buckled out of all recognition." George had performed a similar stunt on the AM-ATB – "the bike was completely unscathed". But apart from such stunts, he confirmed that the suspension isolated the frame and rider from "a lot of vibrational bumps on and off road".

SR, SO And Freewheel Versions

In January 1989 Alex Moulton Limited issued a new price list which mentioned two fully assembled AM-ATBs – the SR (SunTour) model at £1,085 and the SO (Shimano) at £1,295. Carriers for the AM-ATB were listed, the front at £50.95, the rear at £68.95. (Frame skins for AM-ATBs were marketed by Angle Lake Cyclery in the USA but were not catalogued in the UK.)

The 1990 Freewheel mail order catalogue featured that company's own version of the AM-ATB. The headset, hubs, chainset, freewheel and gear levers were all from the Shimano LX range. The triple Superglide chainset had 28, 38 and 48 tooth rings, and the seven-speed freewheel had 13-24 tooth sprockets. The gear range as catalogued was therefore a low 23 to 74", accessed via LX Rapid Action STI levers.

Pedals were Shimano Exage. As usual a Shimano U-brake was fitted to the rear wheel, but the front brake was an Odyssey Pit Bull centre-pull. The brake levers were Shimano. The saddle was a Madison G11 and the handlebar grips were Madison Airgrips – not surprising, as Freewheel were the Madison distributors.

Freewheel's AM-ATB became available in May 1990 and cost £1,295. Despite this, it was **not** their most expensive mail order bike.

More American Views

The following month the whole subject of bicycle suspension was discussed in the American magazine Mountain and City Biking. The reporter stated that "The originality award for suspension goes to the Alex Moulton ATB ... probably the most sophisticated and well thought out suspension bike available."

The August issue of the same magazine gave a detailed review of the bike. It concluded that it was excellent for use on harder surfaces and green lanes, but less well suited to really tough mountain bike riding.

The following July Kaye Krapohl reported in Automobile magazine on a year with an AM-ATB. Kaye was a former Michigan cyclo-cross champion, a pro and amateur racer and 300 mile (480 km) a week cyclist. The bike was described as "delightfully, supremely portable" and "unbeatable downhill". However, on soft ground it was easily overtaken by conventional mountain bikes.

Kaye also found that, "Even when the shock absorbers are adjusted to their stiffest setting, downward thrust on the pedal is absorbed by suspension deflection instead of being turned into crank torque." Nonetheless, the AM-ATB was "a wonderful around-town model". "It is beautifully handcrafted, light, manoeuvrable, and enticing because of its size, wide tyres and shocks [shock absorbers]."

Dutch Acclaim

In 1990 the AM-ATB received a St Valentine's day surprise from the Dutch bicycle industry. On 14 February the bike was given an honourable mention certificate in the Bicycle of the Year awards.

The certificate noted that the ATB was imported by Wim Kok and stated that it was: "A bike of good quality with solid construction and original design. A well-considered concept with front and rear suspension."

The previous May had seen the publication of a three page illustrated review of the AM-ATB in the Dutch magazine Fiets (Bike). The author was Guus van de Beek, who pointed out that "With a Moulton you don't so much buy a bike, more the spirit of the builder, a man with unconventional but absolutely rational concepts".

Among the good points Guus noted about the AM-ATB were its "very great comfort" and "unique handling quality combining stability with great manoeuvrability". He also highlighted its portability, and its very rigid but separable frame. On the debit side his criticisms, apart from the cost, included "energy loss through the wheel springing" when riding hard out of the saddle, the possibility of the derailleur "picking up twigs", and, in the context of the adjustable frame angles, "some understeer characteristic when in the steepest fork position". He also pointed out that the smaller wheels did not roll so well over soft ground.

Guus tested the AM-ATB on a 3,300 metre (2 mile) course with some "substantial, steep humps in it, a little asphalt and a small amount of loose sand". He also rode the course on his 26" wheel Giant mountain bike and timed the two rides, making adjustments in the light of heartbeat monitoring. His conclusion was that on this course the AM-ATB was about 2.6% slower. While pointing out that this was significant in competitive riding, he questioned whether it was of any importance for ordinary leisure riding.

The AM-ATBs imported into the Netherlands by Wim Kok Better Bikes of Utrecht were fitted with Dutch Vredestein BMX tyres. The frame kit sold for 2,500 guilders and fully-assembled bikes cost upwards of 4,500 guilders, depending on specification. The frame and fork were guaranteed for five years.

Antipodean Customisations

By the summer of 1990 MBC member Stephen Parry of Perth, Western Australia had considerably customised his ATB. His aims were twofold: to reduce rolling resistance by using narrower tyres, and to use a complete Campagnolo group set "rather than a hotchpotch of components". He had been put off from using the wider section standard BMX tyres by reports of the Raleigh RSW16 of the 1960s. (Riding this machine, with its 16 x 2" low pressure balloon tyres, was once described as "like waltzing in gumboots".) He also had less need for the greater flotation offered by the wider tyre, because he intended to use the bike mainly on hard surfaces and the occasional gravel road – not for serious off-road use.

To meet his first objective he used Sun Metal 20 x 1.125" rims (ISO code 32-451, a narrow version of the British E5J rim). For the second, he adopted the Campagnolo Chorus group set. The Sun Metal rims are about 30 mm ($1\frac{1}{4}$") larger in radius than the standard recommended AM-ATB rim, and therefore allowed the 50 mm (2") deep Chorus brakes to reach the rims. However, it was necessary to braze on a rear brake bridge in place of the U-brake bosses.

The transmission consisted of 39 and 54 tooth Campagnolo chainrings in conjunction with a SunTour Winner 12-28 tooth freewheel. This gave gears of 28 to 90". The Chorus gear levers were mounted on a small demount bracket which Stephen made from stainless steel and attached to the top carrier mount via an 8 mm stainless socket-head bolt.

The original SR Laprade seat pillar was removed from the stainless steel outer seat post and replaced by the Campagnolo Aero pillar. The ensemble was completed by special front and rear bags made locally.

Stephen bought a second AM-ATB and through the May/June 1991 edition of The Moultoneer passed on two tips to fellow owners. The first was that the alloy locking ring securing the removable tie bar kept working loose during a ride. Mere finger pressure was insufficient to lock the ring for long. He therefore suggested cutting two flats on the ring so that it could be gently tightened by a small adjustable spanner. Alex replied that the size of the locking ring had been increased to 25 mm (1") so that adequate tightening could be carried out without using a tool.

Stephen's second suggestion was that a lock-nut be provided for the bolt of the adjustable rear suspension cam. This would prevent a slight movement in the thread which caused an occasional "clunk" on mounting the bike. Alex replied that a small diameter lock-nut was now fitted for this purpose.

The March/April 1992 edition of The Moultoneer carried an illustrated article by Stephen entitled "The Ultimate Moulton?" It was not clear whether this described his second AM-ATB or further modifications to his original machine, but the bike shown incorporated the rear brake bridge modification referred to above. It was also fitted with Scott triathlon-style handlebars.

Stephen gave three reasons for describing this ATB as the ultimate Moulton. Firstly, choice of wheels and tyres. With the 20 x 1.125" Sun Metal rims he could fit anything from 20 x 1.125" IRC Roadlite EX 100 psi (6.8 atm) road tyres to 20 x 1.375" knobbly BMX tyres. Alternatively, with the standard 20 x 1.5" AM-ATB recommended rims he could use tyre widths from 1.5 to 2.125", including the most commonly available BMX formats. His second reason was the much lower cost of tyres – as little as $9 Aus each when bought 50 at a time, as compared with the Moulton 17 x $1^1/_4$" tyre which then cost Aus $30 or more each. He admitted, however, that the 20" tyres gave poorer acceleration.

Stephen's final reason was the ease of achieving a good range of touring gears, say from 30 to 88". All that was necessary was to fit a standard road racing group set, such as a 12-28 tooth seven-speed freewheel with 42 and 53 tooth double chainwheels. As he put it, "No messing about with tiny cogs or massive chainrings, and all available from your local bike shop! Bliss."

Another antipodean customisation of AM-ATBs was commissioned by Geoff Pratt, an Australian from New South Wales. He and his Cornish partner Gwyneth, better known as Ginny, were keen travellers, and sought the ideal form of transport for exploring parts of the world such as India and Asia. Having used motor cycles, public transport and Shanks's pony, they concluded that "bicycles seemed a good solution". Geoff subsequently described their carefully chosen mounts in Australian Cyclist magazine.

The couple "wanted to wimp it on mountain ranges and through monsoons". This meant they needed bicycles that could fit into "the sardine-tin confines of the local Indian bus". They decided against using their existing diamond-frame touring bikes because they were too large, and had questionable solidity and stability on poor road surfaces. Conventional mountain bikes were rejected as being "slow on the tar, heavy and still physically large".

Geoff and Ginny sought advice from Noel McFarlane, owner of Sydney's Bike Warehouse. He had first-hand experience of cycling across India, including frame failure of a conventional tourist bike. As Geoff wrote later, "He stressed the importance of ride comfort for any third-world travel and recommended that we look at Moulton ATBs as the bike traveller's choice."

The twosome did just that and ended up purchasing a pair of AM-ATBs that were customised for touring India. The machines were assembled by Adrian Lancaster of Calypso Cycles, who also selected the componentry. Geoff specified that it should be of good quality and easily repairable. The front brake and pedals were Shimano 105, the crankset Shimano

600, the headset Tange Seiki and the saddle an Avocet Gel.

For lower rolling resistance and lighter weight, 20 x 1^3/$_8$" tyres were fitted on Sun Metal Mistral E5J format rims, the front wheel being radially spoked. The main drawback with this tyre format was the very close clearance between the tyre and the crown of the sprung front fork. Geoff suspected that they might need to fit tyre-savers (flint catchers) to prevent stones jamming between the tyre and fork crown.

As noted in Chapter 1, for his 1970 ride from England to Australia, Colin Martin chose a Fichtel-Sachs Torpedo Duomatic two-speed coaster hub. Geoff made a choice from the same stable – the Sachs Torpedo Pentasport. As he put it, "This amazing piece of hubbery has five gears and a back-pedal brake!"

With a 52 tooth chainring and a 19 tooth rear sprocket, the Pentasport provided gears of 37, 43, 55, 70 and 82". The couple each intended to carry a smaller spare cog which could be substituted if they ended up doing a lot of riding on the flat. Although the gearing was a compromise, it was enclosed and so was the rear brake. Geoff thought that the Pentasport hub was probably "lighter than the alternative combination of hub, cluster, changer, derailleur, brake and brake lever."

The lack of mudguards, combined with the thinner tyres and absence of derailleurs gave Geoff and Ginny's AM-ATBs a clean, lean and mean appearance. Geoff praised the responsive steering and seemed pleasantly surprised by the effectiveness of the suspension. He wrote: "You don't even feel the bumps! Although I saw the portability as its main asset, I can now see why Noel praised the suspension."

When he wrote his article for Australian Cyclist, Geoff was still saving for his trip to India. He concluded, "They're great bikes, ideally suited to our purpose. It's just that we're on bread and water until the map on the wall becomes a reality!" Two and a half years of Australian recession later (May 1993) Geoff and Ginny were still saving for the Indian trip. However, they were shortly to embark on a tour around Bali. Having had time to get used to the customized ATBs, Geoff reported, "We've found them very practical, well-made and sturdy machines."

Another Hub Gear Conversion

P. A. Evans of Sutton, Surrey rode a conventional ATB for eight years before switching to an AM-ATB. Although he considered the Moulton inferior "when the mud is thick and the going rough", he thought it "ideal for mixed on and off-road outings."

However, he found wheel grip poor on muddy slopes and advised against using tyres with a central ridge for off-road riding. He had used 1.5" tyres to maximise clearance around the wheels and reduce the risk of mud clogging. The Mitsuboshi Silver Star was the best 1.5" tyre he could obtain, but he found it gave little grip in thick mud. The sidewalls also punctured easily.

To reduce the problem of mud being transferred from the rear wheel to the chain and thence to the rest of the transmission, Mr Evans fitted a Sachs Pentacross five-speed hub gear and hub brake. This enabled the "rear brake clutter" to be removed altogether. As the hub gear sprocket was further out from the wheel than the larger derailleur cogs, the chainline was well away from the tyre. This allowed him to revert to a wider rear tyre, a 2.1" Mongoose Bump with a recommended pressure of 65 psi (4.42 atm) – a knobbly tyre which bore the inscrutable legend "For optimum traction use on front only".

To obtain greater clearance for the front wheel, Mr Evans removed the U-brake and fitted a side-pull calliper with arms that curved well clear of the tyre. This enabled him to fit a 1.8" Mongoose tyre, recommended pressure 40 psi (2.72 atm). However, he still found a tendency for the front wheel to jam when he rode through sticky thick mud and leaves.

Mr Evans used a triple chainwheel with 26, 36 and 50 teeth to drive the 18 tooth sprocket of his Pentacross hub: a short-arm rear derailleur mechanism took up the chain slack. This configuration gave him gears of 18, 21, 27, 35 and 41" with the smallest chainring; 25, 30, 38, 49 and 57" with the middle ring; and 35, 41, 53, 67 and 79" with the largest – a total range of 4.4:1.

He described his AM-ATB modifications in the September/October 1992 edition of The Moultoneer, and commented that the ratio of the smallest chainwheel to the hub gear sprocket was 1.4:1, well under the 2:1 minimum recommended by Sturmey-Archer and by Chicken and Sons, the then Sachs importers. I replied that the 2:1 ratio applied to 26-28" wheels, and that smaller wheels are subject to proportionately lower torque. The equivalent factor for a 20" wheel should indeed be about 1.4:1.

Although the Pentacross hub and the wider tyres added some weight to the AM-ATB, Mr Evans felt it was "well worth it for the better grip, brake control and freedom from mud that results." He found that the cable stops provided with the hub and on the bike's frame were fairly easily adapted to allow frame separability to be maintained. The reaction arm of the hub brake needed to be rotated slightly to fit the frame.

Another Third World Tourer

Leigh Wade, then of Paynesville, Minnesota, bought a touring version of the AM-ATB marketed by Angle Lake Cyclery as the "Third World Tourer". His machine was built with a SunTour Dura-Ace cassette hub, the smallest sprockets being an AM two-cog cluster with 10 and 11 teeth. With a 24/33/44 tooth triple chainwheel, the transmission offered gears of 19 to 88".

During 1990 he experimented with a Breeze Cheater fairing, which fitted to the handlebars and fork. He found it satisfactory, with little detrimental effect on the handling. However, he also owned an AM14 with the frame-mounted AM-Zzipper fairing which worked better. (See Chapter 5.) He decided in the end that the Cheater was too much trouble for serious touring.

In comparing the AM-ATB with the AM14, Leigh found the biggest difference was in ride quality:

"The AM14 rides like a sports car, and the ATB rides more like a large sedan (while a normal bicycle rides like a horse-drawn carriage on this scale of comparison). The AM-ATB hybrid with the 1.5" slick tyres has to be the **most comfortable** bike ever made. To me, the ATB also feels more stable on descents (feeling more like a motor cycle than a normal bike)."

He concluded that the AM-ATB was the better machine for loaded touring, especially on rougher terrain or bad roads.

Phase-out

As late as February 1993 the AM-ATB was listed by Bicycling magazine as available from Angle Lake Cyclery for $2,700. In Bicycling's listing of 42 mountain bikes with dual suspension, there were 16 more expensive than the AM: the dearest was a Boulder Defiant TI Ultralite costing $5,999, more than twice as much.

In the UK the AM-ATB had been deleted from Alex's range by April 1992. Pioneering of mountain bike suspension was not his original intention. But although most mountain bikers know nothing of the AM-ATB, it was certainly influential.

As the US magazine Outside put it in April 1991, Alex Moulton's ATB marked the beginning of the mountain bike suspension era. Despite the AM-ATB being "apparently too quaint a design for the radical American mountain biker ... its suspension system altered bicycle design and thinking here in the colonies ..." Three years later history had been rewritten. Mountain Bike Action's March 1994 comprehensive pictorial history of mountain bike suspension made no reference whatsoever to the AM-ATB.

Chapter 8
MOULTON APB
1991-1994

Specifications – Reviews – Customisations

The first hint of the Moulton APB came in a newspaper article on portable bicycles in April 1989. Journalist Peter Greene, writing in The Independent, stated that the Moulton concept "need not lead to a pricey cycle" and that "Moulton might still succeed in challenging old Starley's monopoly in good bicycle design".

Almost a year and a half later Alex Moulton indulged in a little kite flying in the September 1990 edition of the trade magazine Cycle Industry. Interviewed about the Moulton bicycle, he said:

"I don't put down the idea of somebody being interested in making a lower-priced one, lower-cost one, under licence. But certainly what I would never do again is lose control of it. Much better to have absolute control over a thing in small quantities."

In the following month's issue he added:

"It would certainly be possible to make a less sophisticated version of the Moulton bicycle yet containing all the essential features. Of course it would be. And if anyone were interested in doing that, obviously I'd like to talk to them. But certainly I wouldn't want to do it. It's a bore to do everything again in life, isn't it?"

Nine months later it became evident that negotiations were under way. In The Times of 11 June 1991 Callum Murray ended an article about the newly launched AM-GT with this clue: "At the age of 71, Dr Moulton confides that he is once again talking to a large bicycle manufacturer about granting a licence to produce one of his designs. 'Maybe my time has come again,' he says."

Four days later an article in the Financial Times weekend supplement confirmed that something was afoot. In a major piece on Alex's life-style and design philosophy, Christian Tyler noted that, "Moulton believes that the reputation of small wheels can be restored and is working on a cheaper, high-volume model". And the summer 1991 issue of Transport Innovation quoted Alex as saying that in due time a licensing agreement with a large manufacturer might be re-established.

By autumn 1991 a few avid Moulton-watchers deduced that Alex had granted a licence to W. R. Pashley Limited of Stratford-upon-Avon, Warwickshire – coincidentally the town where he was born.

In the September/October 1991 issue of New Cyclist, without giving away any other information, Pashley's then managing director, Tim Pashley, described Alex as "the most influential designer in recent years". About the same time it was rumoured that jigs designed for manufacturing parts of the AM-ATB had been moved to Pashleys. Conjecture therefore grew that the new machine would be closely related to the ATB. This was confirmed in December 1991's issue of Bicycle when Alex told Lucy Taylor, "We shall see some interesting developments from the [Moulton] mountain bike and I can't tell you any more about that."

Early in 1992 Alex agreed that the Moulton Bicycle Club's magazine, The Moultoneer, would be the first in the world to announce the new machine. A loose note was therefore included in the January/February edition revealing that the new bike was called the APB, short for All Purpose Bicycle; that it would have 20" wheels; that it would indeed be made by Pashleys; and that it would be displayed on the Swift Cycles stand at the Cyclex exhibition to be held at Olympia, London from 5-8 March 1992.

The note was dated 11 February and six days later a press release announced that the All Purpose Bicycle was, "As its name suggests, ... for the rider in city, town or country; on good roads or bad."

W. R. Pashley Limited

The choice of W. R. Pashley Limited to make the APB was an interesting one. The company was established in Birmingham during the 1920s by William Rathbone Pashley. "Rath" had been a despatch rider in France during the First World War. His son Richard further developed the company's product range and took a particular interest in tricycle design. Tim Pashley, managing director at the time of the APB launch, is Richard's son. Richard is still on the board of the company, and on the day I visited the factory, he paid a routine visit, arriving on an AM2.

The firm's traditional marketing philosophy was neatly summarised by Tim: "Pashley cycles are distinctive, hand-made, constructed from steel and painted in conservative colours. We don't make BMX, mountain bikes or sports cycles; our speciality is the somewhat unusual – the niche market."

By producing a whole portfolio of niche market products, Pashley are able to organise their production more effectively than most firms

The headquarters of W.R. Pashley Limited, Masons Road, Stratford-upon-Avon. Photo by Tony Hadland.

APB frames at the Pashley factory. Photo by Tony Hadland.

producing a single unusual product. Spreading production over a number of cycle types enables the company to maintain a stable workforce. Employees tend to stay with the firm a long time – 25 years is not unknown.

The Pashley range includes traditional-style British roadsters with hub gears, hub or roller-lever brakes, full chaincases and wicker shopping baskets. There are also tricycles, including a traditional toy trike, and adult small-wheeled shopping and child-carrying tricycles; a tandem; a traditional delivery bike, with small front wheel and huge, frame-fixed front carrier; Post Office delivery bikes; and unicycles. Annual production in 1990 was 12,000 machines, of which half were exported. Many 28" wheel roadsters are shipped to developing countries, such as Nigeria, Afghanistan and Zaire, often as part of aid packages. Export sales account for about a third of Pashley's £2 million annual turnover. Surprisingly, one of the best-selling lines is the unicycle, of which about 1,000 are made each year.

(Incidentally, for the benefit of overseas readers, although Pashley and Moulton both have works near a River Avon, they are not on the same river. Stratford-upon-Avon is on the Warwickshire Avon, while Bradford-on-Avon is on the Wiltshire Avon. The word Avon derives from the old Celtic word for water or stream, as in the modern Welsh word "afon".)

The APB's Hairpin Frame

There had been some conjecture that, for cheapness, the licence-built Moulton would abandon the separable spaceframe concept – perhaps in favour of a single main beam as used in the Moultons of the 1960s and 70s. That, however, would have been backtracking – somewhat out of character for Alex. In reality the APB is a direct descendant of the AM-ATB. Indeed, it is what the AM-ATB was originally intended to be – a rationalised AM, rather than a small-wheeled mountain bike. In design terms, the APB "child" was "father" to the ATB "man".

Although the APB's key frame dimensions are the same as the ATB's, and the same jigs are used, the APB's frame differs in several ways. Apart from the steerer tube, the frame is not of Reynolds 531 tubing, nor are the drop-outs stainless steel. Instead the tubing is high-tensile ERW (Electrical Resistance Welded) steel, and the infill members of the frame's crossed hairpin girders and the X brace in the rear triangle are $^3/_{16}$" (4.8 mm) high tensile round steel bar rather than $^1/_4$" (6.4 mm) tubing.

Also, the seat tube, complete with suspension mountings and bottom bracket, is lower relative to the "hairpin" girders to give a bottom bracket height more suitable for road use, rather than the extra clearance provided for the off-road AM-ATB. Actual bottom bracket height and frame angles when loaded will depend on rider weight, front suspension adjustment, and tyre profile, format and inflation pressure. However, in the **unladen** state a typical APB with no pre-loading

Building an APB frame. Photo by Tony Hadland.

of the front suspension, has a bottom bracket height (to the centre of the crank axle) of about $11^7/_8$" (302 mm). Although about an inch (25 mm) lower than the AM-ATB's, this is still some $3/_8$" (10 mm) higher than the 17" wheel AM's bottom bracket and may be further reduced in future production. The frame angles, about 70 degrees, cannot be varied by adjusting the rear suspension cam, and there is no bellows around the rubber Monosphere, which is held in its mounting by four self-tapping screws, rather than two.

Instead of the ATB's separate tie between the bottom of the seat tube and the base of the head tube, the APB has the more user-friendly AM-style hook joint tie.

According to figures published in technical reviews, the APB's main frame, at 7lb 10oz (3.46 kg) including rear triangle, is 4oz (110 g) **lighter** than the ATB's. However, the APB's front fork, at 3lb $12^1/_2$ oz (1.72 kg) is $5^1/_2$ oz (155 g) heavier than its predecessors, because it has a heavy duty stirrup to take cantilever brakes. On the basis of these figures the complete APB skeleton is only $1^1/_2$ oz (45 g) heavier than the ATB's.

As production proceeded the welding of the hairpins to the head and seat tubes was tidied up. Initially the joints were welded for their complete length, necessitating labour-intensive filing to achieve a passable appearance. Later, to minimise filing, the joint was welded only either side of the head/seat tube, a small gap being left between the curve of the hairpin and the tube. In 1994 appearance was further improved by tack welding the underside of the joint, and neatly infilling the top with braze.

Frame Fittings

Cable splitting for frame separation is by simple turnbuckles. These are a development of those first used on the AM14, and have a wider diameter barrel to accommodate an Allen-headed grub screw to anchor the cut end of the cable. This obviates silver-soldering a brass ferrule onto the cable, making for much easier cable replacement. The usual cable guides and stops are provided.

Some early APBs had integral rear derailleur hangers and all derailleur-geared APBs have a brazed-on fixing for the front derailleur mechanism, to allow for the steep angle made by the chain with the top of the chainwheel. Unlike the AM-ATB, full provision is made for cantilever brakes, except on the APB-3.

However, whereas Mike Burrows had questioned why anyone buying the AM-ATB would want **four** bottle mounting positions, some early purchasers of the APB were a little annoyed that they were offered **none**. It did not go unnoticed that some very much cheaper bicycles were fitted with bottle cage bosses. At the time of writing (June 1994) only the top of the range APB-16 has bottle cage mounts.

The APB-12

The original APB, later renamed (and hereafter referred to as) the APB-12, is supplied in black only, the finish being a matt electrostatic powder coat enamel. The unicrown unsprung front fork has the word Moulton down it in large silver capital letters. The same lettering is used on the forward face of the seat tube (but not on the early demonstrators, nor in the first catalogue). There is a small APB badge with white

lettering on a black background at the top of the seat tube facing forward. About 9" (225 mm) below this badge is a similar one showing the patent references and edged in red. The head tube bears the standard AM head badge.

The black frame finish is complemented by matching saddle, handlebars, stem, hand grips, brake levers, gear levers, cranks, chainwheel trouser guard, pedals and cables.

The APB-12. Photo courtesy of W.R. Pashley Limited.

Transmission

The APB-12 has a 12-speed Shimano SIS indexed derailleur system. The rear mechanism is a Tourney RD-TY20 (not the Deore EX shown in the first catalogue photographs) and both gear levers are basic SIS thumb-shifters. The front mechanism is a better quality Exage 300 suitable for the brazed-on fixing below the rear suspension cone mounting.

The multiple freewheel is a standard threaded-on six-speed unit with 13, 15, 17, 20, 24 & 28 tooth cogs. It is therefore considerably cheaper to replace than the customised blocks used on the 17" wheel AMs. The chain is a Shimano Uniglide. The early demonstrator APB-12s, as featured in the first catalogue and displayed at Cyclex '92, had a huge, gaudy, spoke protector. It looked like something off a 1970 Raleigh Chopper and mercifully was not fitted to production machines.

The chainset fitted to early APB-12s was a Stronglight 190 and had a pair of bolted-on silver-anodised alloy rings with 42 and 52 teeth. The spider and cranks were black plastic-coated steel. Later bikes have a cheaper, heavier all-steel Stronglight chainset with swaged-on (riveted) rings. The bottom bracket is an SKF sealed unit.

With the standard 1.75" tyres, this transmission system offers the following gears:

42T: 30, 35, 42, 50, 56, (64")
52T: (37), 43, 52, 61, 69, 80"

This is essentially a crossover configuration, giving an optimal upward sequence of 30, 35 (+17%), 42 (+20%) (shift to larger chainwheel), 52 (+24%), 61 (+18%), 69 (+13%), 80" (+15%). The range is a modest 2.67:1.

Wheels and Tyres

The APB-12's Rigida alloy wheel rims are of the same BMX format used on AM-ATBs, the USA 20 x 1.75" with ISO code 47-406. This can accommodate not only a 1.75" tyre (typical actual diameter 19.9" (505 mm)) but certain others, such as the 2.125", ISO code 54-406 (actual diameter typically 20.2" (514 mm)). BMX bikes commonly use the wider tyre on the front wheel, the narrower on the rear. Amber-walled (gumwall) 1.75" Arrow Cruiser tyres are fitted to the APB-12.

The hubs are alloy Union bolt-ons, laced to the rims by 36 x 13 gauge stainless steel spokes, arranged "three cross"; that is, each spoke crossing three others attached to the same flange of the hub. This makes for very strong wheels, arguably overbuilt. AM-ATBs' wheels typically had thinner 14 gauge spokes and sometimes the weaker but slightly lighter radial spoking pattern for the front wheel. However, the APB 12's pair of wheels is only $1\frac{1}{2}$ oz (43 g) heavier than the typical USA specification AM-ATB's wheels with Sun Metal M20 rims and Shimano Deore XT hubs. The APB's rear wheel at 3lb $14\frac{1}{2}$ oz (1.77 kg) is a little lighter than the ATB's, whereas at 3lb 12oz (1.71 kg) the APB's front wheel is slightly heavier.

Brakes

The APB-12 was the first Moulton to be marketed factory-fitted with cantilever brakes. When replying to Mike Burrows' critique of the AM-ATB in New Cyclist Alex had commented that "cantilevers seem to me to stick out and catch in things". For the APB-12 basic Shimano Exage Trail SLR "low profile" cantilevers were adopted which minimise this problem. These are operated via matching plastic levers, Shimano type 70GS.

Other Components

The demonstration bikes shown at Cyclex and illustrated in the catalogue had a seat pillar similar to that used on other AMs. However, the production bikes have a 420 mm (16¹/₂") chromed steel seat pillar with a Brooks-style saddle clip. This specially-made pillar is presumably the same diameter as the AM's, 35 mm (1.38"), before plating but ends up 0.2 mm wider afterwards. The top is necked down and fitted with a neoprene plug to hold the Allen key for frame separation. To hold the pump, there is a grommet in the base of the seat pillar, although this was missing from a few early machines. The seat pillar binder bolt has a cam-action quick release lever.

The saddle shown in the first catalogue had each of the support wires formed into a single loop to give slightly enhanced springing without recourse to coil springs. However, the saddle fitted to production machines has conventional support wires and is a foam-padded Selle Italia anatomic type.

The almost straight mountain bike style steel handlebars are made by Italmanubri (ITM). They are 525 mm (20.67") wide, fitted with black grips and mounted in a black 115 mm (4¹/₂) stem, also by ITM.

The Union pedals are a basic, plastic composite, bear-trap type with integral reflectors.

Initial Distribution & Production Target

The arrangements for production of the APB made Alex Moulton Limited responsible for design and manufacture of the tooling, while W. R. Pashley Limited produced the bicycles. Neither company was to sell the APB, either wholesale or retail. In the UK this was the responsibility of APB Distribution, a specially created division of Swift Cycles of Forest Hill, London. The bikes were sent out packed flat, the aim being to get them to customers within four days of receiving the order.

The APB is marketed not as an AM, nor as an Alex Moulton, nor even as a Pashley. Instead, for the first time since the deletion by Raleigh of the MkIII in 1974, the unadorned name Moulton is used.

The recommended price at launch was £499.95. Production commenced in early March 1992. Pashley set a conservative production target of 500 for the first year, which in the event was exceeded by some 50%.

The Launch

The press releases for the APB launch were dated 14 and 17 of February 1992. On 26 February The Daily Telegraph printed an illustrated article by its environment correspondent Toby Moore under the heading "Moulton gets into gear for cycle launch". This showed

Tim Pashley riding one of his company's delivery bikes alongside the river Avon at Stratford, accompanied by his wife Clare on a Moulton APB. Also illustrated was former Chancellor of the Exchequer Lord Hailsham riding a Moulton in 1966. A graph of bicycle sales from 1981 to 1991 showed the steep recent downturn, and there was a captioned silhouette of the APB showing its key features.

The text put the APB in context within the evolution of the Moulton bicycle concept. There were quotes from Michael Woolf of Moulton Preservation and from Alex himself, who pointed out that the APB "will have really most of the advantages of my most expensive designs". The reporter noted that the new machine would sell for "about the same as a good mountain bike, and considerably less than the £1,500 which the cheapest Moulton now costs".

Five days later the Nottingham Evening Post printed a small article under the heading "Bike of the 60s on way back". Like the Telegraph article, it stated that the APB was lighter than its 1960s predecessors. The Nottingham paper noted that the Moulton was "as much of a 1960s icon as the Mini", and quoted Alex as saying, "I do think the [Moulton] bicycle can be a success in the nineties. Right from the beginning, all the bicycles had front and rear suspension, and now you see modern mountain bikes with that feature at the front."

However, Nottingham is the home of Raleigh and the reporter wrote that "Raleigh has doubts about the appeal of the design to a modern audience". A Raleigh spokeswoman was quoted as saying, "We used to mass produce them, but they phased themselves out" – which rather suggests that the Moulton is a cross between a bicycle and a lemming!

On 4 March The Times printed a photograph of two Pashley employees, Gordon Hawkins (now managing director) and Chris Bonell, test riding APBs. Alex was quoted as saying that the APB "will appeal to people who do not want the image a conventional push-bike gives."

The following day he visited the APB stand at Cyclex '92 in London's Olympia. Cycle Trader's report of Cyclex asked "Will this herald the 'return' of the Moulton to its 60s popularity? All of the advantages remain, at a reasonable price for serious traffic-beaters."

In the editorial of the March/April issue of The Moultoneer, I greeted the arrival of the APB:

"The launch of the All Purpose Bicycle marks a major development in the evolution of the Moulton bicycle. It is not the lightest, fastest or most sophisticated of Alex Moulton's designs. It is, however, the most affordable and the first to be mass-produced under licence since 1974.

"A particular attraction to riders seeking a mount for heavy or frequent use, especially those compelled to use badly maintained roads, is the adoption of 20" wheels. ... This wheel format, a standard sprocket cluster and a price tag of under £500 make the APB the nearest thing to a 'people's Moulton' since the demise of the Raleigh-made MkIII."

The same issue pointed out that "AM-ATB owners or prospective purchasers may rest assured that spare parts will continue to be made available by Alex Moulton Limited long after the ATB is deleted from the AM range."

The April/May issue of Cycle Touring and Campaigning carried a report on Cyclex '92 by the CTC's Technical Officer, Chris Juden. He noted the plethora of suspension systems for mountain bikes and bemoaned the "often hasty adaptations of previous unsprung designs". He suspected that "the customer is in most cases paying a great deal of money for the privilege of joining the test team!" He continued:

"There is, however, a British-made suspended bicycle which, unlike **all** these recent developments, has not only been tried and tested over a period of several decades, but was also designed as such from the outset by someone eminently qualified in this field: namely Dr Alex Moulton."

Chris rated the APB "the most exciting product of the show. Truly an all-purpose bicycle and an All Persons Bicycle." Noting that the APB was styled as a mountain bike, he pointed out that "it would be a simple matter to alter the specification to something more efficient for road riding".

By mid May APBs had been exported to the USA, Switzerland and the Netherlands. This was reported on the front page of Midweek, a free newspaper serving the Stratford-upon-Avon area. It also noted that Pashleys had received an enquiry from a Swedish national living in China about the cost of delivering an APB to Beijing.

Optional Extras

The original APB catalogue made no mention of a rear carrier or mudguards. However, The Times of 4 March 1992 showed an APB with both. The Moultoneer for March/April 1992 confirmed that they would be available, the carrier being "very much less expensive than the AM-range carriers, albeit somewhat heavier." Availability of these components was echoed by Cycle Touring & Campaigning's April/May issue.

Mudguards went on sale in late July 1992. They are black-painted steel and made by Spencer, part of the Pashley organisation. Teething troubles were encountered fitting these to early APBs. The rear drop-outs had no fixing eyes and therefore had to be drilled, while the front drop-outs had eyes which were the wrong size for the fixing bolts. Early rear mudguards, once fitted, also tended to vibrate and eventually fracture, because only one pair of stays was used, as compared with the two pairs later fitted. The initial price of a pair of APB mudguards was a modest £12.

Rear carriers did not appear until late August 1992. Again some annoying but minor surgery was needed to fit the carrier to early APBs, including slight shortening of the mounting boss and drilling it out to accommodate the fixing bolt. It was also necessary to fit a longer straddle wire for the rear brake, but this was supplied with the carrier.

The carrier is very much in the tradition of the AM series. However at £28 when launched it was a fraction of the price. It had a much thinner outer member, constructed of thin, round steel bar rather than tubing, reinforced by two additional braces per side.

There was just room between the seat tube and the back of the carrier to fit one of John Long's tailpiece bags. John produced a special version of his bag specially for the APB, which he marketed direct via advertisements in The Moultoneer. He also produced a larger bag for the rear carrier and carry bags for the bike when separated. The latter were initially sold via APB Distribution, the price in April 1993 being £69.95 per pair. (For John Long's 1994 address see Appendix B.)

The rear bags made for the 17" wheel AMs also fitted the APB's carrier quite well. Another option was offered by London MBC member Andrew Beckman, who produced rigid-sided bags similar in concept to those of the 1960s Moultons. These were available from spring 1993 for £25 each, finished in black or silver-grey. (For Andrew Beckman's 1994 address see Appendix B.)

Although it had been stated by Pashleys that a front carrier would be available, the idea was subsequently dropped, only to be resurrected in the summer of 1992. It was autumn of that year before APBs were produced with front carrier fixing points. The front carrier which then became available was, like the rear carrier, similar in principle to that of the AM's.

APB-5

Writing about the APB in the March/April 1992 edition of The Moultoneer I stated:

"A Sturmey-Archer 5-Star hub would provide a 2.25:1 range (say 36 to 80") and could offer a much higher top gear than 80". Indeed a monster 111" would be possible simply by using a 14 tooth sprocket with the 52 tooth chainwheel! It is rumoured that a version of the APB fitted with the 5-Star may well be produced if a reasonable level of demand is detected. As is well known, W. R. Pashley Limited are one of the few British cycle manufacturers totally familiar (and comfortable) with hub gear technology."

The following issue of The Moultoneer confirmed the rumour. A stop press report stated that, in response to demand, a 5-speed alloy hub geared version of the APB would indeed be produced, and that it would sell for the same price as the original 12-speed version. This news was based on a press release that promised the new version would be exhibited at the National Cycle Show, Harrogate on 7-9 June 1992.

Apart from the transmission system the APB-5, as the new bike was dubbed, was identical to the APB-12. The chainset was a simple alloy cotterless type by Solida with no provision for changing the 46 tooth chainring. A black plastic guard flange was fitted.

The Sturmey-Archer 5-Star hub was, in reality, steel-shelled, an alloy version not being available except in combination with a hub brake. On the APB it was fitted with a $1/8$" sprocket with 18 teeth, giving gears of 34, 40 (+18%), 51 (+28%), 65 (+27%) and 76" (+17%). Brazed-on cable guides and stops were provided for the two gear control cables which fed into a single thumb-shifter on the handlebars.

The APB-5. Photo courtesy of W.R. Pashley Limited.

APB-12 and Conventional ATB Compared

The first detailed road test of the APB-12 appeared in The Moultoneer's May/June 1992 edition. It was carried out jointly by Steve E. Michaels, a university lecturer in engineering and Ian Hodgson, the Moulton Bicycle Club's then chairman and technical adviser. The main basis for comparison was Steve's 18 month old Saracen Traverse mountain bike, which cost about the same as the APB-12. The APB was judged against the brochure description: "for the rider in city, town or country; on good roads or bad ... for every rider who appreciates individuality in conception, excellence in design and quality in construction."

The testers noted that on their very early APB the lock-nut that tightens the knuckle joint of the lower frame tie was at a slight angle and therefore "did not provide a very satisfactory joint." The brazing also looked "rather heavy-handed", though not enough to be a serious cosmetic problem.

Whereas the Saracen came supplied with bottle cage mounts, cage, bottle, toe-clips and straps, none of these was provided with the APB. The APB's plastic pedals were thought "cheap and nasty" compared with the Saracen's "reasonable quality Shimano pedals".

The test course consisted of about 10 miles (16 km) of country roads and tracks, during which Steve and Ian switched machines from time to time. The two are of similar stature and did not need to adjust riding position. However, Steve found the seating position of the APB was rather far forward and very upright for his short stature. He also detected some roughness in the transmission.

On metalled roads the APB "rode excellently", the suspension insulating the rider from jarring very effectively. This contrasted with the unsprung Saracen which "transmitted everything back to the rider". The APB's 20" wheels gave much livelier steering, making the Saracen seem "almost ponderous". Yet the APB's steering was significantly less sensitive than a 17" wheel AM, and in Steve's opinion "all the better for that".

Off road the APB coped well with soft mud, ruts and stones. However the Saracen felt more stable, with better traction, less side-slip and "less tendency to fall into holes or become trapped in longitudinal ruts". The testers felt that some of the difference could be overcome by fitting the APB with more heavily treaded tyres, like those on the Saracen. On metalled roads, however, the APB's Cruiser tyres seemed to roll more easily than the Saracen's.

As to gearing, the testers felt that the APB-12's top gear was too low on the road and the bottom gear too high off road. The 21-speed Saracen effectively offered two more gears at each end of the range. The APB-12's indexed gear changing worked reasonably well but, as is often the case with new equipment, needed slight adjustment. The thumb-shifters on top of the handlebars were less conveniently sited than the Saracen's under-bar type, but needed much less effort to shift. It was noted that the gears and other componentry were "of a significantly lower grade to that of the Saracen, and indeed even the lowliest of the AMs".

The APB's braking was described as "impressive throughout, providing smooth, silent retardation, and appearing to be as powerful as you could wish for." The facility to vary the reach of the Shimano brake levers was appreciated but the amount of free movement in the lever bearings was disliked.

The two bikes seemed to be about the same weight, but when it came to crossing a stile, the APB felt easier to handle. However, the testers were concerned about possible damage to its very thin tubing.

Steve and Ian concluded that the APB-12 "can do most things you would want it to, and does them very well." There was some concern about the luggage carrying capacity, but the main criticisms related to the relatively narrow range of gears and the general standard of the components fitted. It was acknowledged that these latter points relate directly to cost, and that the APB-12 was "not particularly expensive by bicycle standards today."

The testers differed when answering the question whether they would buy an APB-12. Ian, who did little off-road riding, preferred to stick with a lighter, easier rolling 17" wheel AM. Steve agreed that the 17" wheel machine was better for his normal road riding and touring, and that a 26" wheel mountain bike was better for serious off-road use. However, he felt he might buy an APB for commuting, or if he needed an AM and could not afford a new 17" wheel one.

200 Miles on the APB

Shortly after writing up the test, Steve did indeed buy an APB-12, subsequently selling his Saracen mountain bike. He was therefore soon in a position to comment in greater detail on the APB's merits and demerits. He published a report on his first 200 APB miles (320 km) in the May/June 1992 edition of The Moultoneer.

On the whole his opinions remained as expressed in the earlier test. His machine seemed to have neater brazing than the original test machine, but poorer paintwork. His first 200 miles (320 km) were completed over some three weeks and included "about 10 rides of various kinds – around town, out in the country, and along a disused railway track which serves as a footpath and cyclepath". On a ride involving a mixture of road riding and several miles of a rough and muddy track, Steve found the APB much more comfortable than a conventional mountain bike, yet it coped with the rough conditions just as well.

On the road Steve felt that he needed lower gears than on an AM7; for example 30" on the APB where he would use 36" on the 17" wheel machine. The APB's 20" tyres rolled significantly less easily than the 17" Moulton-Wolbers.

Steve would rather have paid more money in the first place for the APB-12 to be fitted with better components and a wider gearing range – a reaction shared by many. He added prophetically, "perhaps it leaves open the opportunity to introduce in the future a Deluxe model that overcomes these shortcomings!"

Overall he was delighted with the APB, adding that, "If weather conditions are unpleasant, or I plan to go off road then this is undoubtedly my first choice." He also rated the bike highly for in-town riding, where it would cope well with potholes and where the substantial tyres would be more puncture resistant than 17" tyres. But for longer rides on the road he still preferred the smaller-wheeled AMs.

A Twelve-Speed Commuter ...

Writing in The Moultoneer for May/June 1992, Tony Connor, a Dorset-based cyclist, expressed amazement at the low price of the APB-12. He bought one for his 15 mile (24 km) daily commute, most of which is off road. He had tried using a 17" wheel AM, but was deterred by the frequency of punctures, and ended up using a conventional mountain bike.

An experienced club racing cyclist, Tony considered the APB's frame "beautifully assembled" with an excellent paint finish. His APB-12 weighed 32lb 12oz (14.85 kg), complete with its complement of UK-required reflectors. (Later APB-12s, with the heavier steel chainrings, weighed nearer 33lb 11oz (15.27 kg).) This was about 1lb 4oz (0.57 kg) heavier than a typical AM-ATB fitted with mainly Shimano Deore components.

Tony rightly thought that the additional weight of the APB lay not in the frame but in the components – the seat pillar and saddle clamp alone weighed 1lb 12oz (0.79 kg). He also pointed out that his daughter's unsprung Kona Lavadome mountain bike, which cost about the same as an APB, was only 1lb 10oz (0.74 kg) lighter.

He felt that it should be possible to re-equip an APB to match the weight of the then new 29lb 12oz (13.49 kg) Cannondale Delta V2000 full suspension bike – and that the total cost of the APB plus replacement componentry would be less than half the £1,700 price of the non-separable American bike.

(This theory was soon proved by APB owner Keith Findlay, who achieved the desired weight saving simply by replacing the seat pillar, chainset, handlebars and tyres with lighter components.)

Tony wrote, "The ride comfort is a revelation. I have been seeking out all the worst potholes I can find, and the 20" wheels just soak them up." However, he stressed the need to adjust the front suspension to gain maximum benefit and bemoaned the fact that the relevant instructions were not provided with the machine.

In the past he had time-trialled on a fixed-wheel AM and his recollection was that the 17" wheel machine was nowhere near as comfortable as the APB. He shared the view that a conventional mountain bike was better at coping with the deepest ditches and ridges, but for forest track and bridleway riding he would take the APB every time for its greater comfort.

He felt that some riders might wish to change the tyres and gearing, depending on the intended use. For example, a coarser tyre tread would be desirable for slippery conditions. He intended fitting a close-ratio 13-18 tooth freewheel and a 54/40/28 tooth chainset, thus offering approximately the same range of gearing as the standard APB but with much closer ratios.

... a Single-Speed Commuter ...

Another commuter who took to the APB was David Bailey of Weston-super-Mare. His approach was somewhat different from Tony Connor's. David's route to work, though involving tracks and bridleways, was fairly level. It was therefore not necessary to have variable gearing, and he opted for a single-speed fixed-wheel transmission.

With the co-operation of St John Street Cycles in Bridgwater, David bought an APB-5 and returned all the unwanted components for a refund. He ended up with "a bare frame without a headset". Then, with the assistance of Robin, owner of the cycle shop, David assembled his ideal commuter bike – born out of 14 years of commuting up to 130 miles (208 km) a week.

The upshot was a drop handlebar machine with a single gear of 65". Transmission consisted of a Stronglight chainset with 52 tooth chainwheel (salvaged from an old AM7) driving a 16 tooth sprocket. The bottom bracket employed TA cups and axle with Campagnolo ball bearings.

The wheels had Ukai 1.5" rims built onto Shimano Dura-Ace track hubs with 14 gauge spokes. The tyres were 1.75" RL Edge with a recommended pressure of 100 psi (6.8 atm), although in practice David ran the front tyre at 80 psi (5.44 atm) and the rear at 90 (6.12 atm).

His points of contact with the machine consisted of Shimano SPD pedals, an Avocet Gelflex 20 saddle and 420 mm (16^1/$_2$") Cinelli 64 bars, with Grab-On foam sleeving. The bars were held in a 120 mm (4^3/$_4$") Sakae Cro-mo stem and the headset was Shimano Ultegra. The brakes were also by Shimano – Deore XT cantilevers with 105 aero brake levers.

Being a true commuter machine, mudguards and a decent pump were fitted. The latter was a Zefal HP, strapped under the rear carrier by shortened toe straps. The guards were Poker Cromoplastic, the rear one customised to take a second pair of stays.

David had previously used a variety of cycles to commute to work. For four years he had ridden an AM7, but eventually dispensed with it because of fast tyre wear and poor performance on soft tracks. However, he still used an AM14 for touring and other leisure use.

What then was David's verdict on his "APB-1"? The suspension, having a stiffer spring than the AM14, was less prone to bounce at fast cadences – particularly important in a single-speed machine. He found the ride "wonderfully comfortable", and for commuting the customised APB was, he said, the most suitable bike he had used so far.

... and a Five-Speed Commuter

Nigel Sadler, who became editor of The Moultoneer late in 1992, does not own a car. He relies heavily on his bicycles to get about, be it for business or pleasure. In spring 1993 he bought an APB-5 from Phoenix Cycles of Battersea. By this time the bikes came with proper instructions, which Nigel described as "excellent". They included a glossy A4 sheet with, on one side, 15 photographs showing assembly and adjustment, on the other maintenance instructions similar to those for the AM range.

Writing in The Moultoneer, Nigel described the ride quality and performance of the APB-5 as midway between his 1965 Moulton Deluxe and his AM14-S. The Cruiser tyres were, he said, much more resistant to the "huge amounts of glass to be found strewn all over London's roads". He praised the tyres as a good compromise between on and off-road types, but warned that "the central ridge looses grip in slippery conditions, particularly noticeable on painted road markings, (bus lane white lines, yellow lines etc.) whether wet or dry." (The paint used in the UK for these purposes is often about $1/4$" (6 mm) thick.) He also noted that the Cruisers "seem to have a built-in speed limiting factor, which prevents me from exceeding 30 mph (48 kph), no matter how hard I try or how steep the hill!" This was despite running the tyres at 70 psi (4.76 atm), rather than the recommended pressure of 60 psi (4.08 atm).

Nigel found the Sturmey-Archer 5-Star gear "a delight", with ratios fine for urban riding. The bike's components were, he felt, basic but serviceable. He did, however, have problems with the mudguards and rear carrier. The mudguards were the early type, with only one pair of stays. Nigel warned potential purchasers: "Make sure your dealer specifies and only accept double stays, because you will only have to fit extra stays yourself, or replace the rear mudguard when it has vibrated itself to pieces ..."

The other defect was potentially more serious and concerned the mounting point for a reflector and lamp. This takes the form of a small bridge linking the seat stays of the rear triangle.

If the rear suspension of early machines is fully compressed, this bridge can hit the carrier support strut. It must be said that Nigel had pushed the machine to extremes by riding it down a shallow flight of steps with a load on the carrier. The result was that the bridge bent the carrier strut. Under the weight of the luggage, the strut deformed further until arrested by the rear brake straddle wire. This locked the rear brake on. As Nigel put it, "This could be replicated by hitting a large pothole in the middle of a busy junction!" Nigel suggested to APB owners that they bend the bridge further down to prevent the problem occurring. (The geometry of the APB's rear triangle was subsequently modified to overcome this.)

Nonetheless he praised the APB-5 for being sturdy and sure-footed. "Its feeling of strength gives me confidence, hence riding down a flight of steps – something I would never have dreamt of doing on any of my other Moultons." He added that, "For 30-50 mile (48 – 80 km) a day touring, the APB fits my bill!"

Time-Trialling – on the APB-5!

Even though Nigel Sadler found his APB-5 incapable of exceeding 30 mph (48 kph), Richard Grigsby of Bath Cycling Club rode one to third place in the 1993 "Tin Can Ten". This is an annual time trial for cycles of all types and ages with hub gears ("tin cans").

For a bit of fun Richard borrowed the perfectly standard APB-5 from Dick and Jane Barrow's Bradford-on-Avon Bike Hire. Retaining all the fittings, including mudguards and a kick stand, Richard merely added triathlon bars.

On the day of the race he cycled 30 miles (48 km) to hitch a lift for the long journey to West Leake, Nottinghamshire where the race took place. The course was 10.8 miles (17.3 km) and he covered it in 27 minutes 35 seconds, averaging 23.5 mph (37.6 kph). The first placed rider, on a proper time-trialling machine, was 2 mins 6 secs faster, and the second placed beat him by 1 min 16 secs. Richard ended the day cycling the 30 miles (48 km) back home from his lift.

What would the outcome have been, I wonder, had the APB been stripped and fitted with narrow section tyres and lightweight equipment?

Potential for Development

In the September/October 1992 edition of The Moultoneer, Walsall MBC member Peter Arnold wrote that he saw great potential for developing the APB range. He felt there should be three models: an off-road version, based on the APB-12 but with a smaller inner chainring; a town model, based on the APB-5 but with narrower road tread tyres, mudguards and carrier; and a touring version with drop handlebars, hybrid gearing with a triple chainwheel and five-speed hub, alloy rims fitted with high-pressure narrow-section, mudguards, and front & rear carriers.

By summer 1993 Peter had put his ideas for a touring APB into effect. To his APB-12 he fitted drop handlebars, a Brooks B15 saddle and Haro 1.5" slick tyres, which he reported rolled much better than the original Cruisers. To carry luggage he mounted a lockable Lintek motor cycle box on the rear carrier. His hubs were by Sturmey-Archer: an AT5 rear hub brake/five-speed combination and an Elite front hub brake. The torque arm of the Elite was clipped to the right-hand side of the fork stirrup "on the principle that the hoop was designed to take the considerable stresses of the original cheap steel cantilevers." (However, this adaptation is not factory-approved. Cantilevers impose a balanced load on the stirrup blades, whereas the hub brake reaction arm puts all the load on one blade!)

Discarding the original 52 tooth outer chainwheel, Peter kept the 42 tooth. This drove 25, 17 and 13 tooth sprockets on a Dacon driver (a special replacement sprocket carrier for pre-NIG Sturmey-Archer hub gears, that can be fitted with up to four sprockets, including smaller ones than a standard clip-on Dacon). Peter noted that "the top three 'click-stops' on the original indexed gearing coincide with the three cogs, a useful bonus, though there is a slight clearance problem on the smallest cog".

He considered that the range of gears offered by this hybrid configuration was superior to either an all-hub or all-derailleur system, especially in the lower range. The spread provided was:

25 T – 23, 27, 34, 43, 50"
17 T – 33, 39, 49, 63, 74"
13 T – 43, 51, 65, 82, 97".

Reviews in the Cycling Press

Apart from the CTC's Cycle Touring & Campaigning, the mass-market cycling press initially gave poor coverage to the APB. In The Moultoneer for May/June 1992 I reported that "the plethora of mountain bike magazines, full of articles on suspension for ATBs, seem to have ignored it totally – just as they ignore the fact that Alex Moulton pioneered ATB suspension".

Surprisingly New Cyclist, at the time the best general purpose monthly cycling magazine published in the UK, made no mention whatever of the APB until its June 1992 issue – despite carrying an advertisement for it in the April edition. Whereas the CTC's Chris Juden rated the

APB-12 "the most exciting product" at Cyclex 1992, New Cyclist's Cyclex report totally ignored the bike. However, the magazine made amends with its June issue. The front cover featured a small inset photograph of the APB and the caption "Budget Moulton – on test". Inside the APB received centrefold treatment via an illustrated article entitled "A Moulton for the Masses". The author was Geoff Apps, who noted that a key principle behind the APB-12 was that "a good frame with naff components is better than a naff frame with good components." Nonetheless he felt that the lower priced Moulton involved few compromises.

Having outlined the ancestry of the machine, Geoff turned to build quality. He pointed out that it was difficult to be sure "without stripping the paint off and sawing the bike up" but that "close inspection suggests that the build is good."

As to the components, he saw "nothing 'cheap-and-nasty' about them." However, he did have some slight criticism of the Shimano Exage brakes, which were not as effective as he would have liked. He thought this might be because of the relatively long straddle wires fitted in order to clear the mudguards and carrier stay. He would have liked to have seen hub brakes fitted but appreciated that this would not have been possible within the target price range.

Whereas the APB-12's gearing had attracted some adverse comment from reviewers in The Moultoneer, Geoff considered the range excellent, providing "a nice spinning cadence on gear 10 or 11 on the road, yet a lowest gear of 30" which is easily good enough for most off-road or gradient requirements." He also praised the bike's luggage carrying capacity, noting that the rear carrier was "delightfully easy to fit (and to remove for that matter) with a good wide platform for assorted luggage." A similar front carrier would also be available, he added. So too would be front and rear bags and a transit bag.

The bike Geoff tested was fitted with the Spencer mudguards. He noted that they were curiously short, particularly the rear one, and felt that this would cause anything on the rear carrier to be sprayed with water.

As to ride quality, he reported that the APB rode "like a good quality roadster" but "smoother and nippier". Steering was "fine once you get used to the varying geometry that suspension gives". He advised off-road users to "develop a few counterweighting techniques to avoid front-end-dive."

Geoff concluded by describing the APB-12 as "a sophisticated yet functional machine", "well-designed and worthwhile". The New Cyclist test team approved its all-purpose affordability.

In April 1993 New Cyclist again reviewed the APB, this time as part of a report on four of the most popular portable bicycles. Patrick Field was greatly impressed by the suspension, noting that "hitting a 2" step at 20 mph (32 kph) is hardly noticeable". He pointed out that, while not sluggish, the APB "like many bikes with sprung frames, … will not reward the rider who tries to fight it. It encourages smooth pedalling."

Patrick concluded that, while the APB was not the most portable of the machines on test, it was "an excellent general purpose bike and would serve all the needs of many riders whose ambitions do not extend beyond easy riding on roads or rough tracks."

This drew a response from Tim Pashley, published in the magazine's July 1993. He suggested that Patrick was "labouring under two major misapprehensions"

"Firstly, that the APB's prime purpose in life is to be taken to pieces and stowed away;

secondly, that the APB will not serve the rider whose ambitions extend 'beyond easy riding on roads or good tracks'."

Tim would have preferred the reviewer to have tested the APB "against other general purpose bicycles with larger wheels" rather than against "folding bicycles whose only merits are apparent when they are not being ridden". He enclosed a photograph of the APB being ridden off-road on Dartmoor, which New Cyclist printed alongside his letter.

By this time New Cyclist had featured the APB for a third time. An article in the May 1993 issue by Patrick Field on buying a bicycle gave thirteen case studies. One featured a middle-aged man who had not cycled since his youth. A recurring ankle injury had prevented him playing squash to keep fit.

He tried a mountain bike, a couple of hybrids (crosses between a mountain bike and a roadster), a Brompton folding bike, an AM14 and an APB-12 – which he purchased. Patrick reported that the man "has now been riding almost every day for two months and his ankle is so much better that he has re-entered his squash ladder."

A Thorough Analysis

The October 1992 edition of Cycling Plus included detailed critiques of the AM14 and the APB-12. In each case marks out of seven were given for various aspects of the bikes' performance, design and construction.

The first aspect considered was handling, for which the APB earned six out of seven. The reviewer, cycle journalist and veteran Moulton owner Ben Searle, wrote that the APB-12 felt something like a lightweight mountain bike and that he found himself doing things that he would not try on his usual bike: "On rough paths it came into its own, sailing over the debris beneath". Although the steering was light, Ben found it "less twitchy than the AM14". Once he had adapted to the lighter steering, he found the APB stable at all speeds: it inspired him "with a lot of confidence in town traffic".

Ben then turned his attention to speed. Here the APB-12 scored five out of seven. He found acceleration and hill climbing "good compared to a hybrid or mountain bike", and ascribed this to the ultra-rigid frame. However, the APB was not as lively as the 17" wheel AM. Ben suggested changing to lighter wheels and tyres for long-distance road use, and recommended two BMX specialist dealers as possible sources of such components – Shiners of Bristol and Hot Wheels of Bournemouth.

The APB-12's wheels drew some criticism from Ben who described them as "a misguided attempt at overkill". He argued that thirty-six 13-gauge spokes were unnecessary, especially with suspension, and that "such short, thick, inelastic spokes" were very difficult to tension properly.

Gear performance was the next aspect considered. For this Ben awarded the APB-12 four points out of seven. The rear derailleur worked well enough but was very basic. The front changer was better and gave very good changes. He found the overall ratios adequate for town use but frustratingly low when wanting to exceed 20 mph (33 kph).

Frame design and quality earned the APB five out of seven. Ben reported that mass production of the intricate frame had resulted in little compromise, and that frame alignment was good, despite the difficulties in achieving this in a bicycle with rear suspension. He stated that, because the framing is made from relatively thick-walled high tensile steel tubing, the frame was TIG-welded, rather than brazed. The joints looked "a lot less neat" than those of the 17" wheel AMs but "should be just as strong". Ben wrote that the APB's suspension and fat tyres "did a wonderful job in isolating me from very irregular road surfaces". However, he had difficulty achieving a comfortable riding position, a problem that he thought could be overcome by fitting a shorter handlebar stem.

The early APB-12 scored worst in the area of build and component quality – three out of seven. Ben acknowledged that the makers had got their priorities right by not compromising the frame for the sake of cheapness. He personally would want to replace the rear derailleur mechanism and the saddle, and rebuild the wheels. The Union pedals were criticised for their slipperiness and the fact that toe-clips could not be fitted. However, the Shimano cantilever brakes were praised for their even progression, power and comfortable brake levers. But on the debit side, the brake and gear cable sheaths were too long and the cables had not been greased.

Ben sought second opinions from two other cyclists. Paul Lyons, mountain biking editor of Cycling Plus and a daily cycle commuter, saw the APB-12 as being more suited to the beginner than the experienced cyclist. He felt that the package offered more than the sum of its parts but was a little overpriced. Ines Rodrieguez, a novice cyclist, was impressed by how effective the suspension was. For this rider the APB-12 felt very secure and safe. Having mastered the art of separating and reassembling the frame, Ines found it hard to surrender the bike.

Ben Searle's final verdict on the APB was that it scored a very creditable six out of seven for value for money, and five out of seven overall. Most of all he thought the bike was fun, and yet it was no toy. Like Tony Connor, he considered it "an achievement that the bike, with all the AM features at half the price, is there at all." And he was heartened that the benefits of the Moulton concept were now being made available to a wider public.

Mathematical Beauty

In November 1992 Design magazine featured bicycles, specifically "a triumvirate of the lean, mean vehicle at its most technologically advanced". The machines in question were the Lotus Sport, Spanbike and Moulton APB-12.

Tim Ostler wrote of the latter: "The Moulton has a beauty that is purely mathematical. Three-dimensional triangulation allows it to be superbly rigid, yet demountable in less than a minute. On no other bicycle is the engineering prowess of its designer so instantly visible." He concluded that with the APB, "Moulton's original utility bike of 1962 has returned, re-cast for current market conditions."

The following month the All Purpose Bicycle featured on Alex's 1992 Christmas card. Drawn as always by Brian Walker, it showed a rider on an APB arriving at the Red Lion, Lacock during the MBC Weekend the previous September.

The APB-14

In January 1993 journalists and the cycle trade were invited to attend a press day at The Hall. The main purpose was to launch a new model, the APB-14. As a flash on the corner of the invitation stated, this was "The APB with the superior specifications demanded by press and riders alike."

The press day was Friday 29 January. More than a dozen APBs were on display, along with other products from the Pashley range – including a tandem, tricycle and a mail delivery bike. Parties attending came not only from the UK but also from Japan, the USA, Germany,

Belgium and the Netherlands. Alex Moulton and Tim Pashley gave the visitors a comprehensive audio-visual presentation on the history of the Moulton bicycle concept. As The Moultoneer's then editor Nigel Sadler put it:

"The occasion was not so much the launch of the latest addition to the APB family ... but the telling of a philosophy of a design of bicycle that had been under development for nearly forty years, had been in production in one form or another for over thirty years, and had never been built **without** suspension."

The presentation included video footage showing the production process at the Pashley works. Nigel, who was involved in staging the presentation, wrote: "We saw a rear triangle being formed by robot arm from continuous lengths of steel tube, bending the metal this way and that like a giant paper clip, before it went off to the jigs to be aligned and have the cross braces brazed by hand."

The frame of the new machine was essentially the same as that of the APB-12, apart from minor changes to the rear drop-out to accommodate a different derailleur system. Cosmetically the frame differed only in that the head badge and lettering on the fork and seat tube were in gold rather than silver. However, the paint finish was a superior matt black electrostatic powder coat enamel of exceptional impact resistance – described by one observer as being satin black and rubbery. Alex had decided to retain the black frame colour so that the look of "the little black bike" could more easily become well known.

The APB-14 weighed approximately 29lb 13oz (13.52 kg), some 3lb (1.33 kg) lighter than the APB-12. The weight savings were achieved principally by using lighter handlebars, stem and chainset. The handlebar stem was Cro-Mo and the bars were alloy and much narrower. A better saddle was fitted and the brakes were also of higher specification, being Shimano Altus C10 M-system cantilevers.

The front end of the transmission consisted of a Shimano RX100 chainset with 52 and 42 tooth rings (a 24% difference) and a Shimano Deore LX mountain bike front derailleur. This set-up drove a 12, 14, 16, 18, 21, 24 & 28 tooth Shimano HG70 seven-speed cassette on a Shimano Freehub. The rear derailleur was a road type Shimano RX100. Selection was via Deore XT thumb shifters. Gears thus offered were:

42T: 30, 35, 40, 47, 53, 60, (70")
52T: (37), 43, 50, 58, 65, 74, 87"

Probably the optimal upward changing sequence of this crossover configuration, starting on the smaller chainwheel, would be:

30, 35 (+17%), 40 (+14%), 47 (+13%), 53 (+17%) (shift to larger chainwheel and back one cog), 58 (+9%), 65 (+17%), 74 (+14%), 87" (+17%).

Thus nine speeds could be selected in sequence with an average spacing of 15% and an overall range of 2.87:1.

The press day saw the introduction of a new APB brochure to reflect the expanded range. This followed the style of the original leaflet, being A4 size and featuring the black bicycle on a black background. This time, however, the brochure was in landscape (horizontal) rather than portrait (vertical) format. It no longer referred to APB Distribution, instead giving W. R. Pashley Limited as the supplier. The Pashley connection was further reinforced by the integration of the APB range into the main Pashley catalogue. The recommended prices quoted were £699.95 for the APB-14, £549.95 for the APB-12 and £534.95 for the APB-5, although some dealers gave considerable discounts.

Reviewing the APB-14

The international press day at Bradford-on-Avon was on a Friday. The following morning the APB-14 reached a wider audience via a full page colour article in The Times Saturday Review.

A detailed analysis appeared in the December 1993 issue of Cycling Plus, in a group test of bikes with suspension. This also covered the Radical, Allsop Powercurve, Slingshot and AM-SPEED S. (See page 288.)

Both Moultons were awarded six out of seven for frame performance. No other bike in the group test achieved this score. The APB's suspension was not as soft as the Radical's but coped better with poor road surfaces than most suspension bikes, including big-wheeled ATBs. Off road it did well on all but the roughest terrain, but was "happiest on canal paths and bridleways". The reviewers suggested that the front suspension would be even better if there was less damping on compression than on rebound – "it would then react faster to small bumps without bouncing under power."

On descents the handling was "very reassuring". The steering, though quick, was easier to adapt to than the AM's, and the APB rode like a much lighter machine.

Gear and brake performance rated five out of seven. The 87" top gear, though adequate for most town users, was considered too low. An 11-28 tooth cassette and wider range chainwheels were suggested as a way of achieving a wider range of gears.

Frame quality and design also scored five out of seven. Despite the use of high tensile steel rather than Reynolds 531, the frame was very stiff and finished in "a good, tough paint that is knock-resistant". The separability was greatly admired. As to frame geometry, it was suggested that the frame angles be steepened by about 2 degrees.

Five out of seven was also the score for component quality and choice. It was noted that the APB-14's fittings were a great improvement on the APB-12's. However, there were still "some naff bits", such as the "tacky plastic pedals (an abomination) and the steel seatpin (not much better)".

Overall though, Cycling Plus gave the APB-14 six out of seven both for overall performance and value for money – the best aggregate score in the group test. In summing up, the magazine confided that two of its testers were sufficiently impressed to contemplate buying the APB-14. "It is, after all, a model that comes closest to being a genuine multi-purpose bike – ideal for city, travel and leisure."

The original APB-14. Photo courtesy of W.R. Pashley Limited.

The 1994 Range

After reorganisation of W. R. Pashley Limited in 1993, Adrian Williams became the company's sales and marketing executive. With David Duffield as consultant he expanded the range of APBs considerably.

The APB-12, APB-14 and APB-5 continue as before, the latter now with the single-cable Sturmey-Archer Sprinter hub. An export version of the APB-12, with Grip Shift gear controls, is distributed in the USA by Delta Cycle Corporation of Stoughton, Massachusetts. Delta ship the bike pre-assembled in a carton "nearly ready to ride" for $1,789.

Since May 1994, four new models have been added to the UK range, with recommended retail prices from just under £450 to almost £900.

For the first time an APB is available with narrow section tyres. And for the new models the "little black bicycle" strategy has been abandoned. This was almost certainly a good move: according to one analyst, Henry Ford's "any colour as long as it's black" policy lost the US car maker a market lead that took 50 years to recover!

The new models were launched via a four page A5 glossy leaflet. The cover showed the APB-14 Shimano Plus on a pedestal and bore the slogans "More than an Artform" and "Dynamic by Design". Full page colour advertisements, based on the brochure cover, appeared in a number of cycling magazines and on the back page of Cycle Touring & Campaigning.

The APB-3

The new base model in the APB range has 500 x 28A amber-walled narrow section ribbed tyres on Rigida alloy rims. The front hub is alloy, the rear the Mk5 (lubricated for life) version of the Sturmey-Archer AW wide-ratio three-speed, with the new Nimbus thumb-shifter.

This is the only version of the APB not to be fitted with cantilever brakes bosses, having instead Saccon dual pivot alloy sidepull callipers. It is also the only APB to come with mudguards fitted as standard.

In other respects the APB-3's componentry is similar to the APB-5's. There is a choice of frame colour, "rapid red" or "racing green" – the mudguards, handlebars, stem and saddle being black. Recommended price in 1994 is £449.95.

Building an APB-3. Photo by Tony Hadland.

The APB-3. Photo courtesy of W.R. Pashley Limited.

The APB-14 Sachs

This is a cheaper version of the original and well-received Shimano-equipped APB-14 (now renamed the APB-14 Shimano). Being fitted with Sachs brakes and transmission, it also gives the potential purchaser the opportunity to buy a bike with little or no Far Eastern componentry.

The tyres are similar to those on the APB-12 but are fitted to narrow section Rigida alloy rims built onto Sachs alloy hubs. Transmission range is the same as the original APB-14's but the equipment is by Sachs, the chainset being their 3000 model. The brake levers are Sachs two-finger type and operate Sachs alloy cantilever brakes. Pedals are VP 955A.

The APB-14 Sachs is offered in aquamarine or cerise, and the recommended price in 1994 is £599.95, £100 cheaper than the APB-14 Shimano.

The APB-14 Shimano Plus

The Shimano Plus is an upmarket version of the APB-14, at £749.95 being £50 dearer than the APB-14 Shimano (1994 prices). It answers many of the criticisms of the original APB-14.

Tyres are 20 x 1.75" Michelin Cobras on narrow section Rigida alloy rims. An 11 to 28 tooth cassette is fitted, giving a higher top gear of 94".

The APB-14 Sachs. Photo courtesy of W.R. Pashley Limited.

The APB-14 Shimano Plus. Photo courtesy of W.R. Pashley Limited.

The rider's points of contact with the machine are all improved. Gone are the plastic pedals, replaced by alloy-shelled VP 3385s. The saddle is an aero-anatomic type, and the handlebars are Reynolds 501 with

Zoom Cro-mo stem and polished alloy bar ends. Brake levers are two-finger type.

The APB-14 Shimano Plus is finished in brilliant blue.

The APB-16 SunTour

Top of the APB range is the APB-16 SunTour – again, a chance to buy a non-Shimano equipped machine.

Tyres and wheels are as the APB-14 Shimano Plus, but with SunTour quick release alloy hubs. Overall range of the SunTour transmission is also the same, but more closely spaced, having an eight-speed cassette with 11 to 18 teeth and XC Pro rear derailleur. The brakes are SunTour XC Expert cantilevers.

Saddle, pedals and handlebar configuration are as the APB-14 Shimano Plus, but with purple anodised bar ends. The frame colour is "gunmetal". Toe clips, straps and a bottle cage are supplied.

The recommended price in 1994 is £899.95.

The APB-16 SunTour. Photo courtesy of W.R. Pashley Limited.

Relative Values

In concluding this chapter on the APB, it is interesting to make a price comparison between the base models in the APB and AM ranges. Comparing the APB-3's launch price with that of the original AM2 (adjusting for inflation) shows that in real terms the APB-3 is a third cheaper than the 1983 AM2.

However, since 1983 AM prices have risen about 80% faster than inflation, and if the AM2 were made today, its price would be about three times that of the APB-3. It is clear, therefore, that Alex Moulton has achieved his aim of producing a parallel range of spaceframe Moultons with most of the key features of the AM range, but at substantially lower cost.

Chapter 9
AGAINST THE CLOCK
1983-1993

Aeros – 'Liners – Audax – RAAM – SPEED – Triathlon – Jubilee L

The AM7 notched up its first major speed success on 20 June 1984. In the 30 mile (48 km) Toronto Berolina Criterium, Elgar Vaivars rode the bike to victory against 39 opponents, winning all but one of the lap sprints. Elgar used the AM7 throughout the season and even competed against the great Francesco Moser, finishing with the pack.

Although the Canadian criterium victory pleased Alex Moulton, his speed ambitions lay in another direction. In early spring 1984 he addressed the Road Records Association (RRA) at a dinner to acclaim recent record-breakers. Among the 175 members and guests was John Woodburn, who in 1962 broke the Cardiff-London record on the original Moulton Speed, and who

Elgar Vaivars with his AM7.

later broke the RRA 24 hour and End-to-End (Land's End to John o'Groats) records on conventional machines.

But although nostalgia could have dominated, Alex was not there to talk about the past. Instead he drew attention to the "view of the future" offered by Human Powered Vehicles (HPVs). In recent years his interest in these had been stimulated by HPV speed trials at Brighton and Goodwood. He pointed out that HPVs had produced "a revolution in speed achieved by man-powered vehicles", and rather than ban them altogether, he hoped the RRA would recognise a category for certain HPVs.

The world-wide rules for conventional cycle racing are set down by the Union Cycliste Internationale (UCI), in French. For instance, wheel diameters are governed by UCI Article 49, which translates as: "The wheels of the machine may be of different diameters, respectively a maximum of 700 mm (27.6") and a minimum of 550 mm (21.7"), including the tyre."

The International Human Powered Vehicle Association (IHPVA) was started in the early 1970s after some creative southern Californians tried to enter a streamlined bicycle in a UCI-rules cycle race. They were barred, and in classic Californian style decided to start their own club without restrictive design rules. The IHPVA allows any sort of vehicle as long as it uses only human power, no stored energy and meets certain safety rules.

Alex had experimented with streamlined cowlings before the launch of the first Moulton bicycle. In 1960 he carried out coast-down (free-wheeling) tests on a prototype Moulton bicycle fitted with a rigid glass-fibre cowl protecting only the rider's lower body (similar to the integral front cowling of a 1960s motor scooter). Later that year, at Alex's request, the famous Italian car stylist Pininfarina applied his design flair to an aluminium cowling.

Pininfarina fairing on the first F-frame Moulton, 1960. This is the frame design shown in the 1959 patent drawing, complete with small diameter tubes for the suspension swing arms.

In 1962 John Woodburn tested larger cowls for Alex under racing conditions. The first was constructed of doped linen stretched over a wire frame, and was followed by a rigid glass-fibre cowl.

All these experiments with aerodynamics showed useful gains in speed, ease of propulsion and weather protection. So much so that in 1963 Alex filed GB Patent 1018962 covering a high speed bicycle with small front wheel and large nose cowl. However, he had reservations about safety in cross-winds. Because of this, and the RRA's prohibition of cowls, and the lack of suitable materials for mass production of lightweight cowls, Alex abandoned his work on bicycle aerodynamics for some 18 years, from 1962 until 1980.

The doped linen cowl under test in 1962.

The Millikens

Elgar Vaivars' AM7 was not the only one to do well in Canada in 1984. Another was ridden in the International Festival of the Bicycle (29 May to 3 June) at Hull, across the river from Ottawa. This machine was equipped with a prototype fairing and was the first AM-based HPV used in competition. In a field dominated by streamlined recumbents, it came fourth in the Techno-Cycle Competition, and fourth also in La Grande Pursuit. The designer of the AM's fairing was Douglas Milliken, then 30 years old.

Doug's father, William F. Milliken Jr., had been an aeronautical engineer during World War II for Boeing and other American aircraft companies. After the war Bill Milliken spent 30 years at the non-profit Cornell Laboratories in Buffalo, Western New York State. These were noted for their advanced aeronautical testing facilities, which included transsonic and supersonic wind tunnels. In the 1950s Bill's team pioneered the numerical modelling of automobile handling, using techniques derived from aeronautical practice.

In 1976 Bill established his own consultancy, Milliken Research Associates Inc., which specialises in the horizontal dynamics (handling) of road vehicles. (Anthony Best, whose company occupies the old Moulton factory at The Hall, specialises in **vertical** dynamics (ride). Moulton Developments pioneered research in both ride and handling.)

In the late 1970s Milliken Research Associates were agents for the Moulton Hydragas suspension system during its evaluation by General Motors. Bill took Alex to the former Cornell Aeronautical Laboratory (by then renamed Calspan Corporation) to see its still unique flat bed, high speed tyre tester, which enabled very accurate measurement of tyre forces and moments. While at the labs, Alex noted the wind tunnel facilities.

This led ultimately to Alex sponsoring Bill Milliken's sons Doug and Peter in the aerodynamic design of fairings, leading to the Moulton HPVs. Initially Alex funded a research programme with money he had been awarded in 1979 by the Institute of Mechanical Engineers for winning their James Clayton Prize for outstanding contribution to engineering.

In September 1980 he despatched a Moulton MkIII to Doug. It was the first Moulton Doug had seen and was one of the dozen MkIIIs Alex bought from Raleigh when they ceased production of the bike. It had been converted into a MkIII version of the Stowaway S model of the mid 1960s, complete with Fichtel & Sachs Duomatic two-speed coaster hub. The paint finish was light blue, with black fork and rear triangle, and main beam bore black Moulton Stowaway decals.

As a basis for a high performance HPV, Doug found the Moulton bicycle "an excellent starting point because its small front wheel can turn inside the fairing. Additionally, the suspension reduces road shock and lowers the stress on the fairing supports". Being shorter than a conventional bicycle, the fairing was correspondingly smaller, another advantage.

Doug designed 20 or more fairing configurations for the MkIII. These were mocked-up quickly with welding wire, clear plastic sheeting and lots of tape. The fairings sat on a standard 1960s-style Moulton front carrier (rack) and were attached with jubilee clips (worm-gear hose clamps). Initially coast-down tests were tried, but it soon became clear that small puffs of wind and turbulence from passing vehicles rendered these invalid.

For the wind tunnel tests Doug built a force measuring device and turntable which allowed him to test the bike, complete with rider and fairing, in a small wind tunnel at Calspan Corporation. Dr George Skinner, who ran the wind tunnel, became interested in the project, and in the evenings assisted free of charge.

The turntable allowed the bike to be tested at a range of angles to the wind. Very few wind tunnel tests had been carried out on the effect of cross-winds on bicycles and HPVs. One interesting result, subsequently verified on the road, was the ability to sail. With the right wind and fairing there is enough thrust to move the bike without pedalling.

The result of Doug's research was a confidential report of some 50 pages for Alex, detailing the performance of the fairings, including their behaviour at an angle to the wind. An abstract of the report was published in 1984 by the IHPVA as part of the proceedings of its Second International Human Powered Vehicle Scientific Symposium, held on 22 October 1983.

Looking at the wind tunnel test data, it is interesting to note that the unfaired basic Moulton MkIII was less susceptible to cross-winds than a conventional machine. This was primarily because of the smaller side area of its wheels.

By March 1981 Doug had evolved a three-piece Lexan fairing, known as pre-prototype No.1. Lexan is a polycarbonate sheet made by GE (General Electric), and the material used was approximately $1/25"$ (1 mm) thick. It was fixed to the support framework by Velcro.

The First AM Aero

Doug first attended the International Human Powered Speed Championships (IHPSC) in 1982, while visiting Los Angeles. At the following year's event in Indianapolis, Doug Adamson, a visiting English cycle journalist, showed Doug and Pete Milliken an AM7. This was a press demonstrator subsequently crushed in somewhat mysterious circumstances on the return flight to the UK.

A few months later, early in 1984, Doug received a newly-built AM7, serial number 350001, on which to experiment. For this machine he built another front fairing out of single-curved Lexan sheet. This was in two panels and was designed for flat storage. Like all subsequent Aero-series fairings, it was fixed to the supporting frame by 3M Hedloc fasteners (now discontinued). The frame tubing was $5/16"$ (8 mm) diameter, and a mix of Reynolds 531 and automobile brake tubing. In the best tradition of the 531-framed AMs, it was fixed to the bike frame by bolts with 6 mm Allen heads, for easy fixing and disassembly.

It was this fairing that was used on the AM7 at the Hull International Festival of the Bicycle in 1984. The fairing bore the letters AMA (for Alex Moulton Aero) in 10" (250 mm) high white tape. The bike itself was a basic AM7, complete with mudguards.

Pre-prototype No. 1 fairing, 1st March 1981.
Photo by Doug Milliken.

Jim Glover in Hull, Ottawa 1984 on the AM Aero. Photo by Doug Milliken.

Jim Glover

Doug needed a strong rider for the Hull event, so he sought the advice of Ian Brown, the owner of Ottawa Bikeway, the local AM agency. Before emigrating to Canada, Ian had worked for Alex Moulton at Bradford-on-Avon. Ian suggested Jim Glover.

An elite athlete, Jim had gained valuable experience on the highly competitive Montreal cycle track. He subsequently became a time-triallist and qualified for the 1980 Canadian Olympic team. Unfortunately, because of the boycott of the 1980 Moscow Olympics, he was unable to take part.

At Hull Jim rode the faired AM7 to fourth place in La Grande Pursuit, a 15 mile (24 km) road race. Initially he was placed second in the Techno Cycle Competition but was later marked down to fourth.

Friendly Rivalry

Alex Moulton's intention was to market a fairing for the AM range, for touring and commuting use. In 1983 and early 1984 Doug Milliken was in friendly rivalry with Glen Brown of Zzip Designs to evolve the production design.

Ultimately it was Glen Brown's AM-Zzipper fairing that was adopted. Being curved in two planes, vertically, as well as horizontally, it looked more attractive, and was therefore more easily marketed. (See Chapter 5.)

The Zzipper double curvature fairings are, however, much more difficult to fabricate from Lexan. First the polycarbonate sheet has to be dried for 24 hours to drive off any moisture, otherwise the sheet could permanently "fog" during forming. The sheet is then curved by clamping it to the bottom of a special heating frame and literally blowing a bubble downward at about 400 degrees Fahrenheit (200 degrees Celsius). The final shape is then cut out from the bubble after cooling.

The Aero II and Indianapolis 1984

At the urging of "speed-demon" Jim Glover, Doug reworked the first AM Aero to add a new nose and a dark blue Spandex fabric tail section. Once again, all the kit bolted onto the standard carrier mountings and the resulting machine was called the Aero II. It was specifically built for the 10th International Human Powered Speed Championships, held at Indianapolis in September 1984.

The aerodynamic cape was inspired by one seen on an Easy Racer HPV at the Hull event. It considerably improved the Aero's aerodynamics: so much so that after the IHPSC, Doug, who does not claim to be a strong cyclist, was able with favourable wind conditions to ride 140 miles (225 km) in a day with a touring load.

A conventional close-ratio block was fitted to the Aero II, the smallest sprocket having 12 teeth. With the 75 tooth chainwheel this gave a top gear of 106"

Alex was at the IHPSC to watch Jim Glover's performance in the Aero II. Bicycle Action reported the stir created when in the speed trials on the Indianapolis Motor Speedway the machine achieved 41 mph (66 kph) through the flying 200 metre speed trap, "a remarkable performance for an upright bicycle." It was virtually the same speed posted by a fully-faired Mike Burrows Windcheetah SL recumbent tricycle. In fact, the Aero II achieved an even higher speed of about 43 mph (69 kph) but the result was not officially recorded.

The Aero II proved to be a giant-killer, beating many recumbents and all the big-wheeled HPVs. It created great interest, because most HPV designers had abandoned the normal riding position, believing it impossible to obtain the performance achieved by the Aero.

At the Major Taylor Velodrome, Jim in the Aero II finished 13th in the 4,000 metre individual pursuits. In the 20 km (12 mile) Le Mans start road race, he came fourth, behind three fully streamlined recumbents. Nearby, at Eagle Creek Park, he took sixth place in the 32 km (20 mile) road race, despite a spectacular crash when cornering too tightly. (He slid to the feet of Alex Moulton and Doug Milliken!) In the commuter vehicle competition he came fifth.

Jim Glover in Aero II at Eagle Creek Park road races, Indianapolis 1984, with Andy Pegg in a Mike Burrows Windcheetah in hot pursuit. Photo by C. Michael Lewis.

Glen Brown at IHPSC '85 with his AM7.
Note the aerodynamic stretch girdle.
Photo by C. Michael Lewis.

In Bike Tech magazine the following February, Robert G. Flower stated that hybrid fairings, as used by the Aero (part-rigid, part flexible) were starting to be seen as solutions to some of the difficulties inherent in all-rigid designs. He noted that the Aero was one of the lightest HPVs with almost full fairing coverage – it weighed about 34lb (15.4 kg).

Easy Rolling

Meanwhile, thousands of miles away in Palo Alto, California, technical consultant Eric Hjertberg of Wheelsmith was writing in American Bicyclist & Motorcyclist (September 1984) about bicycle wheels: "Lately we are discovering, as Alex Moulton well knows, that small wheels are not only very efficient but create less wind resistance in use."

In his earliest 1960s experiments with small wheels Alex had not considered the retarding effect of spoke air drag, nor the air drag of tyres and rims: he had concentrated on the rolling resistance of the tyres. However, he had subsequently realised that low wind resistance was another advantage of the small wheel.

Eric Hjertberg and his colleagues received useful assistance from Alex when they were evaluating wheel formats for racing purposes. They concluded that small wheels could be very fast.

The First Moulton 'Liner

At the 1984 IHPSC Alex made enquiries about the cost of a professionally built Kevlar-epoxy composite fairing. This proved prohibitively expensive, so Doug, with enthusiastic support from Jim Glover, agreed to have a go at producing a more cost-effective fairing.

During the winter of 1984/85 Doug carried out further research into aerodynamics. He travelled to California, visiting Glen Brown and

Chet Kyle. Both had designed and built fairings for standard big-wheel bikes and the Kyle Streamliner held the normal-riding-position record in the high 40 mph (70 kph) range. This was remarkable, because until the 1970s fully-faired bicycles had typically achieved no more than 36 mph (58 kph).

Doug discussed the possibility of building a fully-faired AM. Chet Kyle felt that the biggest problem would be handling, because of the fairing's tendency to vibrate or oscillate relative to the bike and rider.

The basis of the new machine was a red-painted early AM7 which Alex sent Doug early in 1985. To let the rider crouch as low as possible, the steering tube was shortened. This resulted in the low-head configuration eventually adopted for the AM-Jubilee, the SPEED and the stainless steel AMs.

To ensure that the belly (floor) pan of the fairing had adequate ground clearance, and for optimum aerodynamic effect, the AM7 needed its bottom bracket height raised by about 2" (50 mm). Therefore the front suspension was raised by adding a pressed stainless steel tube to the base of the head tube; and the rubber rear suspension unit was fitted with an extended alloy cam, about $1^3/_8$" (35 mm) long, to jack up the back of the bike.

To improve the straight-line handling at speed, the front fork was reversed, thus greatly increasing the castor effect. The front suspension was stiffened by shortening the spring by about an inch (25 mm) and adding a spacer above the spring to take up the missing length.

The transmission consisted of an 82 tooth chainwheel, which in top gear drove a 10 tooth AM sprocket. At the target velocity of 52 mph (83.7 kph) this gave a gear of 140" and a crank speed of about 125 rpm. A new 9, 10 and 11 tooth close-ratio gold cluster was used with four standard sprockets, but for maximum efficiency the 10 tooth cog was used as top gear, saving the 9 tooth to catch the chain if it overshifted.

Jim Glover demonstrates the riding position and support structure of the 'Liner. 'Liner III structure is much cleaner, stiffer and better looking.
Photo courtesy of Doug Milliken.

'Liner at Indy 1985.
Left to right: Jim Scandale, Mike Lewis, and inside, Jim Glover – battening down the hatch. Photo courtesy of Doug Milliken, seen here on the right.

A single SunTour Bar-Con handlebar-end shifter was used on very narrow cowhorn type bars, which Doug welded up from steel tube. The cage from a Campagnolo derailleur front changer was banded onto the seat tube to ensure that the chain stayed on the big chainwheel, which was somewhat flexible despite the large bolt circle diameter of the Campagnolo Nuovo Record crankset. (On the Aero II Doug had used a chain retainer of his own design, made of nylon.)

At Alex's request, Doug designed the fairing so that it attached to the bike solely via the standard AM front and rear carriers, and the seat binder bolt. The supporting framework was built of thin diameter Reynolds 531 tubing, with square alloy tube for the ribs that controlled the aerofoil shape.

The front panel, which had to be optically clear, was vertical but curved in top view. It was formed from Lexan. The side panels were cut from plastic foam-cored artist's board (Polyboard, Foamtex or similar), about 1/4" (6 mm) thick.

The most difficult panels to make were the lid sections, which curved in two planes, from front to back and from side to side. The front section of the lid was transparent, but did not need to be optically perfect. It was therefore vacuum-formed from PETG, a modified polyethylene, less likely than polycarbonate to "frost" during forming. The tapered rear section of the lid and the belly pan were vacuum-formed from 1/20" (1.25 mm) high impact polystyrene.

Timber formers were created for the lid and pan panels. These were made from laminated pattern pine, free of knots and abrupt changes of grain direction. For this task Doug enlisted the assistance of one of the world's greatest aeronautical pattern makers, Al Bajorek. Al built the full-size model of the Bell X1 rocket plane, and some of his wind tunnel models are in the Smithsonian Institution, Washington, DC. He came out of retirement specially to assist with the AM HPV project.

To complete the aerodynamic ensemble, the wheels were fitted with Doug's aerodynamic wheel discs, vacuum-formed from high impact polystyrene. It was important to ensure that the wheels were accurately balanced, as at the target speed, they would be spinning at about 1,000 rpm.

The machine was dubbed the 'Liner, short for Streamliner. It weighed about 50lb (23 kg).

The Aero III at IFB '85

The Aero III differed from its predecessor in that it had a red Spandex tail and new front fairing. Jim Glover rode it in August 1985 at the second International Festival of the Bicycle at Hull, Quebec, taking the opportunity to test Doug's new wheel discs.

In the 200 metre sprint heats Jim came second to a hard shell recumbent: in the finals he was fourth overall. And in the 25 mile (40 km) road race around the streets of Hull, he was third behind two recumbent tricycles.

Aero III.
Photo by C. Michael Lewis.

Indianapolis 1985

The opportunity to put the 'Liner through its paces arose at the 11th International Human Powered Speed Championships, held at Indianapolis in late September 1985.

The poster for the event was based on a painting by the IHPVA's artist, C. Michael Lewis of Portland, Maine, who worked for AM dealer Christopher Igleheart of Portland Bicycle Exchange. It showed the Aero II ridden by Jim Glover, leaning round a bend, followed by the Windcheetah, Easy Racer and Lighting X2. Originally the painting, based on a photograph taken at the 1984 IHPSC (see page 210) featured only the Aero and the Windcheetah: the other machines had to be added "to appease certain political factions". But if the poster upset some people, the combination of Jim and the 'Liner on the track was to cause an even bigger stir.

The first day consisted of test runs. The second day allowed the support teams to modify and tune their HPVs, while the riders recovered. Day three was reserved for the championships.

Jim had never ridden the 'Liner. Despite this, the plan was to try to break the world record for the flying 200 metres for an unpaced, fully-faired HPV, with a solo rider in the normal riding position – and preferably to exceed 50 mph (80.45 kph) in the process. The location was the Indianapolis Motor Speedway, home of the Indy 500.

The strategy centred on smooth acceleration and had been computer-modelled by Pete Milliken, using estimated air drag data from Chet Kyle's similar-shaped HPV. For use in the simulation, Jim Glover's power output was measured on a special computer-controlled bicycle dynamometer built by the Millikens.

It was necessary for the rider to achieve 30 mph (48 kph) 1 km (1,094 yds) before the start of the measured 200 metres. From that point smooth acceleration was needed, the rider accurately shifting the gears upwards as pre-specified cadences were indicated by a handlebar-mounted computer. At least, that was the theory. However, Doug had discovered that the original Cateye Solar computer he had been using on the various AM-based HPVs gave erratic readings above about 45 mph (72 kph). This may have resulted from a sensor problem, or from inadequate frequency response in the computer's input stage for such abnormally high speeds. (A Schwinn Paramount computer subsequently proved accurate up to about 1,200 rpm (60 mph/97 kph).)

Fortunately Jim had an excellent memory for cadence and therefore hardly needed a speedometer. The team therefore worked out the gear shift speeds from the gear chart, and Jim used mental arithmetic to calculate his speed.

In HPV events of this type, riders are typically capable of only three good attempts in a day. On the first run Jim started accelerating too late, and achieved 49.3 mph (79.3 kph). He over-compensated on the second run, building up speed too soon, and notching up 49.6 mph (79.8 kph). But on his third run, he broke both the world record and the 50 mph barrier, achieving 50.21 mph (80.79 kph). The fully-faired AM7 was now the fastest streamlined bike in the world on a flying 200 metre unpaced run in still air using the normal riding position.

Rider comfort necessitated some minor refinements to the 'Liner. For example, the transparent section of the lid was partly lined with silver-coloured Mylar sheet to protect the rider from the sun.

Through the 50mph barrier...
Photo by C. Michael Lewis.

Also, it was discovered that the rider typically lost about a US gallon (0.85 imperial gallon, 3.8 litres) of fluid in an hour-long event through perspiration. Over a period of time rider sweat proved to be severely corrosive!

The day after he broke the 200 metre record, Jim Glover rode the 'Liner in a road race. He was in second place until he crashed. Undaunted, he managed to remount unaided (discarding the lid which required taping on from outside the machine) and achieved fourth place. Phil Godkin from Green Bay, Wisconsin, whom Doug Milliken met in the parking lot and invited to ride for him, took the Aero III to second place in the same race. (Phil later rode the Aero IV in the 1991 Milwaukee IHPSC, where he also did well.)

In July the following year Swift Cycles, the premier AM dealer in the UK, started running advertisements in the cycling press proclaiming

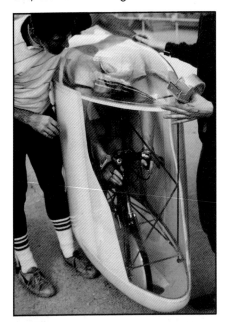

"The World's Fastest Bicycle". The advert featured the AM7, which formed the basis of the 'Liner. Angle Lake Cyclery in Seattle used a similar approach in their AM adverts.

Taping the lid onto the 'Liner at IHPSC '85, Indianapolis.
Photo by C. Michael Lewis.

'Liner at Indy '85,
Left to right: Jim Glover, Jim Scandale, Doug Milliken.
Photo courtesy of Doug Milliken.

Zapple

Although most AM-based HPV racing took place in North America, there was some in England and elsewhere. Four weeks before Indianapolis '85, on the weekend of 31 August/1 September, the Zapple Festival of Human Power was staged at Milton Keynes. Sponsored by a brand of sparkling apple juice, it was an official IHPVA event at which human-powered aircraft and water craft were also scheduled to take part.

Unfortunately blustery winds prevented the aircraft from flying, and considerably impaired the performance of the water craft. As Bicycle magazine put it, "This left the main activity to the land events, and a continuous battle in every event between Moultons and Speedys."

The Moulton racing contingent consisted of Dave Synar and Trevor Bull. They rode Zzipper-equipped standard AM7s with oversized chainwheels. The AMs were HPVs only by virtue of bolting on the commercially-available AM-Zzipper fairing. They therefore had considerably higher aerodynamic drag than the fully enclosed recumbent Windcheetah Speedy tricycles fielded by Mike Burrows.

Nonetheless, in the "round the houses" race the AMs came second and fourth, Speedys taking first and third places. In the practical vehicle event Alex Moulton himself rode an AM14 fitted with Zzipper fairing, front and rear lights, rear basket and frame skins. It was judged third, behind a fully faired Speedy and an unfaired Lighting X2 recumbent.

Alex Moulton with his practical vehicle entry at Zapple.

AM7 with Zzipper fairing at Zapple.

Fast Writer

That summer another AM14 was put through its paces by Hamburg journalist Georg Weden, but this time in the standard, unfaired form. In the 6th VW Radler-Cup event, on the test track at Ehra-Lessien, Lower Saxony, he achieved "one of the first places in the speed test … and in the final endurance test". According to the German magazine Fahrrad Sport & Reisen, Weden clocked 28.2 mph (45.2 kph) and described the AM14 as "sensational".

Versatility

David Gordon Wilson, the well-known British-born expert on cycle technology, based at the Massachusetts Institute of Technology, published a survey of HPVs in the July/August 1986 issue of American Scientist. In the following issue a reader took him to task for not mentioning the Alex Moulton bicycle.

Professor Wilson replied, acknowledging his omission of the "wonderful machine". He added that he owned three Moultons and had "ridden tens of thousands of miles on them, often loaded with, for instance, five-gallon [23 l] drums of oil. No other bicycle built for commuting could do this. At the other end of their range, their performance in IHPVA racing has been truly remarkable."

The 'Liner II – and a New Record

The 12th International Human Powered Speed Championships were held in Vancouver in August 1986 as part of the World's Fair (Expo '86). Nearly 100 HPVs took part but only a dozen or so were able to exceed 50 mph (80.45 kph).

One of these was the 'Liner II. Some 5lb (2.25 kg) lighter than the first 'Liner, it was similar in principle, but slightly shorter. Again, Jim Glover was the rider, and again, he broke the flying 200 metres record, this time taking it to 51.29 mph (82.53 kph). His achievement was all the more remarkable because the course, an

Getting Jim Glover and 'Liner II ready before the record setting 51.29 mph run at Expo '86, Vancouver. On the left is Alex Moulton and behind him Doug Milliken.
Photo courtesy of Doug Milliken.

51 mph – THE WORLD RECORD MOULTON

On August 29th 1986 at the 3rd International HPV Scientific Symposium at Vancouver. A MOULTON ridden by JIM GLOVER broke the world unpaced cycling record with a speed of 51.29 mph over 200m (conventional riding position)

Fairing by Doug Milliken. AM7 special low head. 82 x 10 5-step block, 140" gear. 17" standard Moulton Wolber tyres, 120 p.s.i.

Alex Moulton Limited
Bradford on Avon, Wiltshire BA15 1AH, England. Tel 02216 5895
Fax 02216 4742 (overseas 2216 4742)

The promotional card produced by Alex Moulton Limited
to commemorate the 'Liner II's success.

unopened section of highway, sloped uphill slightly, and was at a lower altitude with denser air than Indianapolis.

Alex was present on 29 August to see the 'Liner's triumph. While in Vancouver he also gave an address to the Third International HPV Scientific Symposium, entitled "The Moulton Bicycle Project from Conception". This was subsequently published as an illustrated booklet.

The 'Liner II was featured on the 1986 Alex Moulton Christmas card. Brian Walker's drawing showed it leaning against the wall of Alex's office.

The Aero III at Vancouver

The flying 200 metres was not the only success for the AM at Vancouver. The Aero III, ridden by Dave Bogdan, a mechanic employed by Angle Lake Cyclery in Seattle, came second in the gruelling 165 mile (265 km) Seattle to Vancouver race. He averaged 25 mph (40 kph) and came in less than ten minutes behind the winner, a rigid-faired recumbent tricycle. Dave beat many other fully-faired HPVs, including the much publicised Bluebell. As Frank Berto put it in his report of the event, published in Bike Tech , "Not too shabby for a standard configuration bicycle".

By this time the Aero III had been fitted with a belly pan, which improved the airflow – and gave early audible warning if the rider was leaning too far on bends! Sandy Bellamy, maker of the special Bel Ami bags for AMs, kindly patched the Spandex fairing, accidentally torn before the race.

After the IHPSC the 'Liner II was taken back to Seattle and shipped to Germany for the Cologne cycle show, which took place a fortnight later. 'Liner II had flown into Seattle as Doug's checked luggage in two boxes and had been assembled at Angle Lake Cyclery, over a couple of days. For shipment to Germany, Dale Clark of Angle

Jim Glover in Aero III, with red spandex tail cone, in the road races at Expo '86, Vancouver. Photo by Doug Milliken.

Lake arranged to have a large wooden crate made so that the machine could be shipped without disassembly, thus saving trouble setting up for the show. The Aero III (ridden by Dave Bogdan in the Seattle-to-Vancouver race) returned as Doug's luggage, these two bikes being the only known full streamliner HPVs to ship this way.

Aero III ready to be shipped home after the road races, Expo '86, Vancouver. Photo by Doug Milliken.

The 'Liner III

Doug Milliken's next project was the 'Liner III. This was based on a white prototype AM-SPEED (see page 236) and therefore weighed a little less than the 'Liner II. The suspension was jacked up in the same way as the red low-head prototype used for 'Liners I and II. Unlike production SPEEDs, the front fork was a unicrown type, similar to that used for the AM-ATB.

The 'Liner III's transmission consisted of 86 and 82 tooth chainwheels driving a close-ratio block. The smallest four sprockets had 9, 10, 11 and 12 teeth, giving gears of 162, 146, 133 and 122" with the larger chainwheel, and half-step options of 155, 139, 127 and 116" with the smaller ring. Therefore, by double shifting, a progression in approximately 5% steps was possible.

'Liner III at the 1989 IHPSC, Michigan International Raceway. Left to right: Doug Milliken, Jim Glover (showing how he enters the 'Liner by by standing on the pit wall) and Jim Scandale. Photo courtesy of Doug Milliken.

The tyres were Moulton-Wolber slicks (see page 238), run at 140 psi (9.52 atm). The handlebars were upturned unrolled drops.

Doug Milliken's calculations showed that the 'Liner III was potentially faster than either of its predecessors. However, it never fully achieved its potential – circumstances always seemed to conspire against it. For example, in 1989 on the Michigan International Speedway, an attempt was made on the hour record. Jim Glover was well up to schedule when the Aero II was blown over by the September wind. In pre-attempt testing Jim had achieved speeds in excess of 55 mph (88 kph).

Nonetheless, earlier in 1989, he rode the 'Liner III to overall winning place at the International Festival of the Bicycle HPV event at Hull, Quebec. Six AM-based HPVs of various types took part against eight other HPVs. Doug fielded three AMs, including the Aero III. He was joined by Will Kennedy's Aero, IHPVA President Marti Daily's AM7 and Jim Glover's AM7, ridden by Gord Fraser, now a Canadian national team member whom Jim coached in Ottawa for several years. The Aero III, which had been fitted with a new purple Ripstop non-porous tail cone for improved aerodynamics, was ridden by various local Ottawa riders.

Jim in the 'Liner III came first in the road race and sprints. Other AMs took second, third and fourth places in the road race. Overall the AM-based HPVs took the lion's share of the winnings.

Wisconsin HPV Hat Trick

In April 1990 the 'Liner III and Aero III took part in the Wisconsin HPV Classic. This was run in very cold weather on the Milwaukee Mile motor track at West Allis.

For personal reasons Jim Glover was unable to take part, so his place in the 'Liner III was taken by "Fast" Freddie Markham, an HPV record-breaking rider. Markham set the fastest time of the day at 48.278 mph (77.679 kph). Fifteen year old Will Kennedy in the Aero III achieved fastest time in the GT class, 33.725 mph (54.264 kph).

A hat trick was completed when Freddie Markham won the one hour time trial in the 'Liner III – despite being blown over by a gust of wind, necessitating removal of the HPV's lid.

In August that year, the International Human Powered Speed Championships were held at Portland, Oregon. In this event young Will Kennedy, in the Dave Kennedy-built Aero, came equal second in the 200 metre time trial, GT class. He achieved 37.47 mph (60.29 kph). Doug Milliken rode his Aero IV in this event but was beaten by Will. (Dave Kennedy, Will's father, is a past president of the IHPVA.)

Left to right: Will Kennedy and Kennedy Aero, Doug Milliken and Aero III (with Ripstop nylon tail) at IHPSC 1990, Portland, Oregon.
Photo by Jean Seay, editor 'HPVA News'.

502 miles in 24 Hours

In the 1991 Wisconsin HPV Classic, Australian Anthony Peden rode the 'Liner III in the Milwaukee Mile and achieved over 50 mph (80.45 kph) in the 200 metre sprints. In the road race Matt Chambers, from California, took the 'Liner III to third place.

But perhaps the most remarkable result was achieved by Gerry Tatrai in Aero IV. (This differed from its predecessor in that it had a new belly pan shape.) Only 10 days earlier Gerry, on a conventional cycle, had come third in his first Race Across AMerica (RAAM). Despite not being fully recovered from this arduous single stage transcontinental race, he won the 24 hour HPV race around the Milwaukee Mile track, covering no less than 502.2 miles (808 km) in Aero IV. In so doing he stopped to sleep a little and to take a shower. Yet he beat the second placed rider by about 100 miles (160 km).

(In 1992 Gerry again came third in the RAAM, but won it the following year, in both cases on conventional machines.)

At Wisconsin in 1992 Jim Glover was reunited with the 'Liner III. In difficult, windy conditions he came second in the 200 metre sprints. The wind also foiled another attempt on the hour record.

'Liner III has now retired to the Moulton Museum at Bradford-on-Avon. It calmly awaits the day when another normal position HPV breaks the flying 200 metres record, at which point it or a successor may just come out of retirement!

The 'Liner III story would not be complete without giving credit to Tim Bigwood who built the SPEED prototype around which it was constructed. Honourable mention must also be made of Jim Scandale, longtime support crew member.

The John Paul Mitchell Systems Run

The John Paul Mitchell Systems Run was a competition for the fastest cycle ride from San Francisco to Los Angeles, a distance of 390 miles (627 km). It was open to HPVs and in 1991 Doug Milliken therefore put together a team. The rider was Elaine Mariolle, a former RAAM women's section winner. She rode the Aero IV and, despite being only 5' 2" (157.5 cm) was able to ride the same AM frame as 6' 1" (185.4 cm) Doug. He simply put on a normal short handlebar stem and lowered the saddle – another example of AM versatility!

The frame was the original one Doug received from Alex early in 1984 (frame number 350001) but now modified to the low steering head/Jubilee configuration.

The team were confident that Elaine could complete the course in 24 hours riding time, given ideal conditions. Unfortunately conditions on Interstate Highway 5 were far from good. On the first day the California Highway Patrol stopped the attempt for four hours while documentation was sorted out. This necessitated an unplanned night in a motel, because of the difficulty of cycling on the Interstate Highway at night.

Elaine reached Los Angeles the following day, 41 hours having elapsed. No time adjustments were allowed for the delays caused by the Highway Patrol, nor for a puncture, and she was given fourth place overall.

Interestingly, most of the other finishers, including the winner, were recumbents using an AM 17" front wheel.

The Kennedy Aero

Sometime after the 1990 Wisconsin Classic, Will Kennedy and his father Dave used some of Doug Milliken's cast-off components to build their own Aero fairing in yellow nylon with black Spandex trim. The Kennedy Aero uses a 1986 standard AM7 frame kit and Doug's original Aero front carrier.

Evolutionary changes from the Aero III include:
- Lexan windscreen extended back further past the rider's shoulders,
- tail strut shortened by 3" (75 mm),
- stiffer rear carrier,
- belly pan closer to the ground (because the AM7 frame has the standard bottom bracket height),
- lower fairing support hoop,

- flexible upper front carrier strut to the windscreen (which seems to reduce wind gust sensitivity),
- cowl top added to front fairing in 1992.

The transmission uses an eight-speed close-ratio block, the smallest sprocket having 9 or 10 teeth, driven by a 64 tooth chainwheel: this gives a top gear of 121" or 109". Alternatively a 68 tooth ring is used, driving an 11 tooth cog, to give a top gear of 105".

Will Kennedy, using the Kennedy Aero, won the road race at the Midwest HPV Series, Columbus, Indiana in 1990. In the same year he won the Waterford Hills, Michigan standing start hill climb. At the 1991 Wisconsin IHPSC he achieved 39 mph (63 kph) in the flying 200 metres.

In the 1992 IHPSC at Yreka, California, Jim Glover, riding the Kennedy Aero, pushed the speed up to a remarkable 45.75 mph (73.61 kph). He also made fourth place in the 25 mile (40 km) time trial.

At the 1993 IHPSC held in Minneapolis, Minnesota, Will won the 1/4 mile (400 metre) drag races, covering the distance in a very creditable 30.02 sec. He came third in the 1 km (0.62 mile) race, GT class, with a time of 1 min. 12.98 sec. – his first competition event on a velodrome. And in the 200 metres, GT class, he came second.

Will Kennedy and the Kennedy Aero at IHPSC '90, Portland International Raceway, Oregon.
Photo by Doug Milliken.

New Zealand Knockout

The ability to convert any AM into an HPV merely by bolting on the "off-the-peg" AM-Zzipper fairing enabled Dave Kelly of Christchurch, New Zealand to take part in the Human Powered Vehicle races held in that city in April 1993. He raced with all the normal fittings on his bike, such as mudguards and even the dynamo lighting system. His only concession to lightness was to remove the carrier!

The first event was a standing start 1 km (0.6 mile) time trial on a banked track. Dave Kelly had never ridden the AM on banking before, but nonetheless came second to a fully-faired recumbent bike, Red October.

Next came a flying 200 metres, where he was again beaten by Red October. The third event was a 6.5 km (4 mile) "round-the-houses". This time Dave beat Red October but lost to another recumbent. The final event was a test of manoeuvrability, a slalom course which Red October did not even attempt – Dave won this easily.

He was therefore the best all-rounder, with one first and three second places. While other contestants loaded their machines into trailers or cars, Dave "put the carrier back on, filled the rear bag with my winnings (four bottles of wine) and rode home". That day the AM14 proved itself truly a multi-role machine!

Training and Coaching on an AM

Jim Glover uses an AM7 extensively, especially when coaching at the national level in Canada. He has little time for those who say you cannot maintain high cadences on an AM:

"When I was coaching Gord Fraser (the national 15 km TT record holder) to ride pursuit, he learned the meaning of the word spin. We would put our bikes in a tiny gear and spin it up for 5 minutes. I would lead (always on the AM7) since the object was to spin; speed would come later with power training.

"After about 3 minutes at 140 rpm, I would sit up and turn round to see how he was doing, maintaining 140 rpm! Then have the insensitivity to tell him to pedal faster! (He was struggling to spin that fast back then.)

"In 1992 at the IHPSC in Yreka I pedalled through the 200 meter speed traps at 144 rpm. I had broken my hip May '91 and had second surgery January '92, so my power wasn't back yet and I relied on my spinning skill.

"The fastest I ever pedalled (the AM7) was downhill in a small gear – 237 rpm! and 78 kph or 48 mph! Only for a few seconds though."

Jim finds the AM an ideal mount for draughting:

"In coaching, I can ride very close to the athlete with my Moulton. My empirical testing suggests a heart rate drop at the same speed (when draughting vs. in free air), to be 15-20 beats per minute. This allows me enough "air" to talk to the athlete when they're going hard and I'm sitting in their draught at 28-30 mph (45-48 kph). You can't get a better bike for wheel sucking.

"Every once in a while other uninformed cyclists ask when I'm going to get a full-size bike. My answer is usually 'I'll get a full-size bike when you can keep up with me on this one!'. I smile politely when I say this of course."

Paris-Brest-Paris

Audax events, known as randonnées, involve riding a set course within prescribed upper and lower time limits. As such, they are not races. However, some can be very demanding. The strict translation of randonée as "ramble" can sometimes be misleading!

The word Audax (Latin for "daring") entered the cycling vocabulary in Italy in 1897. Seven years later the Audax Club Parisien (ACP) was founded, and this developed regulations which were adopted throughout France. Audax United Kingdom (AUK) is a relative newcomer, having been established only seven years before the launch of the AM.

Soon after it was introduced, Alex Moulton's new bike was seen by some Audax riders as ideal for their type of riding, being fast, comfortable and capable of being transported easily to and from events by car or public transport. There was sufficient interest to induce Alex to advertise on the back cover of AUK's magazine, Arrivée.

The four-yearly Paris-Brest-Paris Randonnée, which originated as an open race in 1891, is said to be the toughest Audax. It is certainly one of the biggest mass participation cycling events in the world. Typically two to three thousand riders take part. The route from the French capital to the port of Brest in the west of Brittany and back, is about 755 miles (1,215 km).

Those taking part may elect to try to complete the ride in 90, 84 or 78 hours. The majority choose the 90 hour option, which means starting at 4 o'clock in the morning. A sizeable minority prefer a more civilised start time, electing for the 84 hour option. Only a few, a hundred or so, go for the 78 hours, starting at 4 o'clock in the afternoon. There are no official rest breaks: the clock keeps running throughout.

Most riders have two sets of lights on their bikes, one battery powered, the

Ray Craig at the finish of the PBP, 1983. His mount was a works demonstrator. He was so impressed, he bought his own AM. Photo courtesy of Ray Craig.

other dynamo driven. This is because any rider caught without working lights is disqualified.

In 1983 Ray Craig was among the first AM riders to tackle the PBP, as it is commonly known. He cycled from his home in Berkshire to Southampton, took the overnight ferry to Le Havre, then spent two days cycling at a leisurely pace to the Paris starting point. Electing for the 84 hour option he joined some 900 others who set out at 10 o'clock in the morning.

76 hours and 14 minutes later he was back. He had taken less time than was allowed for the late starting elite. Ray wrote, "The machine proved light, responsive and certainly as fast as any other lightweight on the road."

Two other AM7 riders took part in the 1983 PBP – Frenchman Pierre Maisonneuve and Nick Peregrine, then honorary secretary of the MBC. Nick's time was even better than Ray's – approximately 69 hours!

400 Miles in 24 Hours

On the 21 & 22 July the following year, Ray rode his AM7 almost 400 miles (644 km) in 24 hours. This was in the Mersey Roads Club Subscription 24 hour time trial.

He came seventeenth out of 51 starters. Only 41 riders finished the ride; the fastest covering just over 460 miles (740 km), the slowest a little more than 213 miles (343 km).

On a conventional machine Ray had achieved 427 miles (687 km) in the Wessex Roads Club 24, but that was when he was 10 years younger. His performance on the AM7 was therefore quite creditable.

King of the Mountains

At six o'clock on the morning of 10 September 1984 Ray Craig and three other British Audax riders cycled off from Brindisi on the "heel" of Italy. They were embarking on a 1,370 mile (2,200 km) randonée – destination Calais, northern France. Three more of their companions set off 24 hours later.

After some 60 miles (100 km) Ray got separated from his friends: they were not to see him again for the rest of the ride. Ray arrived in Calais about half past eight the following Monday evening, not knowing whether he was in front of his companions or behind.

In fact, despite fighting head winds much of the way, he had completed the ride from Brindisi to Calais (including all meals, comfort breaks and sleeping) in just 182 hrs. 20 min. This was 13 hrs. 15 min. faster than the next best time, and 16 hrs. 45 min. ahead of the slowest. Ray therefore won the yellow jersey, the prize for outright winner.

Three views of the Mont Cenis Pass, taken during Ray Craig's Brindisi to Calais Audax.
Photos by Ray Craig.

He was also proclaimed "king of the mountains" for his performance on the climbs, which included crossing the Alps. The toughest part was the wearisome 15 mile (25 km) climb up Mont Cenis to an altitude of 6,830 feet (2,083 metres) near the Italian-French border. A photograph of Ray's bike on the Mont Cenis pass was featured on the back of the 1985 AM brochure.

A Big Improvement

While Ray Craig rode an AM7 in the 1983 PBP, Australian Stephen Poole rode a conventional custom-built lightweight. His time then was 80 hours – 3 hrs. 46 min. slower than Ray's. Stephen had not been helped by his clothing and saddle, which had conspired with road shock to shave the skin off his derrière.

Stephen road-tested AMs and was impressed. He therefore converted an AM2 for the 1987 PBP. Fitting triple chainrings, a seven-speed block and other racing components, he created what he called an AM21.

As any HPV may enter the PBP, he made full use of aerodynamic aids. In collaboration with Karl Abbé (who bought Zzip Designs from Glen Brown) he developed a Zzipper fairing with prototype Lycra wrapround girdle. Milliken wheel discs were added, along with frame skins and Lycra shoe covers.

Stephen's fitness levels for the rides in 1983 and 1987 were much the same. However, the 1987 route seemed hillier, and the weather less kind. He faced a head wind and a lot of rain for the first 370 miles (600 km).

The AM21 performed well compared with the custom-made lightweight. The cruising speed was much higher, comfort was superior and hill climbing was at least as good. Acceleration when overtaking was substantially better. As Stephen put it, "The aero bits were definitely vindicated". In fact, he knocked 10 hours off his previous time, a 14% improvement – and the skin stayed on his backside this time!

Stephen said he would ride an AM again in the PBP but would fit larger chainrings: his highest gear in 1987 was 91", which was not high enough for the speed he could achieve. Apart from the machine's poor performance on soft ground, the only drawback was the limited number of outlets from which spares could be obtained. However, he pointed out that the factory was very helpful in this respect.

Reverting to a conventional bicycle seemed very strange to Stephen after riding the AM in the PBP: "I had never realised what horrible things top tubes are, and it now feels most peculiar to ride something that flexes sideways and is rigid vertically, rather than vice versa."

1991 was the 100th anniversary of the PBP. One of several AM riders taking part was 54 year old Fred Weinstein from Toronto, who completed the 90 hour option with seven minutes to spare. Over the years he had suffered an unusually high number of problems with his AM7. Nonetheless, as a heavy and not particularly strong rider, he was pleased with his PBP performance and wrote, "I'm still in love with my machine ..."

Also riding that year was Paul Farren of South Yarra, Victoria, Australia. His mount was an AM7 fitted with a double chainwheel. Paul's verdict? "Wonderful bike!"

Flèche Velocio

In 1988 Alan Sturk of Audax United Kingdom used an AM to take part in the Flèche Velocio. This is an annual Easter ride where participants have 24 hours to complete approximately 225 miles (360 km). Each year the destination is a different French village, where an Easter Sunday "concentration" takes place. Riders form small groups of three to five, and ride to the venue from various starting points along differing routes.

Alan's companions in 1988 were a tricyclist and a couple on a tandem. They set off at midnight from Bellegarde, 25 miles (40 km) south of Geneva. The ride through Provence was frosty and mountainous, the highest peak being 1,560 ft (481 metres). They arrived at their destination, Senas in the Rhone delta, with just 30 minutes to spare. In 23 hours they had ridden 227 miles (366 km), half of it in the dark. This is only 47 miles (75 km) short of cycling from Switzerland to the Mediterranean!

Other Great Rides

Other examples of great rides against the clock undertaken on AMs include:

- Nick Peregrine's Birmingham-Lizard-Birmingham ride, 622 miles (1,000 km) in 59 hours.
- Nick Peregrine & Bryan Chapman's Flèche Velocio from Vichy to Avignon via Le Puy, 249 miles (400 km) in 24 hours.
- Peter van Nuys' ride in The Great Californian Land Rush, 404 miles (650 km) in two days.

(All times and distances approximate.)

The RAAM

Even the toughest Audax events seem tame when compared with the **R**ace **A**cross **AM**erica. At typically 3,100 miles (nearly 5,000 km) the RAAM is almost certainly the longest and toughest single stage bicycle race in the world. What were its origins?

In 1978 John Marino broke the record for riding coast-to-coast across the United States. He immediately decided to instigate a transcontinental race. In August 1982 the Great American Bike Race took place, featuring John and three other male riders. Subsequently the name was changed to Race Across AMerica.

Women competed against males in the 1983 RAAM, and in 1984 a women's division was established. Elaine Mariolle, who won the women's division in 1986 (and was the second fastest woman in the 1991 100th anniversary PBP) described the RAAM as "the craziest thing I had ever heard of".

In 1986 David Bogdan of Kent, Washington State was a 25 year old bicycle mechanic with a penchant for hiking, who worked for Dale and Kelvin Clark's Angle Lake Cyclery in Seattle. He was an AM7 owner and had recently taken up cycling seriously, with a view to entering marathons. That August at the Human Powered Vehicle Speed Championships in Vancouver, Dave's employers introduced him to Doug Milliken. Almost before he knew it, Dave found himself riding the Aero II to second place in the road race from Seattle to Vancouver. (See page 219)

Dave had long been a RAAM fan and wanted to ride an AM in the race. The RAAM was only open to "conventional" bicycles, but founder John Marino of the Ultra-Marathon Cycling Association confirmed that he would allow the AM to compete because of its normal riding position.

Angle Lake Cyclery agreed to be prime sponsor and Dave's family was also very supportive. So, in autumn 1986 Dave took a job in Tucson, Arizona where the climate made it easier for him to train through the winter. Later, as summer approached, he would get a foretaste of daytime desert temperatures on the RAAM, possibly exceeding 40 degrees Celsius (105 Fahrenheit).

In April 1987 Dave took part in the 450 mile (724 km) RAAM Open West race in Tucson to qualify for the RAAM itself. Thereafter he rode 500 to 1,000 miles a week (800 to 1,600 km), in a mixture of short, fast club runs and long solo rides.

Meanwhile, back at Angle Lake, Dale Clark built up three AM-Jubilee prototypes (referred to at the time as AM14 specials) from frame kits and pre-release Wishbone stems supplied by Alex. SunTour were eventually persuaded to donate four sets of components, and other sponsors included McDonalds, the hamburger chain.

Two of the Jubilees were fitted out for Dave. One was equipped with a bias towards hill climbing; the other for descending, being higher geared and having specially-made forearm rests by Kevin King of Seattle. The transmission used SunTour Cyclone derailleur mechanisms, but with Shimano Freehub cassettes, necessary to take the close-ratio AM 9, 10 & 11 tooth triple cogs.

The third machine was for Cherie Moore who also competed in RAAM '87. Sponsored by Two-Wheel Transit of Huntingdon Beach, California, she intended to use the Jubilee for riding over the bumpy flats of Midwest America. However, she suffered neck problems riding a conventional machine early in the race and eventually dropped out.

With a single-stage race such as the RAAM, the support team is all-important. The "Tiny Tire Team", as it was dubbed, comprised nine of Dave Bogdan's friends and relatives, captained by his father George, and including Doug Milliken. The team members' ages ranged from 19 to 60.

Two vehicles were involved. A small van, lent by Chrysler, carried the spare bike, wheels and other components. The crew in the Chrysler shadowed Dave closely, communicating with him via his helmet radio, and passing him food and drink almost continuously. The other vehicle was a motor caravan, which provided the meals and sleeping accommodation for the whole crew.

The team worked round the clock on a shift basis. As Doug put it: "Don't get the idea that the support crew had it easy – imagine taking care of nine people and one very hungry rider for a week and a half in about a hundred square feet [9.5 sq m] of motor home."

On 20 June 1987 the race set off from San Francisco, where Alex Moulton and David Duffield joined the spectators. The destination was Washington, DC – 3,127 miles (5,031 km) and 13 states away. Doug recalled the last minute preparations made in true "night before" fashion: "My memory of that night is a blur of half a dozen Shimano Freehubs and lots of cogs that didn't want to be assembled in the desired order ..."

The first few days had their share of problems. Soon after the start Dave's Jubilee punctured. Because of traffic congestion, he had to wait a quarter of an hour for the support van to reach him. Hence he found himself trailing early on. Also, it took about three days to fine tune his diet to avoid stomach problems. Despite this, he powered his way across California, Nevada (where he slept for the first time on the ride), Utah and into Colorado.

In the Rocky Mountains he climbed well to the highest point on the ride, the continental divide at Berthoud Pass, 11,307 feet (3,449 metres) above sea level. Because of the heat, some riders were unable to climb the pass in daylight. Dave, however, was unfazed by the high temperatures and reached the summit at dusk. The temperature then plummeted to 5 degrees Celsius (40 degrees Fahrenheit), necessitating wrapping up well for the descent to Denver. On such fast and rough downhill rides, the AM's suspension really came into its own.

Entering Kansas, Dave's pace began to slow as the mountains gave way to the Great Plains. He was riding about 250 miles (400 km) a day through this boring, hot and humid terrain on rough roads with only a couple of hours sleep. The Tiny Tire Team therefore had to contrive various morale boosting stunts, such as tearing a map of the USA in half as he reached the midway point of his journey.

Dave Bogdan and the Tiny Tire Team crossing the continental divide, Berthoud Pass, 1987.
Photo by the RAAM crew.

Another shot of Dave Bogdan crossing the continental divide, RAAM '87.
Photo courtesy of Doug Milliken.

RAAM '87 – half way to Washington DC and a map of the USA is torn in two. Photo courtesy of Doug Milliken.

The flat lands continued through Missouri, Illinois, Indiana and western Ohio. In eastern Ohio the terrain finally started to become hillier, reviving Dave's spirits. His riding became stronger again as he traversed West Virginia and a small corner of Virginia. Maryland was the last state he crossed before entering Washington, DC.

Dave reached the finishing line 11 days, 8 hours and 2 minutes after leaving San Francisco. He was 1 day, 20 hrs. and 27 min. behind the winner, and came twelfth out of 35 contestants, of whom only 15 completed. (57% of riders of conventional machines failed to finish.) He had averaged about 276 miles (444 km) per day.

Unlike many successful RAAM riders, Dave completed the race in good physical condition. Doug Milliken attributed this to his physical and mental training (partly directed by Jim Glover, now a top cycling coach in Canada), diet, frequent massages and not least to the AM-Jubilee's suspension. Dave weighed about 10 stone (148lb, 67 kg) and lost only 2lb (0.9 kg) during the race. He was basically back to his normal physical condition within three weeks.

No major mechanical problems were experienced with the bikes during the ride. Standard Moulton-Wolber 17" tyres were used, running at 110 to 120 psi (7.5 to 8.2 atm). Two rear covers were replaced as a precaution because of tread wear, and only four punctures were sustained.

The AM was probably the first non-conventional bike to compete both in IHPVA events and the RAAM.

RAAM '88

The following year Dave Bogdan and the Tiny Tire Team were back in action again. This time they were sponsored by Alex Moulton, Angle Lake Cyclery, SunTour, Wolber, Trico and Samuel Smith. To help finance the attempt, Tiny Tire Team T-shirts were marketed at $12.50. These bore the silhouette of a city slicker racing along on an AM, thus stressing the bike's multi-role capability – you could commute on it, or equally well Race Across AMerica!

(Early versions of the silhouette showed the rider's right hand holding the handlebars and a briefcase. The case was later edited out, presumably for product liability reasons, as AM instructions advise against loose luggage on the handlebars!)

Dave was one of 33 entrants, aged from 15 to 45. Their occupations included professional cyclist, surf reporter, schoolboy, piano technician, truck driver and orthopaedic surgeon.

The prospect of a second RAAM did not daunt Dave, who stated: "Whether riding into the wind, climbing endless hills or having water fights with the crew, it's all fun to me!"

Compared with 1987, the route was slightly shorter but more severe. The total height climbed was again some 75,000 feet (22,900 m). On several days the riders were hampered by temperatures exceeding 38 degrees Celsius (100 degrees Fahrenheit), and they sometimes had to fight strong winds.

Early in the ride Dave again suffered illness. Even so, he covered 646 miles (1,039 km) in the first two days.

Despite the more severe conditions, he completed the 3,073 mile (4,944 km) route in 10 days, 15 hours and 1 minute. This was an improvement of 17 hours over his 1987 speed. He averaged 12 mph (19.3 kph) and 289 miles (465 km) per day, and slept for only 26 hours in total. He improved his position by four places, coming in eighth. Only 14 riders out of 33 starters finished, 61% of riders on conventional machines this time failing to make it.

RAAM '87 – Dave Bogdan on the AM-Jubilee prototype somewhere in Kansas. Note the radio headset. Photo by Doug Milliken.

Dave Bogdan, the AM-Jubilee prototype and the Tiny Tire Team, at the finish of the RAAM '87. Photo courtesy of Doug Milliken.

Again, Dave arrived in good condition, and was one of the few riders able to sign his autograph on arrival at the finish line, thanks to the AM's front suspension.

Alex Moulton witnessed the end of the race in Washington, DC. For several years he and Chet Kyle had wanted to compute the efficiency of humans as power sources. The RAAM gave them the opportunity and during RAAM '88 accurate records were kept of Dave Bogdan's performance.

About 90% of the food he consumed was liquid (Ultra Energy), and he drank about two US gallons (1.7 imperial gallons, 7.6 litres) of water per day. In all he consumed 88,840 calories. His output was 15,415 calories; as a power source he was therefore 17.4% efficient. Chet's study, published in Bicycling, also included Pete Penseyres' winning RAAM '86 performance, which showed an efficiency of 20.3%. Kyle concluded that leading RAAM riders were about as efficient as the best fossil-fuel power stations, and much more efficient than most cars.

Alex commented: "Mankind would be hard pressed to make any automotive vehicle as efficient as a man on a bike. Moreover, our fuel is non-fossil, pleasant to consume, and easily renewable."

Dave's epic ride inspired the design of the 1988 Alex Moulton Christmas card by Brian Walker. It showed Dave riding the AM across a map of the USA labelled with the route and key facts about the ride.

Today (1994) Dave Bogdan works for a sports wheelchair manufacturer in Tacoma, Washington. He and his wife Erin still ride Moultons, a SPEED and an AM7, but mostly for weekend recreation.

The Prototype AM-SPEED

The bike Dave Bogdan rode on his second RAAM was specially engineered. While retaining most of the key features of the AM range, it weighed only some 21lb (9.5 kg). It was known as the SPEED, the name being spelt all in capitals – not as an affectation but to differentiate it from the Moulton Speeds of the 1960s. The first three prototype SPEEDs were

RAAM '88 – Dave Bogdan descending one of the many hills as he nears the finish on the SPEED. Photo by Alex Moulton.

Dave Bogdan with the AM-SPEED prototype at the finishing line of the RAAM'88.

Dave Bogdan smiles as he approaches the finishing line.

"The Tiny Tire Team' T-shirt.

built partly unjigged by Tim Bigwood. One was Dave's main RAAM machine, another his standby, and the third formed the basis of the 'Liner III HPV.

The SPEED's frame was lighter than the standard AM frame for three reasons. Firstly, the kingpin joint was eliminated, as separability was not necessary for an all-out road racing machine. Secondly, smaller diameter Reynolds 531 tubes were used for the spaceframe. And finally, instead of using the long, wide diameter stainless steel seat pillar, the seat tube was elongated and necked down to take a standard short seat pin.

Being built of the thinner tubing, the rear triangle was stiffened by additional corner braces between the lower mudguard bridge and the chainstays.

The Production AM-SPEED

The production version of the SPEED was launched in the USA via Angle Lake Cyclery on 7 September 1989, and displayed at the IHPVA Symposium in Adrian, Michigan nine days later. The following weekend it was unveiled at the Moulton Bicycle Club annual meet at Bradford-on-Avon.

However, the SPEED was not marketed in the UK until the following spring (1990), all early production being exported. It was illustrated in New Cyclist's autumn 1989 issue and full page AM advertisements featuring the SPEED appeared in the magazine's spring, summer and autumn issues the following year. A 1990 promotional card for Alex Moulton Limited featured a drawing by Brian Walker of an AM-SPEED rider greeting a driver in "the new Rover Metro (100) with its Moulton Interconnected suspension".

In a departure from the "one frame fits all" philosophy, the SPEED could be ordered with a seat tube height of 19, 22 or 25" (48.3, 55.9 and 63.5 cm). The low head tube could be ordered in a "tall" version, 2" (50 mm) higher than normal.

The frame (25" version) weighed 5lb 1.oz (2.32 kg) without the front fork. It had bosses for two water bottles (front and rear of seat tube), the usual cable guides and stops, a front derailleur mount, and fittings for mudguards. The fork weighed 2lb 11oz (1.23 kg). Typical weight of a fully equipped 18-speed AM-SPEED was 22lb 7oz (10.18 kg).

The AM-SPEED.

For added lightness the SPEED used a non-adjustable version of the Jubilee's Wishbone handlebar stem, the Fixbone. Like the Wishbone, the Fixbone was built from chrome-plated Reynolds 531 tubing. It was made to order in any of 30 versions, there being three lengths (S = 90 mm, M = 140 mm and L = 190 mm, approximating to 3^1/$_2$", 5^1/$_2$" and 7^1/$_2$") each having 11 choices of angle relative to the steering axis (from 0 to 90 degrees in increments of 9 degrees, designated 0 to 10). A Fixbone fitting chart explained the options and related them to the seat tube and steerer heights.

The wheels were also lighter than usual. They had only 20 spokes (the prototypes had 16!) and those on the front wheel were bladed for lower wind resistance. Typical weight for the rear wheel was 2lb 13 oz (1.29 kg), and for the front, 2lb 1^3/$_4$ oz (0.94 kg).

The tyres were a new slick (treadless) version of the Moulton-Wolber 17". Designated C3 and designed to run at 140 psi (9.52 atm), they were complemented by special Boulain natural rubber tubes.

Back in November 1983 Chet Kyle had reported to Alex on tests he had carried out in California on the standard 17" tyre with the tread shaved off. Chet found that at 120 psi (8.2 atm) the treadless tyre had a 17% lower rolling resistance. Later the proper slick version of the 17" tyre was evolved as part of the development work for the General Motors Sunraycer solar-powered car.

Having pioneered six-speed derailleurs in the 1960s, Alex gave the SPEED the world's first nine-speed freewheel. This was the product of his collaboration with the Swiss Wilfred Hugi. It married Hugi's precision cassette hub and six of his hardened aluminium sprockets (in whatever sizes you wanted from 12 to 28 tooth) to an AM cluster comprising 9, 10 and 11 tooth steel cogs, finished in black oxide. (Later clusters had a gold finish.)

The Hugi hub has four sets of bearings, two in the conventional positions to support the wheel, and one at each end of the block. Heavy-duty 7 mm (0.28") pawls are incorporated in the freewheel mechanism.

(The first batch of production SPEEDs required a replacement Hugi axle. Instructions for this are contained in Alex Moulton Limited's Service Sheet No.5, dated May 1990.)

The SPEED's standard chainwheel was a specially-made AM 62 tooth ring with the 130 mm bolt ring diameter introduced by Shimano for racing cranksets in the early 1970s. The standard rear derailleur was a SunTour GPX. A special Moulton index disc was used to convert a SunTour Superbe derailleur lever for nine-speed use. A pair of these levers was supplied, complete with a fixing plate, which mounted on the upper frame truss, just behind its junction with the head tube.

Apart from the frame, Fixbone stem, wheels, tyres, rear derailleur, sprocket cluster, gear levers and chainwheel, every other piece of equipment on the SPEED could be to customer choice, provided it was compatible. Therefore the SPEED was commonly supplied in frame and wheel kit form.

The SPEED was deleted from the AM range at the end of 1993, being replaced by the AM-Triathlon (see below). The stainless steel SPEED S remains in production and is described in Chapter 11.

Reviews of the SPEED

The US magazine ID (International Design) commended the SPEED in its design review of 1990. A jury of designers concluded that the machine was "pushing materials and engineering boundaries beyond conventional limits". And in 1993 the German magazine Radmagazin Tour ran a five-page colour feature on the SPEED by H. C. Smolik, who concluded that in most respects the bike was "very good".

Doug Roosa reported in detail on the SPEED in Bicycle Guide's June 1990 issue. The machine he tested was supplied and built by Angle Lake Cyclery from a frame kit. It had a Specialized alloy sealed headset and Modolo Professional 44 cm (17.3") wide anatomic bend drop handlebars on an L5 Fixbone stem (ie. Long reach, 45 degree). The pedals were Look PD-66 clipless, the seatpost a 27.2 mm (1.07") diameter, 180 mm (7.09") long American Classic and the saddle a Selle Italia Turbo. Brakes were SunTour Superbe Pro 57 mm (2^1/$_4$") reach sidepull callipers, with Dia-Compe AGC250 aero levers.

The rims were American-made Sun Metal Mistral M17s. The spokes had aluminium nipples, and were laced radially on the front wheel and two-cross on the rear. The front spokes were aerodynamically bladed.

Apart from the Hugi-Moulton nine-speed block, and ultra-narrow Rohloff chain, the transmission was all SunTour; the 175 mm (6.8") crankset, rear derailleur and levers all being Superbe Pro. A SunTour Sprint front changer mechanism operated on 46 and 57 tooth circular chainwheels. (The article incorrectly referred to the smaller chainwheel as having 47 teeth.)

The sprocket cluster gave eight single tooth steps from 9 to 16, with a three tooth step to the 19 tooth largest cog. Gears offered were:

46T: 41, 49, 52, 56, 60, 65, 71, 78, (87")
57T: (51), 61, 65, 69, 75, 81, 88, 97, 108"

This crossover configuration offered an upward changing sequence as follows:

41, 49 (19% increase), 52 (+7%), 56 (+7%), 60 (+8%), (shift to larger chainwheel and shift down three cogs) 65 (+8%), 69 (+7%), 75 (+8%), 81 (+8%), 88 (+9%), 97 (+10%), 108" (+11%).

Doug noted that, although the riding position of the SPEED is standard, riding an AM could never be normal, because of other people's reactions.

"Ride a Moulton through town and you might as well be riding with your hair on fire, Everybody reacts in some way – some do a double take, others yell (mostly pre-teen boys whose comments range from 'Hey, look at that cool bike,' to 'Hey, look at that stupid bike'). Most just look in amazement."

He added that the SPEED's road manners were not normal either, and that it took several rides to get used to them. This mostly had to do with the very light wheels.

"The combination of low wheel inertia, high tire pressure, and minimal air drag results in a remarkable feeling that there are simply no wheels at all. The ease with which the SPEED accelerates has to be experienced to be believed.

"On the other hand, the SPEED's wheels pack so little inertia that they deflect with the slightest nudge, whether that nudge comes down through the handlebars or up from the road."

Doug pointed out the need to adapt riding style to allow for the suspension. He recommended simply ignoring all but the very worst of bumps: "stay in the saddle, hold the line, and pedal away ...let the suspension do the work". As someone once said, it was like "riding a velvet-covered I-beam".

(That someone was Max Behensky, a Moulton owner from the Santa Cruz area of California, who helped Doug Milliken at the Vancouver IHPSC in 1986.)

Doug Roosa stressed the need to evolve a smooth pedalling action that did not excite the suspension. It was like learning to spin smoothly on rollers: "Ultimately, the SPEED rewards smooth pedaling, preferably from the saddle."

The SPEED's ability to draught more closely than conventional machines, its fast handling and superior road-holding would make it a terror in any road race, Doug concluded. He said it set new standards in traction: "Riding the SPEED down a high-speed descent is a religious experience. I can arc through corners at speeds and lean angles I wouldn't dare on a regular bike."

However, all this came at a high price – $4,200. The SPEED shown in Doug Roosa's review bore a decal reading "Handbuilt – Untouched by robotic hands", and he pointed out that a quality frame with 60 hand-brazed joints could not be made cheaply. The rest of the bike reflected "Moulton's spare-no-expense execution" in which quality abounded "from front to back". The freewheel assembly and chain alone accounted for $610.

Doug's article produced two very different reactions in the letters pages of Bicycle Guide's December 1990 issue. Leigh F. Wade, sometime Moulton Bicycle Club contact in the USA, wrote from Paynesville, Minnesota congratulating the magazine on its honest reporting and quality photography. However, he warned readers that once they got used to an AM and the advantages it offered, they might never be able to return to a conventional bike. He also cautioned that,"Moultons are very addictive for some reason. After you buy the first one, you want another and another. This gets to be pretty expensive at two or three thousand bucks a crack."

The other letter, from David Holzman of Washington, DC was far from complimentary. David accused Doug of uncritical reporting, and claimed that AMs were far too expensive. He also stated that they were slow, and asked why. "Is it the weight and the poor quality of those funky tyres?"

Presumably he was unaware that three months after Doug's SPEED review was published, the HPV world hour record had been broken on Moulton-Wolber 17" tyres!

The Bean

Although Alex Moulton does not normally sell his 17" tyres for use on other manufacturer's machines, he sometimes makes an exception for HPV designers. For example, he supplies tyres for the front wheels of Mike Burrows' Speedy recumbent tricycles.

One vehicle that was spectacularly successful using the 17" tyre was the fully-faired recumbent Bean, designed and built by Miles Kingsbury and his father John. This front wheel drive machine had a drag coefficient (ie. the non-dimensional efficiency of the shape) of 0.07. Indeed, Miles claimed that the Bean's drag was "similar to an Audi's wing mirror".

On 8 September 1990 at the Millbrook Proving Ground, Ampthill, Bedfordshire, 25 year old Pat Kinch riding the Bean broke the world HPV record for the greatest distance covered in one hour by a solo rider (previously held by "Fast" Freddie Markham in Gold Rush). Pat travelled 46.69 miles in the hour, using a 181" gear at about 88 rpm. The tyres used were Moulton-Wolber C3 slicks, as fitted to the SPEED. Miles calculated that they gave the Bean an extra 1 mph (1.6 kph) over the standard Moulton 17" tyre.

This was the first time the hour record had been broken outside the USA. In May 1992 the same team broke the 200, 500 and 1,000 metre and the mile HPV records, in each case using Moulton-Wolber C3 slicks. A speed of 56.94 mph (91.62 kph) was achieved during the 500 metre record-breaking run.

A Time-Triallist's View of the AM7 and SPEED

Richard Grigsby of the Bath Cycling Club was loaned an AM7 demonstrator early in 1988 for evaluation and modification for racing use. The machine was essentially a standard AM7 tourer but with a larger chainwheel. Richard, then about 32 years old, had never ridden a Moulton before. Sceptical fellow members of the BCC dubbed it the "Pogo Stick".

Richard rode the AM7 on a mixture of club runs, training rides and shopping trips. In late February he produced a report for Alex, setting out what he saw as the machine's good points for time trialling, and highlighting areas for possible future refinement. He praised the handling, cornering, braking and ride comfort. Descending seemed to him faster than on a conventional machine, but climbing hills steeper than 1 in 10 (10%) "increased the workload on the arms and shoulders". And a more forward saddle position would have suited him better.

Richard concluded that the AM7 was suitable for use as a time-trial machine subject to the following modifications and adjustments:

1) Fitting high, close-ratio gears.

Richard Grigsby on the modified AM7, riding in the National 25 Mile Championship, 1989. Photo by Graham Cole.

2) Ensuring the classic prone racing position could be achieved.

3) Inflating tyres to at least 120 psi (8.2 atm).

4) Reducing the weight, if possible, to aid hill climbing.

5) Fitting upturned low profile handlebars on a Wishbone stem (or fitting time trial extension bars and elbow rests).

6) Increasing front damping, but not locking the suspension.

During the 1988 racing season he admitted that he "couldn't get the hang of the AM7", and preferred to race on his low profile time-trial bike. Nonetheless he won the cycle "split" in the Springfield Triathlon, held at Corsham near Bath – his first victory on the Moulton.

Over the following winter Richard commuted and trained on the AM, and rode it on club runs. He increasingly appreciated its qualities, and used it extensively in the 1989 racing season. He modified the machine, adding low profile handlebars and C3 slick tyres running at 140 psi (9.52 atm).

Now Richard started achieving reasonable times, including a 22 min. 10 mile (16 km) time trial and a 56 min. 22 sec. 25 mile (40 km) time trial – both at average speeds in the order of 27 mph (43 kph). Other successes included a 15 mile (24 km) time trial completed in 34 min. 15 sec., and a 5 mile (8 km) time trial done in 11 min. 48 sec. When competing he noted "a great deal of subtle animosity" from riders of conventional bikes, and commented: "Competing under this pressure was not easy".

At the end of the 1989 season, Richard was given the chance to ride a prototype SPEED. His fellow Bath Cycling Club members quickly nicknamed it the "White Meccano Set". This bike was equipped with 62 and 52 tooth chainwheels, and nine sprockets from 9 to 17 teeth. The gears offered were:

52T: 52, 55, 59, 63, 68, 74, 80, 88, (98")

62T: (62), 66, 70, 75, 81, 88, 96, 105, 117"

As with the SPEED tested by Doug Roosa, this was a crossover configuration. However, the spacing between the gears lacked the US-built machine's big jump at the low end, and had a slightly closer percentage shift when crossing over from one chainwheel to the other. A typical upward changing sequence would be:

52, 55 (increase of 6%), 59 (+7%), 63 (+7%), 68 (+8%), 74 (+9%), (shift to larger chainwheel and down one cog) 81 (+9%), 88 (+9%), 96 (+9%), 105 (+10%), 117" (+11%).

Richard reported that the SPEED felt like a short wheelbase time-trial bike, but without "that disconcerting fish-tailing when pedalling rapidly downhill or over rough road surfaces". The front suspension damping could be varied, so that "the comfort of the ride varies from that of a rigid road bike to that of a thoroughbred fat tyred tourer". The non-adjustable rear suspension had "no detrimental effect on racing" but had "the wonderful bonus of absorbing the drilling road vibration normally felt through the saddle".

The frame's stiffness became apparent when climbing hills, and Richard found the cornering gave "great confidence".

Triathlon

Late in the 1989 season Richard competed on the SPEED in the Reading Team Triathlon: "It was during this event that the 'Where's your shopping basket?' question (foolishly) came out. My retort 'Ask me afterwards!' turned out to be most prudent as I had got around the 25 mile (40.2 km) course four minutes faster than the joker in question." In fact, Richard achieved the seventh fastest speed out of 200 competitors.

The following year, 1990, saw Richard and fellow Bath Cycling Club Joe Beer both using the SPEED for triathlons. In the hilly cycling split of the Fowey Triathlon in Cornwall, Richard came first out of 180 competitors. He also came third in the cycling split of the Kingswood Triathlon out of some 400 competitors and was only nine seconds behind a 1st Category roadman.

In a 10 mile time trial the SPEED enabled him to improve his time to around 22 min. 15 sec. However, he was disqualified for using triathlon handlebars, banned at the time by the Road Time-Trials Council.

Joe Beer came third overall in the South West Biathlon against 49 other competitors. In 1991 he also used the SPEED in Canada, where he was top amateur (and fourth overall) in the short course Capriole Triathlon.

Joe found the SPEED substantially better than his classic lightweight, except on unpacked gravel surfaces. Apart from giving a more exhilarating ride, the SPEED accelerated and decelerated more easily, was easier to control on difficult descents, climbed and cornered better, and

Saturday 6th July 1991
THE IRONBRIDGE
RONMAN TRIATHLON
anised by: 220 Magazine

was more comfortable. It was also easier to mount and dismount – important in triathlons.

Overall Joe felt the SPEED gave him an advantage of two to three minutes in the bike split of a triathlon. Richard summed it up neatly: "They do say 'it's the legs that win', but why waste effort riding an antique, when you can ride a kinetic art-form?"

Richard Grigsby on the AM-SPEED in the 1991 Ironbridge Ironman Triathlon. Photo courtesy of Richard Grigsby.

The AM-SPEED S

On Friday 29 January 1993 the SPEED S was launched at an International Press Day at The Hall. (The APB14 was launched at the same event.) The SPEED S was a stainless steel version of the SPEED, which built on the techniques evolved by Alex for construction of the AM-GT. Typically weighing 21lb 15oz (9.95 kg), it cost £2,900 at launch.

Cycling Weekly described it as giving "incredible acceleration and Rolls-Royce ride". In Cycling Plus's group test of five suspension road bikes, including the Slingshot and the Allsop Powercurve, only the SPEED S scored maximum points for overall performance.

As the SPEED S is one of the series of stainless steel AMs, it is described in further detail in Chapter 11.

Richard Grigsby and the AM-SPEED.
Photo courtesy of Bath Evening Chronicle.

Richard Grigsby on the AM-SPEED. He added duplicate brake levers to the tri-bars to conform to the RTTC's "ludicrous" Rule 54.
Photo courtesy of Richard Grigsby.

The AM-Triathlon with wishbone fully extended.

The AM-Triathlon

Spring 1994 saw the launch of a new SPEED derivative, the AM-Triathlon. This has the same smaller diameter 531 tubing as the SPEED but with a separable frame, available in one seat tube height only. There is no provision for a rear carrier and mudguards are not fitted.

Instead of a built-to-order Fixbone stem, the Triathlon has an adjustable Wishbone. The standard AM seat pillar is fitted. Chainset and brakes are Shimano 105, and the titanium bottom bracket set is by Royce. Derailleurs are SunTour.

The 20-spoked wheels are built on Hope hubs, the rear hub being modified by Alex to take his special small sprockets (the Hugi hub no longer being available to him). 16-speeds are offered, the range being either 25 to 98" or 31 to 117", depending on whether the customer orders a 52 or 62 tooth larger chainwheel.

The Triathlon is available in a choice of seven colours and weighs about 22lb (10 kg). The recommended price is £2,500. As with all 1994 AMs other than the AM5, a frame kit is available to selected dealers.

During summer 1994 a works Triathlon was fitted with front suspension damping that could be adjusted by the rider while the bike was being ridden. The front suspension's rear dampers were loosened or tightened by a pair of forward-facing levers linked to a stirrup on the end of a control rod running up to the handlebars.

The AM-Jubilee L

Closely related to the Triathlon is another new model launched simultaneously, the Jubilee L ("Light"). The principal differences are that it comes with mudguards and rear carrier mountings. The bike is therefore marginally heavier.

The Jubilee L costs the same as the Triathlon and the same colour options apply.

The AM-Jubilee L.

Research Continues ...

Meanwhile aerodynamic research continues. In January 1994 Doug Milliken accepted an invitation to take part in an annual wind tunnel test session at Texas A & M. This was hosted by Steve and Anne Hed of Hed Designs, manufacturers of disc wheels. Steve Hed has owned an AM7 since shortly after the bike was launched.

Doug was accompanied by Jim Glover and Dave Kennedy. Other eminent guests included Boone Lennon, designer of Scott USA's aero handlebars, Peter Enright of Phil Wood, and Greg LeMond's new trainer, Adrie van Diemen.

Texas A & M's wind tunnel fan is (somewhat eerily) a propeller from the Enola Gay, the B-29 Superfortress that dropped the atomic bomb on Hiroshima. The four-bladed prop has been trimmed down to 12 feet in diameter (3.8 m) and is driven by a 1,500 horsepower (1,100 kw) electric motor. Although the tunnel is really intended for aircraft use, it also works well at lower speeds, having a very sensitive poise-weight balance system and extremely competent staff.

The testing gave further insights into the sail effect of the streamlined Moultons in even modest cross-winds. It also revealed that both configurations of the Moulton Aero, Doug Milliken's Aero IV and the Kennedy Aero, have similar drag, but for different reasons. Using the knowledge thus gained, Doug set to work on an Aero V, with a view to testing it in summer 1994.

Perhaps most interesting to time-triallists was the discovery that an unfaired AM had essentially identical drag figures to a very fashionable "aero" time-trial machine. The latter had streamlined tubing, aero cable routing and 700C spoked wheels. Both machines were ridden by Jim Glover, who used the arms-out position on Scott clip-on bars. His position was measured to ensure it was the same in each case.

From Derision to Amazement

Despite all the great speed achievements recorded in this chapter, ignorance of the AM's potential is so great that the Moulton rider often has to face scepticism and derision. But this can easily be transformed into amazement on the part of deriders, and exhilaration for the rider, as this brief tale shows.

Michael Doube of South Australia was an enthusiastic participant in the 7th Great Victorian Bike Ride, 1990. The event brought together some 3,500 cyclists for nine days of riding and fun. He was the only AM rider, although there were two other cyclists with older Moultons.

One of the events was a race in the small town of Leongatha. Michael decided to take part on his AM14S. When he lined up for the start he received "much loud and derisive comment".

But, as he put it: "The cheers were louder and the disbelief palpable when I finished second, inches away from winning, just behind a former professional track champion and local hero .... It may look, to the untrained eye, like a toy bike, all small tubes and tiny wheels, but it can sure move!"

Will Kennedy in the Kennedy Aero at IHPSC '93, National Sports Center, Blaine, Minnesota. Photo by Doug Milliken.

Chapter 10
TOURING
1983-1993

Asia – Australia – Europe – North America – Africa

Although the Alex Moulton bicycle is unusually versatile, it is arguably best as a tourer. In the ten years following its introduction, writer Peter Knottley covered some 70,000 miles (112,000 km) on his AMs, and a number of other cycle tourists travelled tens of thousands of miles on the machines. The 1994 Alex Moulton catalogue states that "over a million rider-miles a year are currently ridden world-wide on the AM series alone", much of which must be touring.

Earlier chapters made passing reference to great tours undertaken on AMs, such as Nick Peregrine's early exploits in the Pyrenees. This chapter takes a closer look at the AM's performance as a touring machine, with the emphasis on the reported views of the riders.

An AM14 equipped for a fortnight's touring, Lochranza, Isle of Arran.
Photo courtesy of Peter Knottley.

Turkish Delight

One of the first cycle tourists to adopt the AM was Robert Ludan, US Consul in Izmir, Turkey. In autumn 1983 he made a 10 day, 400 mile (644 km) tour of Bohemia, then in Czechoslovakia, on his newly purchased AM7.

The consul had to make a few minor adjustments of the hubs, and found the bike's handling was improved by keeping most of the luggage weight on the rear carrier. Writing to Alex Moulton he stated that the design, workmanship, and overall performance of the AM7 were "consistent with the high praise that the bike has received in various written reviews".

Race to the Himalayas

About the time the AMs were launched, CTC tour leader Tom Race was completing plans for his most ambitious tour yet. His aim was to cycle across an island (Sri Lanka), a kingdom (Nepal) and a (sub)continent (India). He would be crossing the Himalayas in winter and his research indicated that the roads throughout the tour would generally be rough.

Tom dismissed the idea of using a mountain bike. After a 20 mile (32 km) trial ride he realised how great the tyre drag was and wrote, "Perish the thought that I should ever have to turn those great 'cartwheels' round for over 3,000 miles (4,830 km)."

What he needed was a bike that was light, very strong, with good luggage carrying capacity and very tough wheels. Seeing the review of the AMs in the July 1983 issue of Bicycle, he contacted Alex for further details. The AM's portability was an added attraction, especially as Tom's journey would involve nine flights, some in light aircraft. After due consideration he bought an AM7.

After a few laden trial runs along the south coast of England, he flew off to Sri Lanka shortly before Christmas 1983. On the island he was amazed at the poor road surfaces, which appeared unrepaired since colonial days. "Pot-holes and ruts everywhere, the roads are awash with rainwater," he noted. He cycled north along the canals of Negombo, and then went inland to the ruined jungle cities. The hill country particularly took his fancy, especially the climb up the Ramboda Pass. Tom then followed the superb coastline for over 100 miles (161 km) before turning inland to the Yala National Park.

In all he travelled 1,200 miles (1,930 km) in Sri Lanka which proved "a punishing test for the wheels, suspension and frame". Nonetheless, "All were in remarkable shape."

In January 1984 Tom flew to Nepal, where he found scenery "so beautiful as to defy description". He rode along the Katmandu Valley, cycled to Nagakot to view Mount Everest and visited numerous Hindu and Buddhist temples.

The road over the Himalayas to India was newly built and in good condition. Tom followed it to Pokhara before turning south into India's poorest and most backward state, Utah Pradesh.

This proved flat, dreary and boring. He seemed to spend much of the time riding into a head wind, and was glad of the smaller frontal area of the loaded AM7, which had no protruding panniers to catch the wind. Because of the heat, most of his riding had to be done in the early hours of the morning. Nonetheless, he averaged 120 miles a day (193 km).

After making a 124 mile (200 km) detour to reach the holy city of Varanasi on the river Ganges, he was greatly disappointed by its squalidness. Shortly afterwards he contracted bacterial dysentery and was robbed of a bag containing several rolls of irreplaceable film. Nonetheless, he made it to Delhi where he cheered up, enjoying both the city and its food.

Tom concluded that for a warm island to explore by bike, the cyclist would do better visiting Corsica, Cyprus or Crete than Sri Lanka with its appalling roads. As for India, his only comment was "Never again!" But Nepal, with its comparatively good roads and superb scenery, was "the start of a love affair".

As for the AM7, he wrote:

"I am confident that no other bike could have managed it so easily. The wheels stayed true throughout the whole of the tour and the tyre life was simply astonishing. Over 3,000 miles [4,827 km] for the front, and the back a very creditable 2,200 [3,540]. Its two halves cut through bureaucratic hassle that often confronts the would be traveller. In my view it is the most versatile cycle that I have ever owned. Now, all other cycles seem, by comparison, to be obsolete."

Some four years later Peter Greene wrote an article for The Independent on his experiences with a CTC cycling tour of Iceland. He reported that the tour leader came on an AM which had by then covered 27,000 miles (43,400 km). That leader was Tom Race, whose other great AM rides included 1,100 miles (1,800 km) in Israel and Egypt, and 2,000 miles (3,200 km) in Kenya, Tanzania and Zanzibar.

Across the Nullarbor Plain

In October 1984 Ron Shepherd rode his AM7 the 1,740 miles (2,800 km) west from Adelaide, South Australia to Perth, Western Australia. He followed the Eyre Highway, which includes a stretch of 1,200 miles (1,930 km) across the Nullarbor Plain. This gets its name from the Latin for "treeless" and there are no towns either, merely roadhouses.

However, as Ron pointed out, it was no longer as wild as it had been: "Now there is a sealed road all the way and you are never more than a day's ride from food and water". He thought that maybe 50 to 100 cyclists a year make the crossing through the flat plain covered with saltbush and spinifex (a coarse, spiny-leaved grass).

Ron's ride was trouble-free, and he completed the journey in 19 days, averaging more than 90 miles (145 km) a day. He reported that he was helped by favourable winds and by his AM7, which he described as "both fast and comfortable".

From Hartlepool to Australia

In August 1985 Alan Holden set off on his AM7 from his Hartlepool home to visit an old friend – "the fact that he lived in Australia seemed neither here nor there".

Answering an advertisement in a cycling magazine, Alan teamed up with three other cyclists, intending to reach Singapore in six months. But by the time he got to Athens, he had become separated from his companions, and had to wait four weeks for a new back wheel to be sent out from England. The original had been repaired in Italy but, with 10 broken spokes, was now beyond hope. Alan explained:

"The rear wheel began popping spokes from the beginning of France, two or three I think. No doubt my amateur repairs and the over-loaded baggage (70 lb [32 kg]) resulted in three spoke holes ripping out. The Italian repair was a complete bodge, egg-shaped and offset, with spokes sticking out of the nipples by $1/4$" [6 mm]".

After some cycling in Turkey, and unable to get a visa to cycle through Iran, Alan flew from Athens to Bombay, a city with which he fell in love. From there, he took the train to Agra, where he visited the Taj Mahal before setting off on his bike for Nepal via Delhi.

Despite initial heat exhaustion and the "Delhi belly", Alan soon became acclimatised to cycling in India – "sharing the road with maniac drivers and anything else with wheels, hooves or feet". He was nonetheless delighted to reach Nepal, with its quiet roads and better food.

As a devotee of the mountaineer Chris Bonington, Alan was keen to do some trekking in the Himalayas. He got as high as 17,000 ft (5,200 m), at one stage suffering a severe bout of snow blindness. But his biggest surprise during three months in Nepal happened at dawn one morning, on the top of an 8,200 ft (2,500 m) pass. There he found two of his original travelling companions, watching the daybreak! A celebratory reunion was held in Katmandu before they again parted company.

From Nepal Alan cycled back into India, to Darjeeling and West Bengal. The food and roads were better than before, but Alan suffered a severely infected leg, caused by scratching an insect bite, which required hospital treatment.

After five lazy weeks in Bengal, and fully recovered, Alan cycled to Calcutta. One of the most enjoyable parts was the 30 mile (48 km) downhill run from Darjeeling to Siliguri – "non-stop all the way, never pedalled nor touched the brakes, just one long gentle descent." In all it took seven days to reach Calcutta, followed by a week in bed with "Delhi belly" or possibly hepatitis.

Alan then flew to Bangkok via Rangoon, Burma. He was not allowed to use his bike in Burma ("can't have tourists wandering around the country stirring up the masses") and had to leave it at the airport while he visited the sights. When he returned to reclaim it, Alan could not find the receipt, and had to bribe the customs chief with a bottle of whisky!

After a pleasant fortnight in Bangkok, he cycled south again some 1,500 miles (2,400 km) to Singapore. While riding through Thailand he stayed overnight in Buddhist monasteries, which showed a side of Thai life rarely seen by tourists. He finally arrived in Singapore 15 months after setting out from England, and then flew direct to Sydney.

Despite his misadventures, Alan described his journey thus: "No wars, no bandits, no ruffians or jail, just a good time all the time." But his travels were far from over: he spent "three more years bouncing around Asia", which included visiting Sumatra, New Zealand, many parts of Australia and revisiting Thailand. A keen lensman, he took some 2,600 photographs during his travels, some of which have been exhibited in Hartlepool and Bristol.

Sarawak, Borneo – the kind of load and road an AM7 can handle – provided it doesn't rain.
Photo courtesy of Alan Holden.

Brunei – Alan Holden with the beer (and bike?) that reaches places others cannot reach.
Photo courtesy of Alan Holden.

Alan Holden and AM7 in the thick jungle of
Sumatra.
Photos courtesy of Alan Holden.

Alan Holden and his loaded AM7 in New Zealand (cool weather) mode.
Photo courtesy of Alan Holden.

Alan's bike was an AM7 fitted with a clamped-on front derailleur mechanism to give 14 speeds. The rear derailleur was a SunTour Le Tech with the cable pulling from the front, rather than the back. This, with Simplex levers, gave "a super smooth change".The Regina freewheel started slipping in Turkey but warm weather in India cured the problem, and enabled him to keep going until a spare sent out from England caught up with him.

Alan usually carried four spare tyres, but as many as seven in India. This was not difficult, as they were easy to slip over the rear bag. Why so many? His experience of tyre life was the opposite of Tom Race's, tyres typically lasting less than 400 miles (640 km). The problem was usually carcase failure rather than tread wear.

In all Alan suffered about two dozen punctures, but only two were "regular through the tyre", probably because he was using Mr Tuffy anti-puncture tape. Others, however, were caused by this tape chafing the inner tube, or by blebbing of the tube near the valve (these were the early screwed-on valves). OKO puncture sealant used in the inner tubes tended to congeal in the valves during repairs and ruined two otherwise sound tubes.

"Hooded brakes on dropped bars are a dead loss in India," Alan recalls, "just can't reach the brakes fast enough in the crowded streets. Also long descents would cause cramp trying to hold onto the brakes. Though the dropped bars were comfortable enough, I can only recall using the drops a dozen times. I've since changed the bars, or rather turned them upside down and chopped the drops off."

The front suspension of Alan's AM7 seized up in India, but a local engineering shop cured this by slightly reducing the diameter of the swollen guide bearing. (This can be done with emery paper!) It happened again in Australia but cured itself.

Apart from demonstrations, the frame was separated only four times out of necessity. After Air India bent some parts, Alan always left the AM7 in one piece so that it could be recognised as a bicycle. He never paid any extra for taking the bike on a aeroplane, though came close a few times.

"On the whole, the Moulton-made bits (that is, the frame and racks) lasted without murmur: it was other people's bits that broke. Apart from running out of inner tubes in Nepal, I was never brought to a halt. ... Wheels never buckled, even though I went down some very big pot-holes. The design of the AM meant I could carry awkward baggage (such as other bikes!) and all manner of bits and bobs ..."

Alan is "wedded to the Moulton concept". Funds permitting, he would "shoot off tomorrow" on another transcontinental expedition, but not on 17" tyres. An APB or AM-ATB "with 20" tyres which can be got anywhere in the world would do nicely", he says.

Cretan Craters

Nigel Sadler toured Crete on his AM14S in autumn 1986. The Cretan country roads are noted for their roughness, and he wrote, "it was good to know that I had a strong front line of defence in the suspension for the few unavoidable cavities". Despite the narrowness of the mountain roads, and the sharp hairpin bends, he took some corners at 30 mph (48 kph). "The only fear was the loose roadside gravel, that the high pressure tyres just cut into and slid wherever the whim took them."

Therefore, when he tried a little off-road mountain climbing, Nigel reduced his tyre pressures somewhat, to allow the wheels to ride over the gravel rather than cut into it.

In 450 miles (724 km) Nigel's AM suffered no punctures. Despite some reservations about the quality of finish and fit, he found the frame skins very useful as "an invaluable receptacle for small frequently required items", including spare water bottles.

A Corsican Conversion

London businessman Dennis Romer (see also page 105) was introduced to the AM14 when, late in 1986, Monty Young of Condor Cycles pushed one into his office. Dennis, an experienced cycle tourist, told Monty that he would not be seen dead on "one of those horizontal Eiffel Towers on wheels". Nonetheless he was stuck with it – the customised white bike with his name sign-written on the seat tube was a Christmas present from his business partner!

The following summer Dennis's favoured Hetchins lightweight was being overhauled. He therefore decided to take the AM14 for a solo tour of Corsica, an island he had explored by bike many times before.

He found packing "Madame Eiffel" into her carrying bags for the flight quite difficult and bemoaned the lack of instructions. However, on arrival at Ajaccio airport he was pleasantly surprised at how quick and easy it was to assemble the machine, despite his lack of mechanical aptitude. "Within 25 minutes I was ready for the adventure," he reported.

Dennis's only problems concerned the Fichtel & Sachs cable connector for the rear derailleur cable. Being designed for the lightly loaded cables of hub gears, it proved inadequate for the comparatively savage stresses sometimes imposed under touring conditions by derailleurs. (Subsequently Alex introduced a stainless steel turnbuckle to replace the plastic-bodied F&S connector.)

Dennis found that on steep and sometimes windy mountain descents the well-laden bike held the road "beautifully", enabling him to "corner in complete safety", despite once touching 38.5 mph (61.9 kph). His conclusion "after touring the most arduous mountains in Southern Europe," was that "this Alex Moulton is the finest machine I have ever had the pleasure and comfort to use".

End-to-End

In May 1987 Yorkshire-based artist Tim Barker spent a fortnight cycling from Land's End to John o'Groats. His mission was to raise funds through sponsorship for the Campaign for Nuclear Disarmament and for War on Want.

Tim rode an AM7 and covered 1,087 miles (1,749 km), mostly on quiet country lanes. He recalled: "The weather varied from blazing sunshine at the start in Cornwall and Devon, to five days of head winds and then into Scotland where the weather changed with altitude. On the last day a fierce westerly blew, which made the last 100 miles to John o'Groats quite demanding."

Another rider who did the "End-to-End" on an AM7 was Dave Westwood of Birmingham.

AMs in Eire

Linda and David Bailey toured the Irish Republic on AMs in summer 1988. She rode an upgraded (14 speed) AM7, he an AM14 built from a frame kit and equipped mostly with Campagnolo components.

In twelve days the couple covered 650 miles (1,045 km), taking in Waterford, Cork, Killarney, Dingle and Limerick. The AMs' suspension "very much proved its worth" on the poor road surfaces. However, the badly maintained surface dressing of chippings produced "a lot of vibration". Reducing the damping of the front suspension helped considerably to overcome this.

(Nigel Sadler made similar comments about certain English roads, and added: "The road surface that produces this effect is recently resurfaced country roads that have gone beyond the 'loose chippings' stage but have not fully compacted.")

The Baileys suffered no mechanical problems and no punctures. They attributed the latter to use of tyre savers (flint catchers – see page 273). David wrote: "We have used mudguard-mounted tyre savers for the last two years, and in many thousands of miles have suffered only one puncture ... We can now confidently use the Moulton tyres until there is no tread at all without any cutting up."

He recommended fitting the tyre savers with just a small amount of pressure on the tyre, and good all-round contact.

An Aussie, an AM and the Alps

Australian teacher Michael Doube spent 1988 working in England on exchange. He made good use of his five week summer break by riding his AM14S on the European mainland.

Michael started by packing the bike into its carry bags, putting his belongings into the front and rear bags, and travelling by public transport from Oxenholme, Cumberland to Paris, via British Rail, the London Underground, British Rail again, the Newhaven-Dieppe ferry and SNCF (French railways). "It was so easy," he recalled.

Having explored Paris by bike, Michael travelled by train to Clermont Ferrand in central France. From there he followed the Tour de France for four days, fulfilling a lifetime's ambition. He even rode to the start of a stage with some of the Tour riders, one of whom demanded a demonstration of the AM's suspension.

Michael then took the train to Perpignan and cycled through Andorra and over many of the classic Pyrenean passes, including Le Col du Tourmalet (6,934 ft (2,115 m)). From Tarbes he travelled by rail to Montpelier and toured Provence. Making the tough, hot ascent of Le Mont Ventoux, he was touched to see fresh flowers at the spot where Tommy Simpson died on the Tour de France.

(Simpson, widely regarded as England's greatest post-war racing cyclist, had test-ridden an early Moulton Speed at London's Herne Hill track in 1963. He expressed his willingness to race on it, were he not under contract to Peugeot. Four years later he died on the mountain.)

From Nice Michael travelled by train to Venice to rendezvous with friends. He commented, "With a conventional bike I believe I would have had some aggravation – with the Moulton I had no worries at all, as the bike rode above me in the luggage rack and no one was aware that I had a bike with me."

After a spell in Venice, Michael travelled by rail back to France. He then cycled from Amiens to the French coast, before returning to Cumberland by boat and train.

Michael concluded that the AM14S was "a wonderful touring bike, fast and efficient and with many advantages compared to a conventional machine". It was "the ideal bike to combine cycling with Europe's fast and efficient train system". Its componentry was markedly better than that of the basic AM7, and it "functioned with absolute reliability". Of all the bikes that he had tried, "the Moulton alone is unaffected by carrying a load".

There were, however, "little things that annoy". The worst of these was the absence of the rear derailleur's stop screw, removed on the

AM14 so that the short cage had sufficient wind-up capacity. The first time he punctured and removed the rear wheel he "watched in disbelief as the chain tied itself in knots". Thereafter he carried a spare screw to insert before removing the wheel.

Michael later modified his original AM7 for Alpine touring, fitting a 62, 52 and 42 tooth triple chainwheel and a 12 to 26 tooth SunTour freewheel. The front changer was a SunTour 4050 XCE and the rear a Shimano Deore LX. Top Australian frame builder Brian Hayes added the necessary braze-ons, such as the front derailleur mount and additional cable stops and guides. He also refinished the frame.

The CLB brakes were replaced with double-pivot Shimano 105s, which Michael found lighter to use, yet considerably more effective. The narrow GB drop handlebars were discarded in favour of wider Cinellis, the GB Stelvio RTE stem being reamed out an extra 1 mm (0.04") to accommodate the Italian bars.

The front suspension was also upgraded, by fitting a heavy-duty progressively wound spring supplied by Angle Lake Cyclery of Seattle. Michael commented, "The new spring is an improvement on the softer, original spring, and there is now no bottoming out when braking on a steep descent as before."

Trains and Boats and Planes

In 1988 Nigel Sadler used the portability and separability of his AM14S to the full in a tour of Canada. Most of his riding was in Nova Scotia, especially in the Cape Breton region. Some days he covered more than 100 miles (161 km) in the sparsely populated territory, and was glad of the fatigue-reducing suspension. By way of contrast he also did battle with the tramlines of Toronto and the appallingly rutted roads of Montreal, where again the suspension helped.

Nigel travelled fully laden, "with both front and rear bags bulging" and even the pockets in the frame skins in use. He became very proficient at unloading his luggage, separating the bike and packing it into its carrying bags. Eventually he got the time down from about half an hour to "as little as five minutes if the train was due to leave in six!"

The modes of public or motor transport used during his tour were London Underground, Lockheed Tristar, motor car boot (trunk), VIA (Canadian railways), AMTRAK (US railways), VIA bus, floating bridge and car ferries. The AM travelled free on all except the London Underground and the Prince Edward Island ferries. As Nigel put it, "Try doing that on an ordinary bike!"

A Hub Gear in Tuscany and Umbria ...

In 1991 Kevin Lawley used his AM5 for cycle camping in Italy. He joined an organised tour, and travelled by train from London to Pisa while the bikes were conveyed by truck.

The route covered some 450 miles (725 km) and included San Gimignano, Siena, Sarteano, Lago di Bolsena, Orvieto, Assisi, Gubbio and Florence. Typical daily mileage was 45 miles (72 km) and Kevin's AM5 suffered only one puncture.

The previous year Kevin's hub gear had failed terminally, and throughout the Italian tour he was concerned lest disaster strike again. Fortunately it did not, and he noted that "despite its relatively high lowest gear, the AM5 was quite a good hill climber". As for the descents, "the AM was marvellous" and "sure-footed on the hairpin bends".

...and in Brittany and Normandy

Former Olympic cyclist and record-breaker Jack Lauterwasser once reminded me, "It's not the miles covered that's important, it's the miles enjoyed." That the enjoyment of cycle touring does not necessitate covering immense distances, or crossing daunting mountain ranges, was demonstrated in 1992 by Jean and George Coulouris.

Jean and George made a short tour of Brittany and Normandy, she on an AM7, he on an AM5. They travelled by train from London to Portsmouth and then by overnight ferry to St Malo in Brittany. Using the quieter roads, they toured the Emerald Coast west of St Malo before turning inland to Dinan. Thereafter they visited Mont St Michel before heading for Cherbourg via Avranches and Granville.

The Coulouris's did not pre-book their accommodation but, by using lists provided by the local tourist offices, generally had no difficulty finding bed and breakfast. They averaged 50 miles a day (80 km) and "the bikes were a great success". The only problem was that George's rear wheel broke four spokes.

He weighed about 15 stone (210 lb/95 kg) and the Moulton Bicycle Club's Technical Advisor, Ian Hodgson, suggested fitting 8BA brass washers between the Sturmey-Archer hub flange and the spoke head. This reduces the length of spoke head cantilevered beyond the thin pressed steel flange.

Palo Alto to Beverly Hills

In the summer of 1991 Channell Wasson of Palo Alto, California cycled from his home at the southern end of San Francisco Bay to Beverly Hills, the exclusive suburb of Los Angeles. At the age of 58 he completed the 451 miles (726 km) in five days.

Channell's bike was an AM7 fitted with the AM-Zzipper fairing. He considered that the fairing definitely reduced wind resistance. "I enjoyed riding behind it and will continue to use it", he wrote. Freewheeling downhill at speeds of up to 44 mph (71 kph) he found the bike stable, provided that he kept his hands "wide on the handlebars or on the drops". Hands near the stem brought on "an alarming shimmy to the front wheel".

Channell bemoaned the lack of tyre choice for the 17" wheel. In Californian conditions he had experienced rapid tread wear, particularly on the rear tyre, after the first 400 or so miles (640 km). He had fitted ordinary 16" inner tubes with Schraeder valves (enlarging the valve holes in the rims accordingly) because of easier availability, wider choice, greater durability and the ease of inflation from air-lines at petrol (gas) stations.

During the ride he suffered four punctures before fitting new tyres. He also broke two spokes on the freewheel side of the rear wheel. He concluded, nonetheless that the AM7 was "a great touring bike" and the one he reached for "when doing any serious riding".

London to Moscow

Serious riding was certainly what Channell Wasson did the following summer, when he took part in an organised ride from London to Moscow. The tour lasted five weeks and took him through England, France, Belgium, The Netherlands, Germany, Poland, Belarus and Russia.

Most of Channell's 30 fellow riders were thirty to forty years younger than him and rode conventional machines. Nonetheless, he kept up with them fairly well. They rode in packs, taking turns to draught, cruising at 14 to 20 mph (22 to 32 kph). On average the party covered 80 to 110 miles (129 to 177 km) a day for five or six days, then had a rest day.

Channell used the 2,160 mile (3,475 km) tour to test his ideas for improving the durability of the 17" tyres. After much experimentation he cleaned the rubber thoroughly and spread a coating of urethane caulking cement over the outer surface of the tyre. (This adhesive is similar to that used to install car windscreens.) He continued using ordinary non-Moulton inner tubes with Schraeder valves, and fitted a leather gasket around the valve stem to protect it from being cut by the rim.

During the entire tour he had no punctures and noticed no difference in the rolling characteristics of the tyre. He changed the rear tyre once, following sidewall failure in Germany, but generally rode the bike "hard with abandon", including a 50 mph mountain descent and "tram tracks which we banged across at good speeds!". On arrival in Moscow the thin urethane coating was still intact.

Channell Wasson concluded that his well-used AM7 was "a wonderful bike for this trip" and "certainly the most comfortable". Given "attention from one with reasonable mechanical aptitude" it was "most serviceable, cunningly conceived and really quite an amazing machine."

Pedalling in the Porongorups ...

Silvia Klemenz and Jeremy Knowles, from Perth, Western Australia, spent a fortnight in 1991 cycle camping in the south-western corner of Australia. They rode their bikes, an AM14 and an AM7 from Bunbury, 100 miles (160 km) south of Perth, through the coal mining area around Collie, across the dry and barren wheat belt around Gnowangarup, and up into the Stirling Ranges and the Porongorups.

Their ride continued to Albany on King George Sound, along the South Coast and back inland to Pemberton, a wool milling centre. They returned to Bunbury through forests of Karri, a giant eucalyptus, and vineyards. In all they cycled some 684 miles (1,100 km), averaging about 53 miles (85 km) a day.

... and Touring the World

That ride was merely a warm-up for a much longer tour. In March 1992 Silvia and Jeremy set out on an aircraft-assisted world tour.

They first flew from Perth to Singapore, then spent five weeks touring the island and its larger neighbour, Malaysia. In all they covered some 930 miles (1,500 km). No major problems were experienced with the AMs. The couple usually stayed overnight in small hotels over shops or restaurants. This necessitated carrying the bikes and luggage "up innumerable flights of stairs". The AMs' easily removed front and rear bags therefore proved a great boon compared with unloading a multitude of conventional panniers.

In April 1992 Silvia and Jeremy flew from Singapore to Athens. There they started a four month 5,600 mile (9,000 km) tour of eastern Greece, European Turkey, Bulgaria, Romania, Hungary, Austria, the Czech Republic and Germany. They found Romania and the Czech Republic the most interesting countries.

The roads on this stage of the tour varied tremendously in quality, from cobbles to sticky asphalt. Three spoke breakages occurred, two on a front wheel, one on the non-drive side of a rear. An annoying click from one wheel eventually led to it being respoked.

However, tyre wear was good, the rear covers lasting for about 2,700 miles (4,300 km), the front for almost the whole tour. The tyres were run at 80-90 psi (5.4-6.1 atm) and Wolber Protec puncture resistant tape was used. Thirteen punctures were suffered, a rate of about one per wheel for every 1,700 miles (2,700 km).

Problems were encountered with the rear carriers. On one bike the threaded stud onto which the strut screws, snapped off early in the tour. The strut could not be tightened correctly onto the stud and had apparently transmitted some eccentric loading to it, causing the weld to shear.

Later the other bike's carrier cross-piece, to which the top of the strut fixes, broke. This seems to have been caused by movement of the bolt in the oversized hole or slot at the top of the strut, leading to metal fatigue.

Both carriers were loaded with approximately the maximum recommended load of 30 lb (13.6 kg). Nigel Sadler, commenting on these problems, reported that he had suffered carrier cross-piece failures on two carriers. He recommended using a thick, hard nylon washer to pack the threaded lug, and suggested frequent checking of the carrier fixings for tightness.

(Australian AM rider Michael Doube drilled two holes in the thumb nut of his AM7's carrier. Into each he super-glued two steel rods to give added leverage when tightening the nut.)

Silvia and Jeremy encountered an even more severe problem with the AM7 a week before the end of the tour. A crack was found about halfway through the chain stay on the drive side, just behind the cross brace. Fortunately the fracture did not worsen over the last few days of the tour. A letter was sent to Bradford-on-Avon from Frankfurt and within four days a new rear triangle had arrived.

Silvia and Jeremy spent the winter of 1992/93 touring in southern Africa, covering some 2,500 miles (4,000 km). They cycled from Harare, Zimbabwe to Cape Town, South Africa via Swaziland and Lesotho. At times the route involved scorching temperatures – over 86 degrees Fahrenheit (30 degrees Celsius) by 8 o'clock in the morning! Steep gradients on unsurfaced roads sometimes proved difficult: the AMs' wheels rolled well when the surface was well compacted, but not when it became gravelly.

The couple took the train back from Cape Town to Harare, where they finished their African sojourn with a short tour of Zimbabwe's Eastern Highlands. By this time they were running short of tyres. They had started out with eight spares, but four were now worn through, two too badly cut to use and the other pair had been stolen.

Africa's poor roads had caused much shorter tyre life than in earlier phases of Silvia and Jeremy's world tour: rear tyres averaged little more than 1,250 miles (2,000 km). But apart from this, and another minor problem with a carrier, "both bikes proved their versatility and worth under touring conditions".

Having ridden a further 6,200 miles (10,000 km) through Germany, Poland, Lithuania, Latvia, Estonia, Finland, Norway, the UK, Belgium and Luxembourg, Silvia and Jeremy toured Mexico, Belize and Guatemala. At the time of writing (June 1994) they are in California and intend cycling up to Canada.

An Alpine Birthday Challenge

Swiss Moultoneer Urs Maurer was looking for a special challenge in 1991. It was the year of his fortieth birthday and he wanted to cycle across the French Alps from north to south. Therefore in January he started training on steep slopes to build up his stamina. Over the following eight months he rode some 3,100 miles (5,000 km) in hilly terrain. By September he felt ready for the challenge.

His six day ride took him from Martigny to Manosque via Seez, St Michel, Guillestre, Condamine and St André les Alpes. He rode 404 miles (650 km) and climbed some 41,000 feet (12,500 metres). The highest point on the route was the Cime de la Bonnette, 9,193 feet (2,802 metres) above sea level.

Urs Maurer's machine was an AM14S which he had bought because of its capacity for carrying "the baggage which is indispensable for a ride of several days duration".

Urs Maurer climbing the last mile to the Cime de la Bonnette.
Photo courtesy of Urs Maurer.

Thoughts on "Compleat" Gearing

The pages of The Moultoneer have often contained well-considered articles on optional gearing configurations for AMs used for touring. One particularly interesting proposal published in spring 1992, was put forward by Dave Kelly, an experienced cyclist but then a newcomer to AMs.

He suggested the following performance specification:

- a simple shift pattern,
- evenly spaced shifts of 10 to 14% for the "level ground gears" from 60" to about 85",
- a few higher gears for descents,
- a selection of low gears with wider spaced shifts of up to 20%,
- a lowest gear below 30" and below 20" if possible.

Dave Kelly's suggestion for "the 'compleat' Moulton rider", whether commuter, fast rider or laden tourist, was to use a triple chainwheel with 56, 52 and 38 tooth rings in conjunction with an almost standard AM7 freewheel cluster with 9, 11, 13, 16, 19, 24 and 30 tooth sprockets. This "half-step and granny" arrangement came close to meeting the brief and gave the following options:

38T: 21, 27, 34, 40, 50, (59), (72)

52T: 30, 37, 47, 55, 68, 80, 98

56T: (32), 40, 50, 60, 73, 87, 106".

For fast riding Dave suggested using double shifts between the two larger chainwheels to get small gear steps. For touring he advocated staying mainly on the middle chainwheel, which gives a range of gears similar to the basic AM7's.

Lowdown on Low Gears

Ron Beams was 85 when in The Moultoneer he described the ultra-low gearing fitted to his AM14.

As the years passed, he found walking up steep hills increasingly more difficult than cycling in a very low gear. When riding he liked to maintain a steady cadence of about 60 rpm. He therefore fitted chainrings that would enable him to cycle at walking pace. This necessitated a bottom gear of 17".

Retaining the standard AM14 sprocket cluster, he therefore fitted 30 and 40 tooth chainwheels. The smaller one gave gears from 17" up to 57" for normal touring, the larger from 23" to 75" for flat or wind-assisted rides. This configuration enabled Ron to continue touring well into his 80s, whereafter he used recumbent tricycles.

In his 80th year Ron, and his old friend H. H. "Chater" Willis, were featured on the front cover of Cycling World. They were on a CTC tour of the Lake District and were shown pushing their AMs up the Newlands Pass "in typical overcast and drizzly conditions".

An Octogenarian on the South Downs

In the previous year, 1991, Ron Beams had successfully ridden the whole of the South Downs Way in Sussex unaccompanied. The surface ranged "from smooth grass to very rough flinty chalk", the ridable track often being no more than a 9" (230 mm) wide rut.

For this ride Ron used an AM7 with the mudguards removed. The gearing was modified to give a low of 25" which he used "for many miles". His total mileage was 104 (167 km), of which the South Downs Way constituted 74 miles (119 km). The ride took three and a half days.

Because of the rough surfaces Ron deliberately used worn tyres which he ran at 70 psi (4.76 atm). After 80 miles (129 km) the rear cover, which had suffered sidewall damage, "exploded at a known and patched weak spot in the canvas" and was replaced. No other punctures or tyre damage were sustained, and the wheels were unscathed.

Ron also rode the South Downs Way on a wide-tyred conventional machine, but on balance preferred the AM7.

A Heavy Duty Prescription

Dr Robert Macauley of Edinburgh was one of the first purchasers of an AM7. He found its "stability, carrying capacity and lightness of 'feel' second to none" for fully-loaded cycle camping.

Over the years he made a number of adaptations to his machine with a view to economy and reliability, especially in mountainous terrain and on poorly surfaced roads. Not every high mileage AM rider, nor Alex Moulton, would endorse these modifications. However, they suited Robert very well and demonstrated that AM users can use non-Moulton transmission and wheel components, if they are prepared to give up higher gears and optimal rolling resistance.

For his transmission, Robert adopted a standard 12-34 tooth freewheel and a 47 tooth chainwheel. This gave him a good, fairly closely spaced range of seven gears suitable for heavy touring in hilly terrain, with a low of 24" and a high of 67". The smaller than normal chainwheel also enabled the bike more easily to be packed into the early, ungusseted carrying bags.

Seeking heavier duty and cheaper tyres, and being prepared to accept the inevitably higher rolling resistance, Robert fitted standard British format 16 x 1³/₈" rims and tyres, (ISO/ETRTO code 37-349), the rims being 28 spoke Alesa alloy. This change reduced the bottom bracket height by about $^1/_2$" (13 mm) but did not prove problematic.

(Alternatively he could have used metric 400A tyres and rims. This would have allowed him to use 36 spoke Alesa alloy rims, and would have given a choice of 30, 32 and 37 mm wide tyres all with bead seat diameters of 340 mm. However, availability of 400A tyres is patchy in the UK.)

As for braking, Robert was concerned at the heat build up of the rims on long descents, as were a number of AM riders. He also disliked the sponginess induced by the longer reach callipers necessitated by his smaller 16" wheels. He therefore fitted a Suzue tandem rear hub, specially modified for 28 spoke holes by George Longstaff of Chesterton, Newcastle-under-Lyme. This necessitated spreading the rear drop-out width 10 mm ($^3/_8$") to 140 mm ($5^1/_2$").

Robert retained a calliper brake for the front wheel, but used a Campagnolo drop pivot bolt to allow use of a short reach SunTour Superbe brake.

Across The Roof of England

Laurence Heslop was warden of the Newcastle upon Tyne youth hostel when he bought an AM14T. In July 1992 he embarked on his longest day-ride for 17 years.

It took him via the highest public road in England [2,056 ft (627 m)] to Killhope Cross and back via Allendale, the geographical centre of Britain. The total distance was over 100 miles (161 km) and Laurence climbed some 5,500 feet (1,676 m).

He found that the bike, as supplied by the factory, performed well. It was versatile and in most respects perfect for his needs.

However, he had some minor quibbles. The saddle did not suit him and he had some reservations about the paint finish. He was also troubled by the rear carrier strut rattling. Nonetheless, Laurence confessed himself "a happily converted Moultoneer".

Trans-Canada

Howard Clifford was national adviser on child care to the Canadian federal government and a former director of day care for the city of Edmonton, Alberta. The author of two books on the child care, he was a tireless supporter of non-profit day care. But he suffered a mid-life crisis and, fearing he would become a jaded paper-pusher, decided to ride across Canada on his AM. His objective was to meet children, parents and teachers, thereby encouraging provision of day care.

In May 1992 he set off from the Pacific Coast with the aim of reaching Winnipeg via the Arctic Circle by early September. His plan was to finish the journey in 1993 by riding on to Glace Bay, Nova Scotia.

By August 1992 he was in Edmonton, Alberta, where the local paper described him as looking like "a cross between a Viking and a trim St Nicholas". Howard reported that, "Going by bicycle I've found you get a feel for the land and the way the people feel about the land, and that effects their child-care demands."

The children in the centres he visited loved his stories of cycling and kayaking in the mountains, and the wild animals and children he had encountered. They were also fascinated by his AM, known as Scooter. Howard likened Scooter to "the little engine that could" in the children's story. When the youngsters heard that Scooter had been derided for being too small for the journey across Canada, they were outraged. Many AM owners know that feeling!

Towards the Arctic ...

Although by Alaskan standards not a hard core winter cyclist, Philip Nice of Fairbanks sometimes used his AM-ATB at temperatures in the order of -26 degrees Celsius (-15 degrees Fahrenheit). He reported that even under these conditions the suspension appeared to work satisfactorily.

One Labour Day (5 September) Philip cycled out of Dawson in the neighbouring Canadian Yukon Territory. He headed along the Dempster Highway which runs north-west towards the Arctic Circle. The ride was uphill all the way and the weather, which at that time of year should have been fine, inflicted drizzle followed by a 20 knot head wind (23 mph/37 kph).

Philip camped for the night and on waking found the puddles frozen. Nonetheless, he continued his uphill ride through the Ogilvie Mountains. That night he again camped, and the next morning found that all three of his water bottles had frozen, including one in his tent. In two days he had travelled some 50 miles through the tundra, all uphill and mostly against a strong wind.

At this stage Philip was about 125 miles (200 km) from the Arctic Circle, and in view of the unseasonable weather, he decided to return to Dawson. As he put it, "The Moulton worked fine and, with a fifty mile (80 km) downhill ride with a tail wind, was very enjoyable".

... and on the Equator

No less than seven AM riders were among the 34 CTC members who toured Kenya in spring 1991. The tour lasted just over a fortnight and was led by Tom Race, this time on a conventional machine. From their starting point at the Kenyan capital Nairobi, the party rode to Kisumu 20 miles (32 km) south of the Equator on Lake Victoria. They travelled via the Rift Valley and the 11,004 ft (3,354 m) Mau Summit. From Kisumu they rode to the Equator line at Maseno, where they were photographed together on 7 April 1991.

The riders then transferred by train and coach to Malindi near the mid point of the Kenyan coast. Thereafter they cycled along the coast towards the Tanzanian border, via Mombasa, finishing the tour at Diani Beach.

Three members of the party had bought AMs having been impressed by Roger Shelbourne's AM14 on a CTC tour of Nepal: David Payne, Rick Coleman and Ted Wright rode an AM7, AM14 and a Jubilee respectively. The other AM riders on the Kenyan tour were Kate Wregglesworth and Wolf Bergman (both on ATBs), Bernard Davenport and Tony Warran.

The only mechanical damage sustained by an AM on the tour was a broken SunTour derailleur. The pivot bolt stripped its thread and could not be repaired. The chain was therefore shortened and the rider, Ted Wright, successfully completed the ride on a single gear of 62".

Moultoneers on the Equator, 1991.
Photo courtesy of Tony Warran.

Alan Holden (right) with his AM7 on the Equator in Sumatra. Also shown is Echo Cuncord, who was walking the length of Indonesia. Photo courtesy of Alan Holden.

On Pilgrimage

The following year two veterans of the equatorial tour, Tony Warran and Bernard Davenport, were joined by a third AM rider, Harry Potter for a ride along part of the old pilgrimage route to Santiago de Compostela in north-west Spain. Santiago translates as St James, and the city houses the shrine of St James the Great, beheaded in AD44. According to ancient legend the apostle preached in Spain and his body is said to have been taken by sea to Santiago for burial. In the middle ages many English people made pilgrimages to the apostle's shrine.

The three AM riders, all grandfathers, set off from Bordeaux in south-west France. Tony Warran's wife Mary and a friend followed with a "sag wagon". The symbol of St James is a scallop shell, so the riders each wore one on a ribbon round his neck. Every city and town along the route had its own rubber stamp to mark the cards carried by the pilgrims, and thereby prove that they had made the arduous journey.

The route of some 600 miles (965 km) involved baking heat and some mountainous terrain. At one point the pilgrims were about 4,900 feet (1,500 m) above sea level. Much braking was needed on the descents, with frequent stops to allow the rims to cool down.

The pilgrim cyclists finished their ride by attending a feast day celebration at Santiago cathedral, where Prince Felipe of Spain gave an address.

Earlier that year (1992) another AM rider, Nicol Smith, had written of his pilgrimage ride to Santiago. He retired from his job as Wiltshire's county solicitor and rode all the way to Santiago from his home in the village of Edington.

Nicol rode a five year old AM7 which was checked over at Alex Moulton's factory. Two new tyres were fitted and Nicol carried a spare cover and two spare inner tubes.

His route took him first to Poole, Dorset, where he caught the ferry to Cherbourg. He then cycled down through France, joining the old pilgrimage route from Paris near Poitiers. He proceeded to Bordeaux, then via Roncesvalles, Burgos and Leon to Santiago.

Nicol took four weeks to complete the 1,269 miles (2,042 km). At the end of his ride his rear tyre was still useable.

Flying with an AM

Through the late 1980s and early 1990s the pages of The Moultoneer contained many articles and letters on the best way of taking an AM by aeroplane. Alan Gordon's article, published in the Summer 1993 issue, was probably the best and most comprehensive. The following notes incorporate much of his advice.

If protection of the bike is the first priority, the best solution is to separate the bike and pack it into a stout cardboard carton of the type used by Alex Moulton Limited for air freighting (39 x 22 x 12"/ 990 x 559 x 305 mm). The box should be clearly marked "bicycle". However, you cannot ride the bike to the airport if it is in a box, and you probably cannot carry the box on the bike with all your other luggage. Also, after your outward flight you either have to store the box for the return journey, or procure another one before flying home. Furthermore, both the carton and the bike will count as checked baggage weight, which can be a problem on many routes.

Using the carrying bags is not a good idea, as they will be thrown around like any other luggage. Instead, if the carton solution is not adopted, the AM should be left as a recognisable bike. In this case the problems faced by the AM rider are the same as those faced by riders of conventional bikes.

The airline should be asked in advance what its requirements are for packing. The minimum requirement will be that the pedals are either removed or refitted facing inwards. You should also be prepared to turn the handlebars through 90 degrees. It is common sense to remove baggage and any easily damaged or detached equipment, such as pump, lights, computer and bottles.

You may be required to deflate the tyres, however unnecessary this may seem. But, while it may be counter-productive to object too strongly, you should be able to get away with leaving just a little air in the tyres, so that the bike can be wheeled more easily. Airline policy on deflating tyres is not consistent. For example, I was allowed to leave the tyres of my AM7 inflated when flying from Heathrow to Edinburgh on British Airways, but had to deflate them for the return journey on the same airline. Similarly, when Geoff Meade took his AM7 from London Heathrow to Washington, DC, he had to deflate the tyres, but not for the return trip. This caused him to ask, "Does the US restrict imports of foreign air?"

Unless you wrap vulnerable parts of the bike, you should expect some cosmetic damage, such as scratched paintwork. The AM's paint is much more scratch resistant than many finishes used on bikes (Brian Hayes, frame builder for the Australian Institute of Sport, described it as the toughest he had ever come across) but it is not invulnerable. Bubble wrap or pipe insulation can be used as protection. Alternatively, the whole bike can be put into a large, heavy duty polythene bag. As Alan Gordon pointed out:

"This will afford a little protection, will prevent the bike getting tangled up with other luggage and if anything falls off, it will remain in the bag. This is the preferred method with several airlines. What is more, the bag is easy to stow away in your luggage, so you can do the packing at the check-in desk and keep the bag with you ready for your return journey."

Tyre Care and Cluster Wear

Tyre wear obviously depends on a number of factors apart from the qualities of the tyre itself – rider and luggage weight, road surface, frequency and harshness of braking, tyre pressure, even the weather can have a bearing. However, the experience of high mileage AM riders suggests that under touring conditions on good road surfaces a 17" rear tyre will typically last for about 2,200 miles (3,540 km) and a front tyre some 3,500 miles (5,630 km). This works out at a little over 1p a mile for the covers at 1993 UK prices.

Some riders claim better mileage, as much as 5,000 miles (8,050 km) for a front tyre; others less than 400 miles (640 km) for a rear tyre. Naturally, if the carcase of a supple, high pressure tyre gets cut, its life is likely to be significantly shortened through the resulting deformation. The flint-infested edges of damp Chiltern lanes and the glass-strewn major highways of California are therefore less tyre-friendly than areas where the soil is flint free, or where a deposit is paid for glass bottles and jars, as in eastern Europe.

There are two main defences against carcase cuts. The first is to fit tyre savers, otherwise known as flint or thorn catchers. These consist of a wire about the thickness of a spoke bent to the profile of the tyre. This brushes the tyre lightly in such a way that, if a flint, thorn, tack or stone gets caught in the tread, it will in most cases be flicked out before it has a chance to cause a puncture. The wire is usually suspended on a pair of thin, flexible polythene tubes clipped to the mudguard or fixed to the brake pivot bolt. (On a bike without mudguards, a single polythene tube may be used with a T-shaped wire.)

The other defence is based on the truism that, if you do not ride over sharp objects, you are unlikely to get a puncture. Like many British cyclists, as a youngster I was trained to ride as close to the curb as possible and this became second nature. Riding an AM I am tempted to keep even closer to the curb than on a conventional bike, because the suspension and stronger wheels can cope with the ruts and drainage grilles that would soon write off narrow section 700Cs. However, the amount of detritus – flints, broken glass, tyre carcase wires and nails – a foot (300 mm) from the curb is usually very many times what it is three feet (900 mm) from the curb. I have therefore retrained myself to ride further into the road whenever traffic conditions permit: the result is noticeably fewer punctures.

Rubber cuts more easily in the wet, so I am very cautious about riding through puddles when I don't know what is lurking under the water.

I also don't use the AM for riding on rough flint roads as this can fatally damage a brand new carcase. If mammoths could be killed and skinned using chipped flint, think what it can do to a thin piece of nylon cording coated in rubber!

Wolber Protec anti-puncture tape can reduce the puncture rate considerably. However, being inside the tyre, it will not stop carcase cuts, and some sharp objects will pass through it or through the unprotected sidewalls, just as they will through tyres that incorporate Kevlar barrier layers. (Bullet-proof vests may be made of Kevlar but it does not follow that a thin layer of Kevlar will stop all punctures. My experience of 700Cs shows that it does not!)

As for the special AM clusters of small derailleur sprockets, after ten years of using them Peter Knottley stated:

"I have never discovered their limit. It is always the chain which goes first, and one cannot renew that without renewing the sprockets (or vice versa). A chain will go for up to 10,000 miles [16,000 km], so sprockets will also (and I spend a lot of time in high gears, ie. small sprockets)."

Peter Knottley on his AM14 in Scotland.
Photo courtesy of Peter Knottley.

Another high mileage AM user, Roger Taylor, reckoned to get about 6,000 miles (9,650 km) out of an AM cluster. Taking 8,000 miles (12,900 km) as a compromise between Peter's and Roger's figures, produces a running cost for silver clusters of about 1p a mile at 1994 UK prices.

Allowing for the higher wear rates sustained in urban cycling, through tyre damage, and frequent acceleration and braking, Ben Searle's estimate of about 3p a mile at 1992 UK prices for 17" tyre covers and silver clusters would seem fairly accurate for the typical AM rider.

The APBs, with their easily available and inexpensive tyres and derailleur blocks, therefore look increasingly attractive to budget-minded tourists wishing to enjoy the advantages of the Moulton concept.

Wind Assisted Rides

Finally, what about those who would love to tour the world by bicycle but who are not free to do so? Many people are prevented by family, financial and physical circumstances from undertaking epic tours like those described in this chapter. This is where an 80 page A5 booklet by Moulton Bicycle Club member Richard Hutchins comes in.

Its full title is self-explanatory – "Quiet, 'wind assisted' Cycle Routes between BR [British Rail] Stations covering 3,500 miles [5,632 km] and using 126 'Trailways', 10 Canal Towpaths, 8 Forest Tracks and Bridleways and Minor Roads devised for the Old and People with Young Families".

Richard is a retired solicitor with a great love of outdoor pursuits. The author of the standard work on the British countryside legislation of 1949, he worked for Derbyshire County Council during the establishment of the Peak District National Park.

The idea behind his wind assisted rides book was that, while it occasionally rains when meteorologists forecast fine weather, and they are sometimes wrong about the strength of the wind, they are almost always right about its direction. Hence, Richard and his collaborators devised routes which generally give riders the backing of the wind while they pedal, allowing the train "to take the strain" on the way back.

Each route is typically a day's ride, and all have been checked by the author or his collaborators. The booklet followed an earlier, more modest effort and was published in 1991.

Richard strongly recommends the use of folding or separable cycles for use on British Rail. He himself uses Moultons, as do three of his collaborators – Mike Hessey and Nigel Sadler, who assisted with the word processing and artwork respectively, and John Grimshaw, founder of Sustrans, the national cycle path project based in Bristol.

In 1993, writing in Cycling Plus, John said of his bike: "There's only one bicycle for someone like me. That's a Moulton, isn't it? I couldn't possibly do this job without a high-quality bike that splits up for the train. So Moulton's AM7 has been a godsend ..." A year later John was seen riding an APB specially fitted with a Shimano seven-speed hub.

The late H. H. "Chater" Willis was similarly enthusiastic about the AM7. In a letter to Cycletouring seven years earlier, he wrote that the solution to the train problem "lies in the train-portable cycle, and I smugly admit to having the best sort, a Moulton AM7. For almost any sort of riding it is a first-class machine ..."

And in his 1990 book "Get Away by Bike", writer and broadcaster Les Woodland summed up the AMs as follows: "The new Moultons aren't cheap but very few people switch back to conventional bikes once they've tried one. They're superb for travel with luggage."

March 1994 – Ray Craig's AM7 on the summit of Crown Range Road, the highest through route in New Zealand. The 20 miles (32 km) of gravel track reaches 3,670 ft (1,120 m). Note stuffed kiwi on handlebars! Photo courtesy of Ray Craig.

Chapter 11
STAINLESS STUNNERS
1991-1994

AM-GT – One-Off Titanium 'Moulton' – AM-SPEED S – AM-GTS

On 4 June 1991 the Queen and Prince Philip visited the Design Council in London to view the exhibition "100 Years of British Invention". Alex Moulton was invited to attend and had a stand featuring his innovative automotive suspensions, the 1960s Moulton bicycle and, of course, the AM.

On spying Alex, Prince Philip said, "Ah, a real live inventor! The trouble is, if you attend too many shows like this, you will end up fossilised in one of these cases!"

Eight days later Alex was back in London proving he was not yet ready to become a museum exhibit. In the recently restored vaults of the Royal Society of Arts (RSA) he unveiled the tenth model in the Alex Moulton bicycle range, the AM-GT.

Intended for "universal use by the most discerning of riders", it differed from its predecessors in that its frame was built largely of unpainted polished stainless steel aerospace tubing. The GT was, Alex said, "a further and significant step in the evolution of my aspiration to make 'The Advanced Bicycle System' (TABS) for any adult cycling use."

The RSA is the home of the Faculty of Royal Designers for Industry, of which Alex was once master. The society's vaults provided an ideal studio setting for the new machines, which were set off against graphic displays charting the evolution of the Moulton bicycle. Among those present were the directors of Alex Moulton Limited: the Duchess of Westminster, George Llewellyn, Ron Miles and Julian Hartnoll, Alex's nephew.

Television crews covered the event and the launch was accompanied by in-depth articles in The Times and the Financial Times. Other coverage included news items in Design Week and New Cyclist. Design Week also ran a full page feature on the new machine.

The AM-GT with day carrier.

Frame Tubing

The difficulties Alex had encountered earlier in assuring a supply of suitable Reynolds 531 tubing for the AMs led him to investigate other options. His search ended at Fine Tubes Limited, a Plymouth firm specialising in tube manufacture for the aerospace and nuclear industries. For the GT he selected their small diameter aerospace grade 304 stainless steel tubing.

The GT capitalises on experience gained with the AM-SPEED in using even smaller diameter tubes than the original AMs. Apart from the front suspension stirrup and the seat tube, all visible tubes are unpainted, polished stainless steel and silver brazed – every joint is on display. Hence the machine's visual appeal derives from its very structure, rather than from any superficial surface treatment. In this respect it differs significantly from the chromium-plated S range of the 1960s, the most expensive interpretations of the Series 1 & 2 Moultons.

The GT's seat tube, steerer and suspension stirrup are Reynolds 531. The colour of the stirrup and seat tube can be selected by the purchaser: the choices being black, British racing green or any colour from the current AM paint range – steely grey, blue, Ferrari red or yellow. (Originally the stirrup was available in black only.)

Use of thin stainless steel tubing helps contribute towards a grand tourer that is some 10% lighter than the original AM-Jubilee. The frame is extensively re-engineered and not merely a replica of the original AM frame. For example, the kingpin mechanism is considerably slimmer. Like the slimline kingpin of the AM-ATB or APB, it is operated by an Allen key, in this case 5 mm. But the GT's kingpin is captive and therefore easier to use. (A similar slimline kingpin is used in the AM-Triathlon and AM-Jubilee L.)

A Pivotal Issue

The rear suspension pivot of all previous AMs is immediately behind the bottom bracket. This minimises variations in wheelbase as the suspension moves up and down. In the late 1980s, as mountain bike designers took increasing interest in bicycle suspension, a vogue developed for rear suspension swing arms with pivots raised above the bottom bracket.

The aim in most cases was to keep the suspension pivot in line with the upper section of the chain, thus eliminating any leverage between the chain and the pivot. This reduces the tendency for the rider's pedalling action to move the suspension up and down. Such "Biopacing" can waste energy and reduce rear wheel adhesion in muddy conditions.

(The prototype Cannondale/Magic Motorcycle mountain bike "Coda Magic", shown at the 1993 Las Vegas Interbike Bicycle Show, used an idler pulley to align the chain with the suspension pivot. The idler, however, must absorb a little energy, bearing in mind that a pair of derailleur pulleys typically rob the rider of about 1% of his output.)

In practice the theoretical advantages of raised suspension pivots are compromised somewhat by the use of multiple chainwheels – only one size can be optimal. Also, with most raised pivot designs, wheelbase fluctuations are substantially worse than with the pivot immediately behind the bottom bracket.

In some designs the pivot is raised substantially **above** the upper section of chain. The aim here is to use tension in the chain during pedalling to restrain movement of the suspension, the suspension becoming "active" only when the rider freewheels. The prime disadvantage of this configuration is that it imposes colossal loading on the chain when a bump is encountered.

About 1990 Alex experimented with a raised pivot version of the AM rear suspension. This enabled comparative tests to be carried out, involving time-triallist and triathlete Richard Grigsby as test rider.

Richard aggressively rode a bike fitted with the original low pivot suspension up a very steep incline, Brassknocker Hill, in the wet. Despite using high pressure 17" slick (treadless) tyres, he managed to achieve only slight "non-inhibiting" wheel slip. The raised pivot suspension offered no significant advantage, and as it had inherent disadvantages, was therefore abandoned.

The GT's Suspension

The GT's the rear suspension pivot is **very slightly** higher than on earlier AMs. It is as if Alex were saying to other suspension designers, "I hear what you say, salute your efforts but don't really agree".

In fact, there is a serious reason for slightly raising the pivot. It means that, without altering the basic geometry of the original AM rear triangle, the rear suspension's rubber Monosphere is mounted slightly higher up the seat tube. This enables the cone housing to make a foundation for the carrier fixing (see below). It also brings the central axis of the Monosphere into better alignment with the horizontal beam of the frame, thus distributing the stress in the frame more efficiently.

The GT's rear triangle incorporates additional corner braces linking the chainstays to the bridge immediately ahead of the wheel, as in the AM-SPEED. The front suspension also differs from that of earlier AMs, the fork blades being parallel-sided rather than tapered, for greater rigidity. This design feature, first seen in the AM-ATB, was introduced across the AM range in 1993.

There is a choice of front suspension spring: either the standard AM unit, or an uprated short stroke race spring. The latter has a shorter, stiffer coil and an alloy spacer to make up the length.

Details of the AM-GT.

Components

The wheels used on the GT each have only 20 spokes. They are radially spoked, except for the dished (freewheel) side of the rear wheel which is built two-cross (each spoke crossing two others). The customer has the choice of standard Moulton-Wolber high pressure 17" tyres or the Moulton-Wolber C3 slicks, introduced for the AM-SPEED.

The hubs were originally Hugi with sealed bearings. In February 1990 the US magazine Bicycle Guide described Swiss engineer Wilfred Hugi's standard cassette hub as "a freewheeling mechanism that spins like the tumblers in a Swiss bank vault". The world's first nine-speed freewheel, developed for the AM-SPEED, resulted from Alex's collaboration with Wilfred Hugi (see page 239). For the GT's rear hub they worked together again, this time to produce an eight-speed touring block using a Moulton silver cluster with 9, 10 and 11 teeth, and five light alloy sprockets in sizes up to 28 teeth.

Later the special Hugi hubs became unavailable and instead British-made Hope hubs were used, the rear again being specially modified.

In conjunction with a Rohloff or Sedis super-narrow chain and a 62/52 tooth double chainwheel the eight-speed block offers a sixteen-speed range of 31 to 117". Alternatively, if a 52/42 tooth chainset is specified, the range is 25 to 98". The indexed gear levers can be frame-mounted, handlebar-end or thumbshifter type. The rear derailleur mechanism is a SunTour GPX, the front a SunTour SL.

The bottom bracket axle set is a 115 mm (4.53") British-made titanium unit by Royce Racing, with twin sets of sealed, pre-adjusted ball bearings. Cups and lock rings are machined from 30 tonne tensile aluminium alloy. The Royce crank arm bolts automatically fill the GT's SunTour Superbe Pro crank, obviating the need for dust covers.

Titanium is also used for the GT's seat pillar. This incorporates a continuously variable screw-jack type micro-adjuster for the saddle, instead of the SR Laprade cradle used on other AMs.

Brakes were initially Shimano Ultegra 600 side-pulls, later changed to 105s. New cable connectors (turnbuckles) for the brakes and gears were introduced on the GT. These, described in greater detail on page 177, soon became available on other AMs, Moulton APBs and as a retro-fit item.

Like the Jubilee, the GT is fitted with Alex's patented Wishbone handlebar stem, in either 140 (5^1/$_2$") or 190 mm (7^1/$_2$") lengths. Reach is adjustable and indexed. The GT's stainless steel Wishbone is more graceful than the Jubilee's chrome plated Reynolds 531 stem, and somewhat lighter.

Handlebars can be drops, flats or the special Loveday type introduced for the AM14T. Saddles and pedals are to choice from the options used in the AM range.

Carriers and Bags

The GT's rear carrier was a new design, launched with the bike. The carrier platform is Reynolds 531 and similar to the original AM pattern but reversed (upstand at the back) and tilted at about 25 degrees to the horizontal. It is somewhat reminiscent of the 1969 Moulton Marathon's rear carrier. The main objective of this configuration is to bring more of the load into the wheelbase, thus improving stability.

The carrier platform's two central main tubes run from the base of its upstand (where they are furthest apart) to the seat binder bolt, by

A phalanx of AM-GTs at the GT launch in 1991, each with the wishbone stem adjusted differently. Photo by Tony Hadland.

which they are attached to the bike. A horizontal stainless steel underframe serves as a support strut.

The underframe consists of a pair of tubes with zigzag infill, a visual extension of the horizontal girder of the bike's main frame. The two forward ends of the tubes incorporate internally expanding collets which plug into a pair of mount tubes resembling oversized cable guides, one either side of the rear suspension rubber cone. The underframe can be used as a secondary carrier, for small items such as a cape.

To enable a rear reflector and lamp to be fitted clear of the sloping carrier upstand, the carrier incorporates a tail loop, which gives the appearance of a continuation of the carrier's two central main tubes.

A stainless steel day carrier is available for the GT. However, as the collet fixing system is not adequate in its own right for the cantilever load imposed, a light stainless steel strut is provided to give additional support.

A prototype GT rear bag was demonstrated at the launch. This was expandable, its midriff containing a "bellows" section which could be compressed and zipped up if the full capacity of the bag was not required. In the reduced height mode, the bag was reasonably rigid,

AM-GT with optional Loveday handlebars.

thus overcoming a criticism of the standard AM rear bags. The top flap was similar to that of the earlier bags, with loops for tieing on a cape or tent. The GT bag was black with a red-edged silver trim line around its circumference. For those who preferred an open basket on the rear carrier, there was a specially made optional Sedgemoor wicker basket.

Also displayed was a prototype GT front bag, like the rear bag finished in black. It dispensed with the need for a carrier by wrapping around the head tube, rather like a pannier set on its side, and fixing to the front carrier mountings by bolts passing through cleated holes in the inner faces of the bag. The net effect was to reduce weight and keep the luggage within the wheelbase of the bike for better stability under load. Also wind resistance was reduced by the rounded front of the bag.

A special GT front carrier, prototyped in 1994, provides a platform for a similar front bag. The standard AM front carrier can, of course, be fitted to the GT.

Price and Weight

Typical weight of the basic GT was quoted as 23^3/$_4$lb (10.8 kg). The price at launch was £2,500, the highest yet for an AM. However, as Peter Hall of Design Week pointed out, it was only £375 (18%) dearer than a top of the range Muddy Fox mountain bike. By spring 1993 the GT's price had risen to £2,900: for the same price you could buy a dual suspension mountain bike (GT RTS-1) that weighed about 4lb (1.8 kg) more! So, although the GT was expensive, it was not uniquely so.

Because of the price, Alex did not foresee a large market for his new model. He stated that, in any case, he was not inclined to produce more than a limited number of high quality machines. So saying, he stressed that the new machine was fully tooled, and therefore skilled labour intensive, rather than craftsman dependent.

Brochures and Advertising

A double-sided colour leaflet in the usual AM format was produced for the GT, as was a pale yellow fold-out leaflet depicting for the first time the full AM range. Line drawings showed the various models, pride of place being given to the AM-GT.

This leaflet was designed by Nigel Sadler, who created the various graphic displays for the GT launch. One of his wallboards charted the GT's "Pedigree of Advanced Engineering" showing its descent from the Moulton bicycle of the 1960s. A4 copies of the pedigree were distributed at the launch.

A half-page advertisement featuring the AM-GT was run by Swift Cycles Limited of Forest Hill, London in New Cyclist, commencing July/August 1991.

Press Reaction

On the whole the British broadsheet newspapers, in reporting the GT launch, concentrated on Alex rather than the bike. The most comprehensive design-oriented article was Peter Hall's in Design Week, which gave a reasonably detailed description of the machine.

Bicycle Trade & Industry was most enthusiastic, stating that, "With this new gleamer we may even be seeing a Moulton hanging in an art gallery." (Something which had actually happened in Manchester some years earlier with a 1960s Moulton!) In Blueprint, Sebastian Conran wrote that the AM-GT "exudes Formula 1 glamour and sniper rifle aesthetics. If M were briefed to equip James Bond with a bike, this would be it."

Sixteen months after the bike's UK launch, the Japanese glossy magazine Begin included a six page colour feature on Alex and his bicycles under the heading "The Great Labels". The AM-GT, beautifully photographed, was featured on the first page of the article.

The Cyclists' Touring Club's technical officer, Chris Juden, writing in Cycle Touring & Campaigning and taking a more practical view, found it hard to accept the "jaunty tilt" of the rear carrier. He would have preferred an improved version of the original AM carrier. Nonetheless, he felt the AM-GT represented value for money:

"Its price should be compared not with other bicycles, assembled as they are from a standard kit of parts, but with other highly-engineered pieces of machinery. How much would a similar sized aircraft component cost? Whatever the figure may be, I'm certain more satisfaction can be gained from riding an AM-GT, not to mention just looking at it."

(Subsequent analysis as a "bit of fun" by Alex and another eminent engineer revealed that the AM-GT does indeed come cheap when compared weight for weight with an airliner!)

The most detailed review of the GT was a three page illustrated article in the racing-oriented magazine Performance Cyclist International, published in August 1993. Steven Robinson stated that the frame contained "more triangles than the Toblerone factory" and looked "like a GCSE [General Certificate of Secondary Education] metalwork project".

He considered the gear changing and derailleur mechanisms were relatively poor for such a costly bike. Some of the gear spacings were, he added, too far apart for the performance rider. Low speed stability was "quite poor", demanding "maximum rider concentration", and acceleration was, he said, disappointing. All this led Steven to conclude that the bike was not built for racing – which was broadly correct.

On the credit side, Steven praised the GT's exceptionally smooth ride and well-engineered frame separability. Braking was powerful and responsive. Stability at speed was good and cornering was excellent.

The bike excelled in the areas of comfort, manoeuvrability and portability. It was, Steven felt, almost the ultimate utility machine. He concluded, "It's just a pity that what began life as a bicycle for universal appeal has evolved into one that only Japanese businessmen can afford."

But that was to ignore that it had also evolved into the APB, a Moulton at a fraction of the GT's cost. When Steven's article was published you could buy **five** APB-12s for the price of an AM-GT, and still have change!

User Feedback

The Summer 1993 issue of The Moultoneer carried a report from Dr Douglas G. Ismay of Chaniers, France. He had bought an AM-GT and stated that, "were it not for this brilliantly conceived bike" he would have had to give up cycling altogether – Douglas suffered from rheumatoid arthritis in his wrists and hands.

By using the most upright setting of the wishbone stem, and having the handlebars raised a further 7" (180 mm) by Chas Roberts of Croydon, he achieved "a completely sit up and beg position", reducing the pressure on his wrists. The suspension also eliminated the worst of the jarring at the handlebars.

Douglas praised the lightness of the bike, but suffered problems with the front derailleur throwing the chain off in lowest gear. He was also decidedly unimpressed by the sloping rear carrier.

Despite these criticisms, he found the bike "a great joy to ride", adding: "When I am out with a group, I am in a superior position with less effort."

The One-Off Titanium "AM"

The AM-GT's titanium seat pillar was supplied by One-Off Titanium Inc. of Florence, Massachusetts – a company specialising in custom fabrication, machining and welding of titanium. Mike Augspurger, the custom bike builder who runs One-Off, became interested in Moultons about 1990, after riding a friend's.

In summer 1991 Doug Milliken introduced Mike to Alex: the two got on well. They went cycling in hilly Western Massachusetts, then visited Mike's shop in Boston, where Alex was particularly interested in some destructive testing of titanium being undertaken there.

Mike expressed an interest in building a titanium AM-style non-separable machine. Alex allowed him to proceed and supplied certain unique components. It took Mike about two months, working part-time, to build the frame-set. The front fork assembly and rest of the frame each weighed about 1lb (450 g) less than the corresponding parts of the AM-Speed.

Alex was somewhat concerned about product liability, and in November 1991, issued Mike with this disclaimer for use with the titanium machine: "While I have not licensed, approved of, tested or even seen the One-Off Titanium bike which you have made, I am interested in your experiment. To assist you in this One-Off experiment I have enabled our Moulton components to be made available to you in this one instance."

The One-Off titanium
"Moulton".
Photo courtesy of Mike
Augspurger.

Right: Front fork
detail and far right:
rear suspension
detail of the One-Off
machine.
Photos courtesy of
Mike Augspurger.

Mike reckoned that he would have to charge about $6,000 (approximately
£4,000) to make another AM-style One-Off frame-set, including seat
pillar – which puts the price of the AM-GT into perspective. He added
that, "Compared to Moultons, all other bikes are the same. Trying to
compare differences between 'regular' bikes becomes pointless hair
splitting after spending an afternoon with Moulton."

AM-SPEED S

As noted in Chapter 9, the AM-SPEED S was launched with the Moulton APB-14 at an International Press Day at The Hall on Friday 29 January 1993. It mixes the constructional techniques of the AM-GT with the non-separable frame concept of the AM-SPEED. The result, as Cycling Plus put it, is "the ultimate fast Moulton". It was priced appropriately at £2,900, rising in common with the AM-GT to £2,950 in 1994.

Typical weight of a complete machine is 21lb 15oz (9.95 kg). The main frame including rear triangle weighs 5lb 2oz (2.33 kg) and the front fork 2lb 11oz (1.22 kg), making a total frame-set weight of 7lb 13oz (3.55 kg). In common with other 17" wheel Moultons, the nominal head and tube angles are $72^1/_2$ degrees.

Transmission typically consists of a SunTour Superbe Pro crankset with 62 and 52 tooth chainwheels on a Royce titanium bottom bracket, driving via an eight-speed cassette via a Rohloff chain. The rear derailleur mechanism is usually a Shimano Dura-Ace, the front a SunTour Edge, and the "downtube" shift levers are AM-modified SunTour.

As with the GT, early hubs were Hugi, later ones Hope – in both cases the rear being specially modified to take the special AM 9, 10 and 11 tooth sprocket cluster. Other cogs are typically 12, 13, 15, 17 and 19 tooth (although the wider gearing of the GT is quoted in the 1994 catalogue). The gears offered by this configuration are:

52T: 47, 52, 59, 68, 74, 80, 88, (98)

62T: (55), 62, 70, 81, 88, 96, 105 & 117"

This is basically a crossover system suitable for time-trialling and triathlons. The optimal upward changing sequence would probably be 47, 52 (+12%), 59 (+13%), 68 (+15%), 74 (+8%) (shift to larger chainwheel and back one cog), 81 (+9%), 88 (+8%), 96 (+9%), 105 (+10%), 117 (+11%).

The rider's points of contact with the AM-SPEED S are typically 16 " (420 mm) wide Cinelli 66 drop handlebars on an AM-GT adjustable Wishbone stem, Shimano Ultegra pedals, and a Flite titanium chassis saddle on a conventional diameter USE seat post.

The SPEED S is available in three seat tube heights, as was the now deleted SPEED. Mudguards are not fitted and there is no provision for carriers.

Reviews of the SPEED S

One of the first cycle writers to comment on the SPEED S was Scot Nicol. In April 1993, in the US magazine Velo News, he reported that the new AMs "are a team time trialist's dream, as the small wheels allow the racers to get extremely close to one another – it feels like being on the back of a tandem."

The AM-SPEED S.

Like many before him, Scot noted that riding a lightweight AM is very different from riding a conventional machine: "On one hand, you can accelerate like a rocket; but out-of-the-saddle work causes the suspension to bob up and down. This is not necessarily bad, just different."

Over in France, Velo Tonic carried a brief report on the AM-SPEED S in its August/September 1993 issue. It seemed that French race ace Christian Taillefer might be testing the machine, which was said to be ideal for descents in the cycling World Cup.

Back in the UK, Cycling Plus comprehensively tested the AM-SPEED S as part of its group test of suspension bikes, published in December 1993. Frame performance and frame design/quality were both awarded six points out of seven: "The frame is beautifully crafted – all the joints are on display and you can really feel the quality."

Head and seat tube alignment, and front fork alignment were excellent; the rear triangle was good. However, it was suggested that a longer "top tube" length be made available for taller riders, and that the seat and head tube angles be steepened. A little more fork trail was also suggested, so that the steering would be less twitchy with tri-bars.

Most of the magazine's testers felt that the suspension absorbed some power, especially on hills, but acceleration was described as "superb", due to the light 20 spoke wheels. "A faster descending bike would be hard to find despite very light steering", concluded Cycling Plus, "Comfort overall is far better than any other high performance bike."

Gear performance was also given six out of seven. The main criticism was a tendency for the chain to stick between the chainwheels when shifting from the large ring to the small.

The Shimano 105 dual-pivot side-pull brakes were considered somewhat downmarket for such an expensive machine. But despite a lack of fine modulation, they were "plenty powerful enough", and earned the bike five out of seven for brake performance.

Componentry was described as "a bit of a funny mix", earning just four points. The tyres were accused of poor wet grip, but the adjustability of the handlebars, the Hugi hubs, Royce bottom bracket and SunTour chainset all won praise.

Cycling Plus's overall conclusion was that the AM-SPEED S deserved seven out of seven for performance, a rare accolade and the best in the group test – which included the Slingshot, Allsop Powercurve, Radical and Moulton APB-14. However, as is often the case with expensively refined equipment, it came last for value for money, scoring only four out of seven.

The AM-GT with GT rear carrier. CAD drawing by Nigel Sadler.

Alex Moulton reveals the bike that became known as the GTS, at the MBC Weekend, Bradford-on-Avon, 1993.
Photo by Mike Hessey.

AM-GTS

The MBC's annual Bradford-on-Avon Weekend in September 1993 saw the debut of a further refinement of the stainless steel AM. The unnamed prototype, revealed at the club's annual dinner, was claimed to be the first separable AM to weigh less than 10 kg (22lb).

Later referred to as the AM-GTS, the concept machine incorporates special narrow hubs for lower wind resistance and quieter running, the rear hub incorporating a silent freewheel mechanism. The hubs were developed by Alex Moulton and Paulo Kiefe. Paulo, a Portuguese-born Swedish national, is the production engineer behind the ultra-compact, short-range, folding MicroBike (not to be confused with the Radnall Micro of the 1970s).

The GTS has a single chainwheel and an eight-speed derailleur. A chain catcher is fitted to prevent the chain riding off the top of the chainwheel. The unusual and eye-catching US-made crankset is by Magic Motorcycle.

At the same dinner Alex announced that he had abandoned development work on recumbents. After a lengthy second flirtation with the idea of a recumbent AM, he had returned to the opinion he formed in the 1950s – that the conventional riding position was, on the whole, better in terms of balance and muscle use.

And so the Moulton story continues. This account ends in June 1994, but will surely not be the last word on this fascinating, controversial and unique marque. At the AM-GT launch Alex made it clear that his was a continuing quest:

"From **my conviction**, I state unequivocally that a bicycle is one of the most fascinating and unlikely creations handed to us from the last century. It represents to me an unending engineering challenge to improve on its performance, convenience and 'pleasure to have and to use'."

Nobody can say he hasn't tried!

Dave Duffield and Alex Moulton celebrate 30 years of the Moulton Bicycle at the MBC Weekend, Bradford-on-Avon, 1992.

Appendix A
MAINTENANCE
&
GEAR TABLES

In most respects adjustment and maintenance of AMs and APBs is no different from that of conventional bicycles. There are a number of good books available that can be referred to on general cycle maintenance, such as "Richard's Bicycle Book" by Richard Ballantine (Pan) and "The Bicycle Book" by Geoff Apps (Salamander Books).

This Appendix therefore concentrates on commonly encountered adjustment and maintenance requirements **specific** to AMs and APBs. For the more esoteric aspects of maintenance, or if in doubt, refer to the factory, or to the Moulton Bicycle Club's Technical Adviser.

FRAME SEPARATION & GENERAL MAINTENANCE

Frame separation and general maintenance instructions should be supplied with all new bikes and hence are not reproduced here. Anyone with a second-hand machine lacking these instructions, may obtain a copy from Alex Moulton Limited. The instructions issued by the company for 17" wheel AMs were written in 1983 for the original AM2 and AM7. The following text, up to and including the section on adjusting the Wishbone stem, is based on a note issued by Alex Moulton Limited and covers additional points applying to later models.

LATER 17" WHEEL MODELS

Allen Keys

Some models use 5 mm and 2 mm Allen keys, which are supplied under the seat instead of a 6 mm key. To keep the 5 mm key in place, it should be **tucked in front of the seat rail** (it is taped in the correct location at time of shipment). A 6 mm key is also supplied in the tool kit.

Cable Separation

The gear levers no longer remove on a demount plate as shown in the instructions. Instead special threaded disconnects (turnbuckles) allow you to separate the cables before separating the frame. When the bike is split, it is a good idea to **tape over the disconnects** to keep them from scratching the frame.

If the O-rings on the cable disconnects require replacement, $^{1}/_{4}''$ (6 mm) internal diameter rings from a hardware store plumbing department may be used.

An extra set of cable stops (near the headset) may have been brazed on by the factory for optional fitting of handlebar mounted shift levers.

Carriers on Stainless Steel AMs

The rear carriers attach by means of internally expanding collets. The day carrier has a small stay below, unlike the day carriers on 531-framed AMs. The large carrier includes a long bolt which replaces the original seat pillar binder bolt. The reflector hangs below the rack.

To install the collets, loosen up the special tapered-seat Allen bolts (but don't remove them). Push the carrier into the mount tubes (brazed onto the side of the rear suspension Monosphere) until it is seated against the shoulder at the front end of the mount tubes. At the same time, work the support (stay or seat pillar binder bolt) into position.

The horizontal portion of the rack will fall right in line with the top of the frame when the collets are properly seated. Once the rack is in the correct position, tighten the tapered Allen bolts and the other support bolt.

Wishbone Stem: Adjustment and Changing Handlebars

To change the effective extension length, loosen the horizontal clamp bolt that passes through the serrated washers. The circlip over the head of this bolt will force the serrations open, allowing adjustment of the stem.

Should it ever become necessary to remove the handlebars from the stem, the wishbone must be disassembled. First, loosen the pinch bolts at the bars. Then loosen the clamp bolt that passes through the serrated washers and work the arms along the bars as the centre section is forced apart. If the arms are not slid along the bars at the same time as the centre is opened, the arms may become cocked and lock onto the bars. Slide the arms off the ends of the bars.

SERVICING THE REAR SUSPENSION

Normally the rear suspension is maintenance free. However, under exceptional circumstances looseness can occur either at the pivot bearing or where the apex of the rear triangle is bolted to the rubber Monosphere. As a preventative measure, never mount the bike by scooting, as this imposes high eccentric loads on the suspension. (It is also unkind to the chainset and bottom bracket bearings of any machine.)

Loose Pivot Bearing

(Based on a service note issued by Alex Moulton Limited.)

Insufficient load in the bolt can cause the hardened steel sleeve to rotate at the ears of the bottom bracket tube, so that the bearing incorrectly works between the sleeve and the bolt, which can result in wear of both and consequent bearing looseness.

The correct working is when the sleeve is pinched between the ears so that it is fixed and functions as the hardened steel journal of the bearing with the sintered Oilite bushes rotating with the rear fork tube.

Insufficient load in the bolt can be due to the nut stripping or overtightening. Since 1987 a $5/16$" UNF Nylok nut with greater overall height has been fitted as standard, giving an increased recommended torque setting of 20lb/ft (27.12 Nm or 2.76 kgf/m). The use of this taller nut with its greater torque capacity, and removal of the washer at the head end of the bolt, will usually remedy the problem.

Looseness at the Rubber Cone (Monosphere)

(Based on notes by Harry Routledge.)

If play is found between the alloy cam (apex of the rear triangle) and the rubber cone, first remove the self-tapping screws either side of the cone's steel housing on the back of the seat tube. The rear triangle can now be swung down, allowing the cone to part company with its housing.

Inside the rubber cone is a 2BA Allen bolt which has worked loose. Tighten it with an Allen key.

Swing the rear triangle up again, so that the rubber cone returns to its housing. Reinsert the self-tapping screws.

(Ideally this task should be carried out with the main frame of the bike held on a work-stand or suspended from the ceiling.)

Softening of the Rear Suspension

This is rare but indicates an internally ruptured Monosphere which should be replaced. Failure to do so may result in the Monosphere's bolt piercing the back of the seat tube within the Monosphere housing. Later Monospheres have a "nose" moulded into the rubber around the bolt head to help prevent this.

To release the defective Monosphere loosen the 2BA Allen bolt referred to above.

SERVICING THE FRONT SUSPENSION

This section is based primarily on a guidance note by Angle Lake Cyclery of Seattle, updated in 1992 and approved by Alex Moulton Limited. Other information from Alex Moulton Limited and the author has been incorporated.

To Adjust and Maintain the Front Suspension

1. The starting position for suspension frequency is when the leading link nuts are just snug against the link plates so vertical motion is not restricted and there is no side play. The front and back nuts of each link (not the middle nuts) can then be adjusted to dampen the suspension frequency.

   For best performance on high frequency bumps, such as a road dressing of coarse granite chippings, simply leave the nuts adjusted as for the starting position. For greater damping, with the suspension reacting only to larger, low frequency bumps, tighten the four nuts by an equal amount. A small amount of tightening makes a big difference to the damping. Indeed, if desired, the front suspension can be locked solid by this means.

2. Spring pre-load is properly adjusted when, with the rider on the bicycle in riding position, leading link plates are approximately parallel to the ground. The spring pre-load should not be adjusted with more than $5/8$" (16 mm) of thread showing.

3. Light lubrication should only be carried out when the fork is overhauled. (See instructions below.)

4. A thorough cleaning should be done periodically in proportion to use and environmental conditions.

To Disassemble the Front Suspension

1. Remove front wheel, brake calliper and mudguard (fender).

2. Remove the six 8 mm nuts and steel washers from the leading link plates. Remove stainless leading links and friction washers. Set aside in safe place.

3. Slide stirrup and spring assembly out of main fork and steerer tube.

   Note: The spring base plug (guide bearing) is hygroscopic and may swell, sticking in the steerer tube. If the base plug is tight within the steerer tube but stays attached to the height adjuster, emery paper may be used to lessen the diameter of the base plug by the minimum necessary to make it free sliding.

If the base plug is stuck in the steerer tube, there are two recommended methods of removal. Whichever you choose, bear in mind that the plug expands more (and therefore sticks more tightly in the steerer tube) under hot conditions than cold. So if the job seems unduly tough, it may be best to "cool it" – in every sense!

a) The author's preferred method: The handlebar stem is removed and a piece of $^1/_4$" (6 mm) steel rod, 12-15" long (305-380 mm) is dropped down the steerer tube. The rod is then tapped gently with a hammer to knock out the base plug. The lower end of the rod should be rounded off with a file to protect the thin-walled Reynolds 531 steerer tube. Care should be taken, as the base plug is under pressure from the spring and may come out with considerable force.

b) Angle Lake Cyclery's preferred method: Obtain a long thin wood screw, drill a small starter hole in the base plug, and start the wood screw in the hole. Grasp onto the screw perpendicular to the fork with Vise Grip pliers (Mole wrench or similar) and tap on the pliers with a hammer to draw out the plug.

Note that with method b) replacement of the plug is necessary. With method a) it should be possible to reduce the plug's diameter with emery paper and reuse it.

Later ATBs (1990 onwards) have thicker-walled steerer tubes, and therefore use a smaller diameter base plug. It is wise to measure the old plug diameter before ordering a replacement.

4. Carefully clean all surfaces with a safe, biodegradable solvent. Then clean out the solvent with a dry cloth.

To Reassemble the Front Suspension

1. Lightly grease the spring with a high quality bicycle grease such as Phil Wood or thick lithium grease. Do not grease the spring base plug, as it is graphite impregnated and needs no lubrication. Lubricating it may cause the plug to swell and in time the suspension will seize.

2. Grease the spring pre-load adjuster threads and screw the adjuster all the way down. If your bicycle is equipped with a pre-load adjuster lock ring (which prevents the adjuster creeping down the thread over a period of time, and which is standard on later machines), it should be installed on the fork prior to the adjuster.

Note: The rubber-faced suspension stop (fork stirrup bushing) should not be used as a lock ring. It should be screwed tightly onto the top of the fork crown, otherwise suspension travel will be impeded.

3. Place the small rubber boot over the spring pre-load adjusting barrel. The spring base plug can now be installed on the pre-

load adjusting barrel with a light tap from a soft mallet. Place the spring inside the steerer tube. Clean the inside of the steerer tube below the spring of any residual grease.

4. Slide the stirrup sub-assembly into the steerer tube. If the machine is an ATB or APB, don't forget to fit the rubber bellows.

5. The leading link washers should be clean and light blue in colour. They may be cleaned with a Teflon-based spray lubricant and a soft rag. If they are heavily soiled, use a fine (soap free) steel wool followed by the soft rag. During assembly, lightly lubricate the leading link washers with the same Teflon-based lubricant used to clean them.

6. Install the brake calliper and mudguard. There should be a small spacer between the stirrup and the mudguard bracket to prevent interference between the mudguard and fork. Also, check the alignment of the mudguard so it does not rub on the main fork.

7. Install the front wheel.

Note: For safety, as well as proper front suspension performance, any front hub quick-release lever must be installed out of the way of leading link travel.

The remaining notes are by the author.

CURING SHIMMY

1. Do not hang loose bags from the handlebars. Only light, well-damped loads should be carried on a front carrier.

2. Check that the front wheel is true and that the hub bearings are correctly adjusted, with a minimum of play. The tyre should be in good condition, correctly inflated and properly seated on the rim.

3. Ensure that the front suspension is correctly adjusted as described above, with no lateral play in the leading links, and no excessive wear in the link pivots.

4. Ensure steering head bearings are in good condition. Adjustment should be just the "tight side of right", so that the steering is smooth but without the slightest hint of sloppiness in the bearings.

5. If after steps 1-4 shimmy is still encountered, contact the factory.

   Over the years greater rigidity has been designed into the front suspension, which should further minimise any tendency to shimmy. Fully-boxed leading links were introduced in the late 1980s, and parallel-sided forks, first used on the ATB, are standard on all AMs from 1993.

LOOSENESS IN THE CAPTIVE KINGPIN

It is not uncommon to find slight looseness in the frame joint of a 17" wheel AM fitted with the original captive kingpin. This is caused by compression of the pressed steel cap on the left end of the kingpin and is not related to the number of times the frame is separated. It results in marginally insufficient length of thread on the kingpin to draw the joint tightly together.

The joint is very forgiving of this and there is no significant risk of structural collapse. Nonetheless, the situation should be remedied as soon as possible, as the bike's handling may be adversely affected. Fortunately the problem is quickly and cheaply overcome by fitting a thin washer under the kingpin's steel cap.

For this purpose the kingpin must be removed by unthreading and detaching the thin wire guide rod below it. (The rod has a screwdriver slot cut in its head.) The washer must have an internal diameter a little over $7/8$" (22 mm) and a thickness of about $1/16$" (1.5 mm). A large brass sump plug washer or a nylon tap-to-basin washer will work well.

AVOIDING REAR CARRIER PROBLEMS

This note concerns 17" wheel AMs with Reynolds 531 frames.

1. If the carrier strut is slightly loose on its threaded stud when aligned correctly with the bolt on the underside of the carrier, the strut will rattle. Fitting a suitable washer over the stud will cure the problem. A nylon plumbing washer or brass sump washer is suitable: it should have an internal diameter of just over $1/2$" (13 mm). The washer should be no thicker than necessary and filed down to ensure correct alignment of the strut.

2. If the carrier strut is an early one and therefore fitted with a forked end (rather than a hole), the carrier bolt may jump out of the forked end if the bike hits a particularly large bump at speed. Overcome this problem by having a stout steel washer brazed to the slotted end. Ensure that the hole in the washer is no bigger than necessary to accommodate the carrier bolt.

3. Frequently check that the carrier thumb nut is as tight as possible. Failure to do so will permit movement at this point. This can lead to metal fatigue of the carrier bolt, or worse, of the cross-piece to which it is attached. This in turn could lead to the carrier collapsing onto the rear wheel.

BRAZE-ONS

Be extremely wary of adding braze-ons, such as additional cable guides and stops or bottle cage mounts. Thin-walled chain stays and cantilevered seat tubes can easily be weakened. Seek advice from the factory.

CHAIN PEG

If you have a derailleur-geared AM with a single chainwheel, fit the special bolt-on chain peg. It is very light, neat and unobtrusive. More importantly, it could prevent a chain that has fallen off the chainwheel getting trapped under your rear wheel, and causing loss of control.

VALVE HOLES

The valve holes in pre 1990 AM rims should be reamed out slightly from 6mm (0.236") to 6.8mm (0.268"). This will allow the newer style moulded valve stem of Moulton-Wolber inner tubes to seat correctly.

TYRE PRESSURES

If you don't use a pressure gauge, your tyres are probably under-inflated. You are gifted indeed if you can tell the difference between 60 and 90 psi (4 and 6 atm) by squeezing a tyre between forefinger and thumb. You are also a masochist if you regularly use a hand-held pump to achieve the pressures needed to get the best performance out of the 17" tyre.

For home use the only sensible solution is a good quality track pump with integral gauge – you will never regret buying one. For commuting or short pleasure rides, treat the pump supplied with the bike as a thief-resistant get-you-home device. When touring, a decent 18" (460 mm) frame-fit pump sits neatly within the spaceframe without the need for extra clips or toe straps to keep it in place.

High tyre pressures are an essential part of the Moulton design philosophy: the inevitable consequence of under-inflated tyres is an under-performing bike!

AM-GT, factory fitted with Sturmey-Archer 5-Star hub gear. This bike was built to special order. Photo courtesy of Max R. Knobel.

GEAR TABLES

The following tables give the gearing, in inches, for various sprocket and chainwheel combinations (including some very rare extremes) for 17" and 20"/500 x 28A wheels. Note that these are nominal wheel sizes – actual diameter, especially in the case of 20"/500 x 28A wheels, may vary somewhat.

Multiplication factors for hub gears are given below.

Gear	F+S 2-speeds	F+S 3-speeds	S-A 3-speeds (since 1964)	F+S 5-speeds	S-A 5-speeds	F+S Super 7	Shimano SG-7
1	1.00	0.74	0.75	0.67	0.67	0.59	0.63
2	1.36	1.00	1.00	0.78	0.79	0.68	0.74
3		1.36	1.33	1.00	1.00	0.81	0.84
4				1.28	1.27	1.00	0.99
5				1.50	1.50	1.24	1.15
6						1.48	1.34
7						1.69	1.55
		1.8	1.8	2.2	2.2	2.5	2.5

Gear Chart in inches for 17" Wheels

Number of teeth on sprocket

Number of teeth on chainwheel

	9	10	11	12	13	14	15	16	17	18	19	20	21	22	23	24	25	26	27	28	29	30	31	32	33	34
21	40	36	32	30	27	26	24	22	21	20	19	18	17	16	16	15	14	14	13	13	12	12	12	11	11	11
22	42	37	34	31	29	27	25	23	22	21	20	19	18	17	16	16	15	14	14	13	13	12	12	12	11	11
23	43	39	36	33	30	28	26	24	23	22	21	20	19	18	17	16	16	15	14	14	13	13	13	12	12	12
24	45	41	37	34	31	29	27	26	24	23	21	20	19	19	18	17	16	16	15	15	14	14	13	13	12	12
25	47	43	39	35	33	30	28	27	25	24	22	21	20	19	18	18	17	16	16	15	15	14	14	13	13	13
26	49	44	40	37	34	32	29	28	26	25	23	22	21	20	19	18	18	17	16	16	15	15	14	14	13	13
27	51	46	42	38	35	33	31	29	27	26	24	23	22	21	20	19	18	18	17	16	16	15	15	14	14	14
28	53	48	43	40	37	34	32	30	28	26	25	24	23	22	21	20	19	18	17	16	16	15	15	15	14	14
29	55	49	45	41	38	35	33	31	29	27	26	25	23	22	21	21	20	19	18	18	17	16	16	15	15	15
30	57	51	46	43	39	36	34	32	30	28	27	26	24	23	22	21	20	20	19	18	18	17	16	16	15	15
31	59	53	48	44	41	38	35	33	31	29	28	26	25	24	23	22	21	20	20	19	18	18	17	16	16	16
32	60	54	49	45	42	39	36	34	32	30	29	27	26	25	24	23	22	21	20	19	19	18	18	17	16	16
33	62	56	51	47	43	40	37	35	33	31	30	28	27	26	24	23	22	22	21	20	19	19	18	18	17	17
34	64	58	53	48	44	41	39	36	34	32	30	29	28	26	25	24	23	22	21	21	20	19	19	18	18	17
35	66	60	54	50	46	43	40	37	35	33	31	30	28	27	26	25	24	23	22	21	21	20	19	19	18	18
36	68	61	56	51	47	44	41	38	36	34	32	31	29	28	27	26	24	24	23	22	21	20	20	19	19	18
37	70	63	57	52	48	45	42	39	37	35	33	31	30	29	27	26	25	24	23	22	22	21	20	20	19	19
38	72	65	59	54	50	46	43	40	38	36	34	32	31	29	28	27	26	25	24	23	22	22	21	20	20	19
39	74	66	60	55	51	47	44	41	39	37	35	33	32	30	29	28	27	26	25	24	23	22	21	21	20	20
40	76	68	62	57	52	49	45	43	40	38	36	34	32	31	30	28	27	26	25	24	23	23	22	21	21	20
41	77	70	63	58	54	50	46	44	41	39	37	35	33	32	30	29	28	27	26	25	24	23	22	22	21	21
42	79	71	65	60	55	51	48	45	42	40	38	36	34	32	31	30	29	27	26	26	25	24	23	22	22	21
43	81	73	66	61	56	52	49	46	43	41	38	37	35	33	32	30	29	28	27	26	25	24	24	23	22	22
44	83	75	68	62	58	53	50	47	44	42	39	37	36	34	33	31	30	29	28	27	26	25	24	23	23	22
45	85	77	70	64	59	55	51	48	45	43	40	38	36	35	33	32	31	29	28	27	26	26	25	24	23	23
46	87	78	71	65	60	56	52	49	46	43	41	39	37	36	34	33	31	30	29	28	27	26	25	24	24	23
47	89	80	73	67	61	57	53	50	47	44	42	40	38	36	35	33	32	31	30	29	28	27	26	25	24	24
48	91	82	74	68	63	58	54	51	48	45	43	41	39	37	35	34	33	31	30	29	28	27	26	26	25	24
49	93	83	76	69	64	60	56	52	49	46	44	42	40	38	36	35	33	32	31	30	29	28	27	26	25	25
50	94	85	77	71	65	61	57	53	50	47	45	43	40	39	37	35	34	33	31	30	29	28	27	27	26	25
51	96	87	79	72	67	62	58	54	51	48	46	43	41	39	38	36	35	33	32	31	30	29	28	27	26	26
52	98	88	80	74	68	63	59	55	52	49	47	44	42	40	38	37	35	34	33	32	30	29	29	28	27	26
53	100	90	82	75	69	64	60	56	53	50	47	45	43	41	39	38	36	35	33	32	31	30	29	28	27	27
54	102	92	83	77	71	66	61	57	54	51	48	46	44	42	40	38	37	35	34	33	32	31	30	29	28	27
55	104	94	85	78	72	67	63	59	55	52	49	47	45	43	41	39	38	36	35	34	33	32	31	30	29	28
56	106	95	87	79	73	68	63	60	56	53	50	48	45	43	41	40	38	37	35	34	33	32	31	30	29	28
57	108	97	88	81	75	69	65	61	57	54	51	48	46	44	42	40	39	37	36	35	33	32	31	30	29	29
58	110	99	90	82	76	70	66	62	58	55	52	49	47	45	43	41	40	38	37	35	34	33	32	31	30	29
59	111	100	91	84	77	72	67	63	59	56	53	50	48	46	44	42	40	39	37	36	35	33	32	31	30	30
60	113	102	93	85	78	73	68	64	60	57	54	51	49	47	45	43	41	40	38	36	35	34	33	32	31	31
61	115	104	94	86	80	74	69	65	61	58	55	52	49	47	45	43	41	40	38	37	36	35	33	32	31	31
62	117	105	96	88	81	75	70	66	62	59	55	53	50	48	46	44	42	41	39	38	36	35	34	33	32	31
63	119	107	97	89	82	77	71	67	63	60	56	54	51	49	47	45	43	41	40	38	37	36	35	33	32	32
64	121	109	99	91	84	78	73	68	64	60	57	54	52	49	47	45	44	42	40	39	38	36	35	34	33	32
65	123	111	100	92	85	79	74	69	65	61	58	55	53	50	48	46	44	43	41	39	38	37	36	35	33	33
66	125	112	102	94	86	80	75	70	66	62	59	56	53	51	49	47	45	43	42	40	39	37	36	35	34	33
67	127	114	104	95	88	81	76	71	67	63	60	57	54	52	49	47	46	44	42	41	39	38	37	36	35	34
68	128	116	105	96	89	83	77	72	68	64	61	58	55	53	50	48	46	44	43	41	40	39	37	36	35	34
69	130	117	107	98	90	84	78	73	69	65	62	59	56	53	51	49	47	45	43	42	40	39	38	37	36	35
70	132	119	108	99	92	85	79	74	70	66	63	60	57	54	52	50	48	46	44	43	41	40	38	37	36	35
71	134	121	110	101	93	86	81	75	71	67	64	60	57	55	52	50	48	46	45	43	42	40	39	38	37	36
72	136	122	111	102	94	87	82	77	72	68	64	61	58	56	53	51	49	47	45	44	42	41	39	38	37	36
73	138	124	113	103	95	89	83	78	73	69	65	62	59	56	54	52	50	48	46	44	43	41	40	39	38	37
74	140	126	114	105	97	90	84	79	74	70	66	63	60	57	55	52	50	48	47	45	43	42	41	39	38	37
75	142	128	116	106	98	91	85	80	75	71	67	64	61	58	55	53	51	53	51	49	47	46	44	43	41	40
76	144	129	117	108	99	92	86	81	76	72	68	65	62	59	56	54	52	50	48	46	45	43	42	40	39	38

Gear Chart in inches for 20"/500 x 28A Wheel

Number of teeth on sprocket

Number of teeth on chainwheel

	9	10	11	12	13	14	15	16	17	18	19	20	21	22	23	24	25	26	27	28	29	30	31	32	33	34
18	40	36	33	30	28	26	24	23	21	20	19	18	17	16	16	15	14	14	13	13	12	12	12	11	11	11
19	42	38	35	32	29	27	25	24	22	21	20	19	18	17	17	16	15	15	14	14	13	13	12	12	12	11
20	44	40	36	33	31	29	27	25	24	22	21	20	19	18	17	17	16	15	15	14	14	13	13	13	12	12
21	47	42	38	35	32	30	28	26	25	23	22	21	20	19	18	18	17	16	16	15	14	14	14	13	13	12
22	49	44	40	37	34	31	29	28	26	24	23	22	21	20	19	18	18	17	16	16	15	15	14	14	13	13
23	51	46	42	38	35	33	31	29	27	26	24	23	22	21	20	19	18	18	17	16	16	15	15	14	14	14
24	53	48	44	40	37	34	32	30	28	27	25	24	23	22	21	20	19	18	18	17	17	16	15	15	15	14
25	56	50	45	42	38	36	33	31	29	28	26	25	24	23	22	21	20	19	19	18	17	17	16	16	15	15
26	58	52	47	43	40	37	35	33	31	29	27	26	25	24	23	22	21	20	19	19	18	17	17	16	16	15
27	60	54	49	45	42	39	36	34	32	30	28	27	26	25	23	23	22	21	20	19	19	18	17	17	16	16
28	62	56	51	47	43	40	37	35	33	31	29	28	27	25	24	23	22	22	21	20	19	19	18	18	17	16
29	64	58	53	48	45	41	39	36	34	32	31	29	28	26	25	24	23	22	21	21	20	19	19	18	18	17
30	67	60	55	50	46	43	40	38	35	33	32	30	29	27	26	25	24	23	22	21	21	20	19	19	18	18
31	69	62	56	52	48	44	41	39	36	34	33	31	30	28	27	26	25	24	23	22	21	21	20	19	19	18
32	71	64	58	53	49	46	43	40	38	36	34	32	30	29	28	27	26	25	24	23	22	21	20	19	19	19
33	73	66	60	55	51	47	44	41	39	37	35	33	31	30	29	28	26	25	24	24	23	22	21	21	20	19
34	76	68	62	57	52	49	45	43	40	38	36	34	32	31	30	28	27	26	25	24	23	23	22	21	21	20
35	78	70	64	58	54	50	47	44	41	39	37	35	33	32	30	29	28	27	26	25	24	23	23	22	21	21
36	80	72	65	60	55	51	48	45	42	40	38	36	34	33	31	30	29	28	27	26	25	24	23	23	22	21
37	82	74	67	62	57	53	49	46	44	41	39	37	35	34	32	31	30	28	27	26	26	25	24	23	22	22
38	84	76	69	63	58	54	51	48	45	42	40	38	36	35	33	32	30	29	28	27	26	25	25	24	23	22
39	87	78	71	65	60	56	52	49	46	43	41	39	37	35	34	33	31	30	29	28	27	26	25	24	24	23
40	89	80	73	67	62	57	53	50	47	44	42	40	38	36	35	33	32	31	30	29	28	27	26	25	24	24
41	91	82	75	68	63	59	55	51	48	46	43	41	39	37	36	34	33	32	30	29	28	27	26	26	25	24
42	93	84	76	70	65	60	56	53	49	47	44	42	40	38	37	35	34	32	31	30	29	28	27	26	25	25
43	96	86	78	72	66	61	57	54	51	48	45	43	41	39	37	36	34	33	32	31	30	29	28	27	26	25
44	98	88	80	73	68	63	59	55	52	49	46	44	42	40	38	37	35	34	33	31	30	30	29	28	27	26
45	100	90	82	75	69	64	60	56	53	50	47	45	43	41	39	38	36	35	33	32	31	30	29	28	28	27
46	102	92	84	77	71	66	61	58	54	51	48	46	44	42	40	38	37	35	34	33	32	31	30	29	28	27
47	104	94	85	78	72	67	63	59	55	52	49	47	45	43	41	39	38	37	36	34	33	32	31	30	29	28
48	107	96	87	80	74	69	64	60	56	53	51	48	46	44	42	40	38	37	36	35	34	33	32	31	30	28
49	109	98	89	82	75	70	65	61	58	54	52	49	47	45	43	41	39	38	36	35	34	33	32	31	30	29
50	111	100	91	83	77	71	67	63	59	56	53	50	48	45	43	42	40	38	37	36	34	33	33	32	31	29
51	113	102	93	85	78	73	68	64	60	57	54	51	49	46	44	43	41	39	38	36	35	34	33	32	31	30
52	116	104	95	87	80	74	69	65	61	58	55	52	50	47	45	43	42	40	39	38	36	35	34	34	32	31
53	118	106	96	88	82	76	71	66	62	59	56	53	50	48	46	44	42	41	39	38	37	36	35	34	33	31
54	120	108	98	90	83	77	72	68	64	60	57	54	51	49	47	45	43	42	40	39	37	36	36	35	33	32
55	122	110	100	92	85	79	73	69	65	61	58	55	52	50	48	46	44	42	41	39	38	37	35	34	33	32
56	124	112	102	93	86	80	75	70	66	62	59	56	53	51	49	47	45	43	41	40	39	37	36	35	34	33
57	127	114	104	95	88	81	76	71	67	63	60	57	54	52	50	48	46	44	42	41	39	38	37	36	35	34
58	129	116	105	97	89	83	77	73	68	64	61	58	55	53	50	48	46	45	43	41	40	39	37	36	35	34
59	131	118	107	98	91	84	79	74	69	66	62	59	56	54	51	49	47	45	44	42	41	39	38	37	36	35
60	133	120	109	100	92	86	80	75	71	67	63	60	57	55	52	50	48	46	44	43	41	40	39	38	36	35
61	136	122	111	102	94	87	81	76	72	68	64	61	58	55	53	51	49	47	45	44	42	41	39	38	37	36
62	138	124	113	103	95	89	83	78	73	69	65	62	59	56	54	52	50	48	46	44	43	41	40	39	38	36
63	140	126	115	105	97	90	84	79	74	70	66	63	60	57	55	53	51	49	47	45	43	42	41	40	39	37
64	142	128	116	107	98	91	85	80	75	71	67	64	61	58	56	53	51	49	47	46	44	43	41	40	39	38
65	144	130	118	108	100	93	87	81	76	72	68	65	62	59	57	54	52	50	48	46	45	43	42	41	39	38
66	147	132	120	110	102	94	88	83	78	73	69	66	63	60	57	55	53	51	49	47	46	44	43	41	40	39
67	149	134	122	112	103	96	89	84	79	74	71	67	64	61	58	56	54	52	50	48	46	45	43	42	41	39
68	151	136	124	113	105	97	91	85	80	76	72	68	65	62	59	57	55	53	51	49	47	45	44	43	41	40
69	153	138	125	115	106	99	92	86	81	77	73	69	66	63	60	58	55	53	51	49	48	46	45	43	42	41
70	156	140	127	117	108	100	93	88	82	78	74	70	67	64	61	58	56	54	52	50	48	47	45	44	42	41

Appendix B
USEFUL ADDRESSES

Alex Moulton Limited

For details and distributors of the AM bicycle range, and for the current addresses of officers of the Moulton Bicycle Club:

The Hall,
Bradford-on-Avon
Wiltshire
BA15 1AH
England
Tel: 01225 865895 Fax: 01225 864742

W. R. Pashley Limited

For details and distributors of the Moulton APB range:

Masons Road
Stratford-on-Avon
Warwickshire
CV37 9NL
England
Tel: 01789 292263 Fax: 01789 414201

Vidimage Productions

For details of the only range of VHS PAL format videos on the history and development of the Moulton bicycle, send a stamped addressed envelope, or if outside the UK, two International Reply Coupons, to:

Cathedin
Somerford Keynes
Cirencester
Gloucestershire
GL7 6DJ
England

(For NTSC versions of these videos see below.)

Doug Milliken

For details of Aero discs for 17" wheels and of NTSC versions of the Vidimage videos, send two International Reply Coupons, or if in the USA, a stamped addressed envelope, to:

245 Brompton Road
Buffalo
New York
NY 14221
USA
Tel: 716-632-6710

The Lund Packhorse pannier carrier.
Photos courtesy of Paul Lund.

Paul Lund

For details of the Lund Packhorse, a light and compact front pannier carrier for AMs and APBs, send a stamped addressed envelope, or if outside the UK, two International Reply Coupons, to:

117 Foliejohn Way
Woodlands Park
Maidenhead
Berkshire
SL6 3XY
England
Tel: 01628 823960

John Long

For details of tailpiece bags for AMs and APBs, send a stamped addressed envelope, or if outside the UK, two International Reply Coupons, to:

Dovecote Cottage
Hawkhurst Court
Wisborough Green
West Sussex
RH14 0HS
England

Andrew Beckman

For details of rigid bags for AMs, in the style of the 1960s Moulton holdalls, send a stamped addressed envelope, or if outside the UK, two international reply coupons to:

131b Dartmouth Road
London
NW2 4ES
England
Tel: 0181-450 3413

Appendix C
SOURCES

(The many private papers consulted have not been listed.)

PROLOGUE

Biographical Precis - Alex Moulton, Alex Moulton Limited, Bradford-on-Avon, March 1979.

Clifton-Taylor, Alec, *Six More English Towns*, British Broadcasting Corporation, London, 1981.

Hadland, Tony, *The Moulton Bicycle,* second edition, Pinkerton/Hadland, Reading, 1982.

Moulton, Alex, "Innovation", *Journal of the Royal Society of Arts*, London, December 1979.

Roberts, Derek, *Cycling History - Myths & Queries*, John Pinkerton, Erdington, 1991.

Sajo, Caba, *The Moulton Story, Parts 1 & 2*, video, Vidimage Productions, Cirencester, 1991.

Urieli, Israel, "A Mutant AM7", *The Moultoneer*, Coventry, January/February 1992.

van der Plas, Rob, *Bicycle Technology*, Bicycle Books Inc., Mill Valley, California, 1991.

CHAPTER 1

Bell, Roger, "Moulton Metal", *Car*, London, January 1985.

Chronicle of the 20th Century, Longman, London, 1988.

Duffield, David, *Small Wheels, Big Potential, Full Speed Ahead,* video, Vidimage Productions, Cirencester, 1993.

Gayfer, Alan, "Ponies Thought We Were Rather Strange!", *Cycling & Sporting Cyclist*, Sutton, 10 May 1969.

Gayfer, Alan, "The Alex Moulton Story", *Cycling World*, Sidcup, Jauary 1984.

Hadland, Tony, "The Moulton and its Effect on Bicycle Sales in the UK", *The Moultoneer*, Coventry, September/October 1992.

Hadland, Tony, *The Moulton Bicycle,* second edition, Pinkerton/Hadland, Reading, 1982.

"Innovation: Moulton Makes a Better Bicycle ... Again", *Engineering,* London, August 1983.

Knottley, Peter, *Half Way Round,* second edition, Knottley, Cheam, 1982.

Knottley, Peter, "Testing a New Moulton", *Cycletouring,* CTC, Godalming, February/March 1970.

Moulton, Alex, "A Look at Future Design", article in *The Bicycling Book,* Dial Press, date unknown.

Moulton, Alex, *Putting on the Style,* The Wynkyn de Worde Society, London, 1984.

Moulton, Alex, *The Moulton Bicycle Project from Conception,* IHPVA paper, Moulton, Bradford-on-Avon, 1986.

Poslett, Jim, "Experimental Machines", *Moulton Cyclist,* Bristol, Spring 1983.

"Raleigh Buys Moulton - for an Unknown Price", *Daily Telegaph,* London, 8 August 1967.

"Raleigh to Gobble Up Moulton to get Mini-bike it Rejected", *Daily Telegaph.* London, 3 August 1967.

Retail Price Index Queries, Bank of England, London, September 1993.

Surviving Original Moultons, list of serial numbers, models and owners, Moulton Preservation, London, 1990.

"Wisp - All Set to Break Speed Record", Raleigh advertisement, *Motor Cycle & Cycle Trader,* London, 26 May 1967.

CHAPTER 2

Allen, John S., "Understanding Bicycle Tire Sizes", *Bike Tech,* USA, February 1983.

"Alloy Rims from a New British Company", *Cycletouring,* Godalming, February/March 1983.

Bergman, Martin, "ISO Codes and the 17" Wheels", *The Moultoneer,* Coventry, November/December 1992.

Berto, Frank J, *Bicycling Magazine's Complete Guide to Upgrading Your Bike,* Rodale Press, Emmaus, Pennsylvania, 1988.

British Patent Summaries, World Patents Index Library, Derwent, London.

Brown, Sheldon & Allen, John S., "Five New Folding Bicycles", *Bicycling,* Emmaus, Pennsylvania, May 1984.

Gayfer, Alan, "The Alex Moulton Story", *Cycling World,* Sidcup, January 1984.

Hadland, Tony, *The Moulton Bicycle,* first edition, Hadland, Reading, 1980.

Hadland, Tony, *The Moulton Bicycle,* second edition, Pinkerton/Hadland, Reading, 1982.

Hodgson, Ian, "AM Front Suspension Lubrication", *The Moultoneer,* Dudley, Autumn 1989.

"Innovation: Moulton Makes a Better Bicycle ... Again", *Engineering,* London, August 1983.

Kitching, Ron, *Catalogue,* Harrogate, 1970.

Knottley, Peter, "Big Enjoyment from Two Small Wheels", *Cycling,* Sutton, 16 April 1977.

Knottley, Peter, *Half Way Round,* second edition, Cheam, 1982.

Kyle, Chester R., "The Beat of a Rotating Drum", *Bike Tech*, USA, October 1988.

"More About the Moulton", *Cycling,* Sutton, 4 December 1982.

Moulton, Alex, "Aesthetics and Engineering", *Designer,* London, November 1984.

Moulton, Alex, "Moulton Bicycle", *Use of Rubber in Engineering,* (ed. Allen P. W. & Lindley, P. B.), Maclaren, London 1967.

Moulton, Alex, *Putting on the Style,* The Wynkyn de Worde Society, London, 1984.

Moulton, Alex, *The Moulton Bicycle Project from Conception,* IHPVA paper, Moulton, Bradford-on-Avon, 1986.

Moulton, Alex, *The Moulton Bicycle,* Friday Evening Discourse transcript, The Royal Institution, London, 23 February 1973.

Newland, D. E. & Mayne, Philip, "The Newland Folding Bicycle", *Cycletouring,* Godalming, date unknown (summer 1969?)

Ottaway, Mark, "Yesterday's Bike of the Future", *The Sunday Times,* London, 30 March 1980.

Poslett, Jim, "17" x 1$1/4$" Tyres and Inner Tubes", *Moulton Bicycle Club Newsletter,* Bristol, June 1982.

Proceedings of the First Human Powered Vehicle Scientific Symposium, International Human Powered Vehicle Association, USA, November 1981.

Roosa, Doug, "The Bicycle Frame", *Bicycle Guide,* Boston, Massachusetts, June 1991.

Sanders, Daved, "Editorial", *The Moultoneer,* Bewdley, November/December 1990.

Sanders, Daved, "Moulton Bicycle Club Meet 1981", *Moulton Bicycle Club Newsletter,* Bristol, June 1982.

Sanders, Daved, "On a Sunny Weekend", *Moulton Cyclist,* Bristol, Spring 1983.

Sajo, Caba, *The Moulton Story, Parts 1 & 2,* video, Vidimage Productions, Cirencester, 1991.

"Set the Pace for the 1970s", Pavemaster Spacemaster advertisement, date unknown.

Stone, Hilary, "Titanium Nitriding", *Cycling Plus,* Bath, January 1994.

Strutt, Michael, "Some New Angles on the Bicycle", *Financial Times,* London, 13 January 1979.

CHAPTER 3

Andrews, Geoff, "The Air-Portable Micro-Bikes", *The Guardian,* London/Manchester, 29 June 1983.

A Pedigree of Advanced Engineering, catalogue, Alex Moulton Limited, Bradford-on-Avon, 1994.

Assembly Instructions, AM2 & AM7, Alex Moulton Limited, Bradford-on-Avon, 1983.

Berto, Frank J., Bicycling Magazine's *Complete Guide to Upgrading Your Bike,* Rodale Press, Emmaus, Pennsylvania, 1988.

Best, Alastair, "Alex Moulton at Home", *Designer,* London, November 1984.

"Better Than Ever", *Cycling,* Sutton, 9 July 1983.

Briercliffe, Harold, "... and an Ex-Olympian Who is Still Active at 80", *Cyclist Monthly,* Sutton, October 1983.

Briercliffe, Harold, "Brisk Business at Moulton's", *Cycling,* Sutton, 27 August 1983.

"Caught in the Act", *Cycling,* Sutton, 17 August 1984.

Certificate of Ownership/Guarantee, Alex Moulton Limited, Bradford-on-Avon, 1983.

"City Firm Wins Bike Contract", *Gloucester Citizen,* Gloucester, 13 October 1983.

"Crowds Up, Sales Up!", *Cycling,* Sutton, 25 August 1984.

"Cycle Inventor Pedals On", *The Daily Telegraph,* London, 8 January 1983.

Donovan, Dennis, "The New Moulton!", *Cycling,* Sutton, 28 May 1983.

Doughty, Simon, "Something Old, Something New at York Exhibition", *Cycletouring,* Godalming, August 1983.

"Folding Bicycle", *The Times,* London, 20 May 1983.

Gayfer, Alan, "The Alex Moulton Story", *Cycling World,* Sidcup, January 1984.

"Gloucester Finishing", *Finishing,* London, November 1983.

Gordon, Alan, "A Bag to End All Bags?", *The Moultoneer,* London, Summer 1993.

Hadland, Tony, *The Moulton Bicycle,* second edition, Pinkerton/Hadland, Reading, 1982.

Hadland, Tony, "A First Look at the Moulton APB", *The Moultoneer,* Coventry, March/April 1992.

"Harrogate Show Guide", *Cycling,* Sutton, 11 August 1984.

"Harrogate Show Review", *Cycle Trader,* London, July 1983.

Howard, Philip, "Yes, Mr Tebbit, I Certainly Will", *The Times,* London, 3 June 1983.

"Innovation: Moulton Makes a Better Bicycle", *Engineering,* London, August 1983.

Jenkins, Nigel, "A Most Remarkable Machine", *Freewheeling,* Haymarket, New South Wales, Australia, November/December 1983.

Juden, Chris, "Technical Information", *Members' Handbook,* Cyclists' Touring Club, Godalming, 1991.

"Klein, aber Fein", *Radfahren,* West Germany, July/August 1984.

Knottley, Peter, "Counties Create Cycling Routes", *Cyclist Monthly,* Sutton, September 1983.

Knottley, Peter, "Peter Knottley's Show Notebook", *Cycling,* Sutton, 16 July 1983.

Lesseps, "Das Comeback einer Zweirad-Spezialitat", *Frankfurter Allgemeine Zeitung,* Frankfurt, 9 November 1983.

"Maughfling for Moulton", *Cycle Trader,* London, October 1983.

McLain, Lynton, "Bicycle with the Exclusive Touch", *Financial Times,* London, 17 September 1983.

Moulton, Alex, *The Moulton Bicycle Project from Conception,* IHPVA paper, Alex Moulton Limited, Bradford-on-Avon, 1986.

"New 'Moulton' on the Way", *Wiltshire Times & News,* Wiltshire, 7 January 1983.

"News", *Design,* London, August 1983.

On Your Bikes, Episode 1, TV series, John Gau Productions for Channel 4 Television, London, transmitted 21 May 1983.

On Your Bikes, press release, Channel 4 Television, London, May 1983.

"On Your New Bike", *Evening Standard,* London, 13 June 1983.

"Pedal Power Call at Cycleway Opening," *Wiltshire Times & News,* Wiltshire, 22 July 1983.

PHS, reported in *The Times,* London, 16 June 1983.

Poslett, Jim, *The Moulton Bicycle Club Annual Meeting 13/14 August 1983,* leaflet, Bristol, 1983.

Price List, Alex Moulton Limited, Bradford-on-Avon, 1 June 1986.

"Space Frame Stiffens New Folder", *New Scientist,* London, 30 June 1983.

"Spokes-persons", *The Times,* London, 15 June 1983.

Strutt, Michael, "Moulton Unveils 'Advanced Engineering' Bicycle", *Financial Times,* London, 20 May 1983.

"That Old Moulton Magic Back with a Vengeance", *Cycle Trader,* London, June 1983.

The Advanced Engineering Bicycle, colour brochure for AM2, AM7 and accessories, Alex Moulton Limited, Bradford-on-Avon, May 1983.

The Advanced Engineering Bicycle, black, white & red brochure, Alex Moulton Limited, Bradford-on-Avon, 1983.

The Best from Europe, catalogue, R. J. Chicken & Sons Ltd, Dunstable, 1983.

"The New Moulton on Show in April", *Cycling,* Sutton, 22 January 1983.

Thomas, Nigel & Montague, Brian, "Souplesse Oblige", *Bicycle Action,* London, June 1985.

UK Retail Price List, Alex Moulton Bicycles, Bradford-on-Avon, 1 January 1994.

"Unisex", *Sunday Telegraph,* London, 5 June 1983.

Vickers, Graham, "The Harrogate Show", *Bicycle,* London, October 1984.

"View", *The Sunday Times Colour Supplement,* London, 21 May 1983.

Walker, Brian, *Christmas card,* Alex Moulton Limited, Bradford-on-Avon, 1983.

Wilcockson, John, "Join the Chain Gang", *The Sunday Times,* London, 4 December 1983.

CHAPTER 4

100 Best Ever Products, exhibition catalogue, The Boilerhouse, Victoria & Albert Museum, London, 1985.

"A New and Improved Cycling Experience", Alex Moulton Limited advertisement, *Cycletouring,* Godalming, June/July 1984 and elsewhere.

Advertisement for AM Range, *Cycle Sport,* Japan, January 1985.

Advertisement for La Grande Roue, *Velo,* Paris, May 1985.

Andrews, Francis M., "Hands Off 2", *Cycling World,* Sidcup, July 1984.

"Aristokratisches Fahrgefuhl", *Wirtschafts Woche,* West Germany, 7 September 1984.

Audax report, *Cyclotourisme,* Paris, January 1984.

Baldwin, J, "Alex Moulton Bicycles", *Co-Evolution,* USA, March 1984.

Bell, Roger, "Moulton Metal", *Car,* London, January 1985.

"Bicycle Made for Who?", *Technology,* London, 26 September 1983.

Boot, Philip, "Moulton - Supremo!", *Moulton Cyclist,* Bristol, Summer 1984.

Brain, Martin, "Moulton Leg-up", *Cycling World,* Sidcup, August 1984.

Bray, S. P. V., "Small Wheels", *Cycling World,* Sidcup, March 1984.

Bray, Stan et al, "He's Sorry!", *Cycling World,* Sidcup, April 1984.

Bray, Stan, "Small Wheel Wobble", *Cycling,* Sutton, 26 November 1983.

Briercliffe, Harold, "The Making of the Moulton", *Cycle Trader,* September 1983.

Brown, Sheldon & Allen, John S., "Five New Folding Bicycles", *Bicycling,* Emmaus, Pennsylvania, May 1984.

Carlson, "Spleen aus Stahl", *Tour Rund ums Rad,* West Germany, March 1984.

"Classe Touriste", *Velo,* Paris, April 1985.

Crane, Hol, "Bikes of the Year", *International Cycling Guide,* The Tantivity Press, London 1984.

"Das Moulton in Neuauflage", *Radfahren,* Bielefeld, West Germany, March/April 1984.

"Das Moulton in Neuauflage", *Radmarkt,* West Germany, 24 January 1984.

Derven, John, "The Erector Set School of Design", *Bicycle Guide,* Boston, Massachusetts, month unknown, 1985.

Donovan, Dennis, "The New Moultons!", *Cycling,* Sidcup, 28 May 1983.

Evans, David E., *The Ingenious Mr Pedersen,* Alan Sutton, Dursley, 1979.

Fairclough, Isaac, "Cable Braiding", *Cycling World,* Sidcup, August 1984.

Foster, David, "The Love of Two Moultons", *Bicycle,* London, February 1984.

French, M. J., *Conceptual Design for Engineers,* second edition, The Design Council, London, July 1984.

French, Prof. Michael J., "Moulton's New Bicycle", *Engineering,* London, September 1983.

Gayfer, Alan, "Cycling World Test: The Moulton", *Cycling World,* Sidcup, November 1983.

Gayfer, Alan, "The Alex Moulton Story", *Cycling World,* January 1984.

"Gefedert und Handlich zu Verpacken", *Bild Post,* West Germany, 7 July 1984.

Gibbon, David, "Should Auld Acquaintance ...", *Bicycle,* London, January 1986.

Gilman, Claire, "Christmas Gifts", *Bicycle,* London, December 1984.

Hadland, Tony, "Hands Off 1", *Cycling World,* Sidcup, July 1984.

Hadland, Tony, "Rohan Sells the Moulton Bike", *The Moultoneer,* Henley-on-Thames, Summer 1986.

Hadland, Tony, "Streamlining at Bradford-on-Avon", *The Moultoneer,* Henley-on-Thames, Spring 1986.

Hickling, Bill, "Come Join Us on a Bike Man's Holiday", *The Advertiser,* Adelaide, 2 December 1983.

Hoffman, Matthew, "Health, Growth and Fitness", *Time Out,* London, 27 September 1984.

"Innovation: Moulton Makes a Better Bicycle ... Again", *Engineering,* London, August 1983.

"Interesting Bikes", *Pedal Power,* Australia, Summer 1983/84.

"Japanese Opening for Moulton", *Bicycle Times,* Gateshead, December? 1984.

Jenkins, Nigel, "A Most Remarkable Machine", *Freewheeling,* Haymarket, New South Wales, November/December 1983.

Jonasch & Meyer advertisement, *Radfahren,* Bielefeld, West Germany, January/February 1984.

Juden, Chris, "Riding is Believing - the AM7", *Cycletouring,* Godalming, December 1984/January 1985.

Juden, Helen, "International Cycling Guide 1984", *Cycletouring,* Godalming, June/July 1984.

"Klein, aber Fein", *Radfahren,* Bielefeld, West Germany, July/August 1984.

Knottley, Peter, "7000 Miles Just Pottering About", *Cycling,* Sutton, 31 December 1983.

Knottley, Peter, "Even Better! - The New Moulton", *Cycling,* Sutton, 27 August 1983.

Knottley, Peter, "Randonneur", *Spokesman,* Cleveland Wheelers, Cleveland, January 1984.

Knottley, Peter, Letter in "Readers' Letters", *Cycling World,* Sidcup, June 1984.

Knottley, Peter, Letter in "Reader to Reader", *Cycletouring,* Godalming, June/July 1985.

Kuva, Heikki, "Statusta Polkupyoralla", *Techniikan Maailma,* Finland, 2/1985.

"La moulton", *Velo,* Paris, May 1984.

Langley, Jim, "The Remarkable Moulton Bike", *California Bicyclist,* February 1985.

Lesseps, "Das Comeback einer Zweirad-Spezialitat", *Frankfurter Allgemeine Zeitung,* Frankfurt, 9 November 1983.

"Liten Sot Britt", *Dina Pengar,* Sweden, April 1985.

Lumley, Peter, "A Target for Alex Moulton and his Design Team", *Bicycle Times,* Gateshead, August 1984.

Lumley, Peter, "Something Quite Different: Moulton Make It", *Bicycle Times,* Gateshead, July 1983.

"Making an Exhibition of Themselves", *Bicycle Action,* London, March 1985.

Maxwell, Ian, "Harrogate Show", *Fiets,* Amsterdam, September/October 1983.

McDermott, G. P., "It's British - Tyres Apart", *Cycling*, Sutton, 10 September 1983.

McLain, Lynton, "Bicycle with the Exclusive Touch", *Financial Times*, London, 17 September 1983.

Monroe, John, "Technical Tirade: Birdcage Moulton - the Well-Mannered Folder", *Bicycling News Canada*, Vancouver, Summer 1984.

Morris, Stuart, "The New Moultons", *Bicycle*, London, July 1983.

"Moulton Makes a Comeback", *Cyclist Monthly*, Sutton, July 1983.

"Moulton Museum", *Bicycle Action*, London, September 1984.

Moulton, Alex, "Moulton's Mettle", *Architect's Journal*, London, 11 March 1987.

Moulton, Alex, *Putting on the Style!*, The Wynkyn de Worde Society, London, 1984.

Moulton, Alex, Sketch of Die-cast Frame, *Designing*, London, April 1984.

"Moulton-Rader: Exquisit Und Teuer", *Fahrrad Sport & Reisen*, West Germany, August 1985.

Mowle, N. S., "A Great Bike", letter in "Reader to Reader", *Cycletouring*, Godalming, June/July 1985.

"Nygammal Cykelnyhet!", *Cykling*, Sweden, March 1985.

Pennell, A. (Tony) et al, "Moulton Bicycle", letters in *Engineering*, London, November 1983.

Peregrine, Nick, "AM7 Road Test and Review", *Moulton Cyclist*, Bristol, Summer 1984.

Peregrine, Nick, "Moulton Bicycle Club", letter in "Technical Forum", *Cycletouring*, Godalming, August/September 1985.

"Portable Bicycles", *The Bicycle Buyers' Bible*, The Bicycle Cooperative, London, 1984.

Rawlins, P., "Shocked", *Cycletouring*, Godalming, April/May 1985.

"Ride a Moulton", advertisement for Moulton Bicycle Riders' Group, *Freewheeling*, Haymarket, New South Wales, May/June 1984.

Roosa, Doug, "Moulton AM7 - Not a Quadrilateral Bit of Piping", *Bicycle Guide*, Boston, Massachusetts, September 1985.

"Sales Up", *Cycle & Motorcycle Trade Monthly*, September 1983.

"Salon de Londres", *Le Cycle*, Paris, France, 1984.

Scott, David, "Soft-ride Bicycle", *Popular Science*, USA, March 1984.

"Selection", *Design*, London, September/October 1986.

Simpson, Eric, "More than 15,000 Riders Make it Down to Brighton", *Cyclist Monthly*, Sutton, August 1984.

"Smart Alex", *Bicycle*, London, July 1984.

Stanesby, Philip R., "Interest Reawakened", letter in "Reader to Reader", *Cycletouring*, Godalming, June/July 1985.

Strutt, Michael, "Deals on Wheels", *Financial Times*, London, 3 September 1983.

Taylor, Lucy, "Master Moulton", *Bicycle*, London, December 1991.

"That Old Moulton Magic is Back with a Vengeance", *Cycle Trader*, June 1983.

"The Revolutionary Moulton Bicycle", advertisement for Calypso Cycles, *Freewheeling*, Haymarket, New South Wales, May/June 1984.

"The Top 10 Bicycles of 1985", *Bicycle*, London, December 1985.

Tonge, Peter, "The Bicycle as an All-weather, Basic Vehicle", *Christian Science Monitor*, US edition, 17 Sept 1984.

van de Beek, Guus, "Kostbaar Anders", *Fiets*, Amsterdam, January/February 1985.

Vaughan Williams, D., "Stable at All Speeds", *Cycling*, 31 December 1983.

Vickers, Graham, "Brilliant/Fantastic", *Bicycle*, London, January 1986.

Vickers, Graham, "Test Report", *Bicycle*, London, August 1984.

Vickers, Graham, "The Bicycle", *Architect's Journal*, London, 21 January 1987.

Wallacesport feature, *Cycling World*, Sidcup, November 1983.

Wendt, Charlotte, "Cyklarnas Mercedes", *Svenska Dagbladet*, weekend supplement, April 1985.

Willis, H.H., "One Man's Meat", *The Moultoneer*, Henley-on-Thames, Spring 1987.

CHAPTER 5

"A New Moulton at £997", *Cycling*, Sutton, 30 March 1985.

A Pedigree of Advanced Engineering, catalogue, Alex Moulton Limited, Bradford-on-Avon, 1994.

"Alex Moulton Bicycles & Accessories", price list, *The Moultoneer*, Henley-on-Thames, Spring 1986.

"AM Frame Wheel Kits", *AM News*, Alex Moulton Limited, Bradford-on-Avon, May 1986.

AM News, (post North American visit issue), Alex Moulton Limited, Bradford-on-Avon, November 1986.

AM-Zzipper Fairing, leaflet, Alex Moulton Limited, Bradford-on-Avon, 1985.

"AM-Zzipper Fairing", *Moulton Cyclist*, Bristol, Spring 1985.

AM14S/AM14T, leaflet, Alex Moulton Limited, Bradford-on-Avon, 1985.

AM5, leaflet, Alex Moulton Limited, Bradford-on-Avon, 1986.

AM7 Custom Frame Set Special Model, specification form, Alex Moulton Limited, Bradford-on-Avon, 1986.

"American Beauty or Love, Italian Style: Moulton vs. Olomo", *Bicycling*, Emmaus, Pennsylvania, June 1985.

Beams, Ron, "Obituary - H.H. 'Chater' Willis", *The Moultoneer*, Bewdley, November/December 1990.

Berto, Frank J., *Bicycling Magazine's Complete Guide to Upgrading Your Bike*, Rodale Press, Emmaus, Pennsylvania, 1988.

"Breaking Barriers", *Bicycle*, London, May 1985.

"Commentary - Biking by Bus", *Cycling*, Sutton, 25 August 1984.

Dealership lists, Alex Moulton Limited, Bradford-on-Avon, September 1986.

"Dr Alex Moulton - an Engineer and a Gentleman", *Rohan Catalogue,* Milton Keynes, Winter 1986.

"Easy Riders", *Country Living,* London, June 1985.

"Equipment News: Small Change", *Cycling Weekly,* Sutton, 4 September 1986.

Flint, K.J., Carrying Children on an AM, *The Moultoneer,* Dudley, Autumn 1989.

"Folding BR", *Bicycle Action,* London, February 1988.

"Frame Kits", *AM News,* Alex Moulton Limited, Bradford-on-Avon, November 1986.

Front Suspension Adjustment and Service Instructions, Service Sheet No.7, Alex Moulton Limited, Bradford-on-Avon.

Front Suspension Assembly and Adjustment, Service Sheet No.6, Alex Moulton Limited, Bradford-on-Avon, February 1992.

Gear Adjustment - Five Speed Hub, Service Sheet No.2, Alex Moulton Limited, Bradford-on-Avon, 1987.

Glaskin, Max, "DIY Moulton", *Bicycle,* London, January 1987.

Hadland, Tony, "AM Front Suspension", *The Moultoneer,* Henley-on-Thames, Spring 1987.

Hadland, Tony, "Editorial", *The Moultoneer,* Henley-on-Thames, Autumn 1986.

Hadland, Tony, "It's Here ... The AM5!", *The Moultoneer,* Henley-on-Thames, Spring 1986.

Hadland, Tony, "More Speed Success for the AM7", *The Moultoneer,* Henley-on-Thames, Winter 1987.

Hadland, Tony, "Record Breaking Wheel Discs - Now Available", *The Moultoneer,* Henley-on-Thames, Spring 1987.

Hadland, Tony, "Rohan Sells the Moulton Bike", *The Moultoneer,* Henley-on-Thames, Summer 1986.

Hadland, Tony, "Soundproofing AM-Zzipper Fairings", *The Moultoneer,* Henley-on-Thames, Autumn 1986.

Hadland, Tony, "Streamlining at Bradford-on-Avon", *The Moultoneer,* Henley-on-Thames, Spring 1986.

Hadland, Tony, "Streamlining of a Different Kind - a New World Record for the AM", *The Moultoneer,* Henley-on-Thames, Spring 1986

Hadland, Tony, "The Moulton Bicycle Club", *The Moultoneer,* Henley-on-Thames, Spring 1986.

Hadland, Tony, *The Moulton Bicycle.* second edition, Pinkerton/Hadland, Reading 1982.

Hessey, Mike, "The AM5 - a Very Civilised Machine", *The Moultoneer,* Dudley, Winter 1989/90.

Hodgson, Ian, "AM Front Suspension Lubrication", *The Moultoneer,* Dudley, Autumn 1989.

Hodgson, Ian, "More on the AM5", *The Moultoneer,* Dudley, March/April 1990.

Hugi Hub Axle Replacement on Original Batch of SPEEDs, Service Sheet No.5, Alex Moulton Limited, Bradford-on-Avon, May 1990.

Juden, Chris, "New Models for '85", *Cycletouring,* Godalming, June/July 1985.

Leer, Bib & Hadland, Tony, "Gears", *The Moultoneer,* Coventry, November/ December 1991.

Loose Pivot Bearing of Rear Fork (Swing Arm), Service Sheet No.3, Alex Moulton Limited, Bradford-on-Avon, August 1987.

Milliken, Doug, "A Better Concealed Pump", *The Moultoneer,* Henley-on-Thames, Autumn, 1987.

Milliken, Douglas, *Aerodynamic Wheel Disks to Fit Alex Moulton AM7 Wheels,* information sheet, Williamsville, New York 1986.

Moulded Valve Stems in New Tubes, Service Sheet No.4, Alex Moulton Limited, Bradford-on-Avon, 27 April 1990.

"Moulton Puts His Spoke In", *Daily Mail,* London, 1 June 1985.

O'Connor, Phil, "AM14", *Bicycle,* London, January 1986.

"Order Book", *AM News,* Alex Moulton Limited, Bradford-on-Avon, August 1987.

Parry, Stephen, "Improved Pump", *The Moultoneer,* Henley-on-Thames, Spring 1988.

Rearden, Nick, "Shop Window", *Bicycle,* London, September 1986.

Rogers, Byron, "Moulton - the Man and the Machine", *Bicycle Action,* London, June 1985.

"Rohan Sells the Moulton Bike", *Rohan Catalogue,* Milton Keynes, Winter 1986.

Romer, Dennis, "1,000 Miles on a Moulton", *Cycling World,* Sidcup, October 1987.

Romer, Dennis, "AM14 1,000 Mile Test Report", *The Moultoneer,* Henley-on-Thames, Spring 1988.

Roosa, Doug, "Moulton AM7 - Not a Quadrilateral Bit of Piping", *Bicycle Guide,* Boston, Massachusetts, Sept 1985.

Sadler, Nigel, "Faring with a Fairing", *The Moultoneer,* Dudley, March/April 1990.

"Smart Alex", *Bicycle,* London, July 1984.

"Special Award: Most Elegant Bicycle Engineering", *Bicycle Guide,* Boston, Massachusetts, February 1987.

Specification Order Form, Angle Lake Cyclery, Seattle, 1986.

Sticking Guide Bearing, Service Sheet No.1, Alex Moulton Limited, Bradford-on-Avon, 1987 (and later revision).

Stuart, Stephen, "Oxford Moulton Rally No.2", *Moulton Cyclist,* Bristol, 1985.

The Advanced Engineering Bicycle, revised leaflet, Alex Moulton Limited, Bradford-on-Avon, 1986.

Thomas, Nigel & Montague, Brian, "Souplesse Oblige", *Bicycle Action,* London, June 1985.

Tully, Clive, "Bicycle Camping", *Bicycle,* London, June 1984.

UK Retail Price List, Alex Moulton Bicycles, Bradford-on-Avon, 1 January 1994.

Wade, Leigh, "Letter from AMerica", *The Moultoneer*, Dudley, September/October 1990.

Whitt, Frank Rowland & Wilson, David Gordon, *Bicycling Science,* first edition, The MIT Press, Cambridge, Massachusetts & London, 1974.

Willis, H. H., "Chain Derailment", *The Moultoneer,* Henley-on-Thames, Winter 1987.

"Zzipper Fairings", *AM News,* Alex Moulton Limited, Bradford-on-Avon, November 1986.

CHAPTER 6

"£12,000 the batch", *Bicycle Trade and Industry,* 26 January 1990.

A Pedigree of Advanced Engineering, catalogue, Alex Moulton Limited, Bradford-on-Avon, 1994.

AM Jubilee, product leaflet, Alex Moulton Limited, Bradford-on-Avon, 1988.

AM-GT, brochure, Alex Moulton Limited, Bradford-on-Avon, June 1991.

AM News, Alex Moulton Limited, Bradford-on-Avon, January 1988.

AM News, Alex Moulton Limited, Bradford-on-Avon, January 1989.

"AM Tyres", *The Moultoneer,* Dudley, Spring 1989.

AM14, product leaflet, Alex Moulton Limited, Bradford-on-Avon, 1988.

Bailey, Linda, "Punctures Many ...", *The Moultoneer,* Henley-on-Thames, Summer 1987.

Baker, Sue, "Pedal Away for a Night and a Day", *The Observer,* London, 19 June 1988.

Banham, Peter Reyner, "Californian Correction", *The Moultoneer,* Henley-on-Thames, Winter 1987/1988.

Berto, Frank J., *Bicycling Magazine's Complete Guide to Upgrading Your Bike,* Rodale Press, Emmaus, Pennsylvania, 1988.

"Bikes We Couldn't Live Without", *Bicycle Guide,* Boston, Massachusetts, January/February 1989

Bilinski, Jacques, "An AM7 Triple Chainring Conversion", *The Moultoneer,* Dudley, September/October 1990.

Briercliffe, Harold, "Folding Stuff", *Cycle Trader,* London, May 1988.

Briercliffe, Harold, "Two Masterpieces in Red and Blue", *Cycling Weekly,* Sutton, 14 April 1988.

British patent abridgement 2182895, *World Patents Index Library,* Derwent, London.

Bullock, A., "Bags and Tyres", *The Moultoneer,* Bewdley, January/February 1991.

Burnett, A. J., "The Moultoneer Format", *The Moultoneer,* Dudley, Summer 1989.

Doube, Michael, "Tyres", *The Moultoneer,* Dudley, July/August 1990.

"Duchess Backs Young Designers", *Cheshire Observer,* Chester, 17 May 1985.

Duckett, Simon, "Silver Clusters", *The Moultoneer,* Henley-on-Thames, Spring 1988.

Giles, Keith, "Carrying Luggage on an AM", *The Moultoneer,* Dudley, Autumn 1989.

Giles, Keith, "Rims and Things", *The Moultoneer,* Dudley, Summer 1989.

Hadland, Tony, "Carrying Luggage on an AM", *The Moultoneer,* Dudley, Winter 1989/90.

Hadland, Tony, "In Search of Le Petit Bi", *The Boneshaker,* Vol.13, No.118, Alderley Edge, Winter 1988.

Hadland, Tony, "Jubilee Launched and AM Range Further Improved", *The Moultoneer,* Henley-on-Thames, Spring 1988.

Hadland, Tony, "Luggage Options", *The Moultoneer,* Dudley, Spring 1989.

Hadland, Tony, "Moultoneering in California", *The Moultoneer,* Dudley, September/October 1990.

Hadland, Tony, "The Most Moulton Miles?", *The Moultoneer,* Henley-on-Thames, Autumn 1988.

Hadland, Tony, *The Moulton Bicycle.* second edition, Pinkerton/Hadland, Reading, 1982.

Hadland, Tony, *The Sturmey-Archer Story,* Pinkerton/Hadland, Henley-on-Thames, 1987.

Hadland, Tony, "Tyre Tip", *The Moultoneer,* Henley-on-Thames, summer 1986.

"Harvest Thanksgiving", *Bradford-on-Avon parish magazine,* October 1989.

Hedges, Fiona, "Moulton Jubilee Commemorative Envelopes", *The Moultoneer,* Henley-on-Thames, Summer 1987.

Hessey, Mike, "Annual Meeting, Bradford-on-Avon, 23-24 September 1989", *The Moultoneer,* Dudley, Winter 1989/90.

Hessey, Mike, "Bradford-on-Avon Weekend", *The Moultoneer,* Dudley, Winter 1988/89.

Hessey, Mike, "More on KM150", *The Moultoneer,* Dudley, September/October 1990.

Hessey, Mike, "News from Bradford-on-Avon", *The Moultoneer,* Dudley, Spring 1989.

Johnson, C.S., "Silver Clusters (and other matters)", *The Moultoneer,* Bewdley, November/December 1990.

Jubilee feature, *Begin,* Japan, December 1988.

Juden, Chris, "Portable Bicycles", *Cycle Touring & Campaigning,* Godalming, April/May 1990.

Knottley, Peter, "... and Punctures Few", *The Moultoneer,* Henley-on-Thames, Summer 1987.

Knottley, Peter, *Half Way Round,* second edition, Cheam, 1982.

Knottley, Peter, letter, *The Moultoneer,* Bewdley, January/February 1991.

Lawley, Kevin, "KM150", *The Moultoneer,* Dudley, September/October 1990.

Llewellin, Phil, "Genius on Two Wheels, or Four", *The Independent Weekend* supplement, London, 18 August 1990.

Mackey, Niall, "Derailleurs and Transporting AMs", *The Moultoneer,* Dudley, March/April 1990.

McCann, Robert, "Moulton Silver Jubilee", plaque advertisement, *The Moultoneer,* Henley-on-Thames, Summer 1987.

Member "Four-oh-Two", "My New Bike: AM7", *The Moultoneer*, Henley-on-Thames, Summer 1988.

Miles, Ron, *Letter to dealers advising price list changes*, Alex Moulton Limited, Bradford-on-Avon, 9 May 1989.

Moulton, Alex, "Shimmy", *The Moultoneer*, Dudley, May/June 1990.

"Moulton Commemorative Envelope", *Tu Quo Que*, Rohan users' magazine, Milton Keynes, 1987.

"Moulton: The Man and His Machine", *Bath & West Evening Chronicle*, Bath, 11 September 1987.

Mowle, Neil, "Severed Threads", *The Moultoneer*, Henley-on-Thames, Summer 1987.

Parry, Steve, "Modified Moultons", *The Moultoneer*, Dudley, summer 1989.

Pivit, Rainer, "Vibrational Stress on Cyclists", *Human Power*, Indianapolis, Fall/Winter 1988.

"Price List for the Complete AM Range", *The Moultoneer*, Henley-on-Thames, Summer 1988.

Roberts, Derek, "In Defence of the Moulton", Human Power, Indianapolis, spring 1989.

Roberts, Derek, *This Veteran Business*, Third edition, Southern Veteran-Cycle Club, May 1979.

Sadler, Nigel, "Faring with a Fairing", *The Moultoneer*, Dudley, March/April 1990.

Sadler, Nigel, "The Swift Answer to AMs", *The Moultoneer*, Dudley, Spring 1989.

Sanders, Daved, "Jubilee Test Ride", *The Moultoneer*, Dudley, summer 1989.

Searle, Ben, "Is Moulton Still Magic?", *Cycling Plus*, Bath, October 1992.

"Small is Beautiful", CBI News, 20 January/3 February 1989.

Stolarski, John, Letter in *The Moultoneer*, Bewdley, May/June 1991.

Sudjic, Deyan, "Joining the Chain Gang", *The Times Saturday* supplement, London, 12 November 1988.

"The AM-Moulton Marathon", *The Moultoneer*, Dudley, Autumn 1989.

Trinder, I. F., "Clacton Cycle Mail", *The Moultoneer*, Dudley, Autumn 1989.

UK Price List, Alex Moulton Limited, Bradford-on-Avon, February 1988.

UK Price List, Alex Moulton Limited, Bradford-on-Avon, February 1989.

UK Retail Price List, Alex Moulton Bicycles, Bradford-on-Avon, 1 January 1994.

Voss, Hans-Heinrich, "Silver Clusters", *The Moultoneer*, Henley-on-Thames, Winter 1987/88.

Walker, Brian, *Christmas Card 1987*, Alex Moulton Limited, Bradford-on-Avon, December 1987.

Weller, Sue, "Provisioning for the Compleat Cruiser: Don't Forget the Folding Bikes", *Practical Sailor*, Palm Coast, Florida, 15 May 1989.

Wilson, Colin St John et al, "Obituary: Peter Reyner Banham", *The Architect's Journal*, London, 30 March 1988.

Woolf, Michael, "Jubilee Weekend at Bradford-on-Avon", *The Moultoneer,* Henley-on-Thames, Winter 1987/1988.

Wright, Ian, "The AM Marathon", *The Moultoneer,* Coventry, May/June 1992.

CHAPTER 7

1989 Moulton ATB Worksheet, *Angle Lake Cyclery,* Seattle, 1989.

Alex Moulton Bicycles, model and accessory chart, *Angle Lake Cyclery,* Seattle, 1989.

Alex Moulton Mountain ATB, specification sheet, *Angle Lake Cyclery,* Seattle, 1989.

Allen, John S., "Understanding Bicycle Tire Sizes", *Bike Tech,* USA, February 1983.

"AM Price List", *The Moultoneer,* Kidderminster, May 1991.

AM/ATB, colour leaflet, Alex Moulton Limited, Bradford-on-Avon, 1988.

"Announcement of AM/ATB - The 'Moulton Mountain Bike'", *AM News,* Alex Moulton Limited, Bradford-on-Avon, March 1988.

Apps, Geoffrey, "Bike Review", *Making Tracks,* August/September 1988.

"Are We Looking Into The Future?", *Mountain & City Biking,* USA, June 1990.

Baddiel, Dennis, Newman, Punt, *The Mary Whitehouse Experience Encyclopaedia,* Fourth Estate, London, 1991.

Ballantine, Richard, "Beware of Cheap Imitations", *New Cyclist,* London, December 1992.

Ballantine, Richard, "The Joke that Becomes Obvious", *New Cyclist,* London, March 1993.

Bell, Chris, *Egg Rings,* catalogue, Lampeter, February 1990.

Bogdanowicz, Tom, "News", *Bicycle Action,* London, April 1988.

Briercliffe, Harold, "Folding Stuff", *Cycle Trader,* London, May 1988.

British patent abridgement 2204004, *World Patents Index Library,* Derwent, London.

Burrows, Mike (& Moulton, Alex), "The Good, The Bad and The Bouncy", *New Cyclist,* Coldstream, Autumn 1988.

Burton, Ralph, "Suspension of Disbelief", *Bicycle Guide,* Boston, Massachusetts, November/December 1988.

Conran, Sebastian, "The Big Wheel", *Blueprint,* London, October 1988.

Cunningham, Richard & others, "The Shock Facts", *Cycling Plus,* Bath, April 1993.

Davis, Caris, "Seattle, Capital of Grunge", *You Magazine,* London, 7 February 1993.

Davison, Colin, "Born in the UK!", *Mountain Biking UK,* London, May 1992.

Evans, P. A., "APBs and Hub Gears", *The Moultoneer,* Coventry, September/October 1992.

"Fiets van het Jaar 90", *The Moultoneer,* Kidderminster, March/April 1991.

Freewheel 1990, mail order catalogue, Madison Cycles plc, London, 1990.

French, George, letter to Alex Moulton quoted in "Postbag", *The Moultoneer,* Dudley, Summer 1989.

"Great Moments in Bike Design", *Mountain Bike Action,* Mission Hills, California, July 1993.

Greene, Peter, "Latest in an Unfolding Story", *The Independent, Weekend* supplement, London, 29 April 1989.

Hadland, Tony, "Reviews of the ATB", *The Moultoneer,* Henley-on-Thames, Autumn 1988.

Hadland, Tony, "The AM/ATB - the Moulton Mountain Bike", *The Moultoneer,* Henley-on-Thames, Autumn 1988.

Hadland, Tony, *The Moulton Bicycle,* second edition, Pinkerton/Hadland, Reading, 1982.

Hessey, Mike, "News from Bradford-on-Avon", *The Moultoneer,* Dudley, Summer 1989.

Hessey, Mike, "Prices for New AMs", *The Moultoneer,* Dudley, Spring 1989.

Holloway, Hilton, "Good Morning AM", *Bicycle,* London, September 1988.

"Honourable Mentions", *Bicycle Guide,* Boston, Massachusetts, January/February 1989.

"Hot Tubes - Joe Breeze", *Bicycle Guide,* Boston, Massachusetts, February 1990.

"Hot Tubes", *Bicycle Guide,* Boston, Massachusetts, January/February 1989.

Juden, Chris, "Tyres", *CTC Members' Handbook,* Cyclists' Touring Club, Godalming, as at June 1994.

Krapohl, Kaye, "Alex Moulton ATB", *Automobile,* USA, July 1991.

Le Voi, Dr M. E., and Bell, Chris, "Legs Versus Eggs", letter and reply in *New Cyclist,* Coldstream, Winter 1989/90.

McGurn, Jim, "Small is Beautiful", *New Cyclist,* London, May 1993.

"Moulton Launch Their Mountain Bike", *Cycle Trader,* London, August 1988.

"Moulton Set to Launch ATB", *Cycle Trader,* London, April 1988.

"Mountain Biking's Best & Worst Inventions", *Mountain Bike Action,* Mission Hills, California, August 1993.

"Off-road Moulton", *Cycling Weekly,* Sutton, 21 July 1988.

Olsen, J N, "The Moulton Mountain Bike", *Mountain & City Biking,* USA, August 1990.

Parry, Stephen, "ATBs in Australia", *The Moultoneer,* Kidderminster, May 1991.

Parry, Stephen, "The Ultimate Moulton?", *The Moultoneer,* Coventry, March/April 1992.

Parry, Stephen, letter in "Postbag", *The Moultoneer,* Dudley, September/October 1990.

PM, "Moulton ATB Leaked", *Bicycle,* London, June 1988.

Pratt, Geoff, "My Bike - the Traveller's Moulton", *Australian Cyclist,* February/March 1991.

Press release, Alex Moulton Limited, Bradford-on-Avon, June 1988.

"Recommended Specification of Complete ATB", *AM News,* Alex Moulton Limited, Bradford-on-Avon, Spring 1989.

Roosa, Doug, "Alex Moulton Mountain ATB", *Bicycle Guide,* Boston, Massachusetts, August 1988.

Roosa, Doug, "Bicycle Suspensions", *Bicycle Guide,* Boston, Massachusetts, August 1988.

Sadler, Nigel, "The Swift Answer to AMs", *The Moultoneer,* Dudley, Spring 1989.

Samer, P. Yuri, "Bike Suspensions", *Outside,* USA, April 1991.

Searle, Ben, "Is Moulton Still Magic?", *Cycling Plus,* Bath, October 1992.

Shimano 91, catalogue, Shimano Industrial Co. Ltd., Hilden, Germany, 1990.

"Shock Value", *Mountain Bike,* Rodale Press Inc., Emmaus, Pennsylvania, March 1993.

Stone, Hilary, "Climb Every Moulton", *Bicycle,* London, August 1988.

Sudjic, Deyan, "Joining the Chain Gang", *The Times,* London, 12 November 1988.

Taylor, David, *The Bicycle,* television series, York Films Limited, BBC/KRO/ NHK/S4C/TVO/YLE, 1991.

"The Leaders", *Bicycle Guide,* Boston, Massachusetts, January/February 1989.

"The Long & Short History of Suspension", *Mountain Bike Action,* Mission Hills, California, March 1994.

"The Politics & Pragmatism of Mountain Bike Testing", *Mountain Bike Action,* Mission Hills, California, January 1993.

UK Price List, Alex Moulton Limited, Bradford-on-Avon, 1 April 1992.

van de Beek, Guus, "Profiel - Moulton Mountain ATB", *Fiets,* Amsterdam, May 1989.

Wade, Leigh, "Third World Tourer", *The Moultoneer,* Coventry, July/August 1991.

Warran, Tony, "Moultons on the Equator", *The Moultoneer,* Coventry, September/ October 1991.

Zahradnik, Fred, "The '93 Specs", *Bicycling,* Rodale Press Inc., Emmaus, Pennsylvania, February 1993.

CHAPTER 8

1994 Recommended Retail Price List, W. R. Pashley Ltd., Stratford-upon-Avon, April 1994.

A Pedigree of Advanced Engineering, catalogue, Alex Moulton Limited, Bradford-on-Avon, 1994.

Apps, Geoff, "A Moulton for the Masses", *New Cyclist,* London, June 1992.

Arnold, P. D., "Another Variation", *The Moultoneer,* London, Summer 1993.

Arnold, Peter, "APB - the First Impressions", *The Moultoneer,* Coventry, September/ October 1992.

Assembly & Maintenance Instructions for Moulton APB, W. R. Pashley Limited, Stratford-upon-Avon, 1992.

Bailey, David, "A Customised APB Commuting Machine", *The Moultoneer,* London, Summer 1993.

Beckman, Andrew, "Front and Rear Bags for AMs/APBs", *The Moultoneer,* London, Spring 1993.

Bennet, Ken, "The Whole World's a Cycleway with a Collapsible Two-Wheeler", *The Birmingham Post,* 14 April 1993.

Bike of the 60s on the Way Back", *Evening Post,* Nottingham, 3 March 1992.

Camm, F. J., *Every Cyclist's Pocket Book,* George Newnes Limited, London, 1950.

"Coming Into the Fold", *Cycling Plus,* Bath, January 1994.

Connor, Tony, "First Thoughts of an APB Owner", *The Moultoneer,* Coventry, May/June 1992.

"Curse of Small Wheels", *Cycle Industry,* October, 1990.

Field, Patrick, "Bike Buyers' Guide", *New Cyclist,* London, May 1993.

Field, Patrick, "Stow It!", *New Cyclist,* London, April 1993.

Freewheel Cycling Directory, Madison Cycles plc, London, Spring/Summer 1993.

Greene, Peter, "Latest in an Unfolding Story", *The Independent,* London, 29 April 1989.

Grigsby, Richard, "Tiny Tyres Racing Team Rides Again", *The Moultoneer,* London, Autumn 1993.

Hadland, Tony, "A First Look at the Moulton APB", *The Moultoneer,* Coventry, March/April 1992.

Hadland, Tony, "Editorial", *The Moultoneer,* Coventry, March/April 1992.

Hadland, Tony, "Moultons and Moultoneers in the Press", *The Moultoneer,* Coventry, November/December 1991.

Hadland, Tony, "Moultons in the Press", *The Moultoneer,* Coventry, May/June 1992.

Hadland, Tony, "Stop Press", *The Moultoneer,* Coventry, May/June 1992.

Hand Built Bicycles by Pashley, catalogue, W. R. Pashley Limited, Stratford-upon-Avon, 1993.

Juden, Chris, "Cyclex 1992", *Cycle Touring & Campaigning,* Godalming, April/May 1992.

Juden, Chris, "Technical Information", *Members' Handbook,* Cyclists' Touring Club, Godalming, 1991.

Latest Moulton to be Produced in Volume Once More, press release for W. R. Pashley Limited, Broadfield Price & Partners Limited, Birmingham, 9 February 1993.

Local Company to Manufacture Bicycle Favourite, press release for W. R. Pashley Limited, Broadfield Price & Partners Limited, Birmingham, 14 February 1992.

McGurn, Jim, "Small is Beautiful", *New Cyclist,* London, May 1993.

Michaels, Steve E. & Hodgson, Ian, "The New APB - A Road Test", *The Moultoneer,* Coventry, May/June 1992.

Michaels, Steve E., "An APB - the First 200 Miles", *The Moultoneer,* Coventry, May/June 1992.

Michaels, Steve E., "Fitting Mudguards to an APB", *The Moultoneer,* Coventry, September/October 1992.

Michaels, Steve E., "Fitting the Rear Carrier to the APB", *The Moultoneer*, Coventry, November/December 1992.

Model RD-TY20 Trouble Shooting, Shimano, current 1992.

Moore, Toby, "Moulton Gets Into Gear for Cycle Launch", *The Daily Telegraph,* London, 26 February 1992.

More than an Artform, APB catalogue, W. R. Pashley Limited., Stratford-upon-Avon, May 1994.

Moulton APB, leaflet, Delta Cycle Corporation, Stoughton, Massachusetts, 1994.

Moulton APB - the Range, catalogue, W. R. Pashley Limited, Stratford-upon-Avon, 1993.

Moulton APB to be Unveiled at Cyclex '92, press release for W. R. Pashley Limited, Broadfield Price & Partners Limited, Birmingham, 17 Feb 1992.

Moulton APB, first catalogue, APB Distribution, London, February 1992.

Moulton Gets Into Gear With an Addition to the Range, press release for W. R. Pashley Limited, Broadfield Price & Partners Limited, Birmingham, undated c. May 1992.

"Moulton Looks at Joint Deals", *Cycle Industry,* September 1990.

Murray, Callum, "Little Wheel Turns Full Circle", *The Times,* London, 11 June 1991.

"New Bike is World News", *Midweek,* Stratford-upon-Avon, 20 May 1992.

Nicol, Scot, "Talking with Alex Moulton: 30 years of Dual-Suspension", *Velo News,* Brattleboro, Vermont, 5 April 1993.

Nuttall, Nick, "The Next Stage in the Cycle", *The Times Saturday Review,* London, 30 January 1993.

Ostler, Tim, "Two Wheels Good", *Design,* London, November 1992.

Pashley, T. J., "Category Query", letter in *New Cyclist,* London, July 1993.

"Pedalling Back", *The Times,* London, 4 March 1992.

Pennington, Hazel, "Pashley Peculiars", *New Cyclist,* London, September/October 1991.

Price, Nick, *Launch of the New Moulton APB-14 Bicycle,* press day invitation, Broadfield Price & Partners Limited, Birmingham, January 1993.

Quality and Style are W. R. Pashley Hallmarks, press release for W. R. Pashley Limited, Broadfield Price & Partners Limited, Birmingham, 9 February 1993.

Read, Peter, Sturmey-Archer - *The First 90 Years - Exploded Hub Gear Drawings,* Read, Milton Keynes, 1994.

Retail Price Index Queries, *Bank of England,* London, September 1993.

Sadler, Nigel, "Happiness is a Bike Called Battersea", *The Moultoneer,* London, Summer 1993.

Sadler, Nigel, "The Moulton APB-14", *The Moultoneer,* London, Spring 1993.

Sadler, Nigel, "The Second Coming of the Improved Bicycle", *The Moultoneer,* London, Spring 1993.

Sadler, Nigel, *The Moulton Flyer,* London, Spring 1993.

Sajo, Caba, *Moulton APB,* promotional video for Alex Moulton Limited, Vidimage Productions, Cirencester, 1993.

Searle, Ben, "Is Moulton Still Magic?", *Cycling Plus,* Bath, October 1992.

"Showoffs at Cyclex", *Cycle Trader,* London, March 1992.

"State of Suspense", *Cycling Plus,* Bath, December 1993.

"Stop Press - Moulton Bicycle Club World Exclusive", loose slip in *The Moultoneer,* Coventry, January/February 1992.

Taylor, Lucy, "Master Moulton", *Bicycle,* London, December 1991.

"Teaming Up with Pedal Power", *Business Chronicle,* Bath, 8 June 1993.

"The Amazing Mr Moulton", *Transport Innovation,* Summer 1991.

Twydell, Ken, "APB Gear Change?", *The Moultoneer,* Coventry, May/June 1992.

Tyler, Christian, "Private View - Industrial Revolutions of a Country Gent", *Financial Times,* Weekend FT supplement, 15/16 June 1991.

UK Retail Price List, Alex Moulton Bicycles, Bradford-on-Avon, 1 January 1994.

Walker, Brian, *Christmas Card,* Alex Moulton Limited, Bradford-on-Avon, 1992.

CHAPTER 9

"1988 RAAM Cyclists", *Race Across America Magazine,* Tucson, 1988.

51 mph - The World Record Moulton, promotional card, Alex Moulton Limited, Bradford-on-Avon, 1986.

"A Moulton Wins Toronto Race", *Cycling,* Sutton, August 1984.

A Pedigree of Advanced Engineering, catalogue, Alex Moulton Limited, Bradford-on-Avon, 1994.

Abbott, Alan (ed.), *Second International Human Powered Vehicle Scientific Symposium Proceedings,* IHPVA, Indianapolis, 1984.

Alex Moulton Bicycles, leaflet, Alex Moulton Limited, Bradford-on-Avon, 1985.

"Alex Moulton Bike Win (sic) Canadian Race", *Bicycle Business Journal,* September 1984.

Alex Moulton Mountain ATB, specification sheet with Tiny Tire Team T-shirt advert, Angle Lake Cyclery, Seattle, 1989.

AM News, Alex Moulton Limited, Bradford-on-Avon, November 1986.

AM SPEED, leaflet, Alex Moulton Limited, Bradford-on-Avon, 1990.

AM SPEED/Rover Metro, promotional card, Alex Moulton Limited, Bradford-on-Avon, 1990.

"Art. 49", *UCI Regulations,* Union Cycliste Internationale, Leudelange, Luxembourg, as at January 1994.

Ayres, Martin, "Recognise these Machines", *Cycling,* Sutton, 7 April 1984.

Beer, Joseph, "Canada 1991 - the AM SPEED Goes Across the Pond", *The Moultoneer,* Coventry, November/December 1991.

Berto, Frank, "The 1986 IHPVA Championships, Vancouver", *Bike Tech,* Emmaus, Pennsylvania, Winter 1986.

Berto, Frank, "Vehicular Velocity in Vancouver", *Bicycling,* Emmaus, Pennsylvania, April 1987.

Billson, Rick, "The Boulogne Alternative", *The Moultoneer,* Coventry, March/April 1992.

"Best Buy Awards for 1993", *Cycling Plus*, Bath, December 1993.

Clements, Bruno, "Steady Eddy's Gem of a Bike", *Evening Post*, Bristol, 13 June 1991.

Craig, Ray, "Exposing the Flèche", *Moulton Cyclist*, Bristol, Summer 1985.

Craig, Ray, "The P-B-P on AM7", *Moulton Cyclist*, Bristol, Summer 1984.

Crane, Nicholas (ed.), "Organisations", *International Cycling Guide 1982*, London, 1982.

Donaldson, Steven, "A Trike that's Different", *Cycling World*, Sidcup, April 1985.

Doube, Michael, "A Moulton on the Great Victorian Bike Ride", *The Moultoneer*, Kidderminster, March/April 1991.

Doughty, Simon, "Brindisi-Calais (or is 'La Malle des Indes' a 'Pain in the Bum?')", *Arrivée*, No.8, Aldermaston, 1984.

Doughty, Simon, "Brindisi to Calais in Eight Days", *Cycling*, 17 November 1984.

Eliasohn, Mike, "Michael Eliasohn Reports on the Aero in Action", *Moulton Cyclist*, Bristol, Spring 1985.

Fixbone Fitting Chart (B361), Alex Moulton Limited, Bradford-on-Avon, 1990.

Flower, Robert G., "Another Record Year", *Bike Tech*, Emmaus, Pennsylvania, February 1985.

Glaskin, Max, "Speed Fiends", *Bicycle*, London, February 1987.

Grigsby, Richard, "AM7 - Suitable for Time Trialling?", *The Moultoneer*, Henley-on-Thames, Summer 1988 (original report dated 23 February 1988).

Grigsby, Richard, "The Memoirs of a 'Tiny Tyres' Racing Team Member", *The Moultoneer*, Kidderminster, March/April 1991.

Grigsby, Richard, "The Moulton SPEED", *The Moultoneer*, Dudley, May/June 1990.

Grigsby, Richard, "Racing and Training on the SPEED", *The Moultoneer*, Kidderminster, May/June 1991.

Hadland, Tony, "Audax - Moulton Style", *The Moultoneer*, Henley-on-Thames, Autumn 1988.

Hadland, Tony, "More Speed Success for the AM", *The Moultoneer*, Henley-on-Thames, Winter 1987.

Hadland, Tony, "Streamlining of a Different Kind - A New World Record for the AM", *The Moultoneer*, Henley-on-Thames, Spring 1986.

Hadland, Tony, "Moulton Speed", *The Moulton Bicycle*, second edition, Pinkerton/Hadland, Reading 1982.

Harvey, Martin, "Moultons in the Press", *The Moultoneer*, Dudley, November/December 1990.

Hessey, Mike, "AM News", *The Moultoneer*, Dudley, March/April 1990.

Hessey, Mike, "Annual Meeting, Bradford-on-Avon, 23-24 September 1989", *The Moultoneer*, Dudley, Winter 1989/90.

Hessey, Mike, "Moultons in the News", *The Moultoneer*, Dudley, Spring 1989.

Hessey, Mike, "News from Bradford-on-Avon", *The Moultoneer*, Dudley, Autumn 1989.

Hessey, Mike, "News from Bradford-on-Avon", *The Moultoneer,* Dudley, Spring 1989.

Hessey, Mike, "The New SPEED", *The Moultoneer,* Dudley, Winter 1989/90.

"High Speed Moulton", *Bicycle,* London, September 1984.

"History of RAAM", *Race Across America Magazine,* Tucson, 1988.

Hjertberg, Eric, "Wheel Futures", *American Bicyclist & Motorcyclist,* September 1984.

"Hot Tubes: Alex Moulton", *Bicycle Guide,* Boston, Massachusetts, January/February 1989.

"HPV versus Bike", *Bicycle,* London, November 1985.

"Hugi Hub Axle Replacement on Original Batch of SPEEDs", Service Sheet No.5 Alex Moulton Limited, Bradford-on-Avon, May 1990.

"Indianapolis 84", *Bicycle Action,* London, December 1984.

"Jubilee to Celebrate Progression", *Bicycle Trade & Industry,* 23 May 1988.

Kelly, Dave, "AM14 Excels in New Zealand HPV Race", *The Moultoneer,* London, Summer 1993.

Kingsbury, Miles, "Beans Means Miles", *New Cyclist,* Coldstream, May/June 1991.

Kyle, Chester R., *Human Powered Vehicles,* IHPVA, 1982.

Kyle, Chester R., *"The Human Machine",* Bicycling, Emmaus, Pennsylvania, May 1989.

Lai, Garrett, "Road Grit - Blowin' in the Wind", *Bicycle Guide,* Boston, Massachusetts, April 1994.

Lewis, C. Michael, *Human Powered Speed Championship,* poster, Portland, Maine, 1985.

Mersey Roads Club Subscription 24 Hours Ride, results list, Mersey Roads Club, Liverpool, July 1984.

Milliken, Doug, "AM & Dave Bogdan vs. the North American Continent", *The Moultoneer,* Henley-on-Thames, Winter 1987/88 & Spring 1988.

Milliken, Doug, "AMs to Race Across America", *The Moultoneer,* Henley-on-Thames, Summer 1987.

Milliken, Doug, "IHPVA Crossover - The 1987 Race Across America with Tiny Tires", *HPV News,* IHPVA, Indianapolis, Indiana, Sept 1987.

Milliken, Doug, "More on Computers", *The Moultoneer,* Dudley, Summer 1989.

Milliken, Doug, *Moulton Streamliner Chronology,* Alex Moulton Limited, Bradford-on-Avon, 1993.

Milliken, Doug, "The John Paul Mitchell Systems Run", *The Moultoneer,* Coventry, November/December 1991.

Milliken, Doug, *The Milliken Lecture,* September 1990, video, Vidimage Productions, Cirencester, 1990.

Milliken, Doug, *Why We Spent New Year's Eve Outdoors in a Blizzard,* draft article for IHPVA News, March 1994.

Milliken, Douglas, *Aerodynamic Wheel Disks,* product data, Douglas Milliken, Williamsville, NY, 1986.

Milliken, Douglas, "The Moulton Aero", (written May 1984) *Moulton Cyclist*, Bristol, Winter/Spring 1985.

Morris, Brian, "What is Audax?", *Cycle Touring & Campaigning*, Godalming, February/March 1994.

"Moulton Claims New Record", *Bicycle Action*, London, December 1985.

"Moulton Cracks 50 mph", *Cycling World*, Sidcup, December 1985.

"Moulton Sensationell", *Fahrrad Sport & Reisen*, West Germany, August 1985.

Moulton, Alex, *Alex Moulton Bicycle Breaks HPVA World Record*, press release, Alex Moulton Limited, Bradford-on-Avon, 7 October 1985.

Moulton, Alex, "AM Completes Race Across America", *The Moultoneer*, Henley-on-Thames, Autumn 1987.

Moulton, Alex, "RAAM 1988 - Bogdan Slashes 17 hours from '87 Time", *The Moultoneer*, Henley-on-Thames, Autumn 1988.

Moulton, Alex, "RAAM", *AM News*, Alex Moulton Limited, Bradford-on-Avon, August 1987.

Moulton, Alex, *The Moulton Bicycle Project from Conception*, IHPVA paper, Alex Moulton Limited, Bradford-on-Avon, 1986.

Mumford, Frank, "The Gladdest Moment - the 1984 Mersey Roads Club 24", *Arrivée*, No.8, Aldermaston, 1984.

Naegeli, Andreas, "Grosse Leistungen auf Kleinen Radern", *Alex Moulton Bicycles*, Velolaboratorium, Zurich, 1993.

Newton, Edgar, "Magic Moultons", *New Cyclist*, Coldstream, Autumn 1989.

New World Record, press release, Biotrace Systems, High Wycombe, September 1990.

Nicol, Scot, "Talking with Alex Moulton: 30 Years of Dual-Suspension", *Velo News*, Brattleboro, Vermont, 5 April 1993.

Peregrine, Nick, "Le Retour de Petit Velo or the Return of the Toy Bicycle", *Moulton Cyclist*, Bristol, Spring & Summer editions, 1985.

"Polished Moulton", *Cycling Weekly*, Sutton, 3 April 1993.

Poole, Stephen, "An Alex Moulton: The Definitive PBP Bicycle?", *Cycling Push On*, Australia, December 1987 - January 1988.

RAAM 1987 - Another Moulton Achievement, promotional card, Alex Moulton Limited, Bradford-on-Avon, 1987.

RAAM 1988 - Moulton Races Across America, promotional card, Alex Moulton Limited, Bradford-on-Avon, 1987.

"Review 1990", *ID* (International Design), USA, 1990.

Roberts, Simon, "Superbike Tops Four World Records", *Bucks Free Press*, 15 May 1992.

Roosa, Doug, "Alex Moulton SPEED", *Bicycle Guide*, Boston, Massachusetts, June 1990.

"Round-the-Houses Bike Challenge", *Bath & West Evening Chronicle*, Bath, 17 June 1985.

Sajo, Caba, *AM SPEED*, video, Vidimage Productions, Cirencester, 1991.

Samuels, Peter B. & Wilson, David, "Letters", *American Scientist*, September/October 1986.

Sanders, Daved, "Interview with Doug Milliken", *The Moultoneer,* Kidderminster, January/February 1991.

Sanders, Daved, "Liner History", *The Moultoneer,* Kidderminster, March/April 1991.

Sanders, Daved, "Power Output", *The Moultoneer,* Kidderminster, January/February 1991.

Sanders, Daved, "Racing Report", *The Moultoneer,* Coventry, July/August 1991.

Sanders, Daved, "Racing USA", *The Moultoneer,* Kidderminster, January/February 1991.

Sanders, Daved, "Record Attempt", *The Moultoneer,* Kidderminster, January/February 1991.

Sanders, Daved, "SPEED Report", *The Moultoneer,* Kidderminster, January/February 1991.

Sanders, Daved, "World Speed Record", *The Moultoneer,* Kidderminster, January/February 1991.

"Small Cycle Makes Big Impression", *Canterbury Gazette,* 14 February 1992.

Smolik, H. C., "Klein Aber OHO", *Radmagazin Tour,* Germany, 1993.

"State of Suspense", *Cycling Plus,* Bath, December 1993.

Stone, Hilary, "Making the New", *Bicycle,* London, August 1988.

Sturk, Alan, "The Goose Flesh Flèche", *Arrivée,* Fishlake, July 1988.

"The Advanced Engineering Bicycle", Alex Moulton Limited advertisement, *Arrivée,* Audax United Kingdom, Fishlake, July 1988.

"The Bicycle that Gives You Everything", Alex Moulton/Swift Cycles advertisement, *New Cyclist,* Coldstream, Spring 1990 & later issues.

"The World's Fastest Bicycle", Swift Cycles Limited advertisement, *Bicycle,* London, July 1985.

UK Retail Price List, Alex Moulton Bicycles, Bradford-on-Avon, 1 January 1994.

Untitled article on Bean breaking 1 hour record, *Cycling Weekly,* Sutton, 27 September 1990.

Wade, Leigh F. & Holzman, David, "Moulton Jones", *Bicycle Guide,* Boston, Massachusetts, December 1990.

Walker, Brian, *Christmas card,* Alex Moulton Limited, Bradford-on-Avon, December 1986.

Walker, Brian, *Christmas card,* Alex Moulton Limited, Bradford-on-Avon, 1988.

Weinstein, Fred, "1991 Paris-Brest-Paris by Moulton AM7", *The Moultoneer,* Coventry, March/April 1992.

Westwood, Parry, "1925 miles in 151 Hours", *Cycling,* Sutton, 25 August 1984.

Whitt, Frank Rowland & Wilson, David Gordon, *Bicycling Science,* first edition, MIT Press, Cambridge, Massachusetts & London, 1974.

"Why is RAAM So Enticing?", *Race Across America Magazine,* Tucson, 1988.

Zapple report, Fiets, Amsterdam, November 1985.

CHAPTER 10

"Across the World on a Moulton", *Wiltshire Times,* Trowbridge, 13 April 1984.

Bailey, David, "AMs in Eire", *The Moultoneer,* Henley-on-Thames, Autumn 1988.

Barker, Tim, "Tim Barker's Thousand Mile Ride", *The Moultoneer,* Henley-on-Thames, Autumn 1987.

Beams, Ron, "AM14 - the Lowdown on Low Gears", *The Moultoneer,* Coventry, March/April 1992.

Beams, Ron, "I Did It My Way: The South Downs Way by AM7", *The Moultoneer,* Coventry, September/October 1991.

Bochove, Danielle, "Day-care Champion's Long Ride for Answers", *The Edmonton Journal,* Canada, 20 August 1992.

Coulouris, George & Jean, "Touring in Brittany", *The Moultoneer,* London, Summer 1993.

"Cyclist Pedals Home", *The Mail,* Hartlepool, 6 January 1990.

Doube, Michael, "An AM7 Metamorphosis", *The Moultoneer,* London, Autumn 1993.

Doube, Michael, "An Aussie Moulton Tourist", *The Moultoneer,* Dudley, March/April 1990.

Gordon, Alan, "Flying with Your AM", *The Moultoneer,* London, Summer 1993.

Greene, Peter, "Icelandic Cycle Saga on a Tough Pair of Wheels", *The Independent,* London, 4 June 1988.

Grimshaw, John, "Face to Face", *Cycling Plus,* Bath, June 1993.

Hadland, Tony, "Book Review - Quite 'wind assisted' Cycle Routes between BR Stations", *The Moultoneer,* Coventry, May/June 1992.

Hadland, Tony, "Getting the Miles In", *The Moultoneer,* Henley-on-Thames, Spring 1987.

Hadland, Tony, "Moultons in the Press", *The Moultoneer,* Coventry, November/December 1992.

Hadland, Tony, "The Most Moulton Miles?", *The Moultoneer,* Henley-on-Thames, Autumn 1988.

Hageman, Marc, "From the Netherlands", *The Moultoneer,* London, Autumn 1993.

Heslop, Laurence, "Across the Roof of England (with my AM14T)", *The Moultoneer,* Coventry, September/October 1992.

Holden, Alan, *To Begin With ...",* introduction to photographic exhibition held at Hartlepool Central Library, July 1990.

Hutchins, R.N. et al, *Quite 'Wind Assisted' Cycle Routes etc.,* privately published, Bedford, 1991.

Johnstone, Roy, "Well, I'll Be Blowed!", *Saga Magazine,* Folkestone, October 1992.

Juden, Chris, "Technical Information", *CTC Members' Handbook,* Godalming, 1991.

Kelly, Dave, "Some Thoughts from a Newcomer to Moultons", *The Moultoneer*, Coventry, March/April 1992.

Klemenz, Silvia & Knowles, Jeremy, "Perth Moultoneers on the Move", *The Moultoneer*, Coventry, March/April 1992.

Klemenz, Silvia & Knowles, Jeremy, "World Touring with AMs", *The Moultoneer*, London, Spring, Summer & Winter 1993 issues.

Lawley, Kevin, "A Tour of Tuscany & Umbria by AM5", *The Moultoneer*, Coventry, January/February 1992.

Macauley, Dr Robert, "Doctor's Orders", *The Moultoneer*, Coventry, July/August 1992.

Maurer, Urs, "A Moulton Goes Climbing", *The Moultoneer*, Coventry, March/April 1992.

Meade, Geoff, "They Should Tell the President!", *Cycletouring*, Godalming, June/July 1988.

Naegeli, Andreas, *Alex Moulton Bicycles*, Velolaboratorium, Zurich, 1993.

Nice, Philip, "The AM that Came in from the Cold", *The Moultoneer*, London, Summer 1993.

Parry, S. J., "Thoughts on Building an AM14 from a Frame Kit", *The Moultoneer*, Henley-on-Thames, Summer 1988.

Race, Tom, *Magnificent Moulton*, report for Alex Moulton Limited, Bradford-on-Avon, 1984.

Romer, Dennis, "1,000 Miles on a Moulton", *Cycling World*, Sidcup, October 1987.

Romer, Dennis, "An AM in the Mountains of Corsica", *The Moultoneer*, Henley-on-Thames, Summer & Autumn 1988 issues.

Sadler, Nigel, "A Highly Portable AM", *The Moultoneer*, Dudley, May/June 1990.

Sadler, Nigel, "How Much?! - or - Cycle Touring with an AM14", *The Moultoneer*, Henley-on-Thames, Autumn 1987.

Saltzer, Bernice, "An Epic Journey Is Recalled", *The Mail*, Hartlepool, 23 July 1990.

Sant, Ron, "Moultons Across the Equator", *The Moultoneer*, Coventry, November/December 1991.

Searle, Ben, "Is Moulton Still Magic?", *Cycling Plus*, Bath, October 1992.

Shepherd, Ron, "A Nullarboring Ride", *Freewheeling*, Broadway, New South Wales, Australia, date unknown, 1986?

Smith, Nicol, "Pilgrims Path to Santiago", *Times & News Leisure Plus* supplement, Wiltshire, 17 April 1992.

Tierney, Basil, "By the Saints - What a Trip!", *Yours*, Peterborough, May 1992.

Warran, Tony, "Moultons on the Equator", *The Moultoneer*, Coventry, September/October 1991.

UK Retail Price List, Alex Moulton Bicycles, Bradford-on-Avon, 1 January 1994.

Wasson, Channell, "A Moscow Tyre Test Story", *The Moultoneer*, London, Spring 1993.

Wasson, Channell, "Palo Alto to Beverly Hills on the Moulton Bicycle", *The Moultoneer,* Coventry, January/February & March/April 1992.

Woodland, Les, *Get Away by Bike*, Pelham, London, 1990.

CHAPTER 11

A Pedigree of Advanced Engineering, catalogue, Alex Moulton Limited, Bradford-on-Avon, 1994.

AM-GT, leaflet, Alex Moulton Limited, Bradford-on-Avon, June 1991.

"Bike Test: Four Full-Suspension MTBs", *Cycling Plus,* Bath, April 1993.

"Ca Roue?", *Velo Tonic,* Le Plessis-Trevise, France, August/September 1993.

Conran, Sebastian, untitled article, *Blueprint,* London, July 1991.

Hadland, Tony, "Stunning in Stainless", *The Moultoneer,* Coventry, July/August 1991.

Hall, Peter, "Pedalling into Future on Wheels of Progress", *Design Week,* London, 28 June 1991.

"Hugi Hub", *Bicycle Guide,* Boston, Massachusetts, February 1990.

Ismay, Dr Douglas G., "An AM-GT, Deep in France", *The Moultoneer,* London, Summer 1993.

Juden, Chris, "AM-GT at the RSA", *Cycle Touring & Campaigning,* Godalming, August/September 1991.

"Moulton Steals a March", *New Cyclist,* Coldstream, July/August 1991.

"Moulton Wheels in Latest Bike", *Design Week,* London, 14 June 1991.

Moulton, Alex, Opening Remarks at the Launch of the Moulton (AM) GT Bicycle, Alex Moulton Limited, Bradford-on-Avon, June 1991.

Murray, Callum, "Little Wheel Turns Full Circle", *The Times,* London, 11 June 1993.

"New Product Jackpot", *Bicycling,* Rodale Press, Emmaus, Pennsylvania, December 1993.

Nicol, Scott, "Talking with Alex Moulton: 30 Years of Dual-Suspension", *Velo News,* Brattleboro, Vermont, 5 April 1993.

Robinson, Steven, "One of a Kind", Performance Cyclist International, August 1993.

Royce Titanium Bottom Bracket Set, leaflet, Royce Racing (88) Limited, Poole, 1990.

Sadler, Nigel, *Alex Moulton Bicycle's Pedigree of Advanced Engineering,* Alex Moulton Limited, Bradford-on-Avon, June 1991.

Sadler, Nigel, *Alex Moulton Bicycles,* leaflet & price list insert, Alex Moulton Limited, Bradford-on-Avon, June 1991.

Sadler, Nigel, "Tales of Joy ...", *The Moultoneer,* London, Winter 1993.

"Shiney [sic] Dream Bike", *Bicycle Trade & Industry,* 7 June 1991.

"State of Suspense", *Cycling Plus,* Bath, December 1993.

Swift Cycles Limited advertisement, *New Cyclist,* Coldstream, July/August 1991.

"The Amazing Mr Moulton", *Transport Innovation,* London, Summer 1991.

"The Great Labels", *Begin,* Japan, October 1992.

Tyler, Christian, "Industrial Revolutions of a Country Gent", *Financial Times Weekend* supplement, London, 15/16 June 1991.

UK Retail Price List, Alex Moulton Bicycles, Bradford-on-Avon, 1 January 1994.

Wade, Leigh, "One-Off Titanium Moulton", *The Moultoneer,* Coventry, May/ June 1992.

APPENDIX A

Assembly Instructions AM2 & AM7, Alex Moulton Limited, Bradford-on-Avon, 1983.

ATB Separation Instructions, Alex Moulton Limited, Bradford-on-Avon, 1988.

Dunkley, Jerry, "Bright Ideas for Night Riding", *The Moultoneer,* Coventry, March/April 1992.

Front Suspension Adjustment and Service Instructions, Angle Lake Cyclery (Seattle)/Alex Moulton Limited, Service Sheet No.7, Bradford-on-Avon, 1992.

"Inventions", *Mountain Bike Action,* Mission Hills, California, August 1993.

Loose Pivot Bearing of Rear Fork (Swing Arm), Service Note No.3, Alex Moulton Limited, Bradford-on-Avon, August 1987.

Michaels, Steve E., "Fitting the Rear Carrier to the APB", *The Moultoneer,* Coventry, November/December 1992.

Moulded Valve Stems in New Tubes, Service Sheet No.4, Alex Moulton Limited, Bradford-on-Avon, 27 April 1990.

Routledge, Harry, "Rear Suspension Maintenance on AMs", *The Moultoneer,* Kidderminster, March/April 1991.

Some Extra Tips for Caring for Your New Alex Moulton *Bicycle,* information sheet, Alex Moulton Limited, Bradford-on-Avon, January 1993.

Sticking Guide Bearing, Service Sheet No.1, Alex Moulton Limited , Bradford-on-Avon, 1987 (and later revision).

Cartoon courtesy of Bicycle Victoria, the Bicycle Institute of Victoria Incorporated, Australia.

Index